Hong Kong
Macau & Canton
a travel survival kit

HONG KONG

登基銀禧紀念

貳角

香港

CORONATION
ANNIVERSARY

1953

1978

TWENTY CENTS

Hong Kong, Macau & Canton

Published by
Lonely Planet Publications
PO Box 88, South Yarra
Victoria 3141, Australia

Printed by
Colorcraft
Hong Kong

Photographs by
Jim Hart, HKTA, Ian McQueen, Alan Samagalski and Tony
Wheeler

First Published
1978

This Edition
August 1986

National Library of Australia Cataloguing in Publication Data

Clewlow, Carol.
   Hong Kong, Macau & Canton.

   4th ed.
   Previous ed. : South Yarra : Lonely Planet, 1983
   Includes index.
   ISBN 0 908086 74 1

   1. Hong Kong – Description and travel – Guide
   books. 2. Macao – Description and travel –
   Guide books. 3. Canton (China) – Description –
   Guide books. I. Title

915.1'25045

   Carol Clewlow 1978
   Lonely Planet 1981, 1983, 1986

Carol Clewlow A free-lance journalist, Carol started her career with three years of work on the *Belfast Telegraph* in Northern Ireland, first as a news reporter and then as a feature writer. In 1972 her itchy feet got the better of her and she travelled overland through Asia, stopping off for three months in Bangkok on the way and finally ending up in Hong Kong. There she worked for 18 months on the *China Mail*, a now defunct evening newspaper. She also spent some time in Hong Kong dubbing English soundtracks onto kung fu spectaculars, specialising in definitive renditions of the word 'Arrrrrrgggh!' Carol left Hong Kong to travel in South-east Asia, returned to Britain and then came back to Hong Kong to write the original *Hong Kong* guide. She now lives in England.

Alan Samagalski Alan came to Lonely Planet a couple of years ago after a lengthy stay on the Indian sub-continent, having gone astray from the Melbourne University Genetics Department and mixed receptions at Melbourne's Comedy Café and Last Laugh. Initial trips to exotic parts of Australia were followed up with an update on *Hong Kong* and a subsequent trip to China from which he returned loaded with notes, maps and diagrams to co-author *China – A Travel Survival Kit*. Alan has also co-written the Lonely Planet *Indonesia* guide and has contributed to and updated other LP books. He returned to Hong Kong, Macau and Canton to update this book.

THIS EDITION

This is the second opportunity I've had to update the Hong Kong guide. This book was originally researched and written by Carol Clewlow, and since then has gone through a couple of incarnations under the influence of a number of people. The second edition was updated by Jim Hart, with a Canton section added by an Australian student who had lived and studied in China for some time. The third edition was updated by myself, and for the fourth edition I've had the added benefit of a long trip to China on which I've based the expanded Canton section – plus an update trip to Hong Kong, Macau and Canton specifically for this book.

We've had a number of letters carrying useful information from people 'out there,' particularly now that China has opened up – even the odd letter from People's Republic Chinese. With thanks to everyone, and with apologies to anyone who's been left out, I'd like to mention: Geoff Bonsall (Lonely Planet's distributor in Hong Kong, whose taste in fine restaurants is much appreciated every time one of us goes there), Rex Butcher (resident of Cheung Chau Island and much appreciated for some interesting perspectives on the colony), Robert Storey, Ian Donaldson, Rob Mitchell, Irene & Ian Colquhoun, Andraes Becker, Herve Buffiere, R Voltan, Michael Buckley (who co-wrote the Lonely Planet *China* guide, *Tibet*, and the China section in *North-East Asia on a Shoestring*), and to:

J D McEwan, Par Eliasson, Erik Klingzell, Brian Smith, Paul Suhler (USA), Margie Parikh (Australia), Gary Fine & Tamara Joy (USA), Peter Russenberger (Switzerland), Robert Entenmann (USA), Joanne Celens (Belgium), Ed Lyons, Robert Bluestein (USA), Mona Russel (Australia), Gilbert Wong (NZ), Jerome & Regina Pauwels (Belgium), Michael Szonyi (Canada), Bruce T Singer (USA), Helga Schmidbauer (W Germany), Ken Haley, Gina Roncoli (Australia), Dolf Mesland (Holland), Joe Greenholtz (USA), Nord-Jan Vermeer (Holland), Jim Leffman, Kevin Sinclair (Hong Kong), Devra Applebaum (UK), Hoon Koh (Australia), Ola Holmgren (Sweden), Anne Folkungagatan (Sweden), Judy Brichetto (USA), Jerome & Regina Pauwels (Belgium), Fiona Baker (Scotland), Piero Fantini (Switzerland), Matthew Maxwell (UK) and Liza Lee (UK).

This book is also a product of the efforts of the other workers at Lonely Planet: Marianne Poole who had the unenviable task of typing the last edition into the word processor before it was updated; Tony Jenkins whose cartoons have graced the pages of many other Lonely Planet books; Ann Logan for typesetting; Todd Pierce for more typesetting and sharing the map load with Miss Fiona Boyes; Sue Tan for proof-reading and indexing; and finally Ricky Holt, fastest paste-up artist in the west.

AND THE NEXT

Things change – Macau had changed so much since I was last there that it was barely recognisable, and hotels just keep on sprouting up in Canton. Prices also go up, good places go bad, bad places go bankrupt, and sometimes they even get themselves a facelift. So if you find things better, worse, cheaper, more expensive, recently opened or recently shut, then write a letter and tell us about it; *Hong Kong, Macau & Canton* is definitely one book we could do with some more feedback on! As usual, the best letters will score a free copy of the next edition or any other LP guide you prefer.

Contents

Hong Kong

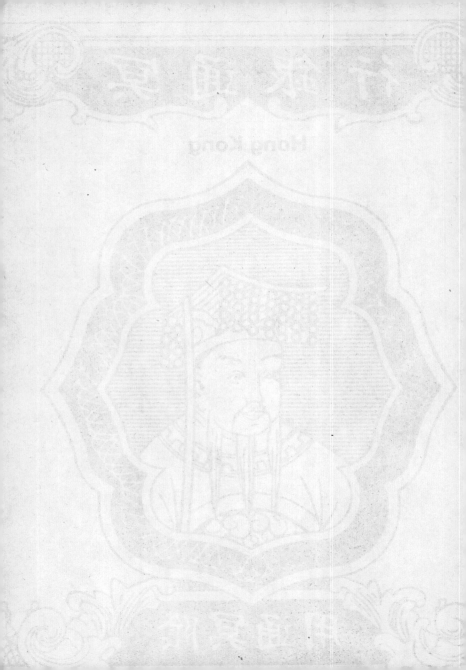

Introduction

Hong Kong is the last British-occupied corner of China, the final chapter of a colonial saga that began almost 150 years ago and will end when the colony is handed back to its former owner in 1997. Most people think of Hong Kong as an island. It is, but not just one; there are 236 islands plus a chunk of mainland bordering the Chinese province of Guangdong – about 1000 square km in all. Much of it is uninhabited while other parts, especially Hong Kong Island itself, are among the most densely populated areas in the world.

Hong Kong Island is the heart of it all, and the oldest part in terms of British history (the British acquired it in 1841). The centre of Hong Kong Island is the business district of Central, where the greater part of the colony's business life goes on. Here new office blocks shoot up almost daily – as do the rents – to accommodate the ever-growing financial elite who want to be a part of the Asian Wall Street.

From Central it's a seven-minute ferry ride across one of the world's great harbours to the Kowloon peninsula on the mainland. The tip of Kowloon is the shopping and tourist ghetto of Tsimshatsui, and beyond that are the high-rise commercial and industrial estates. Beyond Kowloon lie the New Territories, which include not only the mainland part bordering China but also the other 235 islands which make up Hong Kong; together the New Territories form the bulk of Hong Kong territory.

So much for basic geography. Why go to Hong Kong? Contrary to popular belief, it's more than just a place to buy a duty-free musical wristwatch. Hong Kong is one of the world's great trading ports; it is an eye-opener in terms of making the most out of every available square km, since space is Hong Kong's most precious commodity; it supports an almost intact traditional Chinese culture, in contrast to the rest of the mainland where the old culture was attacked and weakened by the Cultural Revolution of the 1960s; there are quiet, empty hills where you can walk for an afternoon and barely see another person; and there are remote villages where the locals still lead rural lives that have changed little over many generations.

Most travel agents and package tours allow a week at the most for visiting Hong Kong – enough time for a whistle-stop tour of a half-dozen attractions plus the obligatory shopping jaunt, but if you give yourself longer and make the effort to get out of Central and Tsimshatsui, you will find a lot more. Hong Kong is only the start; an hour's hydrofoil ride away is the 500-year-old Portuguese colony of Macau. To the north of Hong Kong and adjoining the New Territories is the 'Special Economic Zone' of Shenzhen where the People's Republic has been packing foreign money into development schemes designed to help modernise the entire country. Northwards up the Pearl River is Canton, the chief city of Guangdong Province – a curious mixture of Hong Kong as it was 50 years ago and the new directions China is now taking.

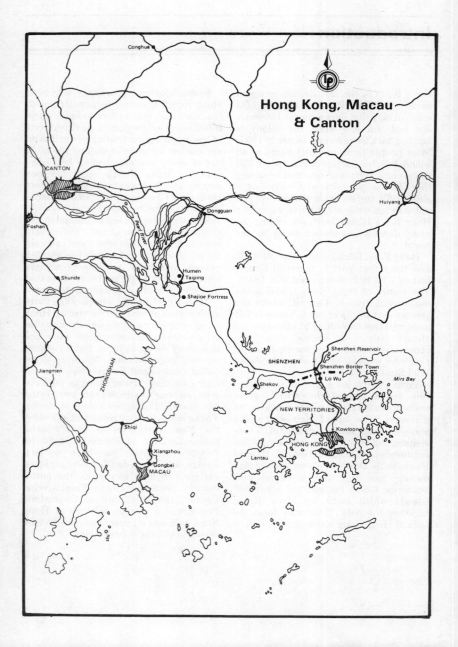

Hong Kong, Macau & Canton

Facts about Hong Kong

HISTORY

'Albert is so amused at my having got the island of Hong Kong,' wrote Queen Victoria to King Leopold of Belgium in 1841. But while her husband could see the funny side of this apparently useless little island off the south coast of China, considerably less amused was the British Foreign Secretary, Lord Palmerston. He considered the acquisition of Hong Kong a massive bungle on the part of Britain's Superintendent of Trade in China, who had negotiated the deal. 'A barren island with hardly a house upon it!' he raged in a letter to the unfortunate Captain Charles Elliot.

The story of Hong Kong really begins upriver, in the city of Canton, where the British had begun trading with China on a regular basis in the late 17th century. They were not the first westerners on the scene; regular Chinese contact with the modern European nations began in the early 16th century when the Portuguese were given permission to set up base in nearby Macau in about 1557. Then a number of Jesuit priests arrived and were allowed to establish themselves at Zhaoqing, a town north-west of Canton, in 1582. Their scientific and technical knowledge aroused the interest of the Imperial court and a few priests were permitted to reside in Beijing. The first trade overtures from the British were rebuffed by the Chinese but Canton was finally opened to trade with the Europeans in 1685.

From then on British ships began to arrive regularly from the East India Company bases on the Indian coast and the traders were allowed to establish warehouses ('factories') near Canton as a base to export tea and silk. The British and French started trading regularly at Canton from the end of the 17th century, the Dutch from 1729, the Danes and Swedes from 1731, and the United States from around 1785.

Even so, the opening of Canton was an indication of how little importance was placed on trade with the western barbarians. Canton was always considered to exist on the edge of a wilderness, far from Nanjing and Beijing, which were the centres of power under the isolationist Ming (1368-1644) and Qing (1644-1911) dynasties. As far as the Chinese were concerned, only the Chinese empire was civilised and the people beyond its frontiers were 'barbarians'; China was the cultural centre, the Middle Kingdom, and therefore other nations had to approach her as inferiors and accept vassalage or pay tribute. The Qing could not have foreseen the dramatic impact which the European barbarians were about to have on the country.

The fuse to the 'Opium Wars' was lit in 1757 when, by imperial edict, a Canton merchants' guild called the 'Co Hong' gained exclusive rights to China's foreign trade, paid for with royalties, kickbacks, fees and bribes. Numerous restrictions were forced on the western traders. They were permitted to reside in Canton from roughly September to March only, and were restricted to Shamian Island on Canton's Pearl River, where they had their factories. They also had to leave their wives and families downriver in Macau, though not all found this a hardship. In addition, it was illegal for foreigners to learn Chinese, or to deal with anyone except the Co Hong. The traders complained of the restrictions they had to work under and of trading regulations that changed from day to day, yet trade flourished nevertheless – mainly in China's favour because the tea and silk had to be paid for in hard cash (normally silver).

Trade in favour of China was not what the western merchants had in mind and in

1773 the British unloaded a thousand chests at Canton, each containing almost 70 kg of Bengal opium. The intention was to balance, and eventually more than balance, their purchases of Chinese goods. The Chinese taste for opium – or 'foreign mud' as it was called – amounted to 2000 chests a year by the turn of the century. The Emperor Tau Kuang, alarmed at the drain of silver from the country and the increasing number of opium addicts, issued an edict in 1796 totally banning the drug trade. But the foreigners had different ideas, and with the help of the Co Hong and corrupt Cantonese officials the trade continued. By 1816 yearly imports totalled some 5000 chests.

Decades later, in 1839, opium was still the key to British trade in China. The emperor appointed Lin Tse-hsu Commissioner of Canton with orders to stamp out the opium trade once and for all. It took Lin just a week to surround the British in Canton, cut off their food supplies and demand they surrender all the opium in their possession. The British stuck it out for six weeks until they were ordered by their own Superintendent of Trade, Captain Elliot, to surrender 20,000 chests of opium – an act which earned him their undying hatred. Lin then had the 'foreign mud' destroyed in public.

Elliot had been under instructions from Lord Palmerston, the British Foreign Secretary, to solve the trade problems with China. Having surrendered the opium, Elliot tried negotiating with Kishen, Lin's representative. When this failed he attacked Canton in what became known as the first 'Opium War.' The attack was ended by the Convention of Chuen Pi, which ceded Hong Kong Island to the British. The convention was due to be signed on 20 January 1841, but never was. Nevertheless, Commodore Gordon Bremmer led a contingent of naval men ashore and claimed the island for Britain on 26 January.

It is said that Kishen was hauled back to Beijing in chains for selling out the emperor. If Palmerston could have done the same to Elliot he probably would have. He believed his empire had been sold short and curtly informed Elliot that he was being replaced by Sir Henry Pottinger. The traders, now holed up in Hong Kong harbour and still smarting at the loss of 20,000 chests of opium, didn't bother to wave the good captain off. Pottinger arrived in August 1842 and sailed straight up the Yangtze River to threaten Nanjing (Nanking). By the end of that month he had brought hostilities to a close with the Treaty of Nanking which – among other things – officially ceded the island of Hong Kong to the British 'in perpetuity.'

That wasn't the end of the fighting. A third 'Opium War' broke out over the interpretation of earlier treaties and over the boarding of a British-owned merchant ship, the *Arrow*, by Chinese soldiers searching for pirates. French troops joined the British in this war and the Russians and Americans lent naval support. The war was brought to an end by the Treaty of Tientsin, which permitted the British to establish diplomatic representation in China. Unfortunately, no one told the person in the street that the war was over, and the first British envoy was fired on as he was making his way to Peking. With this excuse, the fourth and final Opium War was launched in 1859. It was ended the following year by the Convention of Peking, which ceded to the British the Kowloon peninsula (the area of mainland adjacent to Hong Kong Island and as far north as what is now Boundary Road) plus Stonecutters Island just off the western coast of the peninsula.

Hong Kong made its last land grab in a moment of panic 40 years later when China was on the verge of being parcelled out into 'spheres of influence' by the western powers and Japan – all of whom had by then sunk their claws into the country. The British army felt it needed more land to protect the colony, and in June 1898 the Second Convention of Peking presented Britain with the 934 square km of islands and mainland now known as the 'New Territories' on a 99-year lease, beginning 1 July 1898 and ending in 1997.

Despite a shaky start, during the latter half of the 19th century and the early 20th century Hong Kong flourished as a trading centre, an intermediary between China and the rest of the world. Although it was gradually shifting away from trade to manufacturing as its chief activity before WW II, the civil war in China during the 1920s and 1930s and the Japanese invasion of the country in the 1930s hastened the process as Chinese capitalists fled with their money to the safer confines of the British colony. The crunch finally came during the Korean War when the Americans' embargo on Chinese goods threatened to strangle the colony economically. In order to survive, the colony had to develop other industries, including banking, insurance and manufacturing.

When the Communists came to power in China in 1949 they chose to leave Hong Kong very much as it was. Today China has many lucrative investments in the colony including hotels, banks and department stores, and the colony is one of China's principal sources of foreign exchange. At the same time, Hong Kong is completely reliant on China's good will; much of Hong Kong's food comes from the PRC, and most of its water comes from across the border in Shenzhen. The colony could not have been defended had China ever decided to take it back by force; or the Chinese could have simply ripped down the fence on the border and sent the masses to peacefully settle on Hong Kong territory. In 1962 China actually staged what looked like a 'trial run' and sent 70,000 people across the border in a couple of weeks.

However, since Hong Kong was too valuable an economic asset, the Chinese always pulled back or stayed their hand. The problem faced by both the British and the Chinese was the colony's fate once

the lease on the New Territories expired in 1997. At that time the Chinese border would have theoretically moved south as far as Boundary Rd on the Kowloon peninsula, taking in the whole colony except for Hong Kong Island, Stonecutters Island and Kowloon, which – severed from much of its population – would be completely unviable.

If it were purely a problem of economics, both sides would probably leave the colony intact, to continue as it has been. For the Chinese the problem is much deeper than that; Hong Kong is the last survivor of a period of foreign imperialism on Chinese soil (Macau being a somewhat different story) and a symbol of the humiliation of China by Japan and the western powers in the later 19th and early 20th centuries. At that time China was in danger of losing its identity altogether, and becoming little more than a cartographical expression. The Opium Wars had each been ended by an 'unequal treaty' which, among other things, opened more Chinese ports to foreign ships and gave foreigners the right to settle in certain areas and later to travel freely in China. The Chinese were forced to pay large war indemnities, customs tariffs on imported western goods were severely reduced, western diplomats were permitted to take up residence in Beijing, and freedom of movement was eventually accorded to missionaries. Other powers seized Chinese territory (or territory controlled by the Chinese, such as Vietnam – China has a long history of imperialism also) and the Chinese were almost powerless to oppose them. The defeat of the Japanese in WW II and the subsequent defeat of the Kuomintang by the Communists finally cleared out the foreign armies, but China still had to deal with problems left over from the civil war and foreign imperialism. One was Taiwan, where the Kuomintang fled after their defeat on the mainland; the other was Hong Kong, where the need to find a solution was even more pressing as the

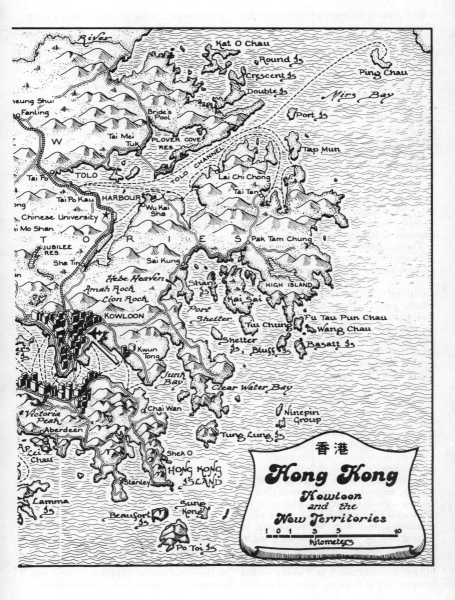

expiry date on the lease loomed closer and closer.

Rather than disembowel the colony and leave both sides with two useless pieces, or hang onto a colony which – arguably – it no longer wants, in September 1984 Britain agreed to hand the entire colony – lock, stock and skyscrapers, including Kowloon and Hong Kong Island – back to China in 1997. Theoretically the agreement between Britain and China will allow Hong Kong to retain its present social, economic and legal systems for at least 50 years after 1997. The Chinese catchphrase for all this is 'One country, two systems,' whereby Hong Kong will be permitted to retain its capitalist system after 1997 while across the border the Chinese carry on with a system they continue to label socialist or communist.

The agreement permits the preservation of Hong Kong's current legal system and guarantees the right of property ownership; allow Hong Kong residents to retain the right to travel in and out of the colony; permits Hong Kong to remain a free port and to continue independent membership of international organisations; and guarantees continuing employment after 1997 for the colony's civil servants (both Chinese and foreigners, including the police). The rights of assembly, free speech, association, travel and movement, correspondence, choice of occupation, academic research, religious belief and the right to strike are all included in the agreement. As one western journalist put it, 'Who else in the world has a 63-year written guarantee of freedom from communism?'

Of course, there's a great deal of scepticism (to say the least) about China's promises to allow Hong Kong to run much of its own affairs after 1997 – and while common sense may be prevailing in Beijing now, no one knows who's going to be making the laws a decade from now. Once China has Hong Kong after 1997 it will run it pretty much as it wants to; but however well it does so, there are no real guarantees that the provisions of the 1984 agreement will be kept.

As for the Hong Kong Chinese – whatever their wishes or desires for their lives after 1997 – they have probably got as good a deal as they could have expected. Of course, not all of them have to become citizens of the People's Republic in 1997 if they don't want to. Hong Kong is a capitalist enclave and those with the money can buy their way out just as other capitalists can buy their way in. Many other countries are positively encouraging the trade in passports as they try to benefit from the scramble of money and talent that's been heading out of Hong Kong – even before any agreements were made over sovereignty after 1997. South American countries simply sell passports – like Paraguay, which flogs them off for US$50,000. US$100,000 gets a person from Hong Kong into Micronesia. Some 10,000 Hong Kong residents a year are resettling in the richer and more secure western nations, the most popular destinations being the USA, Canada and Australia. While most migrations to Australia are connected with family reunions or professional skills in demand, a person from Hong Kong can also buy his or her way into Australia if they can invest a couple of hundred thousand Australian dollars in a business. As for Britain, the flood of immigrants expected from Hong Kong was halted in its tracks, since British immigration laws don't recognise the vast majority of Hong Kong residents as British citizens.

In its brief 160 years Hong Kong has been called many things: a pimple on the arse of China, a half-crown colony, a borrowed place on borrowed time. A monument to laissez-faire capitalism which got its start with the drug trade backed up by foreign warships and armies, the colony has nevertheless managed, for over 35 years now, to maintain its precarious perch on the coast of the world's most populous Communist country – first with the unofficial blessing of the Chinese government and now with their seemingly unabashed encouragement, making all those derogatory labels rather anachronistic. The irony of it all is that what was originally a 'barren island with hardly a house upon it' returns to the Chinese after 1½ centuries as a highly developed city-state.

And what of the opium trade that started it all? It folded by mutual consent in 1907, by which time the trading companies had diversified sufficiently to put their sordid pasts behind them without fear of financial ruin. A second irony is that Hong Kong now has a serious drug addiction problem, with something like 50,000 heroin addicts – a constant reminder of the colony's less than credible beginnings.

GOVERNMENT

Hong Kong is a British territory. Heading Hong Kong's administration is a governor who presides over meetings of both the Executive Council and the Legislative Council.

The Executive Council (EXCO) is technically the major policy-making body of the government. It's composed of top-ranking officials such as the attorney general and the commander of the British armed forces in the colony, together with other members who are appointed either by the governor or on the instructions of the British government. On the next rung down is the Legislative Council (LEGCO), whose job is to frame legislation, enact laws and control the expenditure of government money.

In charge of the day-to-day running of Hong Kong is the Urban Council, whose jurisdiction covers services to the almost four million people living in Hong Kong's urban areas. This body is concerned with street cleaning, garbage collection, food hygiene, hawkers' licenses and the like. The council is composed of 30 members, 15 appointed by the governor and the rest elected by a franchise of nearly a million people.

On the next rung down are the District Boards, set up in 1982 with the intention of giving Hong Kong residents some degree of control over their local area. The boards consist of government officials and elected representatives from the local area. The problem is that these boards have little (if any) real power; the seats are sought after by a small number of candidates who are voted in by the small proportion of the electorate who bothered to register as voters.

Perhaps an indication of the population's enthusiasm for the District Boards were the elections in early 1985 which saw about 476,000 people vote – approximately 34% of the 1.4 million registered voters, out of a potential electorate of 2.9 million.

The staff for all government departments and other areas of administration come under the umbrella of the Hong Kong Civil Service which employs some 173,000 people – of whom around 3500 are expatriates. However, the expatriates fill nearly all the top policy-making positions. Of the 60-odd government departments, 50 are headed by expatriates; and the officer corps in the almost 27,000-strong police force also has a disproportionately high number of expatriates. It has, however, been decided to end the recruitment of British for the top administrative posts and gradually replace them with Chinese in preparation for handing over the colony to China in 1997. The agreement with China decrees that expatriates cannot be heads of major government departments or deputy heads of some departments, although below these levels expatriates may still be employed after China takes over Hong Kong.

Thus, officially speaking, power in Hong Kong is concentrated very much at the top, and in the hands of the British. Exactly how power is really carved up in Hong Kong is much more blurred than a list of the official tasks of government departments – and always has been. In the 19th century it was a popular saying that

Hong Kong was ruled by the Jardine-Matheson trading company, the Royal Hong Kong Jockey Club, the Hong Kong & Shanghai Bank, and the governor – in that order of importance. Although the scope and influence of the top civil servants has increased over the years, the opinion of the the large business companies – both British and Hong Kong Chinese controlled – still carry a good deal of weight. A number of the old trading companies like Jardine-Matheson, Swire's, Hutchison Whampoa and others still survive; most of them are under the directorship of British executives, some of whom are members of the Legislative Council. The rich and powerful are not all British however. The majority of what passes for an upper class in Hong Kong are Chinese, many of them capitalists who fled from Shanghai and Canton before the Communist takeover in China; others are Eurasian, like Stanley Ho, the managing director of the syndicate which runs all casino gambling in Macau.

Where does power ultimately lie in Hong Kong? With powerful figures in the colony itself or with the Chinese government whose good will has allowed Hong Kong to survive for so long? Of course, now that China is due to take over Hong Kong the influence of the People's Republic in the colony is expected to rise even more. The role of the Chinese Communist Party in Hong Kong has a long history, going at least as far back as 1949 when the Communists came to power in China; perhaps earlier. Officially the CCP is called the Hong Kong Macau Work Committee (HMWC) and has always been headed by the director of the PRC's *Xinhua* news agency's Hong Kong branch, which is Beijing's official representative in the colony. Members of the HMWC include top Xinhua officials, representatives of major PRC-based commercial organisations and so on.

Another connection between Hong Kong and China are the 50 or so Hong Kong delegates to the NPC (China's rubber-stamp parliament) and to that other peculiar body, the Chinese People's Political Consultative Conference (the CPPCC). The job of the CPPCC seems to be to confer and consult among each other and provide an image of a united front between China, Macau, Hong Kong and Taiwan. Of these 50 there are 16 delegates to the NPC, all of them top people from Hong Kong's banking, business, commerce, education, trade union, media and other professional worlds – and all of them reliable pro-Beijing people. Exactly what the purpose is of having a number of prominent Hong Kong residents on powerless bodies like the NPC and CPPCC seems to be lost in the inscrutable world of Chinese politics, but presumably it creates an image of support from prominent Hong Kong people for a Chinese takeover of the colony in 1997; and in Hong Kong it's an outward sign of Beijing's seal of approval on certain people.

However, titles and positions are slippery things in China, and often don't convey the real power of their holders at all. With Hong Kong becoming more embroiled with China, trying to describe government and power-arrangements in the colony becomes more like working out a Chinese puzzle than piecing together a British jigsaw.

PEOPLE

Hong Kong has an official population of about 5,500,000, though in fact it's probably closer to six million. That makes Hong Kong, with a total land area of only 1067 square km, one of the most densely populated places in the world. The overall density of the population works out to around 5000 people per square km, but this figure is rather deceiving since there is actually extremely wide variation in density from area to area. Some metropolitan areas of the New Territories have tens of thousands of people per square km – stacked up in multi-block high-rise housing estates – while other areas are only lightly inhabited.

About 98% of Hong Kong's population is ethnic Chinese, most of them with their origins in China's Guangdong Province. About 60% of them were born in the colony. If any groups can truly claim to belong to Hong Kong, they are the Tankas, the nomadic boat people who have fished the local waters for centuries; and the Hakkas, who were farming the present-day New Territories long before Charles Elliot thought about running the Union Jack up a flagpole. The Hakka are a distinct group who emigrated from north to south China centuries ago. The Hakka women can be recognised in the New Territories by their distinctive spliced-bamboo hats with wide brims and black cloth fringes.

The other 2% of the population is made up of *gwailos* – a Chinese word which literally means 'ghost man' but which usually gets translated as 'foreign devils' – mainly westerners and other Asians. The British are the largest group of westerners at 18,000; Americans come in second at 14,000; Australians are third at 8000; and Canadians number about 6000. Of the non-Chinese Asians living here, two of the largest groups are the Filipinos at 27,000 and the Indians at 15,000. There are also sizeable communities of Pakistanis, Japanese, Thais, Indonesians, Koreans, Portuguese, Germans, Dutch and French.

One of the larger non-Chinese Asian groups in the colony is the 4500-man Gurkha force. Nepalese soldiers have served in the British army since 1817 and Hong Kong has been their headquarters since 1971. Guarding the border against the entry of illegal immigrants from China has been the principal reason for Britain's continued recruitment of these troops from Nepal, who bring in close to US$14 million a year for Nepal (about 30% of that country's foreign exchange). No one knows what will happen to the Gurkha force if its job in Hong Kong is taken over by the Chinese army in 1997.

The colony's huge Chinese population is largely a product of the events in China in the first half of this century. In 1851 the colony's population was a mere 33,000. The Qing Dynasty collapsed in 1911 and during the 1920s and 1930s the wars between the Kuomintang, the warlords, the Communists and the Japanese caused Chinese to flee to the safer confines of Hong Kong. By 1931 there were 880,000 people living there. When full-scale war between China and Japan erupted in 1937 (the Japanese having occupied Manchuria several years before) and when Canton fell in 1938, another 700,000 people fled to Hong Kong. The Japanese attacked the colony on 8 December 1941, the same day they attacked Pearl Harbour, and occupied it for the next 3½ years. Mass deportations of Chinese civilians – aimed at relieving the colony's food shortage – had reduced the population to 600,000 by 1945 but the displaced people began returning after the war. When Chiang Kai-Shek's Kuomintang forces were defeated by the Communists in 1949, another 750,000 followed them, bringing the total population to about 2½ million. During the 1950s, '60s and '70s there was a varying flow of immigrants (they're no longer called refugees) across the border from China. In two years alone at the end of the 1970s, the population went up by a quarter of a million as a result of Chinese immigration, some of it legal but most of it not. The rate of this flow varied with the diligence of the Chinese border officials and also with whatever the current policies of Beijing were. Illegal immigration from China is still a big problem.

Hong Kong has also been a destination for over 100,000 Vietnamese (or Chinese-Vietnamese) 'boat people' – several thousands of whom were allowed to stay in the colony, while the vast majority were taken in by other countries. Those who arrived in Hong Kong after July 1982 have been installed in a number of 'closed centres' – effectively prisons which they are not allowed to leave until they can be resettled in some other country. These centres include Chi Ma Wan on Lantau Island where the refugees from southern Vietnam have been grouped together, and Hei Ling Chau which holds those from northern Vietnam. This system of closed centres was designed to end boat peoples' attraction to Hong Kong.

Most recently the Chinese government seems to have quietly relaxed some of its restrictions on citizens exiting the country and Hong Kong has also been soaking up a steady stream of (legal) immigrants from China for the past few years.

ECONOMY

Hong Kong was originally established solely for the purpose of serving the needs of businesspeople, and to a large extent the colony remains dominated by business today. Regarded by some as a paragon of the virtues of capitalism, Hong Kong is a hard-working, competitive, money-oriented society. Its economic policies are a capitalist's dream: free enterprise and free trade, low wages and taxes, a hard-working labour force, a modern and efficient seaport and airport, excellent worldwide communications, and a government which rarely interferes in the running of private business.

The mainstay of Hong Kong's economy is still manufacturing, with perhaps as much as 90% of its manufactured goods being exported. Light manufacturing industries producing mainly consumer goods predominate, with almost 70% of the workforce employed in the textile, clothing, electronic, plastic, toy, watch and clock industries. Textile manufacture alone employs about 40% of all workers in manufacturing industries; another 10% are employed in over a thousand factories producing electronic goods like digital watches and transistor radios. The colony is also the world's largest supplier of toys, which are the mainstay of its plastics industry.

Generally speaking, the trend tends to be towards capital-intensive rather than labour-intensive industries with a cor-responding upward shift in wages and living conditions, but for the time being manufacturing is the most important industry.

Rising labour costs in Hong Kong have induced many investors to look to China as a new source of cheap labour in much the same way as rising labour costs (and trade barriers imposed by western governments against cheap imported goods) in Taiwan, Japan, South Korea and Singapore induced many low-technology manufacturing industries to shift to Thailand, Malaysia, the Philippines or India. While high-tech or heavy industries like ship building and electronics took the lead role in South Korea and Japan (Hong Kong has some large commercial shipping companies but their ships are almost all Japanese-built). The largest proportion of Hong Kong's exports go to the USA, which takes about 45% of the total. Other large export markets are China, Britain, West Germany, Japan, Canada, Australia and Singapore.

' In stark contrast to most other Asian states whose populations are mainly engaged in agricultural production, Hong Kong has a very small agricultural base with only about 9% of the total land area suitable for crop farming. About 2% of the total population is engaged in agriculture or fishing. Most food is imported, though Hong Kong farmers and fishermen produce about 30% of the colony's fresh vegetables, about half of its live poultry, 20% of its live pigs, 12% of its freshwater fish, and about 90% of all its sea fish – Hong Kong has a sizeable ocean fishing industry with about 29,000 fishermen working about 5000 fishing vessels. The rest of Hong Kong's food supply is imported – almost half of it from China.

In fact, because of its limited natural resources Hong Kong has to depend on imports for virtually all its requirements – including consumer goods, raw materials, equipment and fuel. It therefore has to be capable of generating enough foreign exchange through export of goods or by other means in order to pay for these imports. In this regard, one of the colony's greatest assets is its cheap labour force, which allows prices of Hong Kong goods to be competitive on the international market.

Hong Kong's 5½ to six million people include a work-force of some 2½ million – about 1,600,000 men and about 940,000 women. Some 900,000 of these are employed in the manufacturing industry in about 49,000 factories; most of these factories are very small, employing less than 50 people each. About 75% of manual workers in manufacturing industries receive daily wages of HK$74 or more; 25% receive HK$106 or more. Officially, all industries taken into account, the average daily wage works out to about HK$106 for males and HK$86 for women. However, such figures are rather deceiving since many workers are often paid much less than the standard rate; there is no minimum wage. Women make up a sizeable part of the work force in some industries – some 90% of electronics workers are women – but are often paid less than men. Of a work force of some 2½ million people only about 350,000 are unionised, a situation which appears to suit Hong Kong capitalists as much as it does the Chinese government which, arguably, believes that a strong independent union movement could become the focus of mass political discontent and upset the 'stability and unity' of the colony which is of such great importance to China's economic development.

By and large the living standards and wages of most people in Hong Kong are much higher than those of China or most other Asian countries – barring Japan and Singapore. While China aims to increase average yearly income to US$800 per head by the end of the century, in Hong Kong average per capita income is already around US$4000 or more a year. Maximum personal income tax is no more than 15%, company profits tax does not exceed 17% and there are no capital gains or transfer taxes. But the money is not evenly spread and there are great extremes of living conditions in the colony, with thousands of people living in shanty town housing. Despite the massive housing estates you see in the New Territories, huge numbers of people live in squatter huts, tin shacks perched on hillsides without proper sanitation – easy prey for fires and typhoons. Even these shacks don't always come free. Symptomatic of too many people and too little space, there is a brisk (though illegal) trade in the sale of squatter huts. A stone hut will cost about HK$80,000-100,000 and a wooden hut will cost about HK$30,000 – cheap by Hong Kong housing standards but a pathetic situation considering the amount of money that passes through this colony. The relatively low taxation rate is offset by fairly meagre spending on social welfare. There is no national health system, and though costs at public hospitals and clinics are fairly low, everything has to be paid for by the user.

Hong Kong's importance to China is manifold. For the first three decades after the Communist takeover in China in 1949, China was largely content to sell Hong Kong foodstuffs, raw material and fuel. Hong Kong bought the produce and in return provided China with a large proportion of its foreign-exchange earnings, as it continues to do today. Chinese investments in Hong Kong property, manufacturing and service industries possibly amount to a third of all direct foreign investment in the colony, giving China a much greater hold on the colony than might otherwise be thought. The list and the diversity of the enterprises gets bigger every year. About half of all livestock exported by China goes to Hong Kong; Chinese factories trying to upgrade their tools and equipment make Hong Kong one of their first shopping stops since the colony can produce or easily arrange to import what they need; South Korean businesspeople trade with China through Hong Kong middle-men. Trade between Taiwan and China, using Hong Kong as the middle-person, has been going on for years and is getting bigger every year. Taiwan sells light industrial products, electrical appliances, textiles and other consumer goods to China, and buys herbs, seafood, wool and mineral products. The coastline of Fujian Province, adjacent to Taiwan, has also seen a lively direct trade between the two countries, using Taiwanese and Fujianese fishing boats to carry goods. Such links were finally made official in 1985 and Fujian Province will now permit Taiwanese ships to land in Fujianese ports and carry on direct trade.

Nor is China the only country with a profound interest in what happens to Hong Kong after 1997. The Japanese have enormous assets in Hong Kong: Japanese construction companies dominate the building industry in Hong Kong; more than half of Hong Kong's underground railway was built by Japanese companies; almost all the commercial shipping under the control of Hong Kong owners was built in Japan; there are Japanese-owned department stores in the colony and more are planned . . . the list goes on.

No description of Hong Kong is complete without mentioning the tourist industry, which is a big money-earner. The number of visitors to the colony keeps on increasing steadily every year and now stands at just over three million a year. Apart from pulling in more tourists, Hong Kong is also trying to sell itself as an international conference and exhibition centre, and there are plans to build yet another 15 major hotels between now and 1990!

Apart from western tourists, Hong Kong is a favourite destination of visitors from China. In 1980 almost 75,000 Chinese citizens travelled legally to Hong Kong – and the figure more than doubled to around 185,000 in 1984. Of these 185,000 some 28,000 came on organised tours run by a company owned jointly by the China Travel Service (the Chinese national travel organisation) and the Guangdong provincial government. It's not just Chinese from Guangdong Province who visit the colony; CTS also draws its clientele from Jiangsu, Fujian, and Zhejiang provinces, and from as far away as Shanghai, Tianjin and Beijing. A sizeable number of these visitors – perhaps 20,000 a year – are hosted by Hong Kong organisations like the Hong Kong-based Chinese General Chamber of Commerce.

RELIGION

Chinese religion has been influenced by three great streams in human thinking: Taoism, Confucianism and Buddhism. Each of these is more a philosophy than a religion, but all have been inextricably entwined in the popular religion, along with ancient animist beliefs. The founders of Taoism, Confucianism and Buddhism have been deified and the Chinese have worshipped both them and their disciples as fervently as they've worshipped their own ancestors and a pantheon of gods and spirits – the whole lot permeated with sorcery and magic.

Taoism

According to tradition, the founder of Taoism is a man known as Lao Tzu. He is said to have been born around the year 604 BC, but there's some doubt that he ever lived at all. If he did live, then almost nothing is known about him – we don't even know his name. 'Lao Tzu' translates as 'the old boy' or the 'Grand Old Master.' Legends depict Lao Tzu as having been conceived by a shooting star, carried in his unfortunate mother's womb for 82 years, and born as a wise old man with white hair. Another story goes that he was the keeper of the government archives in a western state of China, and that Confucius visited him. At the end of his life, Lao Tzu is said to have climbed on a water buffalo and ridden west towards what is now Tibet, in search of solitude for his last few years. On the way, he was asked to leave behind a

Lao Tzu

by reflection and intuition, orders his life in harmony with the way of the universe and achieves the understanding or experience of Tao. The second kind holds that the power of the universe is basically psychic in nature and that by practising yogic exercises and meditation a number of individuals can become receptacles for *Tao* – they can then radiate a healing, calming, psychic influence over those around them.

In the third kind of Taoism, the power of the universe is believed to be the power of gods, magic and sorcery. Unlike philosophical Taoism, which has many followers in the west, Chinese Taoism is a religion. It has been associated with alchemy and the search for immortality, and partly because of this the Taoists often attracted the patronage of various Chinese rulers before Confucianism gained the upper hand. In fact it's arguable that only philosophical Taoism actually takes its inspiration from the *Tao Te Ching*, and that all the other labels under which 'Taoism' has been practised attached themselves to the book as they developed, using the name of Lao Tzu to give themselves respectability and status.

record of his beliefs, and the product was a slim volume of only 5000 characters – the *Tao Te Ching*, or *The Way and its Power*. He then rode off on his buffalo.

At the centre of Taoism is the concept of *Tao*. Tao cannot be perceived, because it exceeds the senses, thoughts and imagination; it can only be known through mystical insight which cannot be expressed with words. Tao is the way of the universe, the driving power in nature, the order behind all life, the spirit which cannot be exhausted. Tao is the way people should follow to keep in harmony with the natural order of the universe.

Just as there have been different interpretations of the 'way,' there have been different interpretations of *Te* – the power. This has led to the development of three distinct kinds of Taoism in China. One kind holds that the power of Tao is philosophical; the philosophical Taoist,

Confucianism

With the exception of Mao, the one name which has become synonymous with China is Confucius. He was born of a poor family around the year 551 BC in what is now Shandong Province. Confucius' ambition was to hold a high government office and to reorder society through the administrative apparatus. At best he seems to have held several insignificant government posts and though he had his followers his career was permanently blocked. At the age of 50 he perceived his 'divine mission,' and for the next 13 years tramped from state to state offering unsolicited advice to rulers on how to improve their governing. The opportunity to put his own ideas into practice never arose. He returned to his own state on invitation from a new government, but

Confucius

realising that he was too old for public office, he spent the last five years of his life quietly teaching and editing classical literature. He died in 479 BC at the age of about 72.

The glorification of Confucius began only after his death, but eventually his ideas permeated every level of Chinese society – government offices presupposed a knowledge of the Confucian classics, and spoken proverbs trickled down to the illiterate masses. During the Han dynasty (206 BC-220 AD) Confucianism effectively became the state religion. In 130 BC Confucianism was made the basic discipline for training government officials, and remained so until almost the end of the Qing Dynasty in 1911. In 59 AD, sacrifices were ordered for Confucius in all urban

schools; in the 7th and 8th centuries, during the Tang dynasty, temples and shrines were built to him and his original disciples. Under the Sung Dynasty the Confucian bible, *The Analects*, became the basis of all education.

It's not difficult to see why Confucianism became so popular in China. What characterised the China of Confucius' time was the multiplicity of states in perpetual conflict. The long reign of the Zhou dynasty had come to an end around 770 BC as the emperor's power declined and the vassal states asserted their independence. The following centuries were a period of war between these states; the larger ones annexed the smaller ones and by 400 BC only seven remained, locked in a perpetual state of conflict known in Chinese history as the 'Warring States Period.'

Against this background of disorder, Confucius sought a way which would allow people to live together peacefully. His solution was tradition. He believed that there had once been a period of great peace and prosperity in China. This period, he said, had been brought about because people lived by certain traditions which maintained order, and he advocated a return to this way of life.

Confucius did not simply recount the traditions of the past; he devised what he thought were the values necessary for collective well-being. The study of 'correct attitudes' then became the primary task; moral ideas had to be driven into the people by every possible means – in temples, theatres, homes, schools and at festivals, as well as through proverbs and folk stories. Confucius aimed to instill a feeling of humanity towards others and a respect for oneself, a sense of the dignity of human life. Courtesy, selflessness, magnanimity, diligence and empathy – the ideal relationships between human beings – would follow automatically. His ideal person was free of violence and vulgarity, and was competent, poised, fearless and even-tempered.

There are several bulwarks of Confucianism but the one which has probably had the most influence on the day-to-day life of the Chinese is *li*, which has two meanings. The first meaning is propriety— how things should be done, a knowledge of how to behave in a given situation, a set of manners. Behind the concept of li stands the presumption that the various roles and relationships of life have been clearly defined. In the Confucian scheme of things there are five main relationships: father-son, elder brother-younger brother, husband-wife, elder friend-junior friend, and ruler-subject. What you do affects others so you are never alone when you act; your actions must not damage or create conflict for other individuals. The family retains its central place as the basic unit of society (Confucianism reinforced this idea, but did not invent it). The key to family order is filial piety, or childrens' respect for and duty towards their parents. Also embedded in the concept of li is respect for age, which gives everything – people, objects, institutions – their dignity and worth. The old may be at their weakest physically, but they are at the peak of their wisdom, knowledge and experience; respect flows upwards, from young to old. The second meaning of li is ritual. When life is detailed to Confucian lengths it becomes completely ordered with clearly defined rules about how people should act in a given situation.

The tightly bound Confucian society, with strict codes of conduct and clearly defined patterns of obedience, became an inextricable part of Chinese society. Women obeyed and deferred to men, younger brothers to elder brothers, sons to fathers, and age was venerated. Teamed with traditional superstition, Confucianism reinforced the practice of ancestor-worship; Confucius himself is worshipped (though it's debatable whether he's considered a god by the Chinese) and there is a temple to him at Causeway Bay. The strict codes were further held together by the concept of 'face.' Letting down the family or group by falling short of their expectations is a source of great shame for the Chinese. Finally, all people rendered homage to the emperor, who was regarded as the embodiment of Confucian wisdom and virtue and as the head of the great family-nation. Dynasties rose or fell, but the Confucian pattern never changed.

Buddhism

Buddhism was founded in India around the 6th century BC. The founder was Siddhartha Gautama of the Sakyas; Siddhartha was his given name, Gautama his surname and Sakya the name of the clan to which his family belonged. Siddhartha was a prince brought up in luxury, but in his 20s he became discontented with the world when, so the story goes, he was confronted with the spectacle of old age, sickness and death. He despaired of ever finding fulfilment on the physical level, since the body was inescapably involved with disease, decrepitude and death. Around the age of 30 he made his break from the material world, and plunged off in search of 'enlightenment.' After several failed attempts he devoted the final phase of his search to meditation and mystic concentration, and one evening, so the story goes, he sat beneath a fig tree, slipped into a deep meditation and emerged from it having achieved enlightenment.

Buddha founded an order of monks and for the next 45 years preached his ideas until his death around 480 BC. To his followers he was known as Sakyamuni, the 'silent sage of the Sakya clan,' a name which expressed the unfathomable mystery that surrounded him. Gautama Buddha is not the only Buddha, but the fourth, and he is not expected to be the last one.

The cornerstone of Buddhist philosophy is that all life is suffering, that everyone is subjected to the trauma of birth, sickness, decrepitude and death, and that one is always tied to what one abhors (an incurable disease or an ineradicable personal weakness) as well as to separation from what one loves. Real happiness cannot be achieved until suffering is overcome. The cause of unhappiness is desire – specifically the desires of the body and the desire for personal fulfilment. Happiness can only be achieved if these desires are overcome, and this requires following the eight-fold path. By following this path the Buddhist aims for *nirvana*, a state of bliss beyond the limits of mind, feelings, desire and will.

The first step in the path is 'right knowledge', the belief that life is suffering, that suffering is caused by desire for personal gratification, that suffering can be overcome, and that the way to overcome it is to follow the eight-fold path. The second step is 'right aspiration' – passionate involvement with the knowledge of what life's problems basically are. The other steps require that one refrain from lying, idle talk, abuse, slander and deceit; that one show kindness and avoid self-seeking and personal fulfilment in all actions; that one develop virtues and curb passions; and that one practice yoga in order to achieve a personal experience of what lies hidden away within oneself.

Buddhism developed in China during the 3rd to 6th centuries. It was probably introduced by Indian merchants who took Buddhist priests with them on their land and sea journeys to China. Later, an active effort was made to import Buddhism into China. In the middle of the 1st century the religion had gained the interest of the Han Emperor Ming, who sent a mission to the west in search of Buddhism. They returned in 67 AD with two Indian monks, scriptures and images of the Buddha. Centuries later, other Chinese monks like Xuan Zang journeyed to India and returned with Buddhist scriptures which were then translated from the original Sanskrit to Chinese – a massive job involving Chinese as well as foreign scholars from Central Asia, India and Sri Lanka.

Buddhism spread rapidly in the north of China where it was patronised by most of the invading rulers, who in some cases had been acquainted with the religion before they came to China. Others deliberately patronised the Buddhist monks because they wanted educated officials who were not Confucians. In the south Buddhism spread more slowly, carried down during the times of the Chinese migrations from the north. There were several periods during which Buddhists were persecuted and their temples and monasteries sacked and destroyed, but the religion survived. To a people constantly facing starvation, war and poverty, its appeal probably lay in the doctrines of reincarnation and nirvana which were borrowed from Indian Hinduism.

Buddhist monasteries and temples sprang up everywhere in China. These played a role similar to that of the churches and monasteries of mediaeval Europe; they were guest houses for travellers, hospitals, orphanages and refuges. With gifts obtained from the faithful, the monasteries were able to accumulate considerable wealth which enabled them to set up money-lending enterprises and pawn-shops. These pawnshops were the poor man's bank right up until the middle of the 20th century.

At some stage Buddhism split into two major schools. The Hinayana or 'little raft' school (the Buddhism of Sri Lanka, Burma, Thailand and Kampuchea) holds that the path to nirvana is an individual pursuit. It centres on the monks, individuals who make the search for nirvana a full-time profession; man is alone in the world and must tread the path to nirvana on his own. Buddhas can only show the way.

The second school, Mahayana or 'big raft,' is the Buddhism of Vietnam, Japan, Tibet, Korea, Mongolia and China. It holds that since all existence is one, the fate of the individual is linked to the fate of all others. The Buddha did not just point the way and float off into his own nirvana; he continues to offer spiritual help to others seeking nirvana.

The outward manifestation of the difference between the two schools is the cosmology that was either spawned or taken up by the Mahayana school. Mahayana Buddhism is replete with innumerable heavens, hells and descriptions of nirvana; prayers of thanks and prayers for guidance are addressed to the Buddha, combined with elaborate ritual. Buddhist deities were created and the worship of *bodhisattvas*, a rank of supernatural beings in their last incarnation before nirvana, became important. Temples are filled with images of Maitreya, the future Buddha, often portrayed as fat and happy over his coming promotion; and of Amitabha, a saviour who rewards the faithful with admission to a sort of Christian paradise. The ritual, tradition and superstition rejected by Buddha came tumbling back in with a vengeance.

In Hong Kong today there are a number of Buddhist temples and monasteries, of which the most famous is the Po Lin Monastery on Lantau Island. There's also a Temple of 10,000 Buddhas at Shatin and another at the Mui Fat Monastery at Lam Tei, both in the New Territories. In all there are about 360 Buddhist and Taoist temples, shrines and monasteries in Hong Kong.

Chinese Religion

To say that the Chinese have three religions – Taoism, Buddhism and Confucianism – is too simple a view of their religious life. On a day-to-day level the Chinese are much less concerned with the high-minded philosophies and asceticism of Buddha, Confucius or Lao Tzu than they are with the pursuit of worldly success, the appeasement of the dead and the spirits, and the seeking of hidden knowledge about the future. Their religion is inextricably tangled up with what the west regards as superstition. If you want your fortune told, for instance, you go to a temple. Old animistic beliefs combine with Taoism to teach people how to maintain harmony with the universe. Confucianism takes care of the political and moral aspects of life, and Buddhism takes care of the afterlife.

The most important word in the Chinese popular religious vocabulary is *joss* – it means 'luck,' and the Chinese are too astute to leave something as important as luck to chance. Gods have to be appeased, bad spirits blown away and sleeping dragons soothed to keep joss on your side. No house, wall or shrine is built until an auspicious date for the start of construction is chosen and the most propitious location is selected. Incense has to be burned, gifts presented and prayers said to appease the spirits who might inhabit the future construction site.

Fung-shui – literally 'wind-water' – is the Chinese art (or science if you prefer) of manipulating or judging the environment. If you want to build a house or find a suitable site for a grave then you call an expert in fung-shui. Without fung-sui an apartment block cannot be built, freeways cannot be laid, telephone poles cannot be erected and trees cannot be chopped down. Fung-shui is decided by unseen currents that swirl around the surface of the earth and by dragons which sleep beneath the ground, neither of which must be disturbed by humans. If you intend to build a block of flats you must first get the fung-shui priest to survey the site to ensure it doesn't lie on a sleeping dragon; the wrath of a dragon who wakes to find a high-rise apartment block on his tail can easily be imagined. If you can't find a fung-sui person to do the job, then you call Taoist priests who know how to deal with the spirits which would otherwise create trouble. Construction of Hong Kong's underground Mass Transit Railway began with an invocation by a group of Taoist priests who paid respects to the spirits of the earth whose domain was about to be violated.

You also call the priest before you lop down a tree. It might have a spirit living in it and you make a spirit homeless at your

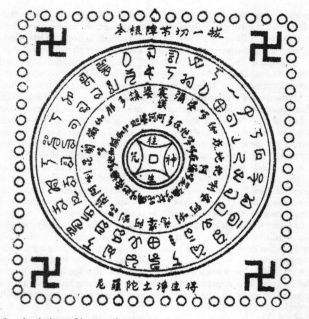

本根障苦切一城

尼羅陀土淨生得

Paper pasted on back door of houses for good luck

peril. Traditionally villages actually planted groves of trees around their settlement for the good spirits to live in. You can still see some of the fung-shui groves in old villages in the New Territories. If you come across a joss stick burning at the foot of a tree, you will know there is a spirit inside – this practice is still common among the Hakka and Chui Chow villagers.

Thus, at its first level Chinese religion is animistic – a belief in the innate liveliness of rocks, trees, rivers and springs. Then there are figures from the distant past where history blends into mythology – like Huang Ti, the Yellow Emperor and mythical founder of Chinese civilisation – who are now worshipped as gods. There are also gods who were real people deified as a result of their actions on earth. Overlaid on these are Taoism, Buddhism and Confucianism. Mahayana Buddhism has developed a whole menagerie of bodhisattvas. Taoism has enlisted hundreds of gods to be worshipped as well as *shin* (spirits) to be placated; it has also developed its own hierarchy of immortals, after the Buddhist bodhisattvas. Glance into any shop or home in Hong Kong and you will see the 'god shelf' with its burning joss-sticks and its statue of Buddha nudging a Taoist house-god. Often you will see the same in temples.

Integral parts of Chinese religion are death, the after-life and ancestor-worship. At least as far back as China's Shang Dynasty (16th to 11th century BC) there were lavish funeral ceremonies involving the internment of horses, carriages, wives and slaves. The more important the person, the more possessions and people had to be buried with him on the grounds that he required them in the next world. The deceased had to be kept happy because his powers to inflict punishments or to grant favours greatly increased after his death.

Even today a funeral can be a lavish event. You can't miss a Chinese funeral. First there's the clash of cymbals and moan of oboes (most unmelodic to western ears). Then comes the clover-shaped coffin and grief-stricken mourners, some paid to weep and many wearing strange 'Ku Klux Klan' outfits with white hoods. A fine spread of roast pigs and other foods, not to be eaten but offered to the gods for the one gone beyond, accompanies the funeral. A gravesite is chosen on the side of hills with a good view for the loved one who must lie there. You can see huge 'armchair'-shaped graves out in the country. At the graveside the mourners burn paper models of material pleasures like cars and boats as well as bundles of paper money, to ensure that the dead person is getting the good things of the first life in the great beyond. Just as during the Shang Dynasty when the dead continue to look after the welfare of the living, the living continue to take care of the dead. The custom was reinforced by the Confucian value of filial piety, but it's probably motivated more by fear than respect for the dead.

Chinese Gods

The important thing to remember is that Chinese religion is polytheistic. Apart from Buddha, Lao Tzu and Confucius there are many other divinities. Every Chinese house has its 'kitchen' or house god, and trades have their own gods too. Students worship Wan-Chung, the deified scholar. Shopkeepers pray to Tsai Shin, god of riches. There are a number of temples in Hong Kong and Macau dedicated to particular gods or goddesses. Some of the important local divinities are described below.

Tin Hau One of the most popular goddesses in Hong Kong is Tin Hau, Queen of Heaven and Protector of Seafarers. In Macau she is known as Ah Ma or Mother. In Taiwan she is known as Ma Jo or Ancestress. In Singapore she is Ma Chu Po or Respected Great Aunt because many fishing people dedicate their children to her.

In Hong Kong, Tin Hau can claim quarter of a million fishing people as followers, and she has about two dozen temples of her own dotted around the colony. The most famous is the Da Miao (Great Temple) at Joss House Bay near Fat Tong Mun. Other Tin Hau temples are on Cheung Chau Island; at Sok Kwu Wan

Hell Banknote

on Lamma Island; on Market St in Kowloon's Yaumati district; on Tin Hau Temple Rd in Causeway Bay; and at Stanley village on the south coast of Hong Kong Island.

Tin Hau is a classic case of the deification of a real person. She was born on an island in Fujian Province around 900 to 1000 AD. The story goes that one day she went into a trance and dreamt that there would be a storm which would destroy all the boats in the fishing fleet. Running down the beach she stared fixedly at her father's boat, which was thus the only one saved when the storm blew up. For deep-sea fishermen the story goes that in her trance she saw that the storm had already hit and that the fleet was in trouble. In spirit she arrived at the scene and began to lead her brothers to safety.

After her death the cult of Tin Hau spread along the coast of China and she became the patron goddess of fishermen. The story goes that in the 11th century two members of her family were shipwrecked on Tung Lung Island in what is now Hong Kong and built a temple for her. Their descendants were responsible for building the original temple at Joss House Bay in 1266. Kublai Khan, the Mongol emperor of China, made her 'Tin Hau' or Queen of Heaven in 1278 – possibly a political move to curry favour with the southern Chinese.

Kuan Yin Tin Hau is primarily a Taoist deity. Her Buddhist equivalent is Kuan Yin (also known as Kwun Yum, and as Kuan Iam in Macau), the Goddess of Mercy, who stands for tenderness and compassion for the unhappy lot of mortals. Kuan Yin temples include those at Repulse Bay and Stanley on Hong Kong Island. There are also some in Macau.

Kuan Ti Soldiers pray to Kuan Ti, the red-faced God of War. Prior to his deification Kuan Ti was a great warrior who lived at the end of the Han Dynasty (206 BC–220 AD) and is worshipped not only for his

The Kitchen God

might in battle but also because he is the embodiment of 'right action,' of integrity and loyalty. The life of Kuan Ti is told in an old Chinese legend called *The Story of the Three Kingdoms*.

A cult developed around Kuan Ti after his death, and by the 7th century the Buddhists had adopted him as one of their own. In the 12th century he was ennobled by the emperor as a 'Faithful and Loyal Duke,' and then as a 'Magnificent Prince and Pacifier.' In 1594 he was made a god by the Ming Emperor Wan Li, who gave him the title of 'Supporter of Heaven and Protector of the Kingdom.' Since then he has been worshipped as the God of War. However, Kuan Ti is not a cruel tyrant delighting in battle and the slaying of enemies; rather, he can avert war and protect people from its horrors.

Kuan Ti is revered not only by soldiers but by many other professions. He is the patron god of restaurants, pawn shops, and of literature; and he is also the patron god of both the Hong Kong police force and secret societies such as the Triad organisations.

Kuan Ti temples in Hong Kong include the one at Tai O on Lantau Island, and the Man Mo (literally 'civil and military') Temple on Hollywood Rd, Hong Kong Island.

Pak Tai Gods for special localities watch over their own little acre. Pak Tai keeps an eye out for Cheung Chau Island, and Wong Tai Sin does the same for a housing settlement in Kowloon.

Like Kuan Ti, Pak Tai is a military protector of the state and there are various stories about his origins. One is that he lived around 2000 BC and was responsible for introducing flood control and drainage systems. Another is that he was placed at the head of a heavenly army to fight two monsters who were ravaging the earth, and having destroyed them was made the First Lord of Heaven. He also holds the title of Emperor of the North, and north being associated with death he is therefore overlord of the realms of the dead. Since the ancestors are the spiritual guardians of their descendants, Pak Tai is the Guardian of Society. When chaos reigns and there is destruction he is believed to descend from heaven to restore peace and order.

On the island of Cheung Chau Pak Tai is revered as a life-giver, for it was through his intervention that a plague which hit the island at the end of the last century was brought to an end. There is a large temple on Cheung Chau, the Temple of Jade Vacuity, dedicated to him.

Tam Kung Tam Kung is a god worshipped only along a small stretch of the southern Chinese coast which includes Macau and Hong Kong. One theory is that he is actually the last emperor of the Southern Song Dynasty (1127-1279 AD) which was overrun by Kublai Khan's Mongol armies. This emperor was a boy of eight or nine years who is now worshipped under the pseudonym of Tam Kung. The story goes that the boy emperor and his retinue paused on the Kowloon Peninsula during their flight from the Mongols and that for some reason he came to be worshipped as a god. A temple for Tam Kung can be seen in Coloane village in Macau.

Wong Tai Sin This god watches over the housing settlement of the same name in Kowloon. Wong Tai Sin had a meteoric rise to success in the colony, having been brought to Hong Kong in 1915 by a man and his son who came from Guangdong Province carrying a painting of him. They installed the painting and an altar in a small temple in Wanchai. A temple for the god was built in Kowloon in 1921 and his popularity grew and grew. One story goes that Wong Tai Sin is a deified shepherd boy. Another theory holds that he may originally have been worshipped as Huang Ti – the mythical yellow emperor and one of the oldest gods of China – but has now come down in status.

The Chinese Temple

Architecturally, the roof is the dominant feature of a Chinese temple. It is usually green or yellow and is decorated with figures of divinities and lucky symbols such as dragons and carp. Stone lions often guard the entrance to the temple. Inside is a small courtyard with a large bowl where incense and paper offerings are burnt. Beyond is the main hall with an altar table, often with an intricately carved front. Here you'll find offerings of fruit and drinks. Behind is the altar with its images framed by red brocade embroidered with gold characters. Depending on the size and wealth of the temple there are gongs, drums, side altars and adjoining rooms with shrines to different gods, chapels for prayers to the dead and displays of funerary plaques. There are also living quarters for the temple keepers.

The dominant colours in a Chinese temple are red, gold or yellow, and green. The orange to red colour range represents joy and festivity. (Red is the colour of marriage and in the old days the bridegroom sent for his bride in a red sedan chair. Today it's a hire-car with red ribbons.) White represents purity and is also the colour of death. Green signifies harmony, of fundamental importance to the Chinese. Yellow and gold stand for heavenly glory. Grey and black are the colours of disaster and grief.

There is no set time for prayer and no communal service except for funerals. Worshippers enter the temple whenever they want to make offerings, pray for help or give thanks. The temple keeper, in casual singlet and sandals, earns his living by selling joss sticks or spirals of joss which are suspended from the ceiling and burn for two weeks.

The temple keeper and/or a medium attached to the temple also charges for interpreting fortune papers. These are numbered to correspond with sticks of wood which the worshipper shakes in a cylindrical box called a *chim* until one falls out. Another way of getting advice from the gods is tossing *sing pui*, two pieces of wood with irregular sides which indicate a positive or negative response to a question. Such forms of fortune-telling are direct appeals to the gods for knowledge about the future – the fall of the fortune sticks or the *sing pui* is regarded as the voice of the gods.

In addition, temples often have shelves filled with the 60 *tai sue*, gods in charge of each year of the Chinese calendar. Worshippers make offerings to the god of the year they were born. If you've ever wondered what year you were born in, here's the chart – but remember that Chinese New Year usually falls in late January or early February, so the first month will be included in the year before.

snake	29 41 53 65 77 89
horse	30 42 54 66 78 90
sheep	31 43 55 67 79 91
monkey	32 44 56 68 80 92
cock	33 45 57 69 81 93
dog	34 46 58 70 82 94
pig	35 47 59 71 83 95
rat	36 48 60 72 84 96
ox	37 49 61 73 85 97
tiger	38 50 62 74 86 98
rabbit	39 51 63 75 87 99
dragon	40 52 64 76 88 00

It is said that the 'Animal Year' chart originated when Buddha commanded all the beasts of the earth to assemble before him. Only 12 animals came and they were rewarded by having their names given to a specific year. Buddha also decided to name each year in the order in which the animals arrived – the first was the rat, then the ox, tiger, rabbit and so on.

Christianity

The Christian community in Hong Kong is estimated to number about 500,000 – about 274,000 Roman Catholics and the rest Protestants, the latter broken up into some 50 different denominations and sects including Lutherans, Baptists, Quakers and Mormons. A list of all of the colony's churches can be found in the yellow pages of the telephone directory. Church services are advertised in Saturday's *South China Morning Post* newspaper.

Sikhism

The Sikhs, from the Punjab province of north-west India, are distinguished by their beards and uncut hair wrapped in turbans. They first came to Hong Kong as part of the British Armed Forces in the 19th century. Because of their generally strong physique, before WW II they comprised a large segment of the Hong

Top: Trams offer a cheap but slow scenic tour of the island (AS)
Left: For a more elevated view take the Peak Tram (JH)
Right: Another Star ferry crosses the harbour (JH)

Top: Freshly caught squid from Cheung Chau (AS)
Left: Flattened chickens in a Hong Kong market (AS)
Right: A fish shop in Macau (TW)

Kong Police Force. (Colonial powers made use of foreigners who would make no alliances with the local population; the British use Gurkhas to patrol Hong Kong's border with China, and before the war the French piece of Shanghai was policed by Vietnamese.) The Sikh temple is at the corner of Stubbs and Queen's Road East in Happy Valley, on the Hong Kong side of the harbour. Religious services are held every Sunday morning.

Islam

There are about 50,000 followers of Islam in Hong Kong. Approximately half of them are Chinese; the rest are from Pakistan, India, Malaysia, Indonesia and the Middle East. The oldest mosque in the colony is the Jamia Mosque on Shelley St, Hong Kong Island, built around the turn of the century and rebuilt in 1915. The newest Islamic landmark is the recently completed and imposing Kowloon Central Mosque on Nathan Rd, not far from Chungking Mansions.

Hinduism

There are about 10,000 Hindus in the colony. Their temple is on Carnarvon Rd, Happy Valley, and a number of Hindu festivals are observed there. The temple is also used for meditation and yoga, as well as for teaching, and often has visiting swamis and gurus. Religious music and recitals are performed every Sunday morning and Monday evening.

Jewish

Hong Kong's Jewish community worships on Friday evenings, Saturday mornings and on Jewish holidays at the Synagogue 'Ohel Leah' in Robinson Rd, Hong Kong Island. The buildings here include a rabbi's residence and a recreation club for the 1000 people in the congregation.

FESTIVALS & HOLIDAYS

Hong Kong's Chinese and western cultures have combined to produce a grand total of 17 public holidays a year. Chinese festivals,

which account for most of the 17, follow the old lunar calendar with its 13 moons of 28 days and are therefore not fixed by western diaries. If you are in Hong Kong at festival time you will soon know it. Everything that moves is packed with the devoted, who are visiting ancestral graves and sites or temples. You can't move on ferries, buses or trains – which is no reason for not joining the crush and going along.

Many of these festivals go back hundreds, if not thousands, of years, their true origins often lost in the mists of time. The reasons for each of these festivals vary and you will generally find there are a couple of tales to choose from. The HKTA has a free leaflet called *Chinese Festivals & Special Events* which will tell you the exact dates the festival celebrations are to be held that year.

Chinese New Year

Chinese New Year marks the start of the lunar calendar and is celebrated either at the end of January or the beginning of February. In the old days it went on for a week or 10 days; nowadays it's a three-day holiday, and though just about everything closes down you won't starve in the tourist areas.

The festival is a family one, with nothing much to see for the visitor. Since it marks the beginning of the new year, houses are cleaned, debts paid off and feuds, no matter how bitter, made up – even if it's only for the day. Pictures of gods are pasted up around the front doors of houses to scare off the bad spirits, all with messages of welcome on red paper to encourage the good ones.

Everyone, by tradition, asks for double wages. The garbage collector, the milk deliverer and so on get *lai see* (lucky money) in red envelopes as tips, which are good reasons for the traditional Chinese New Year greeting *Kung hey fat choi* – literally 'good wishes, good fortune.' If you go to get your hair cut you will find it costs you double in the week leading up to the

New Year. Even cinemas put their prices up. Nor is it the time to go to China; hordes of Hong Kong people cram the trains and every other form of transport to carry them back to the mother country to visit the relatives.

Worth going to see are the huge flower fairs where, on the night before New Year's Day, the Chinese buy lucky peach blossoms, kumquat trees and narcissi from the hundreds of flower sellers (the peach is regarded as a symbol of longevity; the Taoist God of Longevity Sau Shing-kung, with his white beard and enormous dome-shaped head, is believed to have emerged from a peach). Victoria Park in Causeway Bay, Hong Kong Island, is the place to go though it's jam-packed with crowds. Other than that, there isn't much else to see at Chinese New Year. You might catch a lion dance in a local street, and you will certainly see one specially laid on in the top tourist hotels.

Lantern Festival
At the end of the Chinese New Year celebrations, customarily the 15th day of the first moon (middle or end of February), lanterns in traditional designs are lit up in homes, restaurants and temples. This is called Yuen Siu, or the Lantern Festival.

Ching Ming
Celebrated at the beginning of the third moon, usually in April, Ching Ming is very much a family affair almost like Easter. It is a time for visiting graves, traditionally to call up the ancestors and ask them if they are satisfied with their descendants. Graves are cleaned and food and wine left for the spirits, while incense and paper money are burned at the graveside for the dead. Some people follow the custom of pasting long strips of red and white paper to the graves to indicate that the rituals have been performed. The festival is thought to have its origins during the Han period some 2000 years ago, when ancestors' tombs were swept, washed and repaired.

Tin Hau Festival
One of Hong Kong's most colourful occasions, the festival is traditionally held the 23rd day of the third moon – usually sometime in May – and about three weeks after Ching Ming. Tin Hau, patroness of fishing-people, is one of the colony's most popular goddesses. (See the section on Religion above for a description of Tin Hau.)

Junks are decorated with flags and sail in long rows to Tin Hau's temples around the colony to pray for clear skies and good catches. Often her image is taken from the temple and paraded through the streets. Shrines from the junks are carried to the shore to be blessed by Taoist priests.

The best place to see the festival and the fortune telling, lion dances and Chinese opera that follows is at the site of Tin Hau's best-known temple, the Tai Miao Temple in Joss House Bay. It's not accessible by road and is not on the normal ferry route but at Tin Hau Festival time the ferry company lays on excursion trips there. They are, needless to say, packed out. Another major Tin Hau temple is at Sok Kwu Wan on Lamma Island. The Tin Hau temple at Stanley on the south coast of Hong Kong Island was built sometime before the mid-18th century and is the oldest building still standing in Hong Kong.

Cheung Chau Festival
Also known as the Bun Festival of Tai Chiu, this celebration is held in May on Cheung Chau Island, traditionally on the sixth day of the fourth moon. Precise dates are decided by village elders on the island about three weeks before. A Taoist festival (like the Tin Hau festival), it is one of the annual festival calendar highlights.

The Cheung Chau festival was originally held, according to one story, to placate evil spirits who caused a severe storm on the island which, closely followed by a plague, decimated Cheung Chau's population. These spirits are said to be those of thousands of early settlers of the island who were massacred by the notorious pirate Cheung Po Tsai.

There are three or four days of religious observances. On the first day, three 20-metre towers of buns set on bamboo scaffolding are erected on the waterfront outside the Pak Tai Temple (the Temple of the Jade Vacuity). Until a few years ago people would clamber up them trying to get the topmost, luckiest, buns. Because of an accident in 1978, they're no longer allowed to climb the towers and the buns

Joss Paper packet

are now handed out. If you go to Cheung Chau a week or so before the festival you'll see these huge bamboo towers – like the frameworks of rocket-ships – being built in the square in front of the Pak Tai Temple.

A priest reads a dictate calling on the villagers to abstain from meat so no animal will be killed on the island during festival time. On the third day there is a procession with floats, tableaux, people dressed up as legendary characters, stiltwalkers – and a speciality, children apparently floating in space with the aid of cunningly concealed wire harnesses beneath their costumes.

During the celebrations a number of deities are worshipped, including Tin Hau, Pak Tai and Hung Hsing (the God of the South) – all three are of significance to people who make their living from the sea. Homage is also paid to To Tei the God of the Earth, and to Kuan Yin the Goddess of Mercy. Offerings are made to the spirits of all the fish and animals whose lives have been sacrificed to provide food, and during the four days of worship no meat is eaten.

Extra ferries are laid on for the festival, but they're all packed. Still, go if you can. This is a purely Cheung Chau festival and you won't see it anywhere else.

Birthday of Lord Buddha

Also referred to as the Bathing of Lord Buddha, this is a rather more sedate occasion, celebrated on the eighth day of the fourth moon – usually in late May. The Buddha's statue is taken from monasteries and temples and ceremoniously bathed in water scented with sandalwood, ambergris (a waxy substance secreted from the intestine of a sperm whale and often found floating in the sea), garu wood, turmeric and aloes (a drug used for clearing the bowels, made from the leaves of the aloe tree which has fleshy, spiny-toothed leaves). Afterwards the water is drunk by the faithful, who believe it has great curative powers.

Lantau is the best place to go for this event because it has a number of Buddhist monasteries. Most people go to Po Lin since it is the largest and best known of them and extra ferries operate for the crowds. Also go to the Temple of Ten Thousand Buddhas at Shatin or at Lam Tei in the New Territories.

Dragon Boat Festival

Held in June, Thuen Ng – Double Fifth (fifth day, fifth moon) or the Dragon Boat Festival – is a lot of fun despite the fact that it commemorates the sad tale of Chu Yuan, a 3rd century BC poet-statesman who hurled himself into the Mi Lo river in Hunan province to protest the corrupt government. The people who lived on the banks of the river raced to the scene in their boats in an attempt to save him but were too late. Not unmindful of his sacrifice, the people later threw dumplings into the water to keep the hungry fish away from his body.

Today the traditional rice dumplings are still eaten in memory of the event and dragon boat races are held in Hong Kong, Kowloon and the outlying islands. See the races at Shaukiwan, Aberdeen, Yaumati, Tai Po and Stanley, and on Lantau and Cheung Chau Islands. The boats are long and narrow with dragon heads at the prow and dragon tails aft, and are rowed by teams from Hong Kong's sports and social clubs. Traditionally, women are unlucky in a dragon boat but female teams do compete. International dragon boat races are held at Yaumati in Kowloon.

Maiden's Festival

Also known as the Seven Sisters Festival, this celebration for girls and young lovers is held on the seventh day of the seventh moon (about mid-August). It has its origins in an ancient Chinese story about two celestial lovers, Chien Niu the cowherd and Chih Nu the spinner and weaver. One version says that they became so engrossed in each other that they forgot their work. As a punishment for this, the Queen of Heaven decided that they should be separated from each other by being placed on either side of a river which she cut through the heavens with her hair-pin. The King of Heaven took pity on the lovers and said they could meet once a year, but provided no bridge across the river; so the magpies – regarded as birds of good omen – flocked together, spread their wings and formed a bridge so the two lovers could be reunited. At midnight on the day of this festival prayers are offered by unmarried girls and young men to Chien Niu and Chih Nu. Prayers are also directed to Chih Nu's six sisters who appear in another version of the story. The main offerings made to the seven sisters are cosmetics and flowers.

Festival of the Hungry Ghosts

Also known as Yen Lo, this festival is usually held towards the end of August. It's rather like Halloween; the Chinese believe that Yen Lo, keeper of the underworld, allows the ghosts out of hell for 24 hours to roam around the earth. To placate the roving spirits roadside fires are burnt, fruit and food are offered, and at the end of religious observances images of the gods of hell are set on fire along with other decorations made for the festival. On the brighter side there are usually lots of Cantonese opera performances – presumably to give the ghosts one good night out before they go back down below for another year.

Mid-Autumn (Moon) Festival

The Mid-Autumn Festival is held in September, on the 15th night of the eighth moon. Although the observance of the moon is thought to date back to much earlier times, today the festival recalls an uprising against the Mongols in the 14th century when the plans for the revolution were passed around in cakes. Today moon cakes are still eaten. Very sweet, they are filled with a mixture of ground lotus, sesame seeds and dates, and sometimes a duck egg.

Everyone heads for the hilltops, where they light special lanterns with candles in them and watch the moon rise. The Peak Tram is crammed, as is all transport to the New Territories, where hillsides abound.

Birthday of Lu Pan, Master Builder

Master architect, magician, engineer, inventor and designer, Lu Pan is worshipped by anyone connected with the building trade. Ceremonies sponsored by the Builders' Guilds are held at Lu Pan Temple in Kennedy Town, Hong Kong Island. The celebration occurs around mid-to-late July.

Legends say that Lu Pan was a real person, born around 507 BC and later deified. There are a number of stories involving his many inventions for domestic and military use, his assistance to craftspeople and the way he saved buildings from collapse. Other stories are far more fanciful.

Birthday of Confucius

Confucius' birthday is in early October. Religious observances are held by the Confucian Society at the Confucius Temple at Causeway Bay.

Cheung Yeung Festival

The story goes that back in the Eastern Han Dynasty (in the first two centuries AD), an old soothsayer advised a man to take his family away to a high place for 24 hours to avoid disaster. When the man returned to his village he found every living thing had been destroyed and only he and his family had survived. Everyone heads for the high spots again to remember the old man's advice. Public transport is the same as for the Mid-Autumn Festival. The Cheung Yeung Festival is held in mid– to late October.

Lion Dances, Chinese Opera & Puppet Shows

Chinese festivals are not sombre occasions – when the religious rites are over at any festival there is generally a lion dance, some opera or a show by a visiting puppeteer.

Celebrations in Chinatowns throughout the world have made the Lion Dance synonymous with Chinese culture. There is no reason why it should be. The lion is not indigenous to China and the Chinese lion is a strictly mythical animal. Accounts of why it became important vary. One traditional tale says the Buddha was protected on a long journey by a pack of dogs who turned into lions and guarded him. Another dating back 2000 years says a Han Dynasty emperor made the lion holy because he believed a green paper lion had driven away a monster terrorising his country. Centuries later, his counterpart in the Sung Dynasty who had heard the tale suggested his people create a lion dance to try and bring back the good times to his ailing reign. Today's lion dances use kung fu movements. The lion dancers, young men in their teens or early 20s, learn the dance very early and usually belong to local associations or national organisations.

Few festivals are complete without an opera performance. There are probably more than 500 professional opera performers in Hong Kong and hundreds of amateur groups, so no local function has difficulty booking an act. Chinese opera is a world away from *La Boheme* in the West. It is a mixture of singing, speaking, mime, acrobatics, and dancing that often goes on for five or six hours. There are three types of Chinese opera performed in Hong Kong. Among the Chinese culture buffs the creme de la creme is reckoned to be the Beijing variety, a highly refined style which uses almost no scenery but a variety of traditional props. The Cantonese variety is more 'music hall', usually with a 'boy meets girl' theme, and often incorporating modern and foreign references. Most traditional is Chiu Chow, the least performed of the three. It is staged now almost as it was in the Ming dynasty, with stories from Chiu Chow legends and folklore, always containing a moral.

Puppets are the oldest of the Chinese theatre arts and the country has produced some of the finest puppetry in the world. You can see rod, glove, string, and shadow puppets – always magnificently costumed and painted – in Hong Kong. The rod puppets, visible only from waist up, are fixed to a long pole with short sticks for hand movements, all manipulated by the dexterous puppeteer who also sings excerpts of the Cantonese opera usually performed in the course of a puppet show. The puppets are made from camphorwood and the important characters have larger heads than the minor roles – which may or may not help with the plot. Such puppets are thought to have inspired the similar *wayang golek* – or wooden puppets – that you see in Java, possibly first brought to Java by Chinese traders and settlers. Shadow puppets are also found in China as well as in Java, Thailand, Malaysia, India and (presuming some of the puppeteers managed to escape murder by the Khmer Rouge) in Kampuchea. The Chinese puppets, made from translucent leather, cast shadows onto a silk screen. The skills of the puppeteer are passed from father to son, and the performances relate tales of past dynasties.

LANGUAGE

There are about eight major dialects among the Chinese. About 70% of the population of China speaks the Beijing dialect – more commonly known as Mandarin – which is now the official language of the People's Republic. In China it's referred to as *putonghua* or 'common speech' and the Chinese government set about popularising it in the 1950s.

Hong Kong has two official languages, English and Cantonese. Cantonese is a southern Chinese dialect spoken in Canton and surrounding Guangdong Province, Hong Kong and Macau. In Hong Kong Cantonese is used in everyday life, but English is the primary language of commerce, banking and international trade, and is also used in the law courts.

You can get along fine in Hong Kong

without a word of Cantonese – some expatriates live there for years and despite good intentions when they first arrive never learn the language. A phrase book can be useful in Macau, and you should get one if you go to Canton.

The Spoken Language

Cantonese is almost unintelligible to a northerner, as is Mandarin to a southerner. Everyone can read Chinese characters but a Cantonese speaker will pronounce many of the characters differently from a Mandarin speaker. For example, when Mr Ng from Hong Kong goes to Beijing the Mandarin-speakers will call him Mr Wu. If Mr Wong goes from Hong Kong to Fujian Province the character for his name will be read as Mr Wee, and in Beijing he is Mr Huang.

To add to the confusion, Chinese is a 'tonal' language; the difference in intonation is the deciding factor in the meaning of words and if you get the tones mixed up then you can say something entirely different from what you intended. There are only four basic tones in Mandarin but Cantonese has at least nine! Written Chinese has many thousands of characters, but there are only a few hundred syllables with which to pronounce them, so the tones are used to increase the number of word sounds available.

It simply takes a ferry ride or a walk down the street to dispel that myth about the inscrutable oriental. The staccato, noisy language you hear everywhere is Cantonese. It has never been proven that Cantonese has the highest decibel rating of any language in the world, or that it is the only one which can't be spoken in a whisper, but both, you'll soon realise, are distinct possibilities.

The Written Language

Written Chinese has something like 50,000 'pictographs' – characters which symbolise objects or actions. About 5000 are in common use and you need about 1500 to read a newspaper easily. All Chinese use mostly the same characters even though they might pronounce them differently. The Chinese government has also simplified many characters in an effort to make the written script easier to learn and increase the literacy rate in the country. Many of the characters you'll see in Hong Kong are written quite differently from the same ones in China. In China there are also regional variations, with some characters written in abbreviated forms in certain locales but nowhere else.

Written Chinese dates back thousands of years. In the early stages of developing the script, each character stood for a single word. Later, two or more characters were combined to form new characters. Today, 90% of characters in common use are made up of two or more original characters; that is, each character has two or more components.

Each character has a phonetic component which gives some clue to the pronunciation, and an idea component which gives a clue to the meaning. The idea component is called a radical and is often written on the left-hand side of the character. Characters with related meanings will all contain the same radical; for example, the characters for mud, lake, river and oil all contain the radical which represents the character for water. There are somewhat more than 200 radicals and Chinese dictionaries are often arranged according to them.

The phonetic component, like the idea component, is often a character in itself. If you know the pronunciation of the character which the phonetic component is based on, then you can know or approximate the pronunciation of many characters in which that component is used.

Chinese characters are all the same size when written, although some have more strokes than others. All the characters can be constructed using about 13 basic stokes, and these individual strokes are always written in a certain order. Often the difference of one stroke produces an entirely different character with a different meaning. For example, the character for 'large' is 大 but if you add a horizontal line to the top 天 then it means 'sky'; if a dot is added at top-right corner then it becomes 犬 'dog'; and if you cut out the dot and the horizontal line it becomes 'person.' 人

Wade-Giles & Pinyin Systems

One difficulty which westerners have in Hong Kong is pronouncing the romanised place and street names properly. Apart from the problem of getting the tone right, this is partly because the most widely accepted system of romanisation, the Wade-Giles system, does not work very well when it comes to telling you how the Chinese characters should be pronounced. However, in Hong Kong, all street and place names are romanised using this system.

In 1958 the People's Republic officially adopted a system known as 'pinyin' as a method of writing their language using the Roman alphabet. Since the official language of China is the Beijing dialect, it is this pronunciation which is used. The popularisation of this spelling is still at an early stage, and though literate Chinese read and write the same language of course, don't expect them to be able to use pinyin. Off in the countryside and the smaller towns you may not see a single pinyin sign anywhere, so unless you speak Chinese you'll need a phrase book with Chinese characters if you're travelling in these areas. And though pinyin is helpful, it's not an instant key to communication since westerners usually don't get the pronunciation and intonation of the romanised word correct.

The pinyin system has not been extended to Hong Kong yet, but in China it's noticeably used on shop fronts, street signs and advertising billboards. A passing knowledge of the system is of help. Basically the sounds are read as they're pronounced in English. There are a few oddities though:

c is pronounced 'ts' as in *its*
q is pronounced 'ch' as in *choose*
x is pronounced as 'sh' as in *short*
z is pronounced as 'ds' as in *bids*
zh is pronounced as the initial *j*

For example, the second syllable of *Guangzhou* is pronounced so that it rhymes with 'joe'. *Xian* is pronounced 'Shi-arn'. *Chongqing* is pronounced 'Chong ching'.

Footnote

A few Chinese words or phrases have infiltrated the English language. The word 'coolie' comes from the Chinese word *kuli* which means 'bitter labour' and refers to the hundreds of thousands of mostly poverty-stricken Chinese who left the country in the 19th century and wound up building railroads in America or shovelling out the Panama Canal.

The phrase 'gung ho' has been taken into the English language with the connotation of fearlessness and reckless abandon, but in fact it means 'work together.' The credit for adding this phrase to the English language goes to American Marine Colonel Evans Carlson, who spent several months with the Communist forces in China during the 1930s. He later formed the 'Marine Raiders' in the USA, incorporating a spartan physical training programme and an egalitarian code of brotherhood between officers and men based on his observations of the Chinese Communist army. During WW II they carried the Chinese cry 'Gung ho!' back across the Pacific.

Facts for the Visitor

The following information is for visitors to Hong Kong. For information on visas, customs, money and other facts for visitors to Macau and Canton, refer to those chapters.

VISAS

For most people visiting Hong Kong a passport is all that's required.

UK citizens (or Commonwealth citizens who were born in the UK or in Hong Kong) can stay for up to six months without a visa, and it is possible to stay longer. Australians, Canadians and New Zealanders and other British Commonwealth citizens do not require a visa for visits of up to three months. Citizens of most western European countries are permitted to stay for either one or three months without a visa – depending on which country they're from. Americans can stay for one month without a visa.

Officially, visitors have to show that they have adequate funds for their stay, and that they have an onward ticket or a return ticket to their own country. Visitors are not permitted to take up employment, establish any business or enroll as students. If you want to enter for employment, education or residence you must have a work visa unless you are a UK citizen, and even then you officially have to show means of support in Hong Kong.

If you need to apply for a visa you can do so at any British embassy, consulate or high commission. In Hong Kong you can enquire at the Immigration Department (tel 3-7333111) in Hong Kong, which is at 61 Mody Rd, Tsimshatsui East, Kowloon.

CUSTOMS

Although Hong Kong is a duty-free port, there are still items on which duty is charged. These are tobacco, alcohol and petroleum products.

You are allowed to bring in 200 cigarettes or 50 cigars or 250 grams of tobacco, plus one litre of alcoholic beverages and a reasonable quantity of alcohol-containing cosmetics and perfume for personal use. Hong Kong customs are also touchy about fireworks from China or Macau.

Most of all, customs don't like dope of any description, so don't bring any. Hong Kong has a serious drug problem, a relic to some extent of its drug-trading origins, and heroin is widely available. The present tough laws group opium, heroin and cannabis together, and no distinction is made between trafficking and possession. For major offenders there is a provision for life-imprisonment and huge fines. Possession of a dangerous drug or the equipment to smoke it (the Chinese refer to the inhalation of heroin fumes as 'chasing the dragon') can get a sentence of several years plus large fines. So if you're coming in on a flight from suspect places such as Bangkok, be prepared for thorough customs inspections. It always helps to look respectable, of course, but that is no guarantee that you will get through quickly. If any dope is found, you will be arrested immediately and the most you will see of Hong Kong will be your jail cell.

Arriving at Kai Tak Airport is fairly painless and the platoon of immigration and customs officials can move a jumbo load of passengers through pretty quickly. When you leave, there is a departure tax of HK$120 for adults and HK$60 for children between two and 12 years of age. All hand luggage is searched and/or X-rayed and there is the usual metal-detector to walk through.

MONEY

Hong Kong's unit of currency is the Hong Kong dollar, divided into 100 cents.

Notes are issued by two major banks,

the Hong Kong & Shanghai Banking Corporation (which modestly refers to itself as just 'the bank') and the Standard Chartered Bank. Thus there are different banknote designs in circulation, though the notes are completely interchangeable. In 1985 the Hong Kong & Shanghai Banking Corporation started issuing a whole new set of banknotes, smaller than the old notes but in the same denominations and with different designs.

The most common note denominations are $10 (green), $50 (blue) and $100 (red), and there are less commonly used $500 and $1000 notes. Coins are issued by the government in denominations of $5, $2 and $1 (silver) and 50, 20, 10 and 5 cents (bronze).

There used to be a five-dollar note but it's been replaced by the five-dollar coin. Don't count on seeing any 5c coins, as inflation has made them obsolete and they may be withdrawn soon. There are two types of 10c coins in circulation. The old one is almost the same size as the 50c coin and can be easily confused with it. A much smaller 10c coin has been issued to overcome this, and the old coin will probably eventually disappear from circulation. A 1c currency note is issued by the government and you sometimes get it when you change money at a bank.

Exchange Rates
The Hong Kong dollar used to be tied to the pound sterling, but since 1974 it has been allowed to float and is no longer pegged at a fixed ratio to the pound. Now its value tends to follow the US dollar quite closely. At the time of writing the skyrocketing US dollar has pushed the conversion rate up to over HK$7.50 to one US dollar. The exchange rates are given below but bear in mind that these are the rates at a time when the US dollar is very high.

Australia	A$1	=	HK$5.30
USA	US$1	=	HK$7.80
UK	£1	=	HK$11.14
New Zealand	NZ$1	=	HK$4.33
Canada	C$1	=	HK$5.60
West Germany	DM$1	=	HK$3.12
Netherlands	fl1	=	HK$2.73
Sweden	SKr	=	HK$1.02
Switzerland	SF	=	HK$3.68
China	RMB1	=	HK$2.42

Changing Money
You can change foreign cash and travellers' cheques with banks or moneychangers. Banks are open Monday to Friday and half-days on Saturday. Both the Hong Kong Bank and the Standard Chartered Bank are open from 9 am to 4.30 pm on weekdays and from 9 am to 12.30 pm on Saturday. The Heng Seng Bank is open from 9 am to 5 pm and until 1 pm on Saturday. Some banking services stop an hour before the actual closing time of the bank.

You can change money just about any hour of the day or evening at the licenced moneychangers who abound in the tourist areas. Most of the moneychangers are open all day including weekends in the Tsimshatsui district of Kowloon. They will change both cash (notes only) and travellers' cheques.

Exchange rates vary. Change as little as possible at the airport when you arrive, as they have the worst rates. In fact, when you arrive in Hong Kong don't change any more than you absolutely have to at the airport because the rates are abysmal – 10% worse than the real bank rate, which may not sound so dreadful but change even a moderate quantity of money with them and see just how much you lose out! The best rates are given by the banks, second-best by the big hotels, and the worst by moneychangers. The moneychangers may advertise the best rates, but your savings are negated by the big 6, 7 or 8% commissions they tack on in small print.

Remember, a bank or money-dealer will only buy cash off you if they can sell it again at a profit. If there is no chance of someone else buying it then they won't buy it from you. So leave your Omani rials and PNG kina where they belong. West European, American, Canadian, New Zealand, Australian and most South-East Asian currencies are OK in Hong Kong.

Credit Cards

Credit cards accepted by most places are American Express, Bank Americard (VISA), Carte Blanche, Diners Club, JCB, MasterCard and Air Travel. Major charge and credit cards are accepted by many restaurants and shops in Hong Kong. In some instances, shops may try to add a surcharge to the cost of the particular item if you charge your purchase against your card. This is not an acceptable practice and you should contact the card company concerned if it happens to you.

INFORMATION

Two good sources of information in Hong Kong are the Hong Kong Tourist Association (HKTA) and the Hong Kong Student Travel Bureau (HKSTB). First and foremost is the HKTA; generally efficient and helpful, they have reams of printed information which they either give away or sell fairly cheaply.

HKTA Offices in Hong Kong

The HKTA has offices both overseas and in Hong Kong. Those in Hong Kong are at:

Buffet Hall, Kai Tak Airport, Kowloon. Open 8 am to 10.30 pm daily.
Star Ferry Terminal, Tsimshatsui, Kowloon. Open 8 am to 6 pm Monday to Friday and public holidays, and 8 am to 1 pm on Saturday and Sunday.
Connaught Centre, 35th floor, Connaught Rd, Central, Hong Kong Island. Open 8 am to 6 pm weekdays, and 8 am to 1 pm on Saturday.

Telephone enquiries can be made to 3-7225555 from 8 am to 6 pm on weekdays, and from 8 am until 1 pm on Saturday and Sunday. The Airport Information Centre can be contacted at 3-7697765 or 3-7697688. Comments and/or complaints about shops or other organisations which are members of the HKTA can be directed to the Membership Department of the HKTA in the branch in the Connaught Centre (tel 5-244191, ext 278).

The HKTA also has a photo-library on the 32nd floor of the Connaught Building where you can buy slides of Hong Kong for HK$10 each. Be specific about what you want – they've got a couple of filing cabinets full.

The HKTA office at Kai Tak Airport operates a hotel booking service for people who arrive with no place to stay. They don't deal with the real cheapies but they will probably find you a room at a reasonable budget-priced hotel or maybe at the YMCA or YWCA. If you arrive really late at night it can be worth spending a bit more than your usual budget for the first night to avoid hauling heavy bags around the streets – especially as many of the smaller places don't open their doors after midnight.

Useful HKTA publications include *The Official Hong Kong Guide* for HK$10 (the YMCA on Salisbury Rd may give you one free), which has useful lists of airline offices, consulates and embassies, travel-agents and the like. Also available are useful leaflets and booklets on restaurants and eating out in the colony. See the Places to Eat chapter for details.

The HKTA 'fact sheets' are good value – free leaflets on sights and things to do in Hong Kong. These leaflets include the excellent *Six Walks* which gives a run-down on how to see some of the colony's interesting corners on foot; *Places of Interest by Public Transport, Outlying Islands, Beaches, Arts & Crafts Museums, Chinese Festivals* which gives a run-down on festival and holiday dates; *Sightseeing* which details the various guided tours you can take around Hong Kong; and *Tram*

Tour which lists the sights on the tram-line running along the north coast of Hong Kong Island.

If you're physically disabled and want to visit Hong Kong, the HKTA once published a guide with detailed information about facilities available for handicapped people in the colony, difficulty of access to certain hotels and restaurants, and more. They may still produce it so contact them for a copy.

HKTA Offices Overseas
There are a number of HKTA offices overseas. These include:

Australia
Bligh House, 4-6 Bligh St, Sydney, New South Wales, 2000 (tel 02 232-2422)
Britain
125 Pall Mall, London, SW1Y 5EA (tel 01 930-4775)
France
38 Avenue George V, 75008, Paris (tel 720 39-54)
Italy
c/o Sergat Italia, srl Piazza Dei Cenci 7/A, 00186 Roma (tel 656-91-12)
Japan
4th Floor, Toho Twin Tower Building, 1-5-2 Yurakucho, Chiyoda-ku, Tokyo 100 (tel 03 503-0731)
Kintetsu Honmachi Building, 4-28-1 Honmachi, Higashi-ku, Osaka 541 (tel 06 282-1250)
New Zealand
c/o PO Box 2120, Auckland
Singapore
Ocean Building, 10 Collyer Quay, Singapore 0104 (tel 5323668)
USA
333 North Michigan Avenue, Chicago, Illinois 60601 (tel 312 782-3872)
Suite 200, 421 Powell St, San Francisco, California 94102-1568 (tel 415 781-4582)
548 Fifth Avenue, New York, New York 10036-5092 (tel 212 869-5008/9)
West Germany
Weisenau 1, D-6000 Frankfurt 1 (tel 722841/2)

Hong Kong Student Travel Bureau
The Hong Kong Student Travel Bureau (tel 3-7213269) is in Room 1021, 10th floor, Star House, Tsimshatsui, Kowloon, next to the Star Ferry Terminal. They also have offices on the 8th floor, Tai Sang Bank Building, 130-132 Des Voeux Rd, Central (tel 5-414841); and in Room 1812, Argyle Centre Phase I, 688 Nathan Rd, Kowloon (tel 3-900421).

Their main function is to provide students and young travellers with local and overseas tours, visas for China, and other travel services. If you have a student card they can fix you up with cheap student flights to other parts of Asia as well as to Australia, Europe and North America. Even if you're not a student they can still provide you with discount air tickets that are good value!

The travel bureau can help you find cheap accommodation in Hong Kong, or if you've got a valid ISIC or YIEE card they can arrange student discounts at some of the hotels. They offer a variety of sightseeing tours around Hong Kong and issue international student cards and travel insurance as well as Eurail, Britrail and Japan Rail passes, Europe point-to-point rail tickets and Hoverspeed tickets. They arrange sight-seeing tours to China, or can get you a visa if you want to go on your own. They can also help with bookings for transport and accommodation in China.

CLIMATE
Hong Kong is perched on the south-east coast of China, just within the Tropic of Cancer. Although this puts the colony on much the same latitude as Hawaii or Calcutta, the climate is extremely varied with a hot, wet, humid summer and cool winters.

The best time to visit is autumn, from September – when the heat and humidity drops – until December. During this period the weather has a touch of the Mediterranean about it, with a daytime temperature in the mid-20°Cs. But be prepared for rain – it's best to buy or bring an umbrella since a raincoat tends to be sweaty.

After Christmas you will need a jacket

for a couple of months, as it gets chilly when a biting wind sweeps in from China. It can also be damp and drizzly. Official average day-time temperatures of around 18°C belie the fact that it can get quite cold by any standards. You'll certainly discover this if you flop in from Bangkok wearing thongs and a T-shirt! The winter monsoon blows in from the north or north-east and normally begins in September, prevailing from October to mid-March, but can persist until May.

Spring from March to May can be a good time for visiting too, with warm days, mild nights and reasonably low humidity, though it gets stickier as summer approaches. One drawback at this time is the haze and low-altitude clouds that hang around for weeks at a time, partly obscuring The Peak (Shan Teng) so that the view from the top is at best murky and sometimes non-existent.

Summer is from May to September. Day temperatures average 30°C (86°F) from July to September, and the nights aren't much cooler. The humidity is very high, the city gets three-quarters of its annual rainfall, and it's typhoon season – not the best time to visit. The summer monsoon blows from the south or south-west and although it can occur from mid-April until September it is not as persistent as the northern monsoon.

Typhoons

'Typhoon' is the Chinese word for 'big wind'. Hong Kong's worst typhoon struck on 2 September 1937. Well over a thousand junks were sunk and some 2500 people drowned. More than two dozen ocean-going ships were grounded as winds of 267 km an hour lashed the colony. Don't worry, this doesn't happen very often and years go by without Hong Kong getting a direct hit like the one in 1937. Also, the storms no longer arrive unexpectedly.

Typhoons and gales may be caused by tropical cyclones from May to November, and are especially active from July to September. Winds of hurricane strength occur when the eye of the cyclone passes close to the colony.

When a typhoon becomes a possibility, warnings are broadcast continuously on TV and radio. Typhoon signal 1 goes out when there is a tropical storm centred within 740 km of Hong Kong, which may affect the colony. This is followed by signals 3 and 8, by which time offices are closed and everyone goes home while there is still public transport. Even at this stage heavy rain, accompanied by violent squalls, may occur. There used to be other in-between signals with consecutive numbers, but this got too confusing so a simplified system was introduced – hence the odd jumps in the numbering.

After 8, signals 9 and 10 are rare. Nine means that the storm is expected to increase significantly in strength. Ten means that hurricane-force winds are expected. This signal indicates that the centre of the storm will come close to Hong Kong. When the eye of a hurricane passes over an area there is a lull lasting a few minutes to a few hours, followed by a sudden resumption of the destructive winds from a different direction.

Full details of the cyclone warning signals can be found in the Hong Kong telephone directory. Warning bulletins are broadcast at two minutes to and half-past every hour whenever any of the Nos 8, 9 or 10 signals are displayed. If you do not have a radio, or if you miss a bulletin, you can obtain information by phoning the Public Enquiry Service Centre of the City & New Territories Administration at 3-692255.

In addition, signals are hoisted at various vantage points throughout the colony, particularly on both sides of Hong Kong harbour, and there's also a system of white, green and red lights. For details see the telephone directory.

HEALTH

No vaccinations are required providing you are coming from a non-affected area.

Cholera vaccination is required if you have been in an infected area within 14 days prior to your arrival in Hong Kong. However, health requirements can change from time to time so it is best to check the current rules before travelling.

The usual travellers' warning, 'Don't drink the water,' does not apply in Hong Kong. The water supply in the built-up areas can be drunk from the tap quite safely. However, some places in the outlying islands and in the New Territories still draw their water from wells.

As in all tropical countries fruit and vegetables should be washed or peeled before eating; otherwise no particular precautions need be taken. Chinese cooking relies heavily on fresh ingredients so the food is pretty safe, even from the street stalls despite their dubious appearance.

Hong Kong has no national health service, and all medical treatment has to be paid for. There is no free dental or optician service in the colony either. It is well worth taking out a travel insurance policy which covers you for medical expenses, including additional costs incurred if you have to fly home unexpectedly.

If you need medical treatment, both government and private facilities are available. Hospitals favoured by *gwailos* are: Queen Mary Hospital, Pokfulam Rd, Hong Kong Island; Tang Shiu Kin Hospital, Queen's Rd East, Hong Kong Island; and the Baptist Hospital, 222 Waterloo Rd, Kowloon Tong. Most large hotels have resident doctors. Private doctors charge high – often exorbitant – fees on a par with those in western countries. Most pharmacies are open 9 am to 6 pm, some until 8 pm.

READING

Good books on Hong Kong are hard to come by, but there are a couple around which you can use to get an overview of the colony's past and present.

History & Politics

Maurice Collin's *Foreign Mud* (Faber & Faber, UK, 1946) is where it begins; this book tells the sordid story of the Opium Wars.

The Taipans – Hong Kong's Merchant Princes (Oxford University Press, Hong Kong, 1981) tells the story of the westerners – the Taipans, a Chinese word meaning 'big manager' – who profiteered during the Opium Wars. It's a study of Hong Kong's trading houses from the time the first trading companies were set up in Canton and Macau in the 18th century, until the beginning of WW I.

Another aspect of the commercial saga is told in Austin Coates's *Whampoa – Ships on the Shore* (South China Morning Post, 1980), a history of the Hong Kong & Whampoa Dock Company, formed in 1863 and the first great company to be founded in Hong Kong. Coates has written a number of other books, including *Prelude to Hong Kong* which is a scene-setter in old Macau.

The standard history of Hong Kong is *A History of Hong Kong* (Oxford University Press, London, 1958) by G B Endacott. It will tell you not only when and where the founding fathers set foot on the island but when the first sewers were laid.

James Pope-Hennessy's *Half Crown Colony* was by no means popular with local residents. He takes a critical look at Hong Kong, as did one of his forefathers, who did a brief, unloved stint as governor from 1877 to 1882.

Hong Kong's course in the 1960s and early 1970s – with the spectre of the 1997 death warrant looming over it – is told in *Borrowed Place, Borrowed Time* (Andre Deutsch, London, 1976) by Richard Hughes, a *Sunday Times* correspondent who spent years in Hong Kong.

Prior to the signing of the British-Chinese agreement on the handing over of Hong Kong to China in 1997, there was a spate of books speculating about the fate of the colony. Of these, Gregor Benton's *The Hong Kong Crises* (Pluto Press,

London, 1983) raises a few interesting points concerning the attitudes of the British and Chinese governments towards the problem of Hong Kong.

Religion

If you thought the Chinese were heavily into philosophical Taoism, Buddhism or Confucianism, read Jonathan Chamberlain's *Chinese Gods* (Long Island Publishers, Hong Kong, 1983). Chamberlain's book is a very readable account of the nature of Chinese religion – a mixture of Buddhism, Taoism and Confucianism with animist beliefs, ancestor-worship and a whole pantheon of gods still worshipped in Hong Kong today.

Another enlightening book is Frena Bloomfield's *The Book of Chinese Beliefs* (Arrow Books, London, 1983) which deals with a whole range of Chinese religious beliefs regarded by the west as superstition.

Chinese Temple Festivals (South China Morning Post, Hong Kong, 1983) by Ralph P Modder is a rundown of the origins and beliefs associated with the major Chinese religious festivals celebrated in Hong Kong. There's a listing of temple festivals in this guidebook but Modder's book is far more comprehensive.

Fiction

For fiction, why not *The World of Suzie Wong* by Richard Mason? Suzie is, after all, the most famous resident of Hong Kong; and though the book dates to 1957 and the movie to 1960 Suzie seems to have left a lasting impression on popular images of Hong Kong.

The marathon-length *Tai-Pan* (Atheneum, New York, 1966) by James Clavell is a highly romanticised version of Hong Kong's early days and the Jardine-Matheson connection. The sequel to *Tai Pan* is his epic-length book, *Noble House*.

Also set in Hong Kong and China are Robert Elegant's *Dynasty* (McGraw-Hill, UK, 1977) and *Mandarin* (Hamish Hamilton, UK, 1983).

Han Suyin's *A Many Splendoured Thing* is an autobiographical account of a love-affair in Hong Kong just after the Chinese revolution. It provides a few clues to Chinese and western attitudes in the colony.

Living in Hong Kong

If you're going to set up house in Hong Kong, a very helpful book called *Living in Hong Kong* (American Chamber of Commerce in Hong Kong, 1982) is available by writing to the Book Society at GPO Box 7804, Hong Kong. It costs around HK$90 plus mailing charge.

Also useful is *The Single Girl's Guide to Hong Kong* (Lincoln Green Publishing, Hong Kong, 1982) by Jacqueline Mitchell. Lots of good information, from flat-hunting to employment to finding men – and it's fun to read.

Very comprehensive is *Associations, Clubs, Institutes and Societies in Hong Kong,* published by the HKTA and available from their office on the 35th floor of the Connaught Place Building, Hong Kong Island.

Other

The Hong Kong government issues an annual coffee-table-size report card simply entitled *Hong Kong 1985*, *Hong Kong 1986*, etc. It's a useful compilation of Hong Kong statistics which will tell you everything, from how many legal immigrants from China settled in the colony the year before to who owns Ocean Park and how many followers Tin Hau can claim.

A number of old guidebooks have been reprinted in the last few years. An interesting one is the *Hong Kong Guidebook – 1893* (Oxford University Press). Another old account of Hong Kong and Canton is *Kwangtung or Five Years in South China* (Oxford University Press, Hong Kong, 1982) by J A Turner, first published in 1894.

BOOKSHOPS & LIBRARIES

Hong Kong has a number of good bookshops. Probably the best is *Swindon Books*, 13-15 Lock Rd, Tsimshatsui, with a substantial range of books on Hong Kong and China. They also have a branch in the Ocean Terminal, Tsimshatsui.

Times Books, on Granville Rd near the corner with Nathan Rd, Kowloon, sells both Chinese and English books and has many travel books.

Chung Hwa Book Company, M/F 450-452 Nathan Rd, Kowloon, has books in Chinese and is also very good for maps of China. There's a foreign-language book section on the top floor of the shop.

Joint Publishing Company, 6 Queen Victoria St, Central, Hong Kong, specialises in books published in China.

A couple of other bookshops worth trying on the Hong Kong Island side are *Cosmos Books*, basement, 30 Johnston Rd, Wanchai; *Harris Book Company*, Princes Building, Chater Rd, Central; *South China Morning Post Bookshop*, Star Ferry Terminal Building; and the *Hong Kong Book Centre*, 25 Des Voeux Rd, Central. In Tsimshatsui try the *Family Bookshop* in the Ocean Terminal, and the bookshop in the YMCA on Salisbury Rd.

For more reading the Urban Council runs a couple of free libraries, including: *City Hall*, City Hall High Block, Central, near the Star Ferry Terminal; *Kwong Sang Hong Building*, 296A-298A Hennessy Rd, Wanchai; *Yaumati Library*, 250 Shanghai St, Kowloon; and *Waterloo Rd*, 84 Waterloo Rd, Kowloon.

MEDIA

Over 60 newspapers and almost 500 periodicals of one description or another are produced in Hong Kong. Most of these are in Chinese but there are a couple of English-language newspapers that publish either daily or most days of the week, and there is one bilingual paper.

The two major English-language newspapers produced in Hong Kong are the *South China Morning Post* and the *Hong Kong Standard*, available each morning from news agents and street vendors for about HK$2. Also available are the *Asian Wall Street Journal* and the Asian edition of the *International Herald Tribune*. The *China Daily* is produced in China, in English.

There are 10 radio channels in Hong Kong. Five are operated by Radio-Television Hong Kong (RTHK), three by the Hong Kong Commercial Broadcasting Company (CR), and two by the British Forces Broadcasting Service (BFBS). RTHK and CR broadcast in both Chinese and English. The British forces stations broadcast in English and also in Nepali – for the benefit of the Gurkha soldiers stationed in Hong Kong.

Commercial Radio broadcasts its English-language programmes on 1044 kHz. RTHK broadcasts English language programmes on 567 kHz, 91 mHz and 100 mHz. The BBC World Service is relayed on 96 and 105 mHz FM from 6 am to 6.45 am, and from 5 pm to 2.30 am. There are two television stations: TVB Pearl and RTV, both commercial, and most transmissions are in colour.

POST & COMMUNICATIONS

The General Post Office is on your right as you get off the Star Ferry on the Hong Kong side. On the Kowloon side the most convenient post office is at 10 Middle Rd, after the Ambassador Hotel and opposite the high-rise car park. Both of these post offices are open Monday to Saturday from 8 am to 6 pm. All post offices are closed on Sunday and public holidays.

Poste Restante

There are poste restante services at both post offices mentioned above. Mail will be held for two months. If you simply address an envelope c/o Poste Restante, Hong Kong, it will go to the GPO on the Hong Kong Island side. If you want letters to go to the Middle Rd poste restante then you must address them there specifically.

Postal Rates

A letter or postcard sent anywhere within Hong Kong costs HK$0.40 for the first 30 grams.

For air-mailing letters overseas, the world has been divided into two zones. Zone 1 covers mainly India, Pakistan, China, Japan, South-East Asia and Indonesia. Zone 2 covers everywhere else. Airmail rates for letters and postcards are:

	Zone 1	Zone 2
First 10 grams	HK$1.00	HK$1.30
Each extra 10 grams	HK$0.60	HK$0.70

Aerograms cost HK$1 to any part of the world. For letters, postcards and aerograms allow about three to five days for mailings to the UK and the US. Sea mail is slow; allow about six to 10 weeks for mailings to the UK and the US. Some surface parcel rates are:

	One kg	10 kg
Australia	HK$40	HK$115
Britain	HK$55	HK$140
Germany	HK$40	HK$110
USA	HK$30	HK$125

Airmail parcel rates are:

	Up to 500 grams	Each additional or fraction of 500 grams
Australia	HK$51	HK$20
Britain	HK$63	HK$21
Germany	HK$47	HK$21
USA	HK$37	HK$26

For complaints or enquiries about postal services, telephone 5-231071 or 3-884111.

Local Telephone Calls

The telephone system, run by the Hong Kong Telephone Company, is very reliable. Public phones are not common except at obvious public places like the airport, ferry terminals and post offices; they cost HK$1 per local call. All calls from private phones are free. Many shops, restaurants and offices install phones for the use of their customers so if you want to make a call try the nearest coffee bar or fast-food shop. Big hotels, though they provide phones in their rooms, tend to have only pay phones in the lobby.

Hong Kong is divided into three phone areas. If you are calling a different area you must prefix the number with the area code: 3 for Kowloon, 5 for Hong Kong Island, O for New Territories. Telephone numbers are usually written with the area prefix, or sometimes the letter K for Kowloon or H for Hong Kong Island. If the number you want is in the same area ignore the area code prefix and just dial the main number.

For emergency services – police, fire or ambulance – dial 999. These calls are free, even from pay phones. For directory enquiries call 108.

Overseas Calls & Cables (Telexes)

These are handled by Cables and Wireless Offices. You can make overseas calls or send telegrams and cables (telexes) from any of their departments around Hong Kong. You can also make international calls and send telexes from the large hotels (if that's where you're staying), though these will have a 10% service charge.

For overseas phone calls you have three different ways of getting through: operator-connected calls, paid in advance with a minimum of three minutes; international direct dialling, which you dial yourself after paying a deposit, and which you pay for according to the time you use – the rest of your deposit is refunded; reverse charges, which requires a small deposit refundable if the charge is accepted or if the call doesn't get through.

The cost of long-distance calls is listed in the phone directory. Costs of operator-connected calls are: to Australia, HK$63 for the first three minutes and HK$14 for each additional minute; to West Germany, HK$72 for the first three minutes and HK$18 for each additional minute; to Britain, HK$60 for the first three minutes and HK$12 for each additional minute; to the USA, HK$63 for the first three minutes and HK$14 for each additional minute.

Among the more conveniently located Cables and Wireless Offices are:

Mercury House, 3 Connaught Rd, Central. Open 24 hours a day, including public holidays.

GPO Building, Connaught Place, Central. Open Monday to Friday 10 am to 6 pm, and Saturday 10 am to 3 pm.

Hong Kong airport, Terminal Building, Kai Tak Airport, Kowloon. Open 8 am to 11 pm daily, including public holidays.

Hermes House, 10 Middle Rd, Tsimshatsui, Kowloon. Open 24 hours a day, including public holidays.

Ocean Terminal, 1st floor, Room 102, Tsimshatsui, Kowloon. Open 7.30 am to midnight every day, including public holidays.

New Mercury House, 22 Fenwick St, Wanchai, Hong Kong. Open Monday to Friday 8 am to midnight, and Saturday 8 am to 3 pm.

GENERAL INFORMATION

Time

Standard time is eight hours ahead of Greenwich Mean Time, so that when it is noon in Hong Kong the time in other cities (an asterisk means it is the previous day) is:

London	4.00 am
Singapore	11.30 am
Australia (west)	noon
Australia (east)	2.00 pm
Japan	1.00 pm
New Zealand	4.00 pm
USA (Hawaii)	6.00 pm*
USA (west)	8.00 pm*
USA (east)	11.00 pm*

Summer is from late April to late October, when the clocks are put one hour ahead of standard time.

Identification

Visitors to all parts of the colony are required to carry proof of identification of some sort. Residents are expected to carry ID cards at all times, and visitors are advised to carry any sort of identification which includes a personal photograph, such as a driver's licence.

Police & Emergencies

In case of emergency, telephone 999 for police, fire or ambulance. These calls are free from all phones. If you're out and about and need the police urgently, try to find one who is wearing a red shoulder badge, or an officer – they're supposed to speak English.

Electricity

Electricity throughout the colony is 200 volts, 50 hertz (cycles) AC. This is close enough to the sort they use in Britain or Australia, but different from the US. Appliances designed for lower voltages may burn out, though some have a switch for dual operation. Apart from needing the right voltage, some electric motors need the right frequency of current; your 60 hz clock will run slow on 50 hz current.

Tourist hotels often have razor outlets with multi-fittings to suit different plugs and voltages. You can usually obtain adapters for different plugs if you like to travel with an armoury of electrical gadgets. This is all right if your equipment is designed for 200-240 volts – at worst it will run a bit slow – but don't plug in your 110-117-volt electric toenail cutter or it will burn up.

Maps

There are a couple of really good maps of Hong Kong well worth picking up. Some of the best city maps are the *Kowloon Street Plan* and its sister *The Hong Kong Street*

Plan, which you can buy in the bookshops for HK$6 each. These maps are detailed with keys to main buildings and streets.

More detailed is the *Hong Kong – Official Guide Map* printed by the Hong Kong Lands & Survey Department. It's available from the HKTA offices. Marked on it are all the main hotels, commercial buildings and ferry piers, as well as the street names in both English and Chinese. On the reverse side is a good map of the entire colony which you'll find useful if you're going to the New Territories or the outer islands.

If you intend walking on the islands, it's a good idea to get the *Countryside* series of maps, also available from the HKTA offices or from the Government Publications Centre in the General Post Office building on Hong Kong Island.

The map used by most people is the freebie put out by the HKTA and numerous private sponsors. It's covered with advertisements but is very good for finding your way around the Kowloon and Hong Kong city areas, with all the main buildings and streets clearly marked.

Hong Kong maps can also be bought at the Lands Department office on the corner of Nathan and Gascoigne Rds, Kowloon. It's open Monday to Friday from 9 am to 5 pm, and Saturday from 9 am to noon.

Airport Tax

On departure the airport tax is HK$120 per adult, HK$60 per child between two and 12 years of age, and no charge for children under two years. The airlines are touchy about the size of your hand luggage – if it's too big you may have to reclaim your bag or pack and stuff some more in to get your hand baggage down to size. You're allowed one cabin bag that should be able to fit underneath your seat on the plane.

EMPLOYMENT

Stretching the cash? Legally speaking, there are only three groups of foreigners who do not need employment visas for Hong Kong: UK citizens, British passport holders or registered British subjects. Such people are granted a six-month stay on arrival, after which extensions are merely a formality.

As for foreign nationals, including Australians and Americans, to work in Hong Kong you must get an employment visa from the Hong Kong Immigration Department before you arrive. The Immigration Department (tel 3-7333111) is at 61 Mody Rd, Kowloon. Applications for the visas can be made to any British embassy or British consular or diplomatic office. If you arrive in Hong Kong as a visitor and then get a job, you will have to leave the colony, apply for a visa and return when it is obtained. Americans are normally granted a six-month work visa. Extensions should be applied for a month before the visa expires. For further enquiries, contact the Hong Kong Immigration Department (tel 3-733311) at 61 Mody Rd, Tsimshatsui East, Kowloon.

As for finding a job, well, it's true that many people stop off in Hong Kong during their travels to pick up work. The place is full of those who stopped off for a few months to replenish the coffers and found themselves still there 15 years later. However, as in most places Hong Kong's employment situation is by no means as good as it used to be. There is an endless supply of cheap office and factory workers and plenty of college graduates, so to land a decent job you need some degree of skill or a profession not readily available to a would-be employer.

This situation particularly affects western women who are job-hunting. The Hong Kong boss can employ a first-class Chinese secretary for half the wage her western counterpart would ask. It's the same story in shops. Consequently many female westerners end up waiting tables in *gwailo* eating establishments, bar-maiding in pubs, or working in clubs and escort agencies: passable occupations in themselves, but scarcely pathways to the stars financially.

If you're a professional you might try registering with some of the Hong Kong Personnel Agencies. Also check the classified sections of the *South China Morning Post* and the *Hong Kong Standard*.

Qualified teachers (with British passports, or non-British passport holders with a spouse who has one) could try applying to the British Council (tel 5-756501), G/F, Easey Commercial Building, 255 Hennessy Rd, Wanchai, for full-time or part-time teaching posts (including teaching English).

If you're fluent in one or more foreign languages then you might get work as a translator or interpreter. Try *Polyglot Translation* (tel 3-372994), 1B, 230 Prince Edward Rd, Kowloon. Or try *Interlingua* (tel 5-430188), 14/F, Southland Building, 47 Connaught Rd Central.

Occasionally westerners can find work standing around as extras in Hong Kong movies (long hours, little pay but you live another day or two). Some people even try busking, like a British one-man band staying in the Travellers' Hostel last time I was there. He was troubadouring round the world armed with a 12-string acoustic guitar, harmonica, and a back-pack drum and cymbal.

It's fairly easy to pick up work teaching conversational English. This is the one facet of western culture universally desired and Hong Kong residents are no exception. And – no kidding – if you've just dropped out of six years of study at Beijing University with fluent Mandarin under your chopsticks then it might just be worth trying to get a job teaching it in Hong Kong; with 1997 creeping up, learning Mandarin is a big thing now.

Modelling is another possibility for both men and women. Some of the modelling agencies include: *Models International* (5-296189), B5 7/F, Haywah Building, 72-86 Lockhart Rd, Wanchai; and *Irene's Model Booking Service* (tel 5-8917667), Tak Lee Commercial Building, 13/F, 117 Wanchai Rd.

Bar and waitressing jobs are other options. There are numerous British and Australian-style pubs and bars in the colony and people passing through Hong Kong often get jobs in some of them. There's a whole list of places you could try in the chapters on Food and on Nightlife in this book. For females, paid babysitting is a possibility; contact *Rent-a-Mum* (tel 5-243650), 303 William House, 46 Wellington St, Central.

One of the great money-making lurks of travellers in Hong Kong is usually referred to as 'smuggling' but is no more undercover than a pimple on a forehead. The idea is that you cart a bagful of goodies – like one watch, one Walkman, one camera, one ghetto blaster, or some other piece of doozy electronics – to a place like South Korea where imports of such foreign-made goods are heavily restricted. While the big-time smuggling rackets are indeed big-time, there are various smaller operators around Hong Kong who employ westerners to cart the goods to South Korea or Taiwan for them (the customs people there being less likely to stamp the goodies on a western passport, thus requiring you to exit with them). Once there you hand the stuff to your accompanying Hong Kong Chinese, who then zips off to sell them. You either get a fee for this service to free enterprise and go back to Hong Kong to do it again, or else you've gained yourself a free air ticket to South Korea or Taiwan and saved some money.

Warning

Women beware in the Tsimshatsui area; we got a letter from one woman who wrote:

A young Chinese man came to the *Travellers Hostel* looking for an English girl who was after some modelling work. He asked me if I wanted some extra money, offering me escort/film work. I replied 'No' as I was returning home shortly and didn't need money. However, as he persisted and offered me HK$1000 for an evening solely as an escort, I agreed with another girl to meet him the next evening. He turned out to be working as a pimp for Chinese 'high-class' customers. OK, I should have known better; I left as soon as possible amid threats from him and an Indian 'boss' – and quite frankly I was really frightened. My friend interested in modelling stayed, but soon found out that the entire business was just to find European girls for Chinese men.

I'm old enough, and had enough money in Hong Kong to refuse these people who were obviously hoping to intimidate or force us into 'working' for them, but I think perhaps some people would be too scared to say 'No' – they were extremely persistent!

I had gone to see this man – Mr Chan – out of idle curiosity and ended up very frightened! I'd like other women to be warned – they tried very hard to conceal the true nature of their business and Mr Chan is extremely charming and pleasant to start with. They obviously know where to find female travellers (we were approached in the kitchen of the *Travellers Hostel*!

I was really taken in, and having travelled through Asia and Central America, I thought I was pretty good at spotting trouble. Please be warned!

CONSULATES & EMBASSIES

Below are some of the diplomatic missions in Hong Kong. There's a complete list in the yellow pages of the phone directory. Some of the small countries are represented by honorary consuls who are normally business people employed in commercial firms – so it's advisable to phone beforehand to find out if they're available.

Australia
    23rd & 24th floor, Harbour Centre, Harcourt Rd, Wanchai, Hong Kong (tel 5-731881)

Austria
    Wang Kee Building, Pottinger St, Central Hong Kong (tel 5-239716)

Britain
    c/o Overseas Visa Section, Hong Kong Immigration Department, 3rd floor, Mirror Tower, 61 Mody Rd, East Tsimshatsui, Kowloon (tel 3-7333111)

Burma
    Room 2424, Sung Hung Kai Centre, 30 Harbour Rd, Causeway Bay, Hong Kong (tel 5-8913329)

Canada
    14th floor, Asian House, 1 Hennessy Rd, Wanchai, Hong Kong (tel 5-282222)

France
    26th floor, Admiralty Centre, Tower 11, Central, Hong Kong (5-294351)

Indonesia
    2nd floor, 127 Leighton Rd, Causeway Bay, Hong Kong (tel 5-7904421)

Italy
    Room 801, Hutchison House, 10 Harcourt Rd, Central, Hong Kong (tel 5-220033)

Japan
    24th floor, Bank of America Tower, 12 Harcourt Rd, Central, Hong Kong (tel 5-221184)

Korea (South)
    3rd floor, Korea Centre Building, 119-121 Connaught Rd, Central, Hong Kong (tel 5-430224)

Malaysia
    Malaysia Building, Gloucester Rd, Wanchai, Hong Kong (tel 5-270921)

Nepalese Liaison Office
    HMS Tamar, Prince of Wales Building, Harcourt Rd, Central, Hong Kong (tel 5-28933255)

Netherlands
    Room 1505, Central Building, 3 Pedder St, Central, Hong Kong (5-227710)

New Zealand
    Room 3414, Connaught Centre, Connaught Rd, Central, Hong Kong (5-255044)

Pakistan
    Room 307, Asian House, 1 Hennessy Rd, Wanchai, Hong Kong (5-274623)

Philippines
    Room 506, Houston Centre, 63 Mody Rd, Tsimshatsui (tel 3-667610)

Singapore
    United Centre, Queensway, Wanchai, Hong Kong (tel 5-272212)

Sweden
    711 Wing On Plaza, Salisbury Rd, Tsimshatsui East, Kowloon (tel 3-7220333)

Switzerland
    Room 3703, Gloucester Tower, The Landmark, 11 Pedder St, Central, Hong Kong (tel 5-227147)

Taiwan
    c/o Chung Hwa Travel, Room 102, Tak

Shing House, 20 Des Voeux Rd, Central, Hong Kong (tel 5-258315)

Thailand

2nd floor, Hyde Centre, 221-226 Gloucester Rd, Causeway Bay, Hong Kong (tel 5-742201)

USA

26 Garden Rd, Hong Kong (tel 5-239011)

West Germany

21st floor, United Centre, 95 Queensway, Hong Kong (tel 5-298855)

AIRLINES

Listed are some of the airlines which fly into Hong Kong, along with the addresses of ticketing offices on both sides of the harbour. The reservation telephone number (Res) is followed by the flight information telephone number (Info). A large number of airlines are handled by general sales agents, and other airlines which do not necessarily fly into Hong Kong have offices or representatives in the colony. A complete list of airline offices and sales agents can be found in the HKTA's *The Official Hong Kong Guide*.

Air France

Room 2114, Alexandra House, Central, Hong Kong (Res tel 5-248145)

Hotel Regal Meridien, ground floor, Shop G77, Mody Rd, Tsimshatsui East, Kowloon (Res tel 3-684902, Info tel 3-7696662)

Alitalia

Hilton Hotel Shopping Arcade, 2 Queens Rd, Central, Hong Kong (Res tel 5-237047 & 3-7696448)

Air New Zealand

c/o Cathay Pacific, ground floor, Swire House, Central (Res tel 5-640123)

c/o Cathay Pacific, Shop 205, 2nd floor Shopping Arcade, Royal Garden Hotel, 69 Mody Rd, Tsimshatsui (Res tel 3-7236938)

British Airways

Ground floor, Alexandra House, Central, Hong Kong (Res tel 5-775023)

Room 112, Royal Garden Motel, 69 Mody Rd, Tsimshatsui East, Kowloon (Res tel 3-689255)

British Caledonian

BCC House, 10 Queen's Rd, Central, Hong Kong (Res & Info tel 5-260062)

Canadian Pacific

Ground floor, Swire House, Chater Rd, Central, Hong Kong (Res & Info tel 5-227001)

Peninsula Hotel Lobby, Salisbury Rd, Tsimshatsui, Kowloon (Res tel 3-7697113, Info 3-674400)

China Airlines (Taiwan)

Ground floor, St George's Building, Ice House St, Central Hong Kong (Res & Info tel 5-218431)

G5-6 Tsimshatsui Centre, Tsimshatsui East, Kowloon (Res tel 3-674181, Info tel 3-7697732)

CAAC (Civil Aviation Administration of China)

Ground floor, Gloucester Tower, Des Voeux Rd, Central, Hong Kong (tel 5-216416)

Garuda Indonesia Airways

Ground floor, Fu House, 7 Ice House St, Central, Hong Kong (Res tel 5-235181, Info tel 3-7696689)

Japan Air Lines

Ground floor, Gloucester Tower, 11 Pedder St, Central, Hong Kong (Res & Info tel 5-230081)

Harbour View Holiday Inn, Mody Rd, Tsimshatsui East, Kowloon (Res tel 3-7696524, Info 3-666660)

Korean Airlines

Ground floor, St Georges Building, Ice House St, Central, Hong Kong (Res tel 5-235177)

G12-15 Tsimshatsui Centre, Salisbury Rd, Tsimshatsui East, Kowloon (Res & Info tel 3-686221)

Lufthansa

Hilton Hotel Shopping Arcade, 2 Queen's Rd, Central, Hong Kong (Res & Info tel 5-212311)

Ground floor, Empire Centre, Tsimshatsui East, Kowloon (Res tel 3-665201)

Malaysian Airline System

Room 1306, Prince's Building, Chater Rd, Central, Hong Kong (Res tel 5-218181)

Room 014-018, New World Shopping Arcade, Tsimshatsui East, Kowloon (Res tel 3-7697967)

Pan Am

Mezzanine floor, Alexandra House, Central, Hong Kong (Res tel 5-231111)

Ground floor, Empire Centre, Tsimshatsui East, Kowloon (Info tel 3-7697155)

Philippine Airlines

Room 114, mezzanine floor, Swire House, Central, Hong Kong (Res tel 5-227018)

Ground floor, East Ocean Centre, 98

Granville Rd, Tsimshatsui East, Kowloon (Res tel 3-694521, Info tel 3-7696263)

Qantas

Ground floor, Swire House, Central, Hong Kong (Res tel 5-242101, Info tel 5-256206)

Sheraton Hotel Lobby, Nathan Rd, Tsimshatsui, Kowloon (Res tel 3-7698792)

Royal Nepal Airlines

Room 1114-1116, Star House, Salisbury Rd, Tsimshatsui, Kowloon (Res tel 3-699151, Info tel 3-7698591)

Scandinavian Airline System

Room 2407, Edinburgh Tower, The Landmark, Central, Hong Kong (Res tel 5-265978)

Singapore Airlines

Room 115, 1st floor, The Landmark, Central, Hong Kong (Res tel 5-201313)

Ground floor, Wing On Plaza, Tsimshatsui East, Kowloon (Res tel 3-694181, Info tel 3-7696387)

Thai International

Shop 124, 1st floor, World Wide Plaza, Central, Hong Kong (Res & Info tel 5-295601)

Peninsula Hotel Shopping Arcade, East Wing, Salisbury Rd, Tsimshatsui, Kowloon (Info tel 3-7697421)

Getting There

Considering the renowned beauty of Hong Kong Harbour, it's a pity so few people can arrive by ship. The days of a cheap passage on a cargo ship are mostly over. Some cargo ships still call at Hong Kong and have berths for a dozen or so passengers, but they aren't cheap, and naturally they prefer passengers who stay on board for the full journey. So for most of us the beauty of Hong Kong Harbour is first seen not from the deck of a ship but through the window of a jumbo jet or DC-10 as it touches down at Kai Tak Airport. The runway is a single long strip which extends out into the harbour, off Kowloon peninsula. There are plans to build a new airport on Chek Lap Kok island off northern Lantau.

Discount Air Tickets

The air ticket to Hong Kong alone can gouge a great slice out of anyone's budget, but you can reduce the cost by buying some sort of discounted fare which may (or may not) involve restrictions on route, advance purchase requirements, cancellation charges, etc.

Some of the more common cheap tickets include the APEX (Advance Purchase Excursion) tickets which usually have to be purchased two or three weeks ahead of departure, have a cancellation fee, do not permit stopovers and may have minimum and maximum stays as well as fixed departure and return dates.

Another useful method is combined ticketing, where a couple of tickets are issued at the same time to cover several projected trips and therefore guard against fare increases. Also worth considering is a ticket which will take you from point A to point B with multiple stopovers. For example, such a ticket could fly you from Sydney to London with stopovers in Denpasar, Jakarta, Hong Kong, Bangkok, Calcutta, Delhi and Istanbul.

There are a host of other contortions some travel agents go through to sell you a cheaper ticket. Whatever you do, if you buy an air ticket buy it from a travel agent. The airlines themselves don't deal directly in discount tickets, only the travel agents. And always check what conditions and restrictions apply to the tickets you intend to buy!

Round-the-World Tickets

If Hong Kong is just one stop on a round-the-world trip, then consider getting a 'Round the World' (RTW) ticket. These are just what they say – you get a limited period in which to circumnavigate the globe and you can go anywhere the carrying airline goes, as long as you don't backtrack. Some airlines have tickets which last for a year; sometimes two or

56

more airlines team up to provide a round-the-world service.

The best-known RTW ticket is Pan Am's 'Round the World in 180 Days' ticket which gives you 180 days to circumnavigate the globe and you can go anywhere that Pan Am goes, as long as you don't backtrack. Australians should try the Qantas/TWA RTW ticket which covers travel to the US, Europe, the Middle East, Hong Kong and various other cities in the Asian and Pacific region. The economy fare from Australia is around A$2700 and the ticket is valid for one year. Qantas flies you on the Australia-to-Europe leg with stopovers in between; TWA takes you on the London-USA-Australia leg.

Back-to-Front Tickets

These are an interesting consideration if you're not in a hurry and have a Hong Kong connection. Usually this means buying, for example, a Hong Kong-Sydney-Hong Kong ticket but using it to fly Sydney-Hong Kong-Sydney. In other words you use the return coupons before the outward coupon. Such a ticket can be bought in Hong Kong by a friend or by mail or telex if you know a reliable travel agent who deals in discount tickets. It may even be possible to do this with just a one-way ticket. Check prices first as they're not always bargain enough to be worth the trouble – they often cost only a bit less than discount tickets available in your own country. However, the savings may be useful if you want to fly business or first class.

FROM AUSTRALIA

Australia is not a cheap place to fly out of, and even air fares between Australia and South-East Asia are ridiculously high considering the distances flown. However, there are a few ways of cutting the cost.

Among the cheapest regular tickets available in Australia are the advance purchase fares. With these your ticket must be booked and paid for 21 days prior

to departure, and once you're in that 21-day period any change in reservations or cancellation of your ticket incurs a penalty equal to 25% of your fare (although insurance is available to guard against this cancellation penalty). The cost of the advance purchase tickets depends on your departure date from Australia; the year is divided into 'peak' and 'low' seasons, and peak season tickets are more expensive than low season tickets. Peak season only applies from 10 December to 10 January, and the low season is all other times of the year. APEX fares to Hong Kong have a minimum stay requirement of 5 days and a maximum of 60 days. Fares are shown below in Australian dollars.

From Melbourne & Sydney During the peak period the one-way fare is A$750 and the return fare is A$1055. The off-peak fare is A$621 one-way and A$954 return.

For a stay longer than 60 days, the APEX fare is A$1448 return.

From Perth During the peak period the one-way fare is A$633 and the return fare is A$975. The off-peak fare is A$523 one-way and A$807 return.

For more than 60 days it's A$1244 return.

It is possible to get discount tickets and reductions on the cost of APEX and other fares by going to the student travel offices and/or some of the travel agents in Australia that specialise in cheap air tickets. Well worth trying is The Flight Shop (tel 67 6921) at 386 Little Bourke St, Melbourne. They have branches under the name of the Flight Centre in Sydney (tel 233 2296) and Brisbane (tel 229 9958). Also try Student Travel Australia (tel 347 6911) at 220 Faraday St, Melbourne – you don't have to be a student to use their services, but if you are, they'll sometimes have the cheapest available tickets. Also try the student travel offices in the other states.

FROM NEW ZEALAND

There are no longer any direct flights from New Zealand to Hong Kong so the best route now is via Sydney.

Low season return APEX from Auckland to Sydney is NZ$508 and high season is NZ$694.

FROM BRITAIN

Hong Kong suddenly jumped several points on the British and European travel-consciousness scale in 1980 when the London-Hong Kong route opened up and fares dropped like a brick overnight. Previously the route had been the exclusive domain of British Airways, who naturally had little incentive to do any price-cutting. Even Hong Kong's flag carrier Cathay Pacific only flew as far west as Bahrain. Then Her Majesty's government gave up trying to decide which of several contenders should be allowed to also fly the route and instead let them all – Cathay Pacific, British Caledonian and fearless (though now defunct) Freddie Laker – fight it out among themselves. A victory for free enterprise and budget-minded travellers. British Airways, British Caledonian and Cathay Pacific (partly owned by British Airways, which goes to show how absurd some of these restrictions are) fly London-Hong Kong.

Air ticket discounting is a long-running business in the UK and it's wide open – the various agents advertise their fares and there's nothing under the counter about it at all. To find out what's going, check the travel page ads of the giveaway newspaper *The News & Travel Magazine (NTM)* (formerly the *Australasian Express*), *LAM* and the weekly 'what's on' guide *Time Out*. The magazine *Business Traveller* also produces a regular survey listing available air fares throughout the world.

Discount tickets are almost exclusively available in London – you won't find your friendly travel agent out in the country offering exciting deals. The danger with discounted tickets in the UK is that some of the 'bucket shops' (as ticket-discounters are known) are more than a little unreliable, and sometimes the backstairs over-the-shop travel agents fold up and disappear after you've handed over the money and before you've got the tickets, so be very careful.

Two reliable London bucket shops are Trail Finders at 46 Earls Court Rd, London W8; and the Student Travel Association at 74 Old Brompton Rd, London SW7 or 117 Euston Rd, London NW1. Also try Budget Holidays at 40 New Oxford St, London WC1 (tel 01 637 1414); Reho Travel at Commonwealth House, 15 New Oxford St, London WC1A 1BH; Flightdeck at 181 Earls Court Rd, London SW5 (tel 01 370 6437); or All Points Travel at Michelle House, 45/46 Berners St, London W1 (tel 580 0984). The Flight Shop also has an office in London (tel 01 370 6332).

You can expect a one-way London-Hong Kong ticket to cost from around £250, and a return ticket around £450-500. London ticket discounters can also offer interesting one-way fares to Australia with a Hong Kong stopover from around £450.

FROM EUROPE

On the continent, the Netherlands, Brussels and Antwerp are among the best places for buying discount air tickets. WATS, de Keyserlei 44, Antwerp, Belgium, has been recommended. Or try the Swiss agents SOF Travel (tel 01 301 3333) in Zurich, and Stohl Travel (tel 022 316560) in Geneva.

FROM THE USA

You can pick up some interesting tickets from North America to South-East Asia, particularly from the US west coast or from Vancouver. In fact, the intense competition between Asian airlines is resulting in ticket discounting operations very similar to the London bucket shops.

To find cheap tickets, simply scan the travel sections of the Sunday papers for likely-looking agents – *The New York*

Times, San Francisco Chronicle-Examiner and *The Los Angeles Times* are recommended.

The network of student travel offices known as Council Travel are particularly good, and there are also offices of Student Travel Australia (STA) on the west coast.

Typical return fares from the west coast to Hong Kong are around US$650. One-way fares are a bit more than half.

FROM CANADA

Getting discount tickets in Canada is much the same as in the USA – go to the travel agents and shop around until you find a good deal.

In Vancouver a good agent for cheap tickets is Ed Polanin, No 7, 2065W, 4th Avenue. Also in Vancouver try: Kowloon Travel, 425 Abbott St (Chinatown); Westcan Treks, 3415 West Broadway; or Travel Cuts, 1516 Duranleau St, Granville Markets.

Travel Cuts is Canada's national student bureau and has offices in Vancouver, Victoria, Edmonton, Saskatoon, Toronto, Ottawa, Montreal and Halifax. You don't necessarily have to be a student to use their services.

Canadian Pacific Airlines are worth trying for cheap deals to Hong Kong. A San Francisco-Vancouver-Tokyo-Hong Kong flight might cost you as little as US$399 – plus CP Air is a fine airline to fly with. Korean Airlines, which is booked by some of the agents mentioned above, may be able to undercut them, though.

FROM OTHER ASIAN COUNTRIES

There are direct flights between Singapore and Hong Kong. A good place for buying cheap air tickets in Singapore is Airmaster Travel Centre, Tan Kong Tien Building, 87-C Bukit Timah Rd, Singapore 0922. Also try Student Travel Australia (tel 734 7091), mezzanine floor, Ming Court Hotel, Tanglin Rd. Other agents advertise in the *Straits Times* classified columns.

Garuda Airlines has direct flights from

Jakarta to Hong Kong, and from Denpasar to Hong Kong via Jakarta. Cheap discount air tickets out of Indonesia can be bought from travel agents in Jakarta and in Kuta Beach in Bali. You can also buy discount tickets in Kuta for departure from Jakarta. In Bali there are numerous airline ticket discounters around Kuta Beach – several on the main strip, Jalan Legian. Apart from Kuta, Jakarta is the place to go for cheap air tickets out of Indonesia. Kaliman Travel (tel 330101) in the President Hotel on Jalan Thamrin is a good place for cheap tickets. Other agents worth checking are Vayatour (tel 336640) next door to Kaliman, and Pacto Ltd (tel 320309) at Jalan Cikini Raya 24. The agent for AUS (Australian Union of Students) is Travair Buana (tel 371479) in Hotel Sabang on Jalan H A Salim, close to Jalan Jaksa. Any student with an international student card is entitled to an AUS fare, which is usually cheaper than a normal student discount of 25%.

AIR TICKETS OUT OF HONG KONG

Hong Kong is a good place to pick up a cheap air ticket to somewhere else. Again, you have to go to the travel agents for cheap tickets. Remember that prices of cheap tickets change and bargains come and go rapidly, and that some travel agents are more reliable than others. The agents advertise in the classified sections of the *South China Morning Post* and the *Hong Kong Standard* newspapers.

Oddly enough, some of them seem to have zero interest in selling you a ticket. You can do your shopping around by phone; a number of agents are listed below but check the classified ads of the papers for others. There's quite a cost variance among the Hong Kong bucket shops. If you're travelling with kids, you may be surprised to learn that the agents with the cheapest adult tickets may not necessarily have the cheapest children's tickets – even if you're all taking the same flight. Unless you've got the time to get adult tickets from one agent and children's from another, probably the simplest thing to do is go to the agent who offers the lowest total price for all tickets.

Where to Buy Them

A popular place for buying cheap air tickets is the Hong Kong Student Travel Bureau (HKSTB), Room 1021, 10th floor, Star House, Tsimshatsui, Kowloon.

Another popular place is the Travellers Hostel, 16th floor, Chungking Mansions, Nathan Rd, Tsimshatsui, Kowloon.

Also recommended is Travel World, Room 1403, Sam Cheong Building, 216 Des Voeux Rd, Central (tel 5-438876).

A couple of other places worth trying are:

Overseas Travel, Suite 205-6, Commercial House, 35 Queen's Rd, Central (tel 5-246196)

A & J Travel, Room 906, United Overseas Bank Building, 48-54 Des Voeux Rd, Central (tel 5-222153)

Asian Express, Room M4, General Commercial Building, 158-162 Des Voeux Rd, Central (tel 5-440263)

Viking Travel, Room 1006, Mohan's Building, 14 Hankow Rd, Kowloon (tel 3-699568)

Prestige Travel, 4th Floor, Houston Centre, Mody Rd, Kowloon (tel 3-698271)

To Britain & Europe Typical fares direct to Britain and Europe start at around HK$2500. If you're willing to pay more, you can include a number of stopovers on your flight. A fare including Bangkok and Cairo, say, will cost around HK$4200. You should be able to fly into Frankfurt, Paris, Rome, Amsterdam and Zurich. It's worth remembering that at the end of June and in early July, many expatriates fly back to London on holiday. Consequently the planes are booked and it can be hard getting a flight.

To the USA Fares to the US west coast start from around HK$2200 and take you via Taipei, Seoul, Tokyo and Honolulu. Fares to New York start from around HK$2950.

To Australia One-way fares to Australia's east coast start from around HK$3500 and you can fly into Melbourne, Sydney and Brisbane.

To Other Asian Countries Typical one-way fares to Denpasar (Bali) are around HK$2300, and to Jakarta around HK$2700-2900. Better still are the return flights: Denpasar return for about HK$3350-3400, and Jakarta return for about HK$3400. To Bangkok expect to pay about HK$800; to Rangoon via Bangkok about HK$1550; to Manila HK$850; to India from about HK$2300; to Tokyo about HK$900 via Manila; to Singapore about HK$1250 via Manila; to Taipei about HK$800.

Rip-Offs

Be careful when you buy tickets. Rip-offs *do* happen. The territory has always been plagued by bogus travel agents and fly-by-night operations that appear shortly before peak holiday seasons and dupe customers into buying non-existent airline seats and holiday packages. Or you might pay a non-refundable deposit on an air ticket, and when you come to pay the balance they might tell you the price of the ticket has risen.

A popular trick of these operations is to accept a deposit for a booking, and then when you come in to pick up the tickets they say that the flight is no longer available, but there is this other flight which costs X dollars more. If you think you have been ripped off, and the agent is a member of the HKTA, the organisation can apply some pressure (and apparently has a fund to handle cases of outright fraud). Even if an agent is a member of the HKTA it does not have to comply with any set of guidelines.

A law passed into effect in mid-1985

requiring all travel agencies offering outward-bound services to be licensed. It also set up a fund to compensate cheated customers. It could be worth enquiring about if you do get ripped-off.

Getting Around

Hong Kong is a small place with a wide range of public transport, most of it reasonably efficient so getting around is quite easy. The density of the population and the impracticality of private cars (to say nothing of the expense) means that public transport in all its forms is widely used so fares are generally quite low. On the other hand, it means that public transport is often crowded, especially at morning and afternoon rush hours, so avoid these times if you can.

FERRY

There are a number of different ferry services across the harbour, around the coast of Kowloon and the New Territories and to the outer islands.

Star Ferry

The best-known ferry is the Star Ferry operating between Central on Hong Kong Island and Tsimshatsui on the tip of Kowloon peninsula. The trip takes about seven minutes and for most of the day there is a continuous service with several craft so you never have to wait more than a few minutes. The ferries operate daily between 6 am and 11.30 pm.

There are two fares: lower deck is 50c and upper deck is 70c. Tickets are not used; you simply put your money in a coin-operated turnstile at the gateway to the pier and walk through. Some of the machines give change, and there is a change counter at each pier next to the turnstiles.

Top deck is less crowded and has much better views than the bottom deck. It never ceases to amaze me how insistent some travellers are about taking the cheapest class in order to save money, though the difference in price between the two classes is less than US$0.03!

When the ferry arrives at the pier, passengers waiting to board are held

STAR FERRY CREWMAN

behind a gate until those getting off are out of the way. Then the gate is opened and the herd swarms down the ramp to get on. The rush is more out of habit than necessity since passenger load limits mean you can nearly always get a seat if you want one. When the ferry is full the gate is shut, the gangway is raised, ropes are untied, bells ring down below in the engine room, and the ferry chugs out into the harbour, somehow managing to avoid the constant traffic of tugs, barges, tourist cruise 'junks,' police launches and other assorted craft.

Other Cross-Harbour Ferries

If you miss the last Star Ferry between Central and Tsimshatsui, you can get a *walla-walla* – a small motorboat – across the harbour. They run 24 hours a day between Kowloon Public Pier and Queen's Pier Central, both near the Star Ferry pier. These will cost you about HK$5 per person, or HK$45 for the whole boat. By comparison, a taxi from Central to Tsimshatsui via the cross-harbour tunnel will cost you about HK$18 plus HK$10 for the toll on the cross-harbour tunnel (although the driver is allowed to assume he won't get a fare back and charge you HK$20 for the toll).

Another Star Ferry which goes from Central to Hung hom is useful for Kowloon (Hung hom) Railway Station. It runs between 7 am and 7 pm daily at about 15-minute intervals. First-class fare is 70c.

Other cross-harbour ferries include those between Wanchai and Jordan Rd in Kowloon, between Wanchai and Hung hom close to the Kowloon railway station, and between Hung hom and North Point. There's also a vehicular ferry between Jordan Rd and Central, though these days most vehicles use the cross-harbour tunnel.

To the Outer Islands
To visit Lantau, Peng Chau, Cheung Chau, Lamma or any of the other islands, you catch one of the ferries operated by the Hong Kong & Yaumati Ferry Company. These leave from either the Outlying Islands Ferry Pier, Blakes Pier, or the Government Pier, all of which are a few hundred metres to the west of the Star Ferry Terminal in Central. For more information on these ferries see the 'Outer Islands' chapter in this book.

BUS
Hong Kong's bus system will take you just about anywhere you want to go in Kowloon, the New Territories and Hong Kong Island. There is also a bus system connecting all the important centres on Lantau Island.

CMB & KMB Buses
The China Motor Bus Company (CMB) operates the blue and white buses on Hong Kong Island, and the Kowloon Motor Bus Company (KMB) runs the red and cream buses in Kowloon.

Transport Stamps

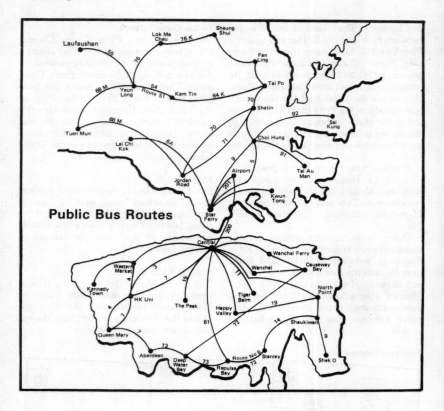

Public Bus Routes

A CMB bus guide, giving routes, fares and service frequencies is available at the CMB Head Office at 510 King's Rd, North Point, Hong Kong Island, at HK$2 per copy. The HKTA has a free handout listing bus numbers and fares from Tsimshatsui and Central to various places of interest in the New Territories, Hong Kong Island and Kowloon – very useful. You can get a copy from their office at the Kowloon side Star Ferry Terminal. Buses run from about 6 am until midnight. Fares range from about 80c for the short routes to no more than HK$5 for the longer ones. For instance, to get from the Jordan Rd Bus Terminal all the way to Lau Fau Shan in the New Territories (two buses) will cost you just HK$5 in all; or from Central to Aberdeen on the south coast of Hong Kong Island is just HK$1.70 via the Aberdeen Tunnel.

You drop the exact fare into the box next to the driver as you board the bus. There are no tickets and no change is given, so keep a collection of small change with you all the time.

Minibus

This is a pale yellow bus with red stripes down the side, which usually seats 14 people. Its final destination is written in both Chinese and English on the sign at

Top: High-rise with junk, Aberdeen (AS)
Left: High-rise with laundry, Chaiwan (AS)
Right: High-rise with bamboo scaffolding, Central (TW)

Top: A market street on Hong Kong island (AS)
Bottom: Downtown Central, Hong Kong island (AS)

the front, but you'll have to squint to see the English squeezed in above the Chinese.

You can hail a minibus just as you do an ordinary taxi. It will stop almost anywhere to pick you up or put you down, but not at the stops for the large KMB and CMB buses or in the restricted zones (such as Central). Fares range from HK$1 to $4.

When you want to get off just yell out anything – the drivers usually don't speak much English. I knew an Australian who used to shout 'kangaroo' and the bus always stopped, but the Chinese say *yau lok* if you want to be correct.

Minibuses to the New Territories can be picked up at the Jordan Rd Ferry Pier in Kowloon.

Maxicab

Maxicabs are like minibuses, but have a green stripe. They operate on routes between the Peak and Central, between Aberdeen and Central/Causeway Bay, and between Shouson Hill Rd and Pedder St.

TRAM

Hong Kong's other great travel bargain, after the Star Ferry, must be its trams – the tall, narrow, double-decker vehicles that trundle their way along the length of Hong Kong Island from Kennedy Town to Shaukiwan and along the short loop to Happy Valley. Trams have been running in Hong Kong since 1904, but the vehicles you see today were built in the 1950s and 1960s using an earlier design.

The trams are not fast but they are cheap. For a flat fare of 60c (dropped in a box beside the driver when you leave – no change) you can go as far as you like, whether it's one block or the end of the line. Children pay 20c. Trams operate between 5.45 am and 12.25 am.

If you can get a seat at the front window upstairs, you enjoy a first-class view of life in Hong Kong as you rattle through the crowded streets. On the other hand, if you don't get a seat (like during the rush

hours) the ride is not so good. The two-storey design means the ceilings are very low – tall westerners find themselves travelling with head bowed and knees bent for the whole trip. The HKTA has a free fact sheet called 'Tram Tour,' which lists sights along the tram route.

Peak Tram

You can't visit Hong Kong without going up to the Peak, and the Peak Tram is the easiest way as well as the most spectacular. The Peak Tram has been going for nearly a century and in that time has never had an accident – a comforting thought if you start to have doubts about the strength of the cable. Everyone thought the Honourable Phineas Kyrie and William Kerfoot Hughes quite crazy when in 1885 they announced their intentions of building a tramway to the top, but it opened three years later, wiping out the scoffers and the sedan chair trade in one go. Since then the only things which stopped it were WW II and the violent rainstorms of 1966 which washed half the track down the hillside.

The bottom station is in Garden Rd, uphill from the Hilton Hotel. From there the tram travels quietly and seemingly effortlessly, hauled by a cable up the steep hillside – actually it's a one-in-two gradient – to the Peak Restaurant, some 360 metres higher. The fare is HK$4 each way. The tram operates every day from 7 am to midnight, and runs about every 10 minutes with three stops along the way. Sometimes there's a free bus connecting the Peak Tram station at the bottom with the Star Ferry.

You may find, as the towering buildings of Central drop away below you, that your brain adjusts to a new attitude so that when the tram stops at a station halfway up you wonder why the buildings there are leaning backwards into the hillside.

MASS TRANSIT RAILWAY (MTR)

Hong Kong's metro system – the first part of which began operation in late 1979 – is its pride and joy. It's fast, clean, efficient

M.T.R. Train

and fulfills its purpose of moving people en masse.

The MTR has four lines. From Central Station on Hong Kong Island the line runs to Admiralty and then goes through an underwater tunnel across the harbour, north under Nathan Rd to Waterloo Station. From there it heads north-west to Tsuen Wan and another branch curves east to Kwun Tong. On Hong Kong Island a line runs west to Sheung Wan and may eventually be extended to Kennedy Town. Another line heads east from Central and Admiralty to Chai Wan via Wanchai, Causeway Bay, North Point and Shaukiwan. There are plans on the drawing board to construct an additional line through eastern Kowloon as well as an extension of the line from Kwun Tong to Junk Bay.

Compared with other Hong Kong transport, the MTR is more expensive. If you just want to cross the harbour from Central to Tsimshatsui, the MTR is at least four times the price of the Star Ferry, with none of the view and is only marginally faster. If you are going further up Nathan Rd, say to Jordan or Waterloo Rd, the MTR is considerably faster than a

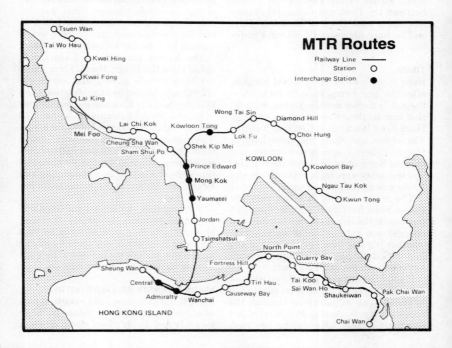

ferry and a bus and only about twice the price. Also, it's air-conditioned, which you may find worth paying for in summer. However, like other Hong Kong transport the trains are crammed with the masses at peak hour, so try to avoid travelling at this time.

Travelling on the MTR is dead easy. You just follow the signs. There is no language problem here, simply because there is no one to talk to. Everything is automated, from the ticket vending machines to the turnstiles. Ticket machines take HK$2, HK$1 and 50c and 20c pieces; they do not give change so you have to feed in the right money. If you put in a HK$5 coin for a HK$4 ticket the next person gets a HK$1 discount!

The plastic tickets resemble flimsy credit cards, with a magnetic coding strip on the back (like the ones used on the BART subway in San Francisco). When you go in through the turnstile the card is encoded with the station identification and is given back to you. At the other end, the exit turnstile sucks in the ticket, reads where you came from and how much you paid, and lets you through if you pass the test. The ticket is retained here to be recycled through the vending machines.

You can't buy return tickets, although the locals use a stored-value or season-ticket for making multiple journeys. The single-journey tickets only have a life-span of 90 minutes, so it's no good buying one to use tomorrow. Fares vary from HK$2 to $4.50. It costs HK$3.50 to cross the harbour. There's also an MTR Tourist Ticket which is valid for HK$15 worth of travel on the MTR. It is available from the large hotels and from the HKTA office in the Connaught Centre and at the Kowloon Star Ferry Terminal.

For information on trains phone 5-250557. For details on the MTR system ask for a free copy of the *MTR Guide Book* from the station information booths. It contains timetables, fare charts and maps showing the location of the stations, as well as information on connecting buses.

The trains run every few minutes from 6 am to 1 am daily. There are no toilets in either the trains or the stations.

TRAIN

Apart from the MTR there is only one train line in the colony, and that is the Kowloon-Canton line which runs from Kowloon to the border at Lo Wu and then carries on into China. Not only is this a good way to get to China, it's a good way to get to various parts of the New Territories. For more details see the 'New Territories' chapter in this book.

There are plans to construct another train line which will do a complete circuit around the New Territories. It will link up with the MTR terminus at Tsuen Wan, head west to Tuen Mun and then circle around to Yuen Long and eventually link up with the Kowloon-Canton railway line.

TAXI

Taxis are red with silver tops in Kowloon and Hong Kong Island, and green with white tops in the New Territories. They're fairly plentiful except at shift change from 3.15 to 4.15 pm and when it rains. There are no additional late-night charges and no extra passenger charges.

The flagfall is HK$5 for the first two km in Hong Kong and Kowloon, and an additional 70c for every further 0.25 km. In the New Territories the flagfall is around HK$4 and the rate per km is slightly lower. There is a luggage fee of HK$1 per bag but not all drivers insist on this – it depends how much stuff you've got.

If you're crossing the Harbour Tunnel you'll be charged an extra HK$20. The toll is only HK$10, but the driver is allowed to assume that he won't get a fare back so you have to pay. Often you will see taxis congregating together with their meters covered. This can mean they came from the other side of the harbour and want to go back. Hong Kong drivers like to stay on the Hong Kong side, Kowloon

Transport facilities

drivers on the Kowloon side. If they do want to go back then you only have to pay HK$10 instead of the usual HK$20 toll.

All taxis have a card on which the 'Top 50 Destinations' are listed in Cantonese, English and Japanese – very useful since a lot of the taxi drivers don't speak English. Even if the card doesn't list your specific destination, it will certainly have some nearby place. The card is usually kept above the driver's sun visor.

If you feel a taxi driver has ripped you off, call the police hotline at 5-277177 and lodge a complaint with the relevant details about when, where and how much. It's unlikely you'll need to, as taxis are strictly controlled and the drivers are licensed. Unlike in other Asian cities, you don't have the problem of trying to get them to use their meters.

AIRPORT TRANSPORT
Bus

There are two airport buses from Kai Tak Airport, one to Kowloon and the other to Hong Kong Island.

Bus No 200 goes to Central on the Hong Kong side. The bus goes via the cross-harbour tunnel and the hotels Excelsior and Plaza, heading up Yee Woo St and Hennessy Rd past the hotels Singapore, Furama and Mandarin. It terminates near the Macau Ferry Terminal. Heading back to the airport, it starts at the Macau Ferry Terminal and picks up passengers outside the Furama, Singapore, Excelsior and Plaza hotels. The fare is HK$4. The first bus to the airport starts at 7.30 am and the last starts at 10.40 pm.

Bus No 201 goes to Tsimshatsui on the Kowloon side. The bus heads from the airport along Gascoigne Rd and turns into Nathan Rd towards Tsimshatsui. It goes past the Park, the Grand, the Miramar, Holiday Inn and Hyatt Regency, and turns into Salisbury Rd, heading up Canton Rd to the Canton Rd Bus Terminus. In the opposite direction, the bus starts at Canton Rd near the Ocean Centre and picks up passengers on Nathan Rd

(opposite the Ambassador Hotel) and at the Hyatt Regency, the Miramar and the Bangkok. The first bus starts at 8 am and the last one at 10.30 pm. The fare is HK$2.50.

No change is given on the buses. Put the right money in the box by the driver as you enter.

In peak-hour traffic the journey from Central could take an hour or more, so allow plenty of time. The same can apply to the Kowloon side. Peak-hour periods in Hong Kong and Kowloon are from 8 to 9.30 am, noon to 2.30 pm, and 4.30 to 6.30 pm Monday to Friday; and 8 to 9.30 am and after 1 pm on Saturday.

If you really want to save money, you can take the ordinary buses No 1A or No 9 from the main road outside the airport to Nathan Rd, but it's hardly worth it.

Taxi

Taxis cost about HK$20 from the airport to the Tsimshatsui area of Kowloon. Across the harbour to Hong Kong costs HK$40 to $45 including the tunnel charge. Right into Central will cost HK$50 to $55.

CAR HIRE

Only someone with a loaded gun could get me behind the wheel in Hong Kong. A territory of 307,000 vehicles, only 1300 km of roads and 15,000 people a year killed or injured on them says something about the joys of motoring in the colony.

If you want to try driving, a number of car-hire companies provide a variety of cars for self-drive or chauffeur-driven rental. You'll find their addresses and phone numbers in the yellow pages of the phone directory, or in the classifieds section of the newspapers. Some of the car-rental companies in Hong Kong are Avis (tel 5-719237), Crown Motors (5-622226), Trinity (5-636117) and National (tel 3-671047). Typical charges from Avis are HK$200 a day for a 1300 Subaru, plus HK$45 for comprehensive insurance. A HK$200 petrol deposit is also required.

You get unlimited km at no extra cost and discounts if you rent for a week or more. Renting cars in Hong Kong ain't cheap. Many car-rental outlets and the big hotels offer chauffeur-driven service, but you could be looking at HK$120 or more per hour. Hong Kong drives on the left – the same as in Britain, Australia and Japan, opposite to the USA and most European countries. Seat belts must be worn by drivers and front-seat passengers.

Anyone over the age of 18 with a valid driving licence from their home country, or an international driving permit, can drive in Hong Kong for up to 12 months. If you're staying longer, you'll need a Hong Kong licence. Apply to the Transport Department Licensing Offices (tel 5-261577) at 2 Murray Rd, Central. At present you don't need to take a driving test.

Parking charges in the Transport Department's multi-storey car parks in Central cost a couple of dollars per hour during the day – cheaper in the evening. Open-air parks are cheaper still but space is at a premium. There are also multi-storey car parks built by private firms in other commercial and residential areas. When there are no signs expressly authorising it, parking is prohibited. Permanent parking spaces are bought and sold in Hong Kong like other real estate.

In fact, driving has been made as difficult as possible because Hong Kong has one of the highest traffic densities in the world – and to slam home the point that cars should be regarded as luxury items (like the more than 500 Rolls-Royces in the colony), the annual vehicle licensing fees for privately owned, petrol-engine cars vary from HK$2300-6700 per year, depending on the engine size. To discourage driving, the government makes it as hard as possible to obtain a licence, with a rigorous practical and written test, high fees and waiting periods months long. A learner's driving licence costs HK$300 and is valid for 12 months; the driving test fee is HK$300; a full driving

licence costs HK$150 and is valid for one year, or HK$450 for a three-year licence. The fee for registration of a motor-vehicle is HK$20. However, the first time you register a private vehicle a tax of 70 to 90% of the vehicles' CIF value (cost, insurance and freightage) is charged. Third-party insurance is compulsory.

RICKSHAW

If you really want to, you can take a rickshaw, but not far. No new licences have been issued for years but a few gnarled, geriatric rickshaw drivers still ply their trade by the Star Ferry concourse on the Hong Kong side of the harbour for the benefit of camera-carrying foreigners. The fare is about HK$10 for five minutes or a few hundred metres, but settle the price first and then ignore the demands for more.

BICYCLE

Bicycles are not recommended for the steep streets and impatient traffic of Hong Kong Island or for the traffic of Kowloon either, but they are suitable for some parts of the New Territories and the outlying islands. There are places on Lantau and on Cheung Chau where you can hire bikes for a few hours or for the whole day; see those sections for details.

WALKING

Despite the onslaught of concrete, glass and steel, Hong Kong presents plenty of opportunity for walking.

There are lots of interesting city walks you can do around Hong Kong Island and Kowloon – the best way of seeing an area. Some of these walks are described in this book. Also useful is the free HKTA leaflet *Six Walks*. One 50-km walk twists and winds across the whole length of Hong Kong Island from Shek-O to Victoria Peak. The 3.5-km peak circuit walk is the starting or finishing stretch.

The outer islands have long been known for their good walks and there are many in the New Territories. Some of these are

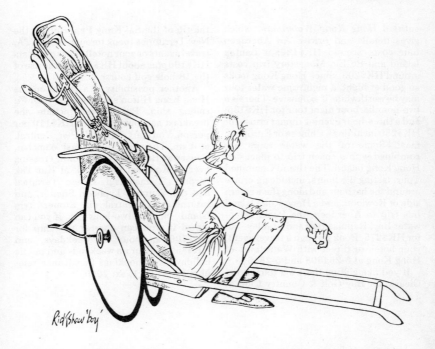

Ricfshaw 'boy'

described in the New Territories and Outer Islands chapters in this book.

Selected Walks in Hong Kong by Ronald Forrest and George Hobbins describes a number of walks of varying lengths on Hong Kong Island, Kowloon, the New Territories and the outer islands.

TOURS

I could go on for pages regurgitating all the available tours of Hong Kong. You can get one to just about anywhere, including the Sung Dynasty village, Ocean Park, Stanley, the outer islands, or the duck farms in the New Territories. Tours can be booked through the HKTA, the HKSTB, travel agents or the large tourist hotels. If you're a student then the HKSTB offers discounts of HK$10 or HK$20 on the cost of the tours. A sample of what's going:

Daily bus tours of Kowloon include the

Wong Tai Sing Temple, the Lung Cheung Rd look-out point (from which there's an unimpeded view across Kowloon to Hong Kong Island and Kai Tak Airport), and the Mongkok and Hung Hom districts. The tour takes 1½ hours and costs HK$40. There are also 3½-hour bus tours around Hong Kong Island for HK$70, taking in places like Aberdeen, Stanley and the factory area of Wong Chuk Hang. If you're short on time then the New Territories tours may be worth considering; a four-hour loop costing HK$80 takes in the Yaumati Typhoon Shelter, the Kam Tin Walled Village, some of the huge new high-rise towns like Shatin, and other sights.

Ferry cruises will take you around the harbour to Aberdeen and to Cheung Chau and Lantau islands. A useful little booklet is available from the HKTA, appropriately entitled *Hong Kong Watertours*, which gives details and prices. An Aberdeen tour costs around HK$180; a Lantau Island and Po Lin Monastery trip costs around HK$200. Since Hong Kong looks so good at night, a night-time water-tour may be worthwhile, if expensive. There's a two-hour harbour night tour for HK$135, and a three-hour evening dinner cruise for HK$230 including a Chinese or European meal. Some of the water tours are combined with a coach trip to places on Hong Kong Island. The Grand Combined Tour, lasting 8½ hours, includes a cruise around the harbour and along the western side of Kowloon, and a Hong Kong Island bus trip to Aberdeen, the Peak, Deepwater Bay, Repulse Bay and Stanley – all for HK$275. Book through a travel agent, your hotel, or direct with Watertours of Hong Kong at 5-254808 and 5-263538.

If you like golfing there's a tour to the Clearwater Bay Golf & Country Club at the tip of the Sai Kung Peninsula in the New Territories (book through the HKTA, travel agents or your hotel). The tour costs HK$190 *plus* about HK$200 for the use of the 18-hole golf course.

Another possibility is a cruise on the Hong Kong Hilton's two-master *Wan Fu* sailing ship. Possibilities include the breakfast harbour cruise for HK$110 per person. You start at Blake's Pier, Central, at 9 am. The ship cruises past Wanchai, Causeway Bay and North Point, crossing over to Kowloon for a look at Kai Tak Airport, Tsimshatsui, Ocean Terminal and the Yaumati Typhoon Shelter, and returning to Central via Stonecutters Island – in all, a two-hour trip. If you can afford it, you can charter the ship for HK$700 an hour on weekdays, and HK$850 an hour on weekends and public holidays. For bookings in advance telephone 5-233111, ext 2009.

Hong Kong Island

The commercial heart of Hong Kong pumps away on Hong Kong Island, where banks and businesses, high-rise apartment blocks and hotels cover a good part of its 75 square km. From the Star Ferry the island looks unbelievably crowded, and on the lower levels it certainly is – but from 400 metres up on Victoria Peak you realise how much space is left.

Most of the unoccupied space is of course more vertical than horizontal, but the demand for buildings is so great that the construction industry is constantly defying gravity to erect more multi-storey monuments to the wonders of reinforced concrete. Glass curtain-walled buildings are one of the more recent architectural fads in Hong Kong; the first such building was the Admiralty Centre on which construction began in 1978. Since then they've sprouted like 'glazed weeds,' as one Hong Kong journalist put it, producing edifices like the Far East Finance Centre, 'a plain slab bedecked in gold-tinted glass, which makes it look something like the ostentatious cigarette lighters many here carry.'

As well as moving up the hill for more building space, Hong Kong keeps on moving out – reclamation along the harbour edge continues to add the odd quarter km every so often, and buildings once on the waterfront are now several hundred metres back. Some of the reclaimed land has been used for new roads to accommodate the traffic which has swamped the old narrow streets.

While Hong Kong Island may appear little more than a menagerie of glass and steel monuments to modern architecture, down at street level – behind the skyscrapers, in the back alleys and small streets – a lot of old Hong Kong manages to carry on pretty much as it has for decades. There are streets full of *dai pai dongs*; there are snake shops with their stock imprisoned in woven baskets stacked on the footpath; there are alleyway shoe-repairmen, fortune-tellers and wine shops selling pickled snakes. There are traditional *dim sum* houses like the Luk Yu on Stanley St which has been around for over half a century, and paper shops which dispense Bank of the Netherworld banknotes to be consigned to the funeral fires of the deceased.

The northern shore of Hong Kong Island is the most heavily built upon part of the island. Moving west to east, there are a number of distinctive districts: Kennedy Town, Sheung Wan, Central (once called Victoria), Wanchai, Happy Valley, Causeway Bay, North Point and Quarry Bay, and Shaukiwan. On the southern coast four of the main centres are Deep Water Bay, Stanley, Repulse Bay and Aberdeen. The major districts along the northern coast of the island are all easily accessible on the recently opened MTR subway line which runs from Sheung Wan in the west to Chaiwan in the east. The rest of the island is connected by an extensive bus network.

CENTRAL

Central is most people's first impression of Hong Kong Island since it's where the Star Ferry lands. As you come out of the Star Ferry Terminal, immediately on your right is the General Post Office, and in front of that is the towering Connaught Centre with its distinctive round windows.

To the left on the waterfront, past the multi-storey car park, is the City Hall, opened in 1971 and consisting of a high block and a low block. The colony's cultural life is embodied here, along with the Museum of Art which contains collections of Chinese art and antiquities.

To reach the main part of Central you have to cross Connaught Rd. Straight

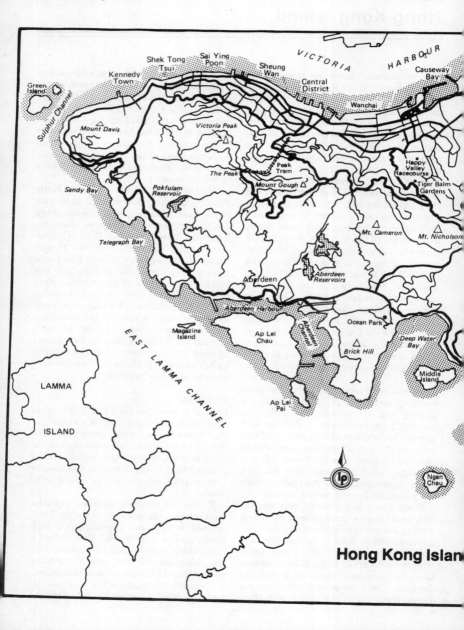

Hong Kong Islan

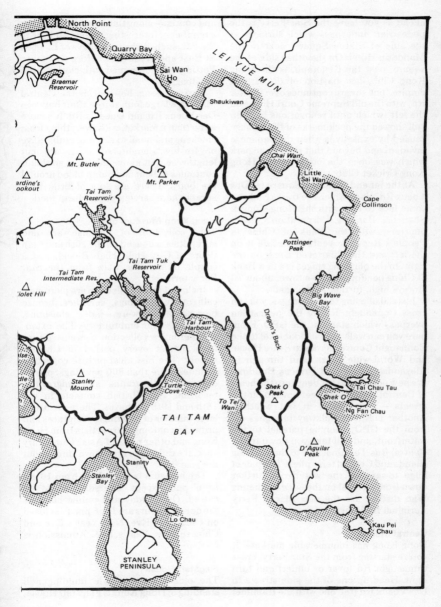

ahead as you leave the Star Ferry is the pedestrian underpass which surfaces at the side of Statue Square, next to the Mandarin Hotel. On the other side of the square, past the Cenotaph, is the Hong Kong Club, last bastion of the British empire. The square continues over Chater Rd, with the old Supreme Court House on the left (which until renovations in 1985 still showed the pock-marks of the damage caused by explosives when the Japanese invaded) and beyond that the public park which was once the home of the Hong Kong Cricket Club.

At the far end of Statue Square (at Des Voeux Rd, along which the trams run) you come face to face with the Hong Kong & Shanghai Banking Corporation's headquarters, with the Bank of China (a People's Republic venture) beside it on the left and the Chartered Bank on the right. In the planning stages is a new Bank of China headquarters – a tower about 70 storeys high, further to the east.

Instead of using the underpass, you can cross Connaught Rd by the pedestrian overpass which starts at the GPO. From here you can walk at first-floor level to the Connaught Centre, across to Swire House and World-wide Plaza, and through to Alexandra House and Princes Building. It's now possible to get deep into the heart of Central before your feet have to hit the streets – very useful in wet weather. Another elevated walkway branches off from the GPO, running parallel to the waterfront, and will take you down to the Central Bus Terminal and to the outlying islands and Central ferry piers. The pair of huge towers on the waterfront further down from Central on the edge of Sheung Wan district are the new Macau Ferry Terminal Buildings.

Central Market

Hong Kong has innumerable markets. If you're starting from the Star Ferry, cross Connaught Rd (over or under) and turn right. Head up one of the side streets to Des Voeux Rd (the one with the tramline)

and continue along this for a bit. There are a number of interesting streets off here to the left, such as the twin alleys of Li Yuen St East and West (just before you get to Pottinger St) crammed with clothing and handbags.

Further along, however, is the Central Market, a large four-storey affair between Des Voeux Rd and Queen's Rd. It's more a zoo than a market, with everything from chickens and quail to eels and crabs, alive or freshly slaughtered. Fish are cut lengthwise, but above the heart so that it continues to beat and pump blood around the body. There are lots of little restaurants here serving good, cheap food.

Hong Kong Museum of Art

This collection of Chinese art and antiquities is housed on the 10th and 11th floors of City Hall (High Block), just a couple of minutes walk from the Star Ferry terminal.

Included in the collection are paintings, calligraphy, rubbings, ceramics, bronze pieces, lacquerware, jade, cloisonné, paper-cuts and embroidery. The extensive ceramics collection contains pieces from almost every period in Chinese history. The historical picture collection includes more than 800 paintings, prints, drawings, lithographs and engravings recording Sino-British contacts in the 18th and 19th centuries. There are also a large number of paintings, sculptures and prints by contemporary artists from Hong Kong and other parts of Asia. Temporary special exhibitions are shown throughout the year.

The museum is open daily from 10 am to 6 pm, except Thursday when it's closed. On Sunday and public holidays the opening hours are 1 to 6 pm. It's closed on Christmas Eve, New Year's Eve and Chinese New Year's Eve. Admission is free.

Flagstaff House

The oldest western-style building still standing in Hong Kong is Flagstaff House, dating back to the mid-19th century. It's situated in the Victoria Barracks – enter from Cotton Tree Drive, which is one of the streets leading up to the Peak Tram Terminus. Today the building houses a Chinese tea ware collection, including pieces dating from the Warring States period (475-221 BC) to the present. The museum is open daily (except Wednesday) from 10 am to 5 pm and is closed on several public holidays. Admission is free. Bus Nos 3, 12, 12A, 17, 23, 23B, 40 and 103 all go up this way.

Government House

On Upper Albert Rd, opposite the Zoological & Botanic Gardens, is Government House, residence of the governor of Hong Kong. The original sections of the building date back to 1858. Other features were actually built to Japanese designs during the war, when Japan occupied the colony and the Japanese governor wanted to establish a residence and administrative centre worthy of his role. If you want to read some more on this, the Japanese architect responsible for the project, Seichi Fujimura, describes it in his book *Constructing Authority, the Governor's House, Hong Kong*. A write-up also appears in the *Far Eastern Economic Review* of 5 July 1984.

Zoological & Botanical Gardens

Hong Kong's Central district is wall-to-wall people during lunchtime; more peaceful are the pretty Zoological & Botanical Gardens. There are hundreds of species of birds, exotic trees, plants and shrubs here. Among the statues is one to the innovative Sir Arthur Kennedy, the first governor to invite Chinese to government functions. If you go to the gardens about 8 am the place will be packed with Chinese toning up with a bit of shadow-boxing on their way to work. The gardens are divided by Albany Rd, with the botanics and the aviaries in the first section, off Garden Rd, and the zoologicals in the other. Admission is free.

The gardens are at the top end of Garden Rd, which leads up from behind the Hilton Hotel. Rather than walking you can take Bus No 3 or No 12 to the gardens from the stop in front of the Connaught Centre on Connaught Rd. The bus takes you along Upper Albert Rd and Caine Rd on the northern boundary of the gardens; get off in front of the Caritas Centre (at the junction of Upper Albert and Caine Rds) and follow the path uphill to the gardens. Alternatively, if you're in Queen's Rd, Central, walk up the Battery Path which starts near the corner of Queen's Rd and Ice House St and curves round past St John's Cathedral. The path comes out on Garden Rd, near the US Consulate and the Peak Tram.

WANCHAI GAP

From the Zoological & Botanic Gardens you could walk west along Robinson or Conduit Rds to Mid-Levels; or you could head east towards the Wanchai Gap District.

For the latter alternative, walk down Robinson Rd (which forms the boundary to the upper part of the gardens) back towards the road interchange at the corner of Garden and Magazine Gap Rds. Like most new roadworks in Hong Kong, this does not offer much footpath for pedestrians. Cross Robinson Rd wherever you can and follow it round to Magazine Gap Rd. Continue up Magazine Gap Rd and cross over to Bowen Rd, which leads off to the left. (Alternatively, you can skip the gardens altogether and catch the Peak Tram one stop to Bowen Rd.)

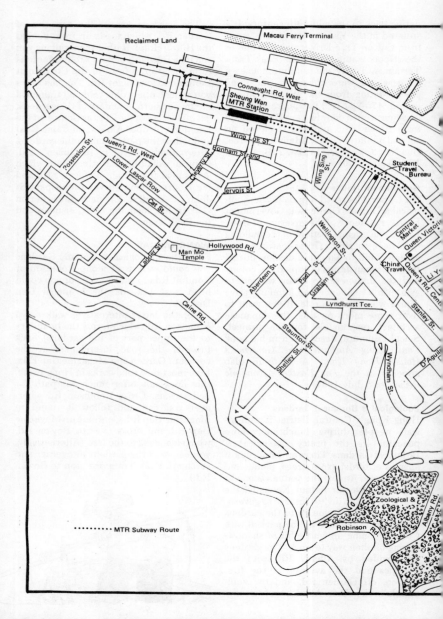

Macau Ferry Terminal

Reclaimed Land

Connaught Rd. West

Sheung Wan
MTR Station

Wing Lok St.

Queen's Rd. West

Bonham Strand

Possession St.

Cleverly St.

Jervois St.

Wing Sing St.

Student
Travel
Bureau

Lower Lascar Row

Cat St.

Ladder St.

Man Mo
Temple

Hollywood Rd.

Wellington St.

Central
Market

Queen Victoria

Aberdeen St.

Peel St.

Graham St.

Lyndhurst Tce.

China
Travel

Queen's Rd. Centr

Li Y

Caine Rd.

Staunton St.

Stanley St.

D'Aguila

Shelley St.

Wyndham St.

Zoological &

MTR Subway Route

Robinson Rd.

Albany Rd.

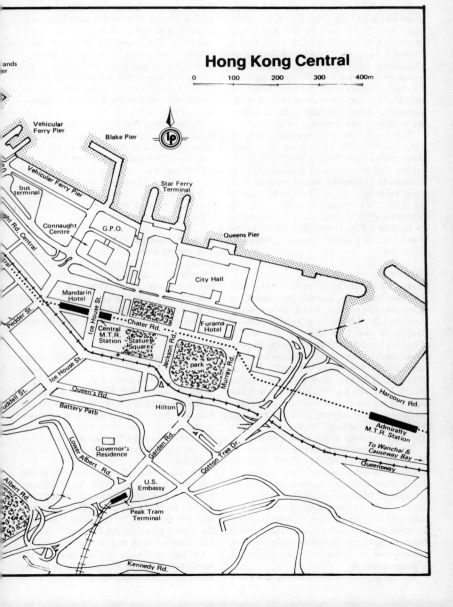

Hong Kong Central

0   100   200   300   400m

Vehicular
Ferry Pier

Blake Pier

Vehicular Ferry Pier

bus
terminal

Star Ferry
Terminal

ands
ier

ght Rd. Central

Connaught
Centre

G.P.O.

Queens Pier

City Hall

Mandarin
Hotel

Ice House St.

Chater Rd.

Central
M.T.R.
Station

Statue
Square

Jackson Rd.

Furama
Hotel

Pedder St.

park

Murray Rd.

Ice House St.

Queen's Rd.

Harcourt Rd.

uddell St.

Battery Path

Hilton

Admiralty
M.T.R. Station

Lower Albert Rd.

Governor's
Residence

Garden Rd.

Cotton Tree Dr.

To Wanchai &
Causeway Bay

Queensway

Albert Rd.

U.S.
Embassy

Peak Tram
Terminal

Kennedy Rd.

Bowen Rd gets narrower, and seems more like a private driveway to the many apartment blocks and the odd mansion or two which crowd the hillside here. In due course it devolves into a footpath through the steep semi-jungle. Along here are many good views over Hong Kong from Central around to North Point. After any rain there is the constant splash of water cascading down the near-vertical storm-water drains which cross the path.

Eventually the path reaches Wanchai Gap Rd, which is more path than road. Just across from here is Maiden's Rock, where unmarried young women pray for husbands during the Seven Sisters' Festival, and where at any time there is sure to be someone burning joss sticks. You can now walk up Wanchai Gap Rd (very steep) to Stubbs Rd and catch Bus No 15 to the Peak, or walk down (equally steep) to Wanchai.

THE PEAK

Everyone should go up to the Peak – first because it's there, second because it's a good way to get Hong Kong into perspective, and third because it provides one of the most beautiful views in the world. From its height of 550 metres you can get a panoramic view of the high-rise lego blocks stretching along the north shore of Hong Kong Island, gaze across the water to the Kowloon peninsula, and watch the aeroplanes taking off and landing on the narrow strip of runway that juts out into Hong Kong Harbour. Beyond that looms the hilly expanse of the New Territories.

The Peak has been *the* place to live ever since the British moved in. The Taipans (a Chinese word meaning 'big manager') built their summer houses up here to escape the heat and humidity (it's usually about 5°C cooler than down below) although they spent three months swathed in mist for their efforts. It's still a good address but these days air-conditioning is considered a more effective form of climate control.

At the top of the tram-line is the Peak Tower, a viewing and restaurant complex with a choice of Chinese and European food. The place is built like an iceberg, one-third above ground and two-thirds below – and is able to withstand winds of up to 270 km per hour. The eating is not cheap but the views are amazing, day or night. High-powered binoculars on the lower balcony cost 50c for a few minutes – worth every cent.

Behind the Peak Tower complex is the Peak Café, a rustic old place which has been there for years and is much more cosy than the Peak Tower. The food in the café is not bad, particularly the Hainan chicken rice. Have a look in the Peak Tower Village, one of these modern shopping resorts where craftspeople sell village arts and crafts.

Walks Around the Peak

You can walk around Victoria Peak easily without exhausting yourself. Harlech and Lugard Rds encircle it. Take off right or left from the Peak Tower and in 45 minutes you will see the whole circle of Hong Kong from the Sai Kung peninsula to Aberdeen, over Cheung Chau, Lamma and Lantau and, on a clear day, even Macau.

You can walk from the restaurant to the remains of the old governor's mountain lodge, about 140 metres higher up the hill along Mt Austin Rd. The lodge was burnt to the ground by the Japanese during the war, but the gardens remain and are open to the public. The views are particularly good and there is a toposcope identifying the various geographical features you can see from here.

For a downhill hike you can walk about two km from the Peak to Pokfulam Reservoir Rd, which leaves Peak Rd near the exit from the car park. This takes you past the reservoir to the main Pokfulam Rd where you can get the No 7 bus to Aberdeen or back to Central.

Or you can walk to Aberdeen. Walk south from the Peak along the Peak Rd for about half a km to an overpass. Go under it

Top: Repulse Bay (AS)
Left: Stanley beach (AS)
Right: Tiger Balm Gardens (AS)

Top: Building junks at Aberdeen (AS)
Bottom: The crowded waterways of Aberdeen (AS)

Peak tram tickets

and then to the right to find Peel Rise, which will take you down for about three km to Aberdeen, passing cemeteries on the way.

Getting There
If you're going up to the Peak, you should go by the Peak Tram – at least one way. The tram terminal is in Garden Rd, Central, behind the Hilton Hotel – 650 metres from the Star Ferry Terminal. The tram trip takes about eight minutes and costs HK$4 (HK$2 for children under 12). Avoid going on a Sunday when there tends to be long queues. See the Getting Around chapter for more details on the Peak Tram.

Alternatively, Bus No 15 from the Central Bus Terminal will take you on a 40-minute trip around the perilous-looking road to the top for just HK$2.50. This is not only the cheapest way but also the most scenic, though the tram trip has much to recommend it. The last bus down to the Star Ferry is at 10.30 pm. Minibuses (maxicabs) leave from the HMS Tamar building, eastern side of City Hall. They charge HK$3 for the trip up to the Peak.

SHEUNG WAN
West of Central (on the right as you come off the Star Ferry) is Sheung Wan (the Western District), which once had something of the feel of old Shanghai about it. The comparison is a bit forced now since much of old Sheung Wan has disappeared under the jackhammers of development, and old stairway streets once cluttered with stalls and street-sellers have been cleared away to make room for more new buildings or the MTR. Nevertheless the area has plenty of interest and is worth exploring.

Past Central Market
Carry on past the Central Market, and about where Central and Sheung Wan merge into each other is Wing On St, also known as Cloth Alley since it's filled with sellers of all kinds of fabrics. A bit further on is Ling Kut St, which is good for toys, costume jewellery, plastic animals and birds. Then there is Wing Sing St, famous for all varieties of eggs, including the 100-year-old ones (which aren't 100 years old but are artificially aged with various ingredients). Finally there is Kwong Yuen St where the flag and banner makers sit sewing.

These streets run between Des Voeux Rd and Queen's Rd, Central (Kwong Yuen St runs between Wing Lok St and Queen's Rd), which is a big shopping area. Look out for the ornate jewellery shops, traditional bridal stores with everything for a wedding, and ivory and silk emporiums.

Snake Shops
Past Wing Sing St, Queen's Rd curves round to the left to be called Queen's Rd West, but if you go straight ahead you will be on Bonham Strand East; veer left opposite Kwong Yuen St for Jervois St. Down here and along Hillier St you will find snake shops. Snakes are considered good things to eat if you want good health, and wine mixed with snake venom is said to be just the thing for keeping out winter chills.

Cat St

Across from Hillier St in Queen's Rd West, and a bit further along, a flight of stone steps used to take you up to Lower Lascar Row, better known as Cat St or Morio Gai. This was once a great place to hunt for 'antiques' and bric-a-brac, but now the old, tiny street with its cramped shops and swinging signs has disappeared under a new commercial high-rise development.

Hollywood Rd

From Queen's Rd, head south uphill to Hollywood Rd. This street has a number of funeral shops selling everything for the best-dressed corpses, as well as wreath and coffin makers. It is also full of furniture shops with antiques of all kinds, from the genuine article to modern reproductions made before your very eyes.

Man Mo Temple

The Man Mo Temple is at the corner of Hollywood Rd and Ladder St. The temple is one of the oldest and most famous in Hong Kong. The Man Mo – literally 'civil and military' – is dedicated to two deities. The civil deity is a Chinese statesman of the 3rd century BC; the military deity is Kuan Ti, a soldier born in the 2nd century AD and now worshipped as the God of War. For more details see the Religion section at the start of this book. Kuan Ti is also known as Kwan Tai or Kwan Kung.

Outside the entrance are four gilt plaques on poles also carried at procession time. Two describe the gods being worshipped and the others request quietness and respect, warning menstruating women to keep away. Inside the temple are two antique chairs shaped like houses used to carry the two gods around at festival time. The coils suspended from the roof are incense cones burnt by worshippers. A large bell on the right is dated 1846 and smaller ones on the left 1897.

The exact date of the temple's con-struction has never been agreed on, but it's certain it was already standing when the British arrived to claim the island as their own. The present Man Mo Temple was renovated in the middle of the last century.

Possession St

Rather than go up Hollywood Rd, you could continue on down Queen's Rd to Possession St. The street is small, but its name recalls that somewhere around here the flag was planted for England after Captain Elliot did his deal with Kishen. The point has never been marked with any sort of memorial, indicating just what the early settlers thought about Elliot handing over their opium to the Chinese. This area used to be much closer to the sea, but it has been pushed inland by land reclamation.

Ladder St

The area around the Man Mo Temple was used extensively for location shots in the film *The World of Suzie Wong*. The building to the right of the temple was used as Suzie's hotel.

The extremely steep flight of steps by the temple is Ladder St. Once upon a time it was crammed with stalls and shops selling everything from beads and bangles to snuff bottles, blackwood furniture, pottery and Mongolian hot pots. Alas, no longer – the stall holders have all been cleared away. Ladder St is well over 100 years old and probably the best example of old Hong Kong remaining in the colony. One reference in an early Hong Kong records book mentions the difficulty in negotiating sedan chairs up the 60 metre plus climb! The steps connect Hollywood Rd to the residential Caine Rd.

After you've explored Ladder St, walk back towards Central along Hollywood Rd and the streets that lead down to Queen's Rd and Des Voeux Rd. Lyndhurst Terrace has shops selling Cantonese opera costumes as well as embroidery and curios.

SHEK TONG TSUI & KENNEDY TOWN

West of Sheung Wan takes you through Sai Ying Pun and Shek Tong Tsui districts to Kennedy Town, a residential and harbour district at the end of the tramline. The chief attraction of Shek Tong Tsui is Hong Kong University's Fung Ping Shan Museum.

Fung Ping Shan Museum

This museum houses collections of ceramics and bronzes, plus a lesser number of paintings and carvings. The bronzes are in three groups: Shang and Zhou Dynasty ritual vessels; decorative mirrors from the Warring States Period to the Tang, Sung, Ming and Ching (Qing) dynasties; and Nestorian crosses from the Yuan Dynasty (the Nestorians were a Christian sect which arose in Syria, and at some stage found their way to China – probably during the Tang Dynasty). A collection of ceramics includes Han Dynasty tomb pottery and recent works from the Chinese pottery centres of Jingdezhen and Shiwan in the People's Republic.

The museum is at the University of Hong Kong, 94 Bonham Rd. Take Bus No 3 from the Connaught Rd Central bus stop in front of the Connaught Centre. Get off at Bonham Rd, opposite St Paul's College. The museum is open Monday to Saturday, 9.30 am to 6 pm, and is closed on Sunday and several public holidays. Admission is free.

WANCHAI

Heading east from Central brings you to Hong Kong's famed Wanchai district. In all the tourist brochure hype Wanchai is still inseparable from the name of Suzie Wong – not bad considering that the book dates back to 1957 and the movie to 1960. Although Wanchai is still Hong Kong's main red-light district, the lights are a bit dimmed these days – with the Vietnam War a multi-billion-dollar bloody memory the bars are no longer crowded with US servicemen getting their R & R.

Lockhart Rd

Instead of brothels and bars, Wanchai is being taken over by high-rise office blocks as they spread out of Central, but a walk down Lockhart Rd will give you a wisp of what it was like when the place was really jumping. You can still find plenty of topless bars, massage parlours and tattooists – but you don't need an appointment any more. Further along Lockhart Rd towards Causeway Bay, the exotic turns to the prosaic and the businesses are more likely to be shops, restaurants and camera stores.

Hong Kong Arts Centre

Also in the Wanchai district is the Arts Centre on Harbour Rd. The Pao Sui Loong Galleries are on the 4th and 5th floors of the Arts Centre and international and local exhibitions are held here year-round, with the emphasis on contemporary art. Opening hours are 10 am to 8 pm daily. Admission is free.

CAUSEWAY BAY

If you catch the tram through Wanchai it will take you to Causeway Bay, home of Hong Kong's most influential *hong* (company), Jardine Matheson (former drug-pushers, home in Hong Kong, assets now safely tucked away from People's Republic hands in Bermuda). This area was the site of a British settlement in the 1840s and was once a *godown* (warehouse) area for merchants and a harbour for fishermen. A good deal of this area has been reclaimed from swamp.

Jardine Matheson Memorials

The old Causeway Bay – *Tung Lo Wan* in Chinese, meaning Copper Gong Bay – has almost disappeared through reclamation. Jardine Matheson set up shop here in 1844, after moving their headquarters from Macau. In fact the area is full of company names and memorials. Percival St, which crosses Hennessy Rd, is named after Alexander Percival, a relative of Sir James Matheson who joined the firm in

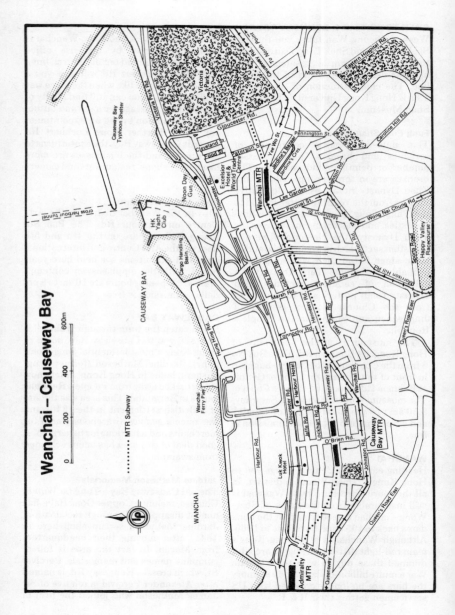

Wanchai – Causeway Bay

1852 and ended up a partner. Matheson St leads off it. Hennessy Rd becomes Yee Wo St, Yee Wo being the name under which Jardine traded in Shanghai.

Jardine Matheson bought heavily in the first land sale in the colony in 1841. They purchased a large tract of land on what was then the waterfront at Causeway Bay and hewed a whole township out of the rock. They built *godowns*, offices, workshops, a slipway, homes and messes for their employees. Today all that remains of the East Point establishment is an old gateway with a couple of plaques. You'll find it up a side-street from Yee Wo St. It's still owned by Jardine Matheson but is now full of modern warehouses.

Two streets to the right behind Yee Wo St are Jardine's Bazaar and Jardine's Crescent, names which recall the old firm. A Chinese bazaar was held on the first. Things haven't changed much. The area is still one of Chinese provision stores, herb stores and cooked-food stalls. Jardine's Crescent has a market too – very good for cheap clothes. Between Jardine's Bazaar and Crescent is the short Fuk Hing Lane where you can stock up on earthenware pots and more of those '100-year-old' eggs.

Other Streets

Nearby Pennington St has a Chinese medicine shop, pawn shops and herbalist tea houses where you can have a bowl of health-giving '24-flavour tea' made from seeds, moss, grass, roots, stems and fungus, all boiled up together. Irving St, off Pennington St, is well known for its soya sauce and wine shops. Russell St off Percival St has an all-day fresh food market.

Waterfront

Today Causeway Bay's waterfront is a mass of junks and sampans huddling in the typhoon shelter. The land jutting out is Kellett Island. It was actually an island until a causeway was built out to it in 1956. Now it's the headquarters of the Royal

Hong Kong Yacht Club. The cross harbour tunnel comes up here too.

Noon-Day Gun

The best known landmark in Causeway Bay is probably the noon-day gun – a recoil mounted three-pounder Hotchkiss built in Portsmouth in 1901. It stands in a small garden in front of the Excelsior Hotel on Gloucester Rd and is fired daily at noon. Exactly how this tradition started is unknown. One story goes that Jardine Matheson either fired it to wish bon voyage to a departing managing director or to welcome an incoming ship. The navy got so enraged that their function had been usurped (or because an ordinary person got a salute reserved for officials) that they told Jardine's to fire the gun every day as punishment.

Noel Coward made the gun famous with his satirical 1924 song *Mad Dogs and Englishmen*, about colonials who braved the heat of the noon-day sun while the natives stayed indoors:

> *In Hong Kong they strike a gong,*
> *and fire a noon-day gun,*
> *To reprimand each inmate who's*
> *in late.*

Jardine's executives stand around the gun on New Year's Eve and fire it off at midnight, to the applause of a colonial gathering.

Food St

Between the Excelsior Hotel and the end of Gloucester Rd is Food St, a modern arcade of restaurants of varied ethnic persuasions. Have a look but don't expect a banquet-like selection of traditional Chinese fare – you're more likely to find the place crowded with Hong Kong Chinese having a family excursion to eat western. However, there are some really good Chinese places here – see the Food chapter for details.

Victoria Park

Victoria Park, between Causeway Bay and Victoria Park Rd, is a large playing field bordered by high-rises. Football matches are played here on weekends and the Urban Services League puts on music and acrobatic shows. Early in the morning it's a good place to see the slow-motion choreography of tai-chi practitioners. Victoria Park becomes a flower market during the Chinese New Year, and it's also worth coming here for the Lantern Festival (see the section on Holidays & Festivals).

Tin Hau Temple

One more thing worth a look in Causeway Bay is a tiny Tin Hau temple on Tin Hau Temple Rd (at the junction with Dragon Rd), behind Victoria Park. Before reclamation, the temple to the seafarers' goddess would have stood on the waterfront. An old bell inside dates back to the 15th century. The temple itself is about 200 years old.

Tiger Balm Gardens

Not actually in Causeway Bay but in the adjacent Tai Hang District are the famous (infamous?) Tiger Balm Gardens. A pale relative of the better-known park of the same name in Singapore, Hong Kong's Tiger Balm Gardens are three hectares of grotesque statuary and appalling bad taste. These concrete gardens were built at a cost of HK$16 million (and that was back in 1935!) by Aw Boon Park, who made his fortune from the Tiger Balm cure-everything medication. He's widely described as having been a philanthropist though perhaps his millions could have been put to a more philanthropic use.

Sad to say, Aw's artistic marvel is in need of repair, the paint peeling and the concrete statues crumbling, making the place look all the more grotesque. If you haven't seen the larger Tiger Balm Gardens in Singapore then this place is worth visiting! There's a jade collection here, but you need to phone in advance if you want to see it (tel 5-616211).

The Gardens are just off Tai Hang Rd, within walking distance of Causeway Bay.

HAPPY VALLEY

Happy Valley has not always lived up to its name. When Hong Kong first began to take root the army was billeted there. However, since the land was low and swampy, malaria broke out and after several virulent bouts the government was convinced that Happy Valley could only be used for a racecourse.

Racecourse

Never before have so many people gathered in one place to lose so much. Apart from a couple of licensed lotteries, racing is the only form of legalised gambling in Hong Kong – which is why Macau is so popular with the gambling-addicted Chinese. The first horse races were held in Happy Valley in 1846, and thereafter races were held once a year. Today there are about 65 meetings per year at two tracks (the other is at Shatin in the New Territories) and about 450 races in all.

The racing season is from September to May. Races are held on most Saturday and Sunday afternoons and on some Wednesday evenings during the season. On- and off-course betting is run by the Royal Hong Kong Jockey Club and you can bet on the Quinella (choosing the first two horses), the Double Quinella (picking the first two horses from two specific races), the Six-Up (out of the day's six races choosing the first or second in each race), and the Treble (picking the winner from three specific races), as well as other combinations.

If you want to sit in the Member's Stand then you can buy a ticket for HK$50 from the Off Course Betting Centre (OCBC) near the Star Ferry Terminal on the Hong Kong side. You'll need to show them your passport. The OCBC is open on Monday from noon to 8 pm, Wednesday from noon to 6 pm (and until 10 pm on racedays),

UNLOADING ICE —
CAUSEWAY BAY

One does not trifle with the affections of a woman with an icepick between her teeth . . . .

Thursday from noon to 8 pm, Friday from noon to 9 pm, and Saturday from 9 am to 7 pm. It is closed Tuesday and Sunday.

The HKTA also has tours to Happy Valley and Shatin. Each costs HK$200 and includes the entrance fee, bus fare and lunch or dinner. Enquire at the HKTA offices or ring 5-244191. If you're a tourist it may be possible to buy a ticket from the Hong Kong Jockey Club (tel 5-7904827) which entitles you to admission to the member's enclosure, bar and restaurant; likewise for the Shatin racetrack.

NORTH POINT

Next up from Causeway Bay is North Point or 'Little Shanghai,' so-called because of the number of Shanghai Chinese who have settled there. It is a densely populated area, clogged with high-rise apartment blocks with scarcely a metre between them.

QUARRY BAY

On to Quarry Bay then, a mainly industrial area centred around the docks. Over 20,000 factories here employ an eighth of the population. Shipbuilding and repairing started in Hong Kong in 1863 with the establishment of Quarry Bay's Whampoa Dock.

SHAUKIWAN

Past North Point is Shaukiwan. Fifty years ago it was a small fishing village; today it has the second largest fishing fleet in Hong Kong, which moors in the typhoon anchorage. Shaukiwan is the home of the Tanka boat people – see them in their traditional black pyjama suits and wide-brimmed straw hats.

Shing Wong Temple

At the Shaukiwan tram terminus is a Shing Wong Temple, undistinguished in architecture but interesting nonetheless. Shing Wong is the city god. His followers believe you must have an efficient city god in your neighbourhood to keep everything running smoothly, and city councillors are supposed to bow in front of him before they take office. The god is also believed to protect the inhabitants against epidemics, famine and invasion.

SOUTHERN & EASTERN COASTS

On the southern coast of Hong Kong Island are a couple of other popular attractions: Stanley, Repulse Bay, Deep Water Bay and Ocean Park, and Aberdeen. Coming over the mountains from Central to the southern coast is a spectacular trip. Even if some of the places on the south coast don't sound all that appealing, the bus ride itself, on a good day, is one of the musts of Hong Kong Island. It's easy to take a round trip by public transport all around the island – starting from Central and taking a bus over the hills to Stanley, and then heading clockwise along the coast back to Central.

Although Hong Kong Island does not have the colony's best beaches, they're conveniently located around the southern and south-eastern coast, from Deep Water Bay to Big Wave Bay, including Stanley and Repulse Bay – see below for details. The protected waters mean you won't find giant surf, but they offer good swimming.

All beaches controlled by the Urban Council or the Urban Services Department are patrolled by life-savers. A red flag means the water is too rough for swimming, and a blue flag means it's unsafe for children and weak swimmers. At most of the beaches you will find toilets, showers, changing rooms, refreshment stalls and sometimes restaurants. The usual life-saving hours are from 9 am to 6.30 pm on weekdays. On weekends at the more popular and bigger beaches, life-saving hours are extended from 8 am to 7.30 pm.

BIG WAVE BAY & SHEK O
Two of Hong Kong Island's best beaches are Big Wave Bay and Shek O; both are on the east coast. To get there take the MTR to Shaukiwan, and from Shaukiwan take Bus No 9 to the last stop. Bus No 14 from Shaukiwan will take you to Turtle Cove on Tai Tam Bay.

STANLEY
The inaptly named Stanley Village is actually the trendy, out-of-town *gwailo* place to live, just 15 km as the crow flies from Central. Once upon a time the village was indeed a village – some 2000 people lived here when the British took over in 1841, making it one of the largest settlements on the island at the time. The British built a prison near the village in 1937 – just in time to be used by the Japanese to intern the expatriates. Today it's used as a maximum-security prison. Hong Kong's contingent of British troops is housed in Stanley Fort at the southern end of the peninsula, which is off-limits to the public.

Stanley Village
There is an OK beach (not as crowded as the one at Repulse Bay) at Stanley Village; a market (open 10 am to 7 pm) selling clothes, furniture, household goods, hardware, foodstuffs and imitation designer jeans; and some cheap food stalls. Because of the *gwailo* community there's a British-style pub, the *Smuggler's Inn*, near the intersection of Stanley Market Rd and Stanley Main St.

Tin Hau Temple
Stanley has a Tin Hau Temple which dates back to 1767. On one of the walls hangs the skin of a tiger killed by Japanese soldiers outside the temple. The temple is on a corner of Stanley Main St, approaching Ma Hang Village.

Kuan Yin (Kwun Yum) Temple
Further up from the Tin Hau Temple is the Kuan Yin Temple in Ma Hang Village. Kuan Yin is the Goddess of Mercy and the temple contains a six-metre statue of her. The statue is sheltered by a pavilion specially built in 1977 following a claim by a woman and her daughter that they'd seen the statue move and a bright light shine from its forehead . . . maybe Stanley isn't such a dull place?

St Stephen's Beach
From Stanley you could take Bus No 73A to St Stephen's Beach a bit further down the coast. Both Stanley and St Stephen's beaches have all the usual facilities. The cemetery at St Stephen's Beach is for military personnel who have died since the British occupation of Hong Kong and during WW II. The oldest graves date from 1843.

Getting There
To get to Stanley from Central take Bus No 6 or express bus No 260 from the Exchange Square Bus Terminus just west of the Connaught Centre. Fares are HK$2 with the ordinary bus and HK$4 with the express bus. The bus to Stanley takes a very scenic trip down Tai Tam Rd to the reservoir, then along the coast at Tai Tam Bay. Bus No 73 connects Stanley with Repulse Bay.

REPULSE BAY
Once upon a time the memorable feature here used to be the Somerset Maugham-ish Repulse Bay Hotel, a splendid old colonial building. Even if you couldn't afford to stay there, it was still worth spending a few dollars to sit on the

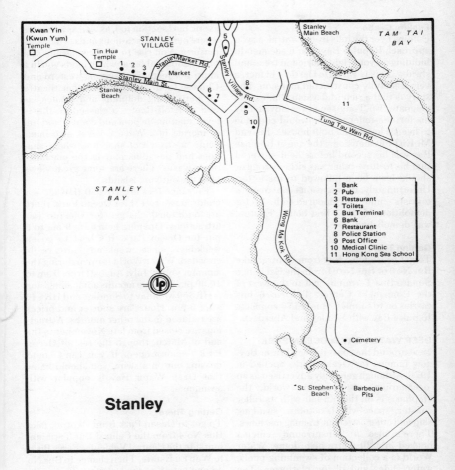

STANLEY VILLAGE

1 Bank
2 Pub
3 Restaurant
4 Toilets
5 Bus Terminal
6 Bank
7 Restaurant
8 Police Station
9 Post Office
10 Medical Clinic
11 Hong Kong Sea School

Stanley

balcony, drink iced tea beneath the huge overhead fans, look out on the bay and envy the comfortable existence of the colonialists. Inside, the heavy brocade, thick carpets and ornate chandeliers made no concession to the orient; Queen Victoria might still have been on the throne. The hotel was ripped down is 1982 and though a block of apartments was to be built on the site, nothing has come of them so far.

Repulse Bay Beach

Today, Repulse Bay's prime attraction is its beach and huge McDonald's. In fact, the beach attracts so many people on hot weekends you're just about swimming in suntan lotion – and to find even a niche in the sand you have to get there early. It's a scenic drive. You could also walk down the coast a bit to Middle Bay and South Bay, about 10 and 30 minutes walk respectively.

Eucliffe Castle

Coming over the hills from Central, as you approach Repulse Bay, you'll see an odd building on your right, buried in trees and shrubs. This is Eucliffe Castle – in fact, a very tastefully constructed mansion. The story is that a rich Malaysian Chinese tin magnate, Eu Tong-seng, was advised by his fortune-teller that he would continue to live, as long as he built houses. Instead Mr Eu built mansions; the one at Repulse Bay was his second before he discovered that his fortune-teller was either wrong or should have been followed to the letter. Unfortunately, the mansion is not open to tourists – and it's rumoured to be up for demolition. Mr Eu's first house, Euston, was demolished.

Getting There

To get to Repulse Bay from Central take Bus No 6 or Bus No 61 from the Exchange Square Bus Terminus just to the west of the Connaught Centre. The No 6 bus carries on to Stanley. Bus No 73 connects Repulse Bay with Stanley and Aberdeen.

DEEP WATER BAY & OCEAN PARK

Next around the coast is Deep Water Bay, now famous for Ocean Park, opened in 1976. Although generally advertised as an 'oceanarium' or a marine world, the emphasis is on the fun-fair with its roller coaster, space-wheel, octopus, swinging ship and other astronaut-training machines. There's also a 'sensurround' cinema housed in a 20-metre-high dome. Water World is a collection of swimming pools, water slides and diving platforms. The place is much more a straight-out amusement park than a marine world.

The complex is built on two levels connected by a seven-minute cable car ride, and looks down on Deep Water Bay below. At the entrance to the park are landscaped gardens with a touch-and-feed section where kids can pet tame llamas, goats, kangaroos and calves. Chinese arts like kung-fu, opera and so on are often staged in the gardens. There's an exotic bird section too, as well as a theatre where penguins, sea-lions and cormorants perform. You rise to the oceanarium in a blue bubble cable car which lands you in a multi-tier restaurant serving western and Chinese food. Nearby is another theatre for performing dolphins and whales, as well as Atoll Reef – a glassed-in, three-level, man-made pool and coral island full of marine life. Wave Cove is also man-made, a stretch of shoreline where sea-lions and penguins play in the machine-made waves. There are some great views over the outlying islands.

Entrance fees are HK$70 (HK$35 for children two to 13) for Ocean Park; there are additional charges for the fun fair attractions. Opening hours are 9 am to 6 pm for Ocean Park. It's best to go on weekdays since weekends are really crowded. Water World is open during the summer (June, July, August) from 9 am to 10.30 pm. In those months adult admission is HK$50 Monday to Sunday, and HK$40 after 6 pm. Hours are shorter and prices are reduced in the other months. Attractions are closed from late November to the end of March, though the rest of Ocean Park remains open. If you can't stand missing out on a swim, you should know that Deep Water Bay is popular with swimmers.

Getting There

To get to Ocean Park from Central, take Bus No 4 from the Central Bus Terminal (outside the Central Vehicular Ferry Pier) to Wah Fu Estate. Then change to Bus No 48 and get off at the last stop. This route takes you via Aberdeen.

Alternatively, take Bus No 70 from the Central Bus Terminal. Get off at Wong Chuk Hang Rd and walk along Ocean Park Rd for about 15 to 20 minutes to the main entrance of the park. Bus No 99 is a direct bus from the Central Bus Terminal to Ocean Park operated only on Sunday and public holidays.

Alternatively, you can buy all-inclusive tickets from the MTR. These include the

ADULT TICKET
成人券

HK$70.00

OCEAN PARK
海洋公園

ADMIT
ONE
ADULT

OPA 884980

Ocean Park ticket

MTR to Admiralty Station, a bus to the park, the entrance fee, cable car fare, and return bus and train.

Bus No 73 connects Ocean Park with Aberdeen to the west and Repulse Bay and Stanley to the east.

ABERDEEN

Aberdeen is called 'Little Hong Kong' by the Chinese and that's all it really is. It was originally a typhoon shelter and a landbase for seafarers – as well as a pirate haunt. Under the British it became an important boat-building port, but today it's promoted as a tourist attraction because of its enormous floating restaurants and innumerable smaller ones serving fresh seafood.

Just off the coast, the island of Ap Lei Chau provides natural protection for the harbour. The island is still a major junk-building centre. The harbour used to be home for 3000 junks (housing some 20,000 people), but there are very few left now – instead there's an enormous housing estate. Today about 53,000 people live at Aberdeen, including 23,000 in Ap Lei Chau and about 6300 on the junks.

The other thing worth noting is the Aberdeen Power Station and its five tall chimneys. Only four of them ever smoke – the fifth is a dummy. The dummy chimney was built because the Chinese word for four – say – is very close to the word for death, so anything to do with the number is unlucky. Or so the story goes. At the junction of Aberdeen Main Rd and Aberdeen Reservoir Rd is a Tin Hau Temple built in 1851.

A bridge to Ap Lei Chau gives a good view of the harbour. It's worth getting a sampan to run you round the harbour. The women who operate them will leap on you, so there's no need to hunt around.

Getting There

A tunnel linking Aberdeen with the northern side of Hong Kong island provides rapid access to the town. From the Central Bus Terminal take Bus No 7 or No 70 to Aberdeen. No 7 goes via Hong Kong University, and No 70 goes via the tunnel. Bus No 73 from Aberdeen will take you along the southern coast to Ocean Park, Repulse Bay and Stanley.

Kowloon

The name 'Kowloon' is thought to have originated when the last emperor of the Song Dynasty passed through the area during his flight from the Mongols. He counted eight peaks on the peninsula and commented that there must therefore be eight dragons here – but was reminded that since he himself was present there must be nine. Kowloon means 'nine dragons' from the Chinese words *kau* for nine and *loong* for dragon. Whether that is the real origin of the name is unknown, but the tradition carries on. Today Kowloon proper is a mere 10 square km or so of high-rise buildings extending from the Tsimshatsui waterfront at the tip of the peninsula as far north as Boundary St.

TSIMSHATSUI

Hong Kong's tourist ghetto lies at the very tip of the Kowloon peninsula in Tsimshatsui. About one square km of shops, restaurants, pubs, topless bars (and others of various degrees of titillation for their customers), fast-food places and camera and electronics stores are huddled together on either side of Nathan Rd. This is where you are most likely to find a place to sleep for the night, whether it's just a bed or a luxury suite.

Star House

If you start your walk from the Star Ferry Terminal, the first building you come to is Star House, home of the Student Travel Bureau, the Macau Tourist Bureau, a Chinese arts and crafts store, a Maxim's fast-food, and other useful and not-so-useful offices and shops.

Ocean Terminal

Just around to the left from Star House, the long building jutting out into the harbour is the Ocean Terminal. The luxury cruise-ship set come ashore here, and to meet their needs the terminal and adjoining Ocean Centre are crammed with very ritzy shops in endless arcades. Not the place for cheap souvenir-hunting but interesting for a stroll, and there are some nice views of the harbour.

Salisbury Rd

The main road in front of Star House and leading away from the ferry is Salisbury Rd. It was once on the waterfront but is now further inland due to the land reclamation works.

Walk along Salisbury Rd for a block or two and you will come to a contrasting pair of establishments. The first one is the YMCA, with a portico over the footpath. Next door is the Peninsula Hotel, Hong Kong's most prestigious watering-hole (it's the one with the fountain and the fleet of green Rolls-Royces out front). The Peninsula is one of *the* places to stay in Hong Kong. Before the war it was part of a chain of prestigious hotels across Asia where everybody who was anybody stayed; the list includes the rather faded and dingy Raffles in Singapore, the Taj in Bombay, and the Cathay (now called the Peace) in Shanghai. Regardless of the Peninsula's historic value, at one time it – like the YMCA – was rumoured to be up for demolition.

The side wings of the Peninsula have shopping arcades at ground floor and basement level, mostly filled with airline offices and expensive boutiques – you can stock up on Gucci leatherware here if your old boots are getting a bit tatty. The hotel's lobby offers high-ceilinged splendour. It is worth paying over the odds for a cup of coffee or a beer here to enjoy the rarefied atmosphere and to spot people spotting other people. The rich and famous are said to stay here; if so, they don't hang around in the lobby.

Over the road from the Peninsula and YMCA is the Hong Kong Space Museum,

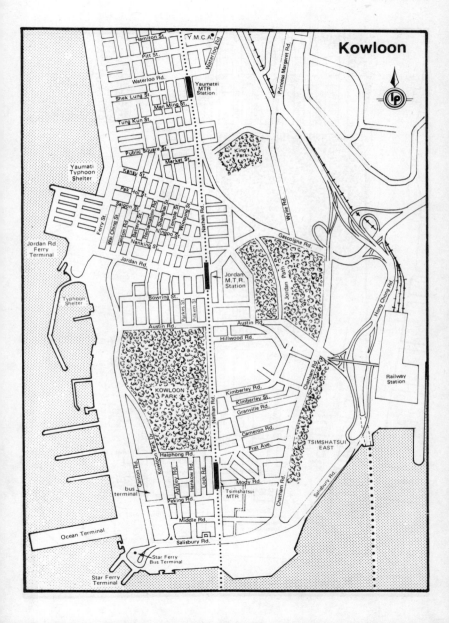

Kowloon

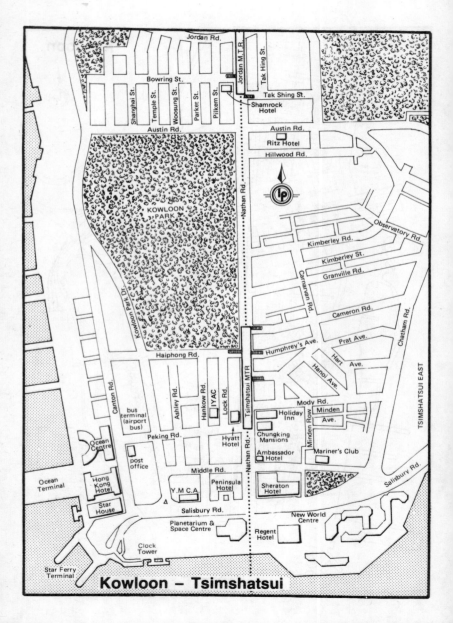

Kowloon – Tsimshatsui

a combination museum with displays of space artefacts and a planetarium; more about it below. As you continue along Salisbury Rd past the intersection with Nathan Rd you'll see several four- and five-star hotels including the Sheraton, the Regent and the New World (plus several levels of sparkling shopping arcades arranged around mezzanine floors).

Nathan Rd

Starting from Salisbury Rd, beside the Peninsula Hotel, is Nathan Rd, the main drag of Kowloon. It extends for about four km to Boundary Rd at the official border with the New Territories.

Nathan Rd is unusually wide for Hong Kong (meaning there is room for more than one lane of traffic in each direction). Named after the governor of the time, Sir Matthew Nathan, it was promptly renamed 'Nathan's Folly' since in those times – just after the turn of the century – Kowloon was sparsely populated and a road of such generous proportions seemed totally unnecessary.

Today the lower end is known instead as the 'golden mile' because of its ability to suck money out of tourists' pockets. Here you'll find almost nothing but hotels, bars, nightclubs, restaurants and shops jammed with the usual assortment of watches, calculators and other zazzy electronics. Explore the side streets, though there the monotony is broken only by jean shops and tailors.

Nevertheless, the area is a convenient one in which to base yourself. This is where most of the cheaper accommodation is located (including the famous – infamous? – Chungking Mansions). At the corner of Hoi Phong and Nathan Rds is the recently completed Islamic Centre, Hong Kong's largest mosque.

There are plenty of buses on Nathan Rd connecting with the Star Ferry. MTR runs under the road with stations near Peking Rd at the southern end, Jordan Rd, Waterloo Rd and Argyle St.

Space Museum

Otherwise known as the Arnold Palmer Centre because it looks like half a golf-ball, this is the peculiar dome-shaped building on Salisbury St at the intersection with Nathan Rd. It's divided into three parts: the Planetarium (Space Theatre), an Exhibition Hall, and a Hall of Solar Sciences devoted to exhibitions of the sun. The museum has the usual sort of exhibits, including a lump of moon rock, models of rocket ships, telescopes, time-lines, videos of moon-walks – all very educational and worth a look. The Mercury space capsule piloted by Scott Carpenter in 1962 is on show here.

The building is closed on Tuesday. Opening times for the Exhibition Hall and Hall of Solar Sciences are Monday, Wednesday, Thursday, Friday and Saturday from 2 to 10 pm; and Sunday and public holidays from 10.30 am to 10 pm. Admission is free. The planetarium has several shows per day (except Tuesday), some in English and some in Cantonese. Check times with the museum or the HKTA. Admission to the planetarium is HK$15. For enquiries phone 3-7212361.

Museum of History

The museum is housed in two late 19th-century buildings (a rarity in themselves in Hong Kong) in Kowloon Park on Nathan Rd. It covers all of Hong Kong's existence from prehistoric times to the present and has a large collection of 19th- and early 20th-century photographs of the city on display.

The museum is open Monday to Thursday and Saturday from 10 am to 6 pm; and Sunday and public holidays from 1 to 6 pm. It is closed on Friday. Admission is free. Enter from Haiphong Rd on the south side of the park. It's a short walk from the Kowloon Star Ferry.

Young's Wax Gallery

In the second basement of the Miramar Hotel is Young's Wax Gallery, a series of wax effigies depicting scenes from Chinese history, as well as modern European personalities. There's even a statue of the 8th-century poet Li Pai, recumbent in a drunken sleep – his chest rising and falling in simulated snores.

The Miramar Hotel is at 134 Nathan Rd, Tsimshatsui. The museum is open daily from 11 am to 7 pm and admission is HK$5. The Miramar Hotel is walking distance from the Star Ferry.

TSIMSHATSUI EAST

Continuing along Salisbury Rd and just at the end of the New World Hotel, you will find Chatham Rd on your left. The large triangle of reclaimed land bordered by Salisbury and Chatham Rds is Tsimshatsui East; once upon a time this whole area was under water. Here you'll find a number of large hotels including a second Holiday Inn, the Shangri-la, the Royal Garden and Royal Meridien. There are numerous commercial office blocks along with a couple of large exhibition centres.

YAUMATI (YAUMATEI)

Immediately to the north of Tsimshatsui is the Yaumati (Yaumatei) district. Its chief attraction is the Jade Market, but there's plenty more to see.

The HKTA produces the very useful *Six Walks* leaflet which gives a rundown of a walk through the Yaumati district, taking in the interesting streets between Jordan Rd and Kansu St. These include Canton Rd (ivory shops, mahjong shops), Saigon St (a street market) and Ning Po St (paper items, including kites as well as paper houses and luxury items for the dead).

Worth checking out is the junk-cluttered Yaumati Typhoon Shelter just to the north-east of Kansu St. The best views are from the upper floors of a nearby highrise! It's possible to hire a sampan and ride around the typhoon shelter – this isn't touristy like riding a sampan around the harbour at Aberdeen on the Hong Kong side, and you get a glimpse from water-level of the gradually disappearing world

Blind street musician

of the boat people. The shelter was built in 1915 after a disastrous typhoon.

Jade Market

Once located at the top end of Canton Rd, the Jade Market has now been moved to the junction of Reclamation and Kansu Sts under the flyover in the Yaumati district, just to the west of Nathan Rd. It's open daily between 10 am and 4 pm (though you may find the sellers packing up and leaving around 1 pm, so go early).

The Chinese regard jade as lucky and as a protection against disease. It symbolises nobility, beauty and purity. Its physical properties have become metaphors for

Top: Student of palmistry, Macau (TW)
Left: At the Po Lin monastery, Lantau (AS)
Right: Street-side calligraphy (HKTA)

Top: The bright lights of Tsimshatsui, Kowloon (JH)
Left: Peking Road, Kowloon (AS)
Right: Near Kai Tak airport (AS)

the Confucian ideal of the noble or superior man: 'Charity is its lustre, bright yet warm . . . wisdom is its pure and penetrating note when struck . . . equity is its sharp edges which injure none,' reads one Chinese dictionary of the 2nd century AD. In the Ming dynasty jade was ground up and drunk in a potion; it was said to keep asthma away and put a gloss on your hair. Today jade is often buried with a loved one because it is believed to slow down the decomposition process. Chinese embalmers used to place jade ornaments on the tongue, chest and other parts of the body before it was buried, and suits made entirely of jade pieces have been uncovered in Chinese tombs. The circular disc with a hole in the middle you see worn around a lot of necks in Hong Kong represents heaven in Chinese mythology. In the old days amulets and talismans of jade were worn by Chinese court officials to denote rank, power and wealth. One emperor was reputed to have worn jade sandals, and another gave his favourite concubine a bed of jade. In Hong Kong it is common to see boat people in old pyjama suits, scruffy street hawkers and amahs on shoestring wages wearing jade bangles beyond the reach of most free-spending tourists. It is also customary for people who have no use for banks to put their money into something tangible like jade. In the Jade Market you can see bangles in two halves, cut from the wrists of dead relatives.

There are two varieties of jade: jadeite and nephrite, both different minerals. While the colour green is usually associated with jade, the milk-white shade is the most highly prized (a debatable point – some say deep green is most prized). Shades of pink, red, yellow, brown, mauve and turquoise come in between – though these can also be produced using artificial dyes. The true test of a piece of jade is said to be its hardness – where the tip of a pocket knife will leave a scratch mark on imitation jade, the genuine item will remain unharmed.

All that said, it's unlikely you'll find a real bargain or a rarity at the jade market. If such specimens did exist neither you nor the Chinese would be able to find it – but the place is definitely worth a look. It's mainly a market for Chinese, not tourists. Even so, bargain hard for all pieces if you intend buying!

To get there take Bus No 9 from the Kowloon Star Ferry Bus Terminal. Get off at Kowloon Central Post Office and walk down to the intersection of Kowloon and Reclamation Sts. Coming over from Hong Kong Island, take the MTR and get off at either Jordan or Yaumati stations.

Tin Hau Temple

On Market St, a block or two to the north of the Jade Market, is a sizable Tin Hau Temple, dedicated to the patron goddess of seafarers. For background on her see the Religion section at the start of this book. The temple is open daily from 7.30 am to 8.30 pm.

Shanghai & Temple Sts

Patronised by the locals, poked around in by curious tourists, favoured by some expatriates who like to buy their underpants here, Shanghai and Temple Sts (which run parallel to each other) are two of Hong Kong's main shopping drags for everyday miscellania. Temple St is at its best in the evening from about 8 to 11 pm, clogged with stalls and people.

NEW KOWLOON

Beyond Kowloon proper is an area of about 30 square km known as New Kowloon, which includes places like Shum Shui Po, Laichikok and Kwun Tong. Strictly speaking, these places are part of the New Territories but they tend to be included in Kowloon in everyday usage of the name. Boundary St marks the border between Kowloon and the New Territories, and is where the border with China was to have been moved in 1997.

The Walled City

The so-called Walled City of Kowloon is not a Ming Dynasty settlement, nor is it to be confused with the walled villages of Kam Tin in the New Territories. These walls only go back to the 19th century, when they were put up to keep a small portion of Kowloon nominally Chinese after it was given to the British. When the Japanese occupied Hong Kong during the war they found that the wall provided a convenient source of stone for building the runway of the nearby airport. There are no walls here today, just a fascinating dense cluster of houses and narrow alleyways.

The city is situated on the north side of Carpenter Rd, which runs into Prince Edward Rd in the Kai Tak district. A simple way to get there would be to take the airport bus to Kai Tak Airport Terminal and walk from there.

Wong Tai Sin Temple

On the upper edge of the Wong Tai Sin housing estate, this temple was built quite recently – in 1973 – but in the traditional style of Chinese temple architecture. It is dedicated to the god of the same name. The image of the god in the main temple was brought to Hong Kong from China in 1915 and was originally installed in a temple in Wanchai until it was moved to the present site in 1921. For some background on Wong Tai Sin see the Religion section at the start of this book. For a very useful description of the temple, building by building, get a free copy of the HKTA Wong Tai Sin fact-sheet.

On a Sunday afternoon the place is crowded with worshippers burning their joss sticks and making offerings of plates of food. Some bring their own carefully prepared dishes, others buy oranges from the numerous fruit stalls that engulf the entrance. The incense is burned, the offerings are made (but not left, since the gods can't be all that hungry and no one wants good food to go to waste), and the fortune sticks are cast. The orange and incense vendors also offer little plastic wind propellers on sticks which make the whole place look as if it ought to be a fairground rather than a place of worship. There is even a sort of sideshow alley, except that all the sideshows are fortune tellers – mainly palmists, physiognomists, and other diviners of one's physical characteristics. Other temples in the grounds are dedicated to various divinities including Buddha, Confucius, the Taoist god Monkey (whose story is told in the 16th century epic *Journey to the West*) and the god of war Kuan Ti.

To get to the temple, take the MTR to Wong Tai Sin Station and follow the directions – it's a three-minute walk north of the station. If you're coming from Hong Kong Island you will have to change trains at Mong Kok Station. The temple is open daily from 7 am to 5 pm. The busiest times here are around the Chinese New Year and on Wong Tai Sin's birthday on the 23rd day of the 8th lunar month.

Laichikok Amusement Park

If you like all the fun of the fair then Kowloon's got the Laichikok Amusement Park, with the usual dodgems and pinball machines, a mini monorail scooting above the treetops, a small zoo and a replica of a Canton lake. Clashing cymbals and other loud noises indicate the Chinese opera performances which start each evening at 8 pm. Performances last about three hours and you can come and go as you please; seats at the rear are free. There is a cinema outside the park but it is not free.

The park is open daily from 11 am to 11 pm and admission is HK$3.50. Try and go during the week if you can, as it's very crowded on the weekends. The imitation Sung Dynasty Village is right next door, so use the same transport – see below for details.

Sung Dynasty Village

Next door to the Laichikok Amusement

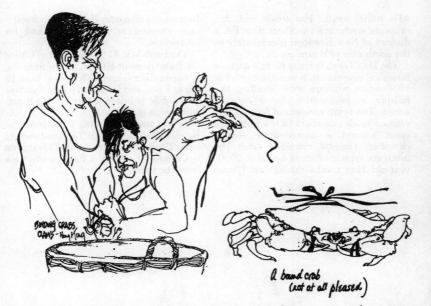

BINDING CRABS CLAWS - Hong Kong

a band crab
(not at all pleased)

Park, the village was once part of it before it was hyped up as an authentic re-creation of a Chinese village from 10 centuries ago. It's a sort of Chinese Disneyland-supermarket where crafts-people and other villagers walk around in period costumes, engaging in Sung Dynasty (960-1279 AD) pursuits such as fortune-telling, blacksmithing, woodcarving and getting married. Candy or pastries can be bought with coupons made to look like Sung money, but if you want a kimono, paperweight or other souvenir from the village shop you'll have to have the genuine 20th-century legal tender. Beneath the Restaurant of Plentiful Joy lies Hong Kong's largest wax museum, which houses figures of people from Chinese history.

You can go on your own on Saturday, Sunday or public holidays for only HK$30 between the hours of 12.30 pm and 5 pm. Stalls with live demonstrations close at 6 pm but you can still visit the wax museum, walk through the village and watch the cultural show scheduled for 7 pm.

Alternatively, you can take a tour during the week. Tour fees (including bus, guide, shows and meal) are: lunch tour HK$135, afternoon tour HK$105 and dinner tour HK$135. For bookings ring 3-7415111, or book through travel agents or the large tourist hotels.

If you're by yourself you can get to the village either by bus or MTR. From the Kowloon Star Ferry Bus Terminal take Bus No 6A, which terminates in front of the Laichikok Amusement Park. From the Tsimshatsui or Central MTR stations take the train to Mei Foo Station. From there head north along Lai Wan Rd and turn left at the junction with Mei Lai Rd. Continue down Mei Lai Rd, at the end of which is the Sung Dynasty Village and the Laichikok Amusement Park.

Lei Cheng Uk Branch Museum & Han Tomb

The Han Tomb at Lei Cheng Uk is a branch of the Museum of History, at the site of an actual late Han dynasty (25-220

AD) burial vault. The tomb and tiny museum are located in Sham Shui Po, a district of New Kowloon immediately to the north side of Boundary St.

The Han Tomb is Hong Kong's earliest historical monument. It was discovered in 1955 when workers were levelling the hillside in preparation for a housing estate. The tomb consists of four barrel-vaulted brick chambers in the form of a cross around a domed-vault central chamber. Objects retrieved from the tomb are typical of those found in 2000-year-old Han tombs throughout China.

Behind the museum is the tomb itself – now encased in a concrete shell for protection.

The tomb is at 41 Tonkin St, Lei Cheng Uk Resettlement Estate, Sham Shui Po. It's open daily (except Thursday) from 10 am to 1 pm, and from 2 to 6 pm. Sundays and public holidays it's open 1 to 6 pm. Admission is 10c.

To get there, take Bus No 2 from the Kowloon Star Ferry Bus Terminal and get off at Tonkin St. The nearest MTR station is Chueng Sha Wan, a five-minute walk from the tomb.

New Territories

To the north of Boundary St on the Kowloon peninsula lie the New Territories, leased from China by Britain for 99 years in 1898. Not only does this lease cover the land joining Kowloon to China, it covers all the outer islands save for tiny Stone-cutters Island off the west coast of Kowloon. For years the thing everyone did in Hong Kong was take a trip to the border and gaze at the hermit on the other side – so you could at least say you'd seen the People's Republic even if you couldn't set foot on it.

While several of the larger islands like Lantau and Cheung Chau get many visitors, the land mass adjoining China is regarded by tourists as something of a misty backwoods – a strange conception because this is where a huge portion of Hong Kong's population lives. All you have to do to stop Hong Kong's factories and skyscrapers is amputate the New Territories; over 1.7 million people – almost a third of the colony's population – live here. In the future more than three million people are to be housed here in a number of townships as well as in seven huge 'new towns' like Tsuen Wan and Shatin. Take away the New Territories – which China could have done in 1997 – and the colony would cease to be a viable state.

The New Territories are not only vitally important to Hong Kong, they're a whole different side of the colony that not enough visitors take time out to see. Even a day is enough for a round-trip by bus out of Kowloon; heading clockwise you can take in some of the vast new towns like Tsuen Wan and Tuen Mun; take a side trip to unique villages like the oyster-producing centre of Laufaushan; cut across to the large Mui Fat Buddhist Monastery at Lam Tei; see the ancient walled villages at Kam Tim; and then curve around back to Kowloon via Shatin and its fabulous racecourse. And that really is only a glimpse of the new Territories; after that there's Hakka villages to explore, the Sai Kung peninsula to walk through, wild Castle Peak to climb and a lot more!

A circular day-trip around the New Territories is only going to use up about HK$25 in bus and train fares. The section below tells you how to do it heading clockwise, starting in Kowloon and working your way around to Tai Po where you can then pick up the Kowloon-Canton railway line and head back to Kowloon via Shatin. If you don't want to do a circular trip there's information on how to get to these places direct from Kowloon.

For updated information on the buses check with the HKTA; they have a printed handout listing transport to and around the New Territories. Details on the Kowloon-Canton railway – along which are places like Shatin, Tai Po, Sheung Shui and the border town of Lo Wu – are given at the end of this chapter.

TSUEN WAN

First stop on the New Territories tour is the industrial new town of Tsuen Wan, 'new town' being an appropriate term because the aim is to make this a largely self-sufficient settlement providing both jobs and housing for the residents. Some 700,000 people live here and when the development is completed in 1993 it will be home to 890,000 – about half of whom are expected to be employed in Tsuen Wan itself.

Nearby is the Kwai Chung container port which handles the third highest volume of goods of any container port in the world. Opposite Tsuen Wan is Tsing Yi Island where housing for 200,000 people is planned. Overlooking Tsuen Wan is Tai Mo Shan, Hong Kong's highest mountain – around 950 metres high.

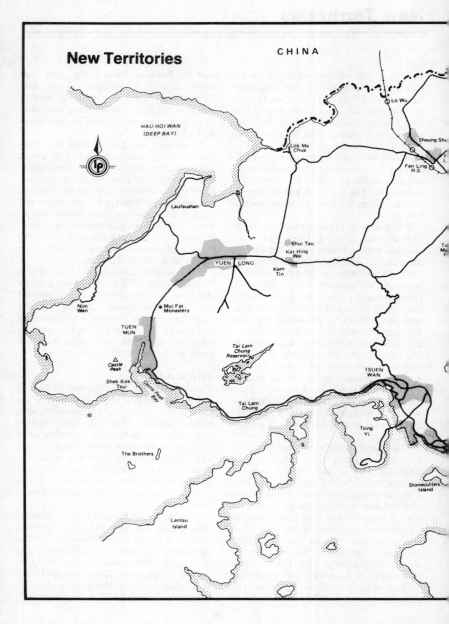

New Territories

CHINA

HAU HOI WAN
(DEEP BAY)

Lo Wu

Sheung Shu

Lok Ma
Chua

Fan Ling
R.S

Laufaushan

Shui Tau

Kat Hing
Wai

YUEN LONG

Kam
Tin

Nim
Wan

Mui Fat
Monastery

TUEN
MUN

Tai Lam
Chung
Reservoir

Castle
Peak

TSUEN
WAN

Shek Kok
Tsui

Tai Lam
Chung

Tsing
Yi

The Brothers

Stonecutters
Island

Lantau
Island

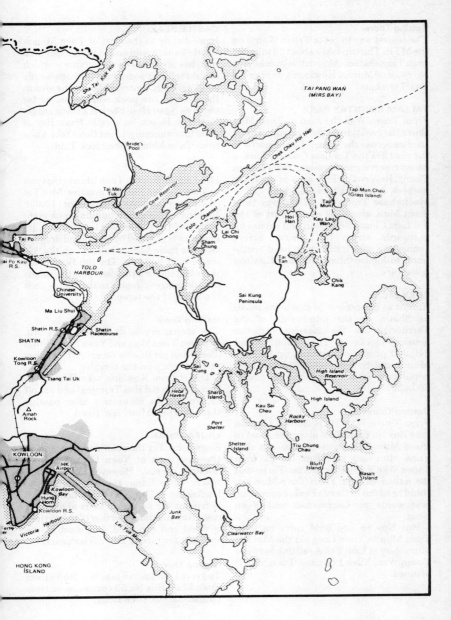

Getting There

The easiest way to get to Tsuen Wan is on the MTR. The trip takes about 20 minutes from Tsimshatsui. Alternatively, take Bus No 68 or 68M from Kowloon's Jordan Rd Bus Terminus.

TAI LAM COUNTRY PARK

From Tsuen Wan the road to Tuen Mun skirts the coast; from the bus you can see Lantau across the water. To the north of the road lies the Tai Lam Country Park, a forest reserve encompassing the Tai Lam Chung Reservoir. This area is good for walkers. A walking trail called the MacLehose Trail runs all the way from Tuen Mun, along the north coast of the Tai Lam Chung Reservoir, and carries on eastwards across the reserve before connecting with trails which head southwards to Jubilee (Shing Mun) and Kowloon reservoirs.

TUEN MUN

Almost as impressive (if that's the word) as Shatin on the other side of the Territories are the massive high-rise housing blocks of Tuen Mun. About 240,000 people are stacked up in Tuen Mun – and by the mid-1990s the total population is expected to be almost 500,000.

Getting There

From Tsuen Wan MTR Station you can take Bus No 68 or 68M along the coast to Tuen Mun. Alternatively, you can skip Tuen Mun and take Bus No 51 from Tsuen Wan Ferry Pier to Kam Tin to visit the walled villages. From Tuen Mun you could head out to Castle Peak, or continue northwards to Laufaushan and Yuen Long.

Bus Nos 68 and 68M carry on from Tuen Mun to Yuen Long via the Mui Fat Monastery at Lam Tei. A rail link between Tsuen Wan, Yuen Long and Tuen Mun is planned.

CASTLE PEAK

Immediately to the west of Tuen Mun is Castle Peak, a wild and mountainous area that has its own rescue service – which should tell you something. Otherwise it's good walking country, although the area to the west of the peak and almost as far north as Ngau Hom Shek is a firing range. Butterfly Beach on Castle Peak Bay is good for swimming; to get there take a bus from Tuen Mun to Shek Kok Tsui.

LAM TEI

Heading north from Tuen Mun brings you to Lam Tei, site of the massive Mui Fat Monastery and its Temple of 10,000 Buddhas. This garish building took eight years and HK$60 million to construct. Its entrance is guarded by two gilded dragons twisting their bodies halfway up the 33-metre-high building. The top floor holds three large golden Buddhas plus thousands of little images clinging to the walls – thus the name of the temple.

Getting There

The monastery is on Castle Peak Rd, between Tuen Mun and Yuen Long. From Tuen Mun get Bus No 68 or 68M – it takes you straight past the temple.

Direct from Kowloon take Bus No 68 from Jordan Rd Bus Terminal and get off in front of the monastery after passing through Tuen Mun New Town.

LAUFAUSHAN

From Lam Tei the road continues on to the new town of Yuen Long, which is nothing special. However, before you reach Yuen Long you can detour to Laufaushan on Deep Bay Coast. Laufaushan is famous for its oyster beds and oyster restaurants. A large portion of the oysters is dried and exported, but most of the shellfish get turned into oyster sauce.

Getting There

To get to Laufaushan take Bus No 55 from Tuen Mun. Bus No 55 continues on from Laufaushan to Yuen Long.

Direct from Kowloon take Bus No 68 from the Jordan Rd Bus Terminal and get off at the end of the line. Then change to Bus No 55 and get off at the last stop.

YUEN LONG

After Lam Tei is the new town of Yuen Long – by comparison with Tsuen Wan or Shatin a minor entity with only about 60,000 people and a planned total population of 150,000 by the end of the century. From Yuen Long you can now head east to the walled villages of Kam Tin, or detour to the north, to the old China lookout point of Lok Ma Chau.

Getting There

Bus Nos 68 and 68M connect Yuen Long to Tuen Mun and Tsuen Wan. Bus No 55 connects Yuen Long to Laufaushan. Bus No 76K connects Yuen Long to Lok Ma Chau. Bus No 54 connects Yuen Long to the Kam Tin walled villages.

Direct from Kowloon, Bus No 68 from the Jordan Rd Bus Terminal will take you to Yuen Long East Bus Terminal. Get off at Yuen Long Main Rd. From here you can walk to Yuen Long West Bus Terminal on Kik Yeung Rd for buses to the Kam Tin walled villages or Lok Ma Chau.

LOK MA CHAU

Lok Ma Chau is ancient history; this is where people used to come to look at China. Now you can actually go to China, which makes peering over the border somewhat pointless.

Getting There

To get to Lok Ma Chau direct from Kowloon, take Bus No 68 from the Jordan Rd Bus Terminal. Get off on Yuen Long Main Rd in Yuen Long. Walk to Yuen Long West Bus Terminal on Kik Yeung Rd. Then change to Bus No 76K. Get off at the junction of Castle Peak and Lok Ma Chau Rds and walk for 20 or 30 minutes to the lookout point. Bus No 76K continues on from Lok Ma Chau to Sheung Shui on the Kowloon-Canton railway line.

KAM TIN

The walled villages of Hong Kong are one of the last reminders that once upon a time the villagers were faced with marauding pirates, bandits and soldiers. There are two walled villages in the Kam Tin region: Kat Hing Wai and Shui Tau. Of the two villages, most tourists go to Kat Hing Wai, however, Shui Tau is bigger and more interesting. Other walled villages in the colony are Kam Hing Wai, Kam Tsin Wai and Shek Tsin Wai.

Kat Hing Wai

Just off the main road is this tiny 500-year-old village, walled sometime during the Ming Dynasty (1368-1644 AD). It's really just one small street with a maze of dark alleyways leading off it. The high street is packed with souvenir sellers. You are not welcome down the side streets.

Shui Tau

For Shui Tau get off the bus on the outskirts of Kam Tin and walk down the road to the left. The 17th-century village is famous for its carved roofs, ship-prow shaped with stone fishes and dragons. Tiny traditional-style Chinese houses huddle inside Shui Tau's walls.

The village was, and still is, the home of the Tang clan who have lived there for centuries. They were high-ranking public servants in the Imperial court of China in the 19th century. The ancestral hall in the middle of the village is used as a school in the mornings but was originally built for the clan to worship its forebears. The small plates on the altar in the inner hall and the long boards down the side list the ancestors. Fish on the roof of the entrance hall represent husband and wife and are put there for good luck. Soldiers painted on the doors guard the entrance.

The Tin Hau temple on the outskirts of the town was built in 1722. Its enormous bell weighs 106 kg.

You will find Shui Tau quiet and the locals friendly. It's definitely worth a look and there are beer stalls scattered around.

For Kat Hing Hai and Shui Tau, take Bus No 54 from Yuen Long West Bus Terminal on Kik Yeung Rd. Bus No 51 connects Kam Tin with the Tseun Wan Ferry Pier if you want to skip the western side of the New Territories.

Direct from Kowloon, the quickest way to get to the walled villages is to take Bus No 68 from the Jordan Rd Bus Terminal and get off on Yuen Long Main Rd. Walk to Yuen Long West Bus Terminal on Kik Yeung Rd, and then take Bus No 54 to the village. Alternatively you could take Bus No 68 or the MTR to Tsuen Wan. From the Tsuen Wan Ferry Pier Bus No 51 goes direct to Kam Tin.

TAI PO

Yet another industrial-residential new town – this time catering mainly to high-technology industries – Tai Po houses something like 120,000 people with housing for an additional 180,000 planned. It's also the site of Tai Po Market, the town having long been a market centre for the surrounding region. Worth checking out is the Tai Ping Carpet Factory where traditional-style Chinese carpets are made.

Getting There

After Yuen Long, Castle Peak Rd becomes Kam Tin Rd and cuts across the neck of the New Territories past the Kam Tin walled villages, Shek Kong and Kadoorie Farm, continuing through Lam Tsuen Valley and on to Tai Po. Bus No 64K will take you from Yuen Long West Bus Terminal to Tai Po via Kam Tin.

In Tai Po, Bus No 64 terminates at Wai Yan St. You can get back to Kowloon two ways: on the electric train from Tai Po Market Station, or on Bus No 70, which leaves from Kwong Fuk Rd.

If you're coming up to Tai Po on the train from Kowloon, you get off at Tai Po Market Station. Or take Bus No 70 from the Jordan Rd Bus Terminal.

PLOVER COVE RESERVOIR

From Tai Po, Ting Kok Rd heads eastward to Tai Mei Tuk at the Plover Cove Reservoir. This is good walking country. You can walk from Tai Mei Tuk to the government field offices and take the road to Chung Mi for a couple of km. Then you follow the stream bed up the valley to Bride's Pool, a picturesque wooded area of streams and waterfalls.

Getting There

Bus No 75K leaves Tai Po from Tsing Yuen St; take it to the last stop at Tai Mei Tuk. Direct from Kowloon take the electric train to Tai Po Market and walk to Tsing Yuen St where you can pick up Bus No 75K.

FANLING, SHEUNG SHUI & THE BORDER

From Tai Po you can head north along the Kowloon-Canton train line. The first stop after Tai Po is Fanling, another new town (population of some 90,000) best known for its golf course and army camps. Visitors can play at The Royal Hong Kong Golf Club course on weekdays. From Fanling visit the Chinese market at neighbouring Luen Wo.

The last stop before the border at Lo Wu is Sheung Shui, worth a wander. The local council hall dates back to 1751 and was once the main ancestral hall of the Liu clan, who settled the village in the 13th century. Its roofs and supports are carved in traditional Chinese patterns of lions and fishes.

SHATIN

Alternatively, from Tai Po you could head south to Shatin via Tai Po Kau. At Shatin they've stacked up enough matchbox-sized flats for 300,000 people. Every time a new block goes up the population rises by 20,000 and it's planned that by the mid-1990's 800,000 people will live here. There are several places worth checking out.

Tsang Tai Uk

If you are keen you could get out and look at Tsang Tai Uk, an old village which has been preserved on the outskirts. The village is back towards Kowloon on the riverbank over the bridge.

Amah Rock

Looking down on Shatin is Amah Rock, a local landmark. The story goes that for many years a fisherman's wife, with her baby on her back, climbed to this vantage point to watch for her husband's return. Eventually the gods took pity on her and transported her to heaven with a lightning bolt which left a rock in her place.

Shatin Racecourse

Shatin is the site of Hong Kong's second racecourse, opened in 1980 after seven years in the making at a cost of HK$500 million and financed by the introduction of night racing at Hong Kong Island's Happy Valley racecourse. Races are held on some Wednesdays and on Saturday and Sunday. If you want to watch from the member's stand, the same arrangements as for the Happy Valley Racecourse apply – see the HKTA or contact the Royal Hong Kong Jockey Club (tel 3-8378315) for a member's stand ticket.

Chinese University Art Gallery

The Institute of Chinese Studies in the Chinese University has an interesting art gallery which houses local collections as well as ones from museums in China. Its main exhibit is an enormous collection of paintings and calligraphy by Guangdong artists from the Ming period to modern times, as well as a collection of bronze seals some 2000 years old and a large collection of jade flower carvings.

The gallery is open weekdays and Saturday from 9.30 am to 4.30 pm, and on Sunday and public holidays from 12.30 to 4.30 pm (closed on some public holidays). Admission is free.

Temple of 10,000 Buddhas

On a hill to the west of Shatin lies this large temple, its most curious exhibit being a mummified body embalmed in gold leaf.

Getting There

From Tai Po, you can take the electric train or Bus No 70 to Shatin. From Shatin you can head back to Kowloon on the electric train. On the way back Lion Rock is on your right – it's at the top of a hill and looks like a lion's head.

To get to Shatin from Kowloon take Bus No 71 from Jordan Rd Bus Station. For the Buddhist temple get off in central Shatin and walk to the Shatin train station. Opposite the station is a sign showing the direction to the steps leading to the temple. For the university art gallery you get off at the stop after the university's main entrance.

Alternatively, take the electric train direct from Kowloon. For the Buddhist Temple you get off at Shatin Station. For the art gallery you get off at University Station (Ma Liu Shui). The university bus meets a train every 20 minutes; get off the bus at the second stop (the Science Centre).

University Station (Ma Liu Shui) is also the place to get off if you feel like a swim at Wu Kai Sha, just across the harbour on the Sai Kung Peninsula. There are about a dozen ferries or sampans a day and the trip only takes about 15 minutes.

SAI KUNG PENINSULA

The Sai Kung Peninsula juts out in a great sprawl to the east of Kowloon and deep into Mirs Bay. It has clear water and some of the best beaches in the colony. Since the beaches are not easily accessible they are largely unspoilt – though some parts are now being developed as resorts. The peninsula is approached by road on the south side and by ferry on the north side. To link up the two sides you have to walk.

Sai Kung Town

The main town in the Sai Kung Peninsula is Sai Kung Town, which was developed as a marketplace for farmers and fishermen of the area. Today the town includes the old fishing village and the new town – about 15,000 people live here now but plans are to expand that to 40,000.

To get there take Bus No 5 from the Star Ferry Terminal to Choi Hung Bus Terminal (past Kai Tak Airport); then change to Bus No 92 for Sai Kung Town. The entire trip takes about an hour.

If you want to follow the road the few km further on you will need a taxi, worth it if you want a swim as there are some good beaches. The road comes to an end at the High Island Reservoir scheme.

Clearwater Bay

From Choi Hung Bus Terminal you can turn south to Clearwater Bay, the most popular resort on the Sai Kung Peninsula but certainly not the best – on weekends it's standing room only on the beach.

Bus No 91 from Choi Hung Bus Terminal takes you to Clearwater Bay. The bus goes along Hammerhill and Lung Cheung Rds to Clearwater Bay Rd, best known as the home of the Shaw film studios which turn out kung-fu movies conveyor-belt style.

Hebe Haven

Taking Bus No 92 to Sai Kung Town, you go past Hebe Haven (Pak Sha Wan). From here you can get a boat over to the tiny peninsula across the harbour to swim off the sandy beach that is as good as it looks from across the bay. The sampan trip should be only a couple of dollars. To get to the islands on the other side of this strip of land you will need to hire a boat for the day, so get a group of people to make up the trip.

TOLO HARBOUR

Rather than take the bus from Kowloon to Sai Kung Town, a far more pleasant way to get there is from the northern side of the

peninsula with a ferry ride down Tolo Harbour. Ferries leave from Tai Po Kau and cruise through Tolo Harbour to Tap Mun Chau (Grass Island) and back again, calling in at various villages on the way. Stops along the way may include Kau Lau Wan, Chik Kang, Tai Tan, Lai Chi Chong, Sham Chung and Shap Sze Hung. Check with the HKTA for ferry times; this could be an interesting trip. There are one or two youth hostels in this neck of the woods – check with the YHA for details.

Tap Mun on Tap Mun Chau is a tiny fishing village. Tai Tan in Tai Tan Hoi Hap (Long Harbour) is the place to get off if you want to walk to Sai Kung Town – a road has been constructed from the High Island Reservoir scheme, and it will take you a couple of hours to walk along to Pak

Tam Chung at the end of the road from Sai Kung Town.

KOWLOON-CANTON RAILWAY

This railway line extends from Kowloon (Hung Hom) Station all the way to Canton, hugging Tolo Harbour for part of the way, and is electrified as far as the border at Lo Wu.

Stations on the Hong Kong side of the border are Kowloon, Mongkok, Kowloon Tong, Tai Wai, Shatin, Fo Tan, University (Ma Liu Shui), Tai Po Market, Fanling, Sheung Shui and the border station of Lo Wu. Ordinary-class train fares from Kowloon Station to the other stations along the line are listed below (1st-class fares are double ordinary-class fares):

Mongkok	HK$1.50
Kowloon Tong	HK$1.50
Tai Wai	HK$2.50
Shatin	HK$2.50
Fo Tan	HK$3.00
University	HK$3.50
Tai Po Market	HK$4.00
Fanling	HK$5.00
Sheung Shui	HK$5.00
Lo Wu	HK$12.00

To get to Kowloon Station take Bus No 5C from the Kowloon Star Ferry Terminal.

The first train of the day departs Kowloon about 5.50 am but only goes as far as Sheung Shui, arriving about 6.25 am. The first train to the border at Lo Wu departs Kowloon about 6.40 am and

arrives at Lo Wu about 7.20 am. The first train from Lo Wu to Kowloon departs Lo Wu at about 6 am, and the last train departs Lo Wu about 11.15 pm.

However, these schedules may vary – there may be extra trains for the New Year period when crowds of people are going to China, or different schedules on weekends and public holidays. A complete timetable and fare sheet is available free from the information desk at Kowloon Station.

Dragon Slaying in the New Territories The story goes that back in the 1930s, a young policeman named W N Darkin was approached by a group of agitated villagers from the New Territories. They begged Darkin to accompany them back to their village on the slopes of Tai Mo Shan to deal with a dragon that was lurking in a grove of trees. The beast was said to be yellow and green, and very large, with a set of monstrous horns. The villagers were obviously frightened, so Darkin trudged up to the village accompanied by two Indian constables armed with rifles. Reaching the grove of trees the policemen were confronted by a gigantic green-and-yellow monster with huge horns. It was, in fact, a huge python which had killed and tried to swallow a water buffalo – but the buffalo's horns had been too big to swallow and were poking out of the snake's distended mouth. Darkin gained immense face by killing the creature, and though he tried to explain to the villagers that it was only a snake, he was known for many years as the policeman who had slain the dragon of Tai Mo Shan. Darkin died several years ago, but the story is recounted in his unpublished memoirs.

The Outer Islands

Take away Hong Kong and you've still got 235 islands – most of which you'd need your own boat to explore, but half a dozen of the larger ones are connected by regular ferry service to Hong Kong Island. The islands vary from the desolate and un-inhabited to the crowded and cramped. Some lie in remote parts of the colony with a bird's-eye view into China, while others lie in the commuter belt, a short ferry journey from Central. You can wander the quiet concrete paths of Cheung Chau, marvel at the almost unspoilt hills of Lantau as you trek from one end of the island to the other, or gape in amazement at the industrial rape being performed on Lamma. If you want to swim you can escape the resort beaches of Hong Kong Island. Out here the beaches are less crowded, and – generally speaking – the water cleaner.

Serious walkers should remember that the high humidity during the spring and summer months is tiring. November, December, January and February are the months for those who like to do more than just stroll. Believe me, clambering up a hillside in 98% humidity can bring on, if not a coronary, a feeling akin to one – even a straightforward walk like the one from Sok Kwu Wan to Yung Shue Wan on Lamma Island feels more like a jog in a sauna if you do it in the heat of the day. On the other hand, it can get very cold on these islands during the winter. Places high up, like the Youth Hostel at Ngong Ping on Lantau, get so cold during winter that it's a good idea to bring a down sleeping bag with you!

Information

If you like a proper tramp to get away from it all, then equip yourself with the excellent 'countryside' series of maps and leaflets turned out by the Crown Lands & Surveys Office. They're not expensive

and you can buy them from the Government Publications Centre in the General Post Office block by the Hong Kong side Star Ferry Terminal. A word of warning from one who's tried. Believe the little broken red line when it says 'steep or seasonally overgrown' and don't try the 'pathway' in sandals or flip flops (thongs to Australians). The free HKTA 'Outlying Islands' leaflet has useful maps, information and ferry timetables; it's available in French, German and Spanish.

Getting There

The major outer islands are linked to Hong Kong by regular ferry services – not for tourists but for locals who work on the mainland and live on the islands. The ferries are comfortable and ridiculously cheap, and many have an air-conditioned top deck. They all serve refreshments. Even if you take a round-trip and don't get off the ferry it's worthwhile. At night the ferry is one of the best ways to see the colony and certainly the most pleasant. The ferries are run by the Hong Kong & Yaumati Ferry Company (HYF).

Most of the ferries leave from the Government Pier or the Outlying Districts Pier, side by side several hundred metres west of the Hong Kong Star Ferry Terminal. The odd ferry also leaves from Blake Pier, which is next to the Star Ferry Terminal on the western side.

The HKTA (tel 5-244191) can advise you of times or you can ring HYF head office (tel 5-423081). The HYF office is at Central Harbour Services Pier next to the Outlying Districts Services Pier. All departure frequencies and times given in this book are approximate – they are meant to be a guide only! However, the HKTA prints leaflets with all the ferry timetables; you can pick up one of these free from the HKTA branch at the Star Ferry Terminal on the Kowloon side.

There is one rule – never go on a Sunday! The islands are day-tripper spots for locals on Sunday and start to fill up as soon as the offices close on Saturday afternoon. Ferries are packed and often double the price, and beaches are crowded at this time. It's much, much better to go during the week when you can still breathe! During the summer in particular the weekend ferries are jammed with people heading for the beaches.

Bring lots of small change with you. For some ferries you buy your ticket before you board, and for others you put the exact fare in a turnstile as you do for the Star Ferry. You can also buy return tickets.

If your time is limited the HKTA runs 'water-tours' taking in a couple of islands at a time – see the Tours section in the 'Getting Around' chapter for details.

Kaido are motorised village ferries that do regular runs on the more remote routes. You can often get a passage on them – or even charter them – from the main piers on the islands.

Cheung Chau

Only a couple of square km in size, Cheung Chau – 'long island' in Cantonese – is 10 km west of Hong Kong, off the south-east tip of Lantau. Archaeological digs have shown that Cheung Chau, like Lamma and Lantau, was inhabited in prehistoric times. The island already had a thriving fishing community 2500 years ago and a reputation for piracy from the year dot – probably started by the earliest Cantonese and Hakka settlers who supplemented their incomes with piracy and smuggling. When Canton and Macau opened up to the west in the 16th century the island was a perfect spot from which to prey on passing ships stacked with goodies. The infamous and powerful pirate Cheung Po Tsai is said to have had his base here in the 18th century.

The piracy and smuggling have gone and about 40,000 people now live on the island – about 10% on the junks and sampans anchored offshore. Fishing is still an important industry for a large number of the island's inhabitants, and the place is noted for its fine seafood. There are several interesting temples – most importantly the Pak Tai Temple, which is the focus of the annual Cheung Chau Bun Festival – and a couple of OK beaches. The tallest building is the six-storey Warwick Hotel, which may be a portent of abominations to come, but while another block of flats seems to appear every day on the already cramped land surface, there are still a few unspoilt headlands where you can get away from the claustrophobia of Hong Kong Island.'

While Cheung Chau is not for serious walkers, it's ideal if you like concrete paths through lush vegetation and butterflies to spot along the way. The island is packed with missionary schools, churches, retreats and youth centres of every denomination and has built up a fair-sized *gwailo* community who have escaped from the rat-race and high rents of Hong Kong Island. There is no traffic noise here; in fact there is no motorised transport other than a battery-powered fire engine (and just 10 years ago a hand-cart did the job). Try not to go on weekends. Cheung Chau is extremely popular with the locals, especially since many of its churches have weekend camps here.

Cheung Chau Village
No longer a village but a small town, the main built-up area on the island is along the narrow strip at the centre of the two headlands that make up the 'dumb-bell'-shaped island. The waterfront is a bustling place any time of day and late into the night. The village is particularly renowned for its evening street restaurants.

Pak Tai Temple (Temple of Jade Vacuity)
There are a number of temples on the island, two of the most interesting being

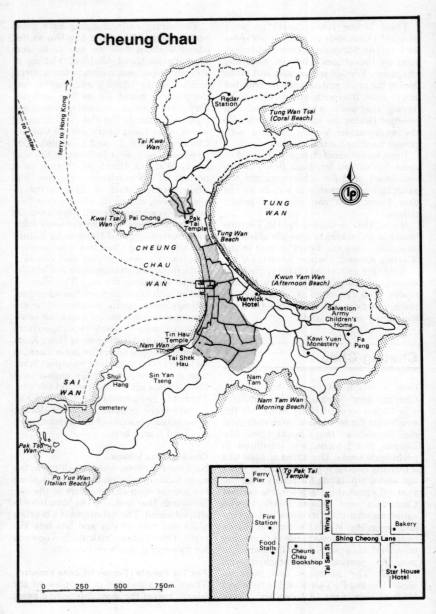

Cheung Chau

Radar Station

Tung Wan Tsai
(Coral Beach)

to Lantau

ferry to Hong Kong

Tai Kwai Wan

TUNG
WAN

Kwai Tsai Wan

Pai Chong

Pak Tai Temple

CHEUNG
CHAU
WAN

Tung Wan Beach

Kwun Yam Wan
(Afternoon Beach)

Warwick Hotel

Salvation Army Children's Home

Fa Peng

Kawi Yuen Monastery

Tin Hau Temple

Nam Wan

Tai Shek Hau

Shui Hang

Sin Yan Tseng

Nam Tam

Nam Tam Wan
(Morning Beach)

SAI WAN

cemetery

Pak Tso Wan

Po Yue Wan
(Italian Beach)

0   250   500   750m

Ferry Pier

To Pak Tai Temple

Wing Lung St

Fire Station

Tai San St

Shing Cheong Lane

Bakery

Food Stalls

Cheung Chau Bookshop

Star House Hotel

Top: Vanishing Hong Kong — an amah and a letter writer (IMcQ)
Bottom: Another disappearing trade — the rickshaw (IMcQ)

Top: Shui Tan village, New Territories (AS)
Bottom: Temple at Shui Tan (AS)

on the waterfront. Turn to your left as you get off the ferry and walk up Kwok Man Rd. You will come to the Pak Tai Temple dedicated to the god Pak Tai – for some background on him see the Religion section at the start of this book. The temple is the oldest on the island and is the focus of the famous Bun Festival held every year.

The story goes that the first settlers from Guangdong Province in China brought Pak Tai, protector of fisherpeople (among other things), with them to Cheung Chau. Carrying the god around the village in the year 1777 is supposed to have scared away a plague. The temple was built six years later. It has a middle court and main hall at the back. At either side of the entrance are two gods upon altars who look after the local people's welfare.

The temple has several historical relics. A large iron sword said to have been forged in the Sung Dynasty (960-1279 AD) stands here. It was dredged from the sea by a local fisherman over 100 years ago and was presented to the god by the islanders. It is regarded as a symbol of good luck and its disappearance from the temple several years back caused great consternation on the island. The person who took it was kind enough to return it when he realised the concern he had caused. There's also a wooden sedan chair, made in 1894, used to carry Pak Tai around the island on festival days, and two pillars hewn out of hunks of granite at the turn of the century which depict the movements of two dragons.

Leading off from the Pak Tai Temple is Pak She St. A few doors down from the temple on this street is a building housing a photo exhibition of the 'floating children' who are carried on poles through the streets of Cheung Chau during the Bun Festival. They are cleverly strapped into metal supports hidden under their clothes so that they appear to be floating in the air. One of the supports is on display here, and includes built-in footrests and a padded seat for the child.

Tin Hau Temples

An indication of the important role fishing has played on this island, there are several Tin Hau Temples here – dedicated to the patron goddess of fisherpeople (see the Religion section at the start of this book for more information about her). One Tin Hau temple is at the southern end of the Cheung Chau village waterfront. The other is at Saiwan on the south-western bulge of the island; you can either walk here or take a *kaido* near the HYF pier. A third is just to the north of the Pak Tai Temple.

Beaches & Walks

To see more of the island, cross to the other side of the island's narrow centre strip, behind the Pak Tai Temple. Heading south along the east coast brings you to Tung Wan Beach, the biggest, most popular but not the best beach on the island – if you do go there the best part is at the far southern end. There are a couple of good restaurants along the beachfront; see the Places to Eat section below for details. Apparently it's possible to hire windsurfers at this beach.

Continuing past the six-storey Warwick Hotel brings you to what is generally referred to as Afternoon Beach. At the end of the beach is a footpath which takes you uphill past a small Kuan Yin (Kwun Yum) Temple dedicated to the Goddess of Mercy. Carry on up the footpath and look for the sign pointing the way to the Fa Peng Knoll. The concrete footpath soon becomes a dirt track which takes you past quiet, tree-shrouded villas.

From the knoll you can walk down to Don Bosco Rd (again look for the sign), which will take you to Nam Tam Beach (Morning Beach) – rocky but good for swimming. Alternatively, if you ignore Don Bosco Rd and continue straight down you come to the intersection with Peak and Kwun Yum Wan Rds. Kwun Yum Wan Rd will take you to Cheung Chau village.

Peak Rd is the main route to the

cemetery, one of the most popular ones in Hong Kong for burying the dear departed. You'll pass several pavilions on the road, built for coffin-bearers who have to sweat their way along the hilly climb to the cemetery. When you get to the cemetery it's worth dropping down to Po Yuen, otherwise known as Italian Beach. It's sandy, unspoilt, quiet and good for swimming. Peak Rd continues to Saiwan, a little village on the south-west bulge of the island. There's a Tin Hau Temple here and if you keep following the path you'll come to some beautiful views of Lantau and **Shek Kwu Chau** Islands. From Saiwan another path leads to Cheung Chau village, or you can go to Saiwan Pier and take a *kaido* back. If you want to walk just follow the path around to the right along the waterfront.

With this walk you will have taken in the most interesting part of the island. It will take a couple of hours, allowing for a swim. Most of the northern headland is deserted, with not much more than a reservoir on it.

Places to Stay

There are at least two places to stay on the island, neither of them cheap. *Cheung Chau Star House* (tel 5-9812186) at 149 Tai Sun Back St was once the old – and comparatively cheap – Pine Hotel. Accommodation is in units with three to five bedrooms each, starting from HK$300 on weekdays, and from HK$400 on weekends and public holidays.

The *Warwick (Wah Wai) Hotel* (tel 5-9810081) is the six-storey eyesore on Tung Wan Beach (come back in 10 years and this place will look like Surfer's Paradise). Singles and doubles go for HK$360 on a weekday and HK$440 on a weekend plus a 10% service charge and 5% tax. There are lower rates in the low season.

Rumour has it that there are some other small hotels on the island but find them if you can . . . .

Places to Eat

A sizeable piece of the western waterfront of Cheung Chau village is lined with restaurants and *dai pai dongs* from where you can watch the world go by and the world can go by and watch you eat. Weekend nights are a great time to be here – it's like a big open-air party. A full Chinese meal for four people should come to around HK$70 to $80. This stretch should also be a good place for morning dim sum.

On the same street as the Star Hotel (see the map) is a good bakery which does tasty munchies. There are a couple of restaurants on the eastern waterfront along Tung Wan Beach. Upstairs and overlooking the bay, try the *Cheung Chau Country Club* which has a Chinese menu listing some cheapish dishes. Off the back of the beach, up Tung Wan Rd, is the *Village Tree Inn*, the local *gwailo* meeting place and western food centre.

Getting There

Ferries to Cheung Chau leave from the Outlying Districts Pier in Hong Kong, with almost 20 departures a day. The earliest ferries depart Hong Kong around 6.30 am, and the last departure is about 11.30 pm. The first ferry to Hong Kong departs Cheung Chau about 5.45 am and the last at about 10.30 pm. The trip takes an hour. Adult fares are: Deluxe class HK$6 on weekdays and Saturday morning; and HK$10 on Saturday afternoon, Sunday and public holidays. Ordinary class HK$4 on weekdays, and HK$6 on Sunday and public holidays.

There is a ferry service from Cheung Chau to Peng Chau via Chi Ma Wan and Silvermine Bay (both on Lantau Island). The first ferry leaves Cheung Chau around 5.30 am and the last at around 10 pm. There are about nine departures per day but some skip Chi Ma Wan or Silvermine Bay or both, or only go as far as Silvermine Bay – so check with the HKTA or HYF before you go if you want to use this service.

Getting Around

Apart from walking you can hire bikes on the island – useful for getting around the built-up area but probably not much use further afield, where it's all uphill. Bicycles can be hired from the shop just to the side of the Pak Tai Temple at HK$6 per hour, though you should be able to bargain a day rate. There's another place on the street which leads up to the temple after splitting off from the main road along the western waterfront – same rates.

A good map of the island is available from the Cheung Chau Bookshop, a short way up the street opposite the fire station. They make the maps themselves. Very useful if you want to do a lot of exploring, the map costs HK$1.

Lamma

In Hong Kong they have a saying: 'If it moves, eat it; if it doesn't, build something on it.' Lamma Island was spared; beautiful and almost wild, it escaped a fate worse than death when plans to build an oil refinery on its northern tip were dropped in 1973. A power station was built instead. Its smokestacks poke up from behind a hill next to the harbour of Yung She Wan. The builders cut 30 or 40 metres off the top of that hill and used the rubble for land reclamation while building the station. That's only half the story. Down south at Picnic Bay, patrons of the Sok Kwu Wan waterside restaurants can watch the island being quarried away before their very eyes – landscape gardening Hong Kong style. With over 200 other lumps of rock to choose from, why Lamma should have been singled out to be pack-raped by progress is beyond me!

Also known as Pok Liu Chau, and thought to have been one of the first to be settled, Lamma was once one of the least spoilt of all of Hong Kong's larger outer islands. It was and still is one of the most accessible islands. South of Hong Kong

Island and east of Cheung Chau, it's about 13 square km in size and supports a population of about 8500, including a number of *gwailos*.

The island is good for walking and swimming and is a favourite weekend mooring spot for *gwailo* junks. It's also a fishing port and you can get good seafood on both ends of the island – particularly at Sok Kwu Wan on Picnic Bay. The chief tourist attraction is the seafood restaurants at Sok Kwu Wan (most of them are modern buildings whereas several years ago they were walk-in canteens, an indication of the money which the island has since come by). Most of the restaurants' clientele is brought over every evening from the mainland in convoys of junks.

Yung Shue Wan

There's not much to this place, though it's the bigger of the two townships. Plastic used to hold body and soul together here; less than a decade ago people in almost every house sprayed a vast assortment of plastic parts for toys and other goods. Now the plastic workshops have vanished

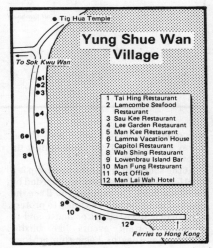

Yung Shue Wan Village

To Sok Kwu Wan

1 Tai Hing Restaurant
2 Lamcombe Seafood Restaurant
3 Sau Kee Restaurant
4 Lee Garden Restaurant
5 Man Kee Restaurant
6 Lamma Vacation House
7 Capitol Restaurant
8 Wah Shing Restaurant
9 Lowenbrau Island Bar
10 Man Fung Restaurant
11 Post Office
12 Man Lai Wah Hotel

Tig Hua Temple

Ferries to Hong Kong

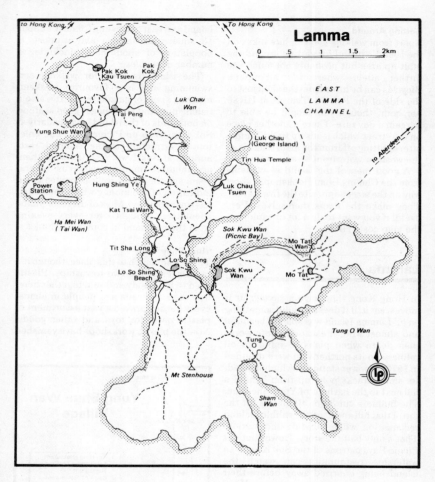

and modern concrete two– and three-storey apartment blocks have sprung up all over Yung Shue Wan.

At the southern end of the township is a Tin Hau Temple, the entrance guarded by two stone lions. On entering you'll see the god To Dei to the left. His job is to protect a particular town, street or house and to record important events like births, marriages and deaths. Facing him is Muen Kuen, the gatekeeper who safeguards the temple from evil. At the centre of the temple is the shrine to Tin Hau – there are two statues of her, the smaller one is removed during festivals and carried in processions. She is flanked by the two smaller figures of her guardians.

Yung Shue Wan to Sok Kwu Wan

From Yung She Wan you can walk to Sok

Kwu Wan on Picnic Bay. The turn-off from Yung Shue Wan to Sok Kwu Wan is just before you get to the Tin Hau Temple. The path takes you through the vegetable gardens to the small beach at Hung Shing Ye – not bad as Hong Kong beaches go but rather crowded on weekends.

The path then skirts the coast, but while it's billed as a footpath it's mostly a dirt and boulder trail and something of a scramble. You can't get lost on it – just follow the trail alongside the grey pipeline that runs southwards. The walk takes about an hour in all – but take a hat and a water-bottle and try to avoid doing it in the heat of the day! Look behind you for a sweeping view of the power station.

There are a couple of beaches on the way. You'll pass Kat Tsai Wan and Tit Sha Long before reaching Lo So Shing. Here you turn left and cross the narrow centre strip of the island to Lo So Shing Village, where you skirt around the inlet to the main southern township of Sok Kwu Wan.

Sok Kwu Wan

Although only a small settlement, Sok Kwu Wan supports about a dozen or more excellent seafood restaurants on the waterfront. There's another Tin Hau Temple as you come into the township from Lo So Shing. From Sok Kwu Wan you can head back to Hong Kong on the ferry, or do some more walking.

The harbour of Sok Kwu Wan is covered with floating fish farms. These are wooden frames from which fish are netted, supported in the water on either tin drums or large pieces of foam. The fisherpeople travel from their vessels to the shore on rafts made of blocks of foam bound together with netting.

The South & East

Most of the southern part of the island consists of the 350-metre-high Mount Stenhouse which you can walk to the top of. There are a couple of good beaches down in the south-west – Sham Wan and Tung O Wan. To get to them you can take the path which leads straight down to Tung O Wan and then down to Sham Wan.

As an alternative you could catch a *kaido* from Sok Kwu Wan to Mo Tat Wan, which is a favourite pleasure spot for the locals. There are two beaches here, both sandy and very quiet during the week. There are about five departures per day from Sok Kwu Wan to Mo Tat Wan – the first at about 6.15 am and the last at about 5 pm. Fares are HK$1 on weekdays and Saturday, and HK$1.50 on Sunday and public holidays. From Mo Tat Wan the *kaido* chugs on to Aberdeen.

Alternatively, you can walk from Sok Kwu Wan to Mo Tat Wan, along a path that runs by the coast – about 20 minutes. Mo Tat village is one of the oldest on the island, and dates back 300 to 400 years.

You can also hike around to Lo So Shing and up to the headland of Luk Chau Tsuen, which has an old temple on the beach. There are rough pathways over Mount Stenhouse, but be prepared for a climb. The coastline here is rocky and it's hard to find somewhere good to swim.

Places to Stay

There are one or two places to stay in Yung Shue Wan, but you'll probably find they don't speak any English and are reluctant to take foreigners. Your best bet might be the *Man Lai Wah Hotel* (tel 5-9820220) just at the start of the HYF ferry pier. Singles and doubles start at HK$140, all with air-conditioning and attached bathroom.

Other places include the *Lamma Vacation House* (tel 5-9820747) on Main St, the road along the waterfront. Also on Main St is the *Wah Kei Restaurant* at No 49 which used to rent rooms but may not do so any longer. Away from the waterfront the *Han Lok Huen Restaurant* (tel 5-9820608) rents out double rooms above their restaurant at HK$200 to $230 per day – all with air-conditioning and attached bathroom.

Places to Eat

Yung Shue Wan has a whole string of good seafood restaurants all the way along Main St. Starting from the ferry pier there's the *Man Fung Restaurant* where noodle dishes begin at HK$11 and chicken, beef, seafood and veggie dishes begin at HK$20. Next to it there's the *Lowenbrau Island Bar* (alcoholic and soft drinks, snacks). As you head around the waterfront there are the *Wah Shing*, *Capitol* (western food), *Man Kee*, *Sau Kee* and *Tai Hing* restaurants.

An evening meal at Sok Kwu Wan is the most fun, and a good way to end off a trip to the island. The restaurants are all in a row along the waterfront, several with tanks full of live fish so you can choose your meal.

Getting There

Ferries from Hong Kong to Lamma leave from the Government Pier on weekdays and Saturday, and from Blake Pier on Sunday and public holidays. The ferries go to Sok Kwu Wan and Yung Shue Wan.

There are about 10 or 11 departures per day for Yung Shue Wan. On weekdays and Saturday the earliest ferry leaves Hong Kong at about 6.50 am and the last at about 10.45 pm. On Sunday and public holidays the earliest departure is around 8.15 am and the last about 10.45 pm. From Yung Shue Wan to Central, the first departure is around 6.25 am and the last around 9.05 pm on weekdays and Saturday; and on Sunday and public holidays the first departure is around 6.50 am and the last around 9.05 pm. Weekdays and Saturday adult fare is HK$3.50, and Sunday and public holidays it's HK$4.

There are around seven or eight departures a day from Central to Sok Kwu Wan, some of which go via Yung Shue Wan. On weekdays and Saturday the first ferry departs Central around 8 am and the last around 10.45 pm. On Sunday and public holidays the first departure is around 7.30 am and the last around 10.45 pm. Coming back from Sok Kwu Wan to Central, on weekdays and Saturday the first departure is around 5.45 am and the last around 9.45 pm; on Sunday and public holidays the first is around 6.05 am and the last around 9.45 pm. Fares are the same as those between Central and Yung Shue Wan.

The best way to see Lamma is to catch a ferry to the north and hike for an hour to Sok Kwu Wan where you can catch the ferry back to Hong Kong. Or pick up the regular Sok Kwu Wan-Mo Tat Wan-Aberdeen *kaido* service.

From Aberdeen there are about five or six *kaidos* a day to Mo Tat Wan and Sok Kwu Wan – the first at about 8 am and the last at about 6 pm. There's also a ferry service – same price, different departure times.

Getting Around

Like Cheung Chau, the island has no motorised traffic, unless you count the rotivators that occasionally take to the paths instead of ploughing the fields. There is one road but it doesn't go anywhere. Concrete paths have been built around the two main villages, Yung Shue Wan in the north and Sok Kwu Wan in the south, but in between communications peter out into rough, winding mountain pathways. You can walk from Yung Shue Wan to Sok Kwu Wan, and there is a *kaido* service between Sok Kwu Wan and Mo Tat Wan – see above for details.

Lantau

Lantau – literally 'broken head' in Cantonese, but referred to as Tai Yue Shan or Big Island Mountain – is twice the size of Hong Kong Island but home to less than 30,000 people, as compared to Hong Kong's population of over a million. Most of those 30,000 are concentrated in just a couple of centres.

Lantau is believed to have been in-

Follow the Sign!

habited by primitive tribes before being settled by the Han Chinese. The last Song Dynasty emperor passed through here in the 13th century during his flight from the Mongol invaders, and is said to have held court in the Tung Chung Valley. The valley takes its name from a hero said to have given his life for the emperor. He's still worshipped on the island by the Hakka people, who believe he can predict the future. Over the years Lantau acquired a reputation as a base for pirates, and is said to have been one of the favourite haunts of the famous 18th-century pirate Cheung Pot Tsai. The island was also important to the British as a trading post long before they got interested in Hong Kong Island.

Lantau is the home of several important monasteries, including the Trappist Monastery and the Buddhist Po Lin Monastery. The Po Lin was rebuilt several years back and now looks more like a Shaw Brothers movie set then a place of quiet retreat. On a hill above the monastery they're building the largest Buddha statue in South-East Asia! Other misdevelopments include Discovery Bay on the east coast where an ant-colony has been built for people who want to ape the western suburban dream – 'Discover the Discovery Bay lifestyle.' There are even plans to build a new international airport on Chek Lap Kok island off the north coast of Lantau, though so far nothing's come of them.

Silvermine Bay (Mui Wo)

This is known as 'Mui Wo' – Five Petal Flower – to the Chinese, but is referred to as Silvermine Bay by westerners because there used to be some old silver mines on the outskirts of the settlement. This is where the ferries from Hong Kong land and where you can catch buses to other parts of the island. There's a beach which tends to be overcrowded and the water tends to be murky, though the township's not a bad place for seafood restaurants. About a third of Lantau's population lives in the township and surrounding hamlets.

There's at least two places to stay here. The *Silvermine Bay Beach Hotel* (tel 5-9848295) has singles and doubles from HK$290 plus 10% tax and service, and prices are higher on weekends. They hire out windsurfers at HK$35 for two hours, canoes at HK$25 for two hours, and beach boards at HK$23 for two hours. Or try the *Sea House* (tel 5-9847757), which has singles from HK$100 and doubles from HK$140.

The *Jolly Roger* is about all that's left of the pirates. It's on the shore at the end of the beach opposite the ferry terminal, and serves European food and drinks. There

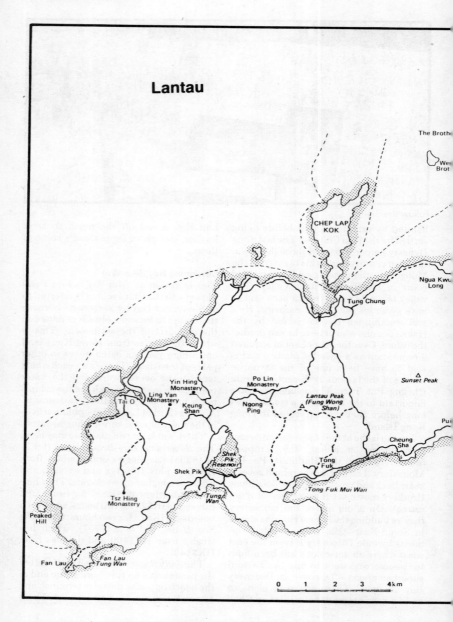

Lantau

The Brothers

West Brot

CHEP LAP KOK

Ngua Kwu Long

Tung Chung

Yin Hing Monastery

Po Lin Monastery

Sunset Peak

Ling Yan Monastery

Tai O

Keung Shan

Ngong Ping

Lantau Peak (Fung Wong Shan)

Pui

Cheung Sha

Shek Pik Reservoir

Tong Fuk

Shek Pik

Tung Wan

Tong Fuk Mui Wan

Tsz Hing Monastery

Peaked Hill

Fan Lau

Fan Lau Tung Wan

0   1   2   3   4 km

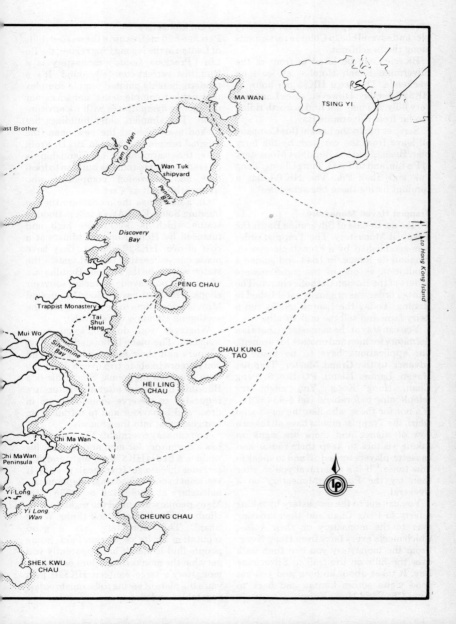

are numerous *dai pai dongs* near the ferry pier and several cheap Chinese restaurants along the beachfront.

Bicycles can be hired in front of the Silvermine Beach Hotel – at least on weekends. They cost HK$5 per hour, or HK$20 per day. However, since Lantau is very hilly you may not find it worth riding too far from Silvermine Bay.

Services run by the Lantau Bus Company all leave from the car park by the ferry pier. Buses go to the Buddhist Monastery of Po Lin, and to Tai O, Tung Chung, Tong Fuk and Shek Pik. The HKTA has a handout listing these bus schedules.

Trappist Haven Monastery

To the north-east of Silvermine Bay is the Trappist Monastery. The Trappist order was established by a French clergyman, Armand de Rance, in 1644 and gained a reputation as one of the most austere orders of the Roman Catholic church. The Lantau order was originally established in Beijing. Today the Lantau monks run a dairy farm and sell the milk locally.

You can stay at the monastery (there is a dormitory for men and another for women), but applications have to be made in advance to the Grand Master, Trappist Haven, Lantau Island, PO Box 5, Peng Chau, Hong Kong. You might try telephoning beforehand (tel 5-9848282). It's not for those who like the gay social whirl; the Trappist monks have all taken a vow of silence and there are signs up asking visitors to keep their radios and cassette-players turned off and to speak in 'low tones.' If it's a carnival you're after then try the Po Lin Monastery on a weekend.

You can get to the monastery by taking a ferry to Peng Chau and then crossing over to the monastery on their *kaido*, which meets every ferry from Hong Kong. From the monastery you can then walk over the hills on the trail to Silvermine Bay. It takes about an hour and you get good views across Lantau and back to Peng Chau and Hong Kong.

Po Lin Monastery

Perched 800 metres up in the western hills of Lantau in the Ngong Ping region, the Po Lin ('Precious Lotus') monastery is a Buddhist retreat-*cum*-fairground. It's a modern, harshly painted temple complex that neither complements, enhances nor in any way sympathises with its environment. The simpler, older buildings are tucked away behind the new ones (the original temple was built in 1921). From here the warm hand of friendship is offered not just to tourists but also to local film and television companies who frequently use it as a set.

On a hill above the monastery they're building South-East Asia's tallest Buddha statue which is 33 metres high and financed by Hong Kong Buddhists at a cost of over HK$20 million. They have made one concession to good taste – the statue will not be the fat, jolly Buddha you often see portrayed in tacky souvenir shops. The Birthday of Buddha, around May, is a good time to be out here (see the section on Holidays & Festivals).

Whatever you do, don't go on a weekend. The place is flooded with day-trippers and their radios and kids, and you're more likely to trip over a dinky toy than a meditating monk. Since this is a Buddhist monastery after all, visitors are requested to observe some decorum in dress and behaviour and to refrain from bringing meat into the grounds.

You can stay overnight. The monastery has a dormitory for men and another for women. A bed is HK$70 per night and that includes three vegetarian meals per day. If you want to make a booking, telephone the monastery at 5-9857426 or 5-9857248. Many people who spend the night do so to climb nearby Lantau Peak (Fung Wong Shan). The monastery has a good reputation for its vegetarian food. Some people find it bland, but apparently you get what the monks themselves eat. In the monastery's large canteen HK$20 gets you a big plate of spring rolls, mushrooms, vegetables and rice.

There are a dozen or so buses daily from Silvermine Bay to the monastery, the first around 8.20 am and the last around 5.50 pm. You take Bus No 2 from the ferry pier as far as the Shum Wat Rd turning circle. There you have to get off and take a connecting minibus up Ngong Ping Rd to the monastery. Adult fares to the Shum Wat Rd circle are HK$3.50 on weekdays and Saturday, and HK$5.50 on Sunday and public holidays. The minibus up to the monastery will cost you HK$1.20 on weekdays and Saturday, and HK$2 on Sunday and public holidays. The views going up are spectacular.

Lantau Tea Gardens

Beside the Po Lin Monastery are the Lantau Tea Gardens, the only tea gardens in Hong Kong. Also run as a resort, it lets you stay overnight and there are horses for hire.

Accommodation rates range from HK$90 per person per night in a room with a couple of beds – more on weekends and public holidays. For bookings telephone 5-9858161. Horseback-riding costs HK$60 per half hour. I'd be hard pressed to recommend actually staying here. Apart from the expensive room rates the video game machines and the roller-skating rink are noisy, though it may be OK on weekdays.

Tai O Village

This is the largest single settlement on the island. A hundred years ago, along with Tung Chung village, Tai O was an important trading and fishing port and exported salt and fish to China. The salt pans are still there but are almost unused. The locals make a living from duck farming, fishing, rice growing, processing salt fish and making shrimp paste.

Tai O is built partly on Lantau itself and partly on a tiny island a few metres from the shore; two women pull a rope-drawn boat across the creek. Although a few of the old-style village houses still stand, most are being replaced by modern concrete block houses. There are still many stilt houses on the waterfront, as well as other shanties including houseboats that haven't set sail for years and have been built on to such an extent they never could again. It's an interesting place. Wander around and look for things like the coffin shop and the Chinese medicine store. The village is famous for its seafood, and has several seafood restaurants. The local temple is dedicated to the God of War Kuan Ti.

There is only one small hotel here, the fairly cheap Po Chu. The sign is in Chinese, but there is a telephone number (9858237) written under the name, so you can recognise it that way. To get there, go across the creek on the hand-pulled boat, then straight up the road in front of you to the T-intersection and turn right. Follow this road for about 10 minutes to the hotel.

There are at least a dozen buses a day from Silvermine Bay to Tai O, the first departing Silvermine Bay around 6 am and the last at around 11.15 pm. The adult fare is HK$4 on weekdays and Saturday, and HK$6 on Sunday and public holidays.

Tung Chung

This farming region is centred around the village of Tung Chung on the northern shore of Lantau. There are several Buddhist establishments in the upper reaches of the valley, but the main attraction is the 19th-century Tung Chung Fort which still has its old cannon pointing out to sea. The fort dates back to the early 19th century when Chinese troops were garrisoned on Lantau. The area was used as a base by the infamous pirate leader Chueng Po Tsai.

You can walk from the Po Lin monastery down to Tung Chung in two to three hours. It's about five km and you can pick up the ferry from Tai O on its way back to the New Territories via Ma Wan island. Or hike from Silvermine Bay to Tung Chung – this takes about 4½ hours and wanders through old Hakka villages before reaching the coast and the farming settlement. Or hike from Tai O to Tung Chung – takes about five hours.

There are five or six buses per day from Silvermine Bay to Tung Chung, the first around 9.35 am and the last around 6.50 pm. Adult fare is HK$3.50 on weekdays and HK$5.50 on Sunday and public holidays.

Cheung Sha Beach & Tong Fuk
Buses head to the Po Lin Monastery from Silvermine Bay along the road that hugs the southern coast. There are long stretches of good beaches from Cheung Sha to Tong Fuk on the south coast of Lantau which get some occasional surf.

Holiday apartments are for rent at Tong Fuk (run by Carousel Ltd, Silver Centre Building, Silvermine Bay, tel 5-9848335). They cost from HK$950 a double for one week.

Numerous buses run from Silvermine Bay to Tong Fuk, the first at about 6 am and the last at about 7.40 pm. Adult fares are HK$2 on weekdays and HK$3.50 on Sunday and public holidays.

Shek Pik Reservoir
At Tong Fuk the bus starts to go inland, along the Shek Pik Reservoir (completed 1963) which provides Lantau with its drinking water. Underwater pipes also supply Cheung Chau and parts of Hong Kong Island with fresh water from this reservoir. It is a pretty place with forest plantations and picnic spots.

There are numerous buses daily from Silvermine Bay to Shek Pik, the first at about 8.15 am and the last at about 9 pm. Adult fares are HK$3 on weekdays and HK$4 on Sunday and public holidays.

Discovery Bay
On the east coast Discovery Bay used to be aptly named until the developers discovered it. The empty beaches have now been developed into a holiday-resort and housing estate.

Penny's Bay
In Penny's Bay is the main yard of one of Hong Kong's most famous boatyards, which specialises in the production of sailing cruisers for the export market.

Yam O Wan
The biggest log ponds in Hong Kong are at Yam O Wan. Here timber from all over South-East Asia is kept in floating storage until required. Large rafts of logs may often be seen being towed by tug towards Tsuen Wan.

Fan Lau
Fan Lau on the south-west tip has a couple of very good beaches and another old fort, very overgrown but with a good view. It's a couple of hours clamber along the coast from Tai O village.

Chi Ma Wan
Chi Ma Wan, the peninsula in the south, takes its name from the large prison there. Also at Chi Ma Wan is a 'closed centre' – a camp housing 'boat people' from southern Vietnam who arrived in Hong Kong after July 1982. There is at least one other closed centre in Hong Kong, at Hei Ling Chau where the boat people from northern Vietnam are kept. These camps are referred to as closed centres because their inhabitants are not allowed out of them at all, and must remain there until they are resettled in another country. You can walk down through the Chi Ma Wan peninsula to the beaches at Yi Long and Tai Long – but arm yourself with a map.

Places to Stay
Details of some accommodation on Lantau have already been given above. There are places to stay at Silvermine Bay, the Trappist Monastery, the Po Lin Monastery, the Lantau Tea Gardens, Tai O and Tong Fuk. Other places to stay are listed below.

The cheapest accommodation on Lantau are the government-run campsites near Pui O, Nam Shan, Pak Fu Tin, Chi Man

Wan and many places along the south coast. The 'Countryside' map or the 'Hostels, Campsites & Other Accommodation in Hong Kong' leaflet from the HKTA will tell you where they are. There is no charge to camp in some of these sites.

A 10-minute walk from the Lantau Tea Gardens is the YHA's *S G Davis Youth Hostel* (tel 5-9857610), which has dormitory beds and a campsite. It costs HK$8 a night and you have to be a YHA member to stay here. For more details on Youth Hostels in Hong Kong see the 'Places to Stay' chapter of this book.

Other top-end accommodation includes the *Sea Breeze Hotel* (tel 5-9847977) at Pui O Beach on the south coast. Double rooms cost from HK$160 on weekdays and from HK$220 on weekends and public holidays.

Getting There
You can take ferries from Hong Kong Central to Silvermine Bay, and from Tuen Mun in the New Territories to Tung Chung, Sha Lo Wan and Tai O. You can also take ferries from Peng Chau to Silvermine Bay via Chi Ma Wan, or take a *kaido* from Peng Chau to the Trappist Monastery on the east coast of Lantau.

The Hong Kong-Silvermine Bay ferries provide the most frequent service. These depart from the Outlying Districts Services Pier in Hong Kong Central. The first departure from Hong Kong is around 7 am and the last is around 11.15 pm. There are about 18 to 20 ferries daily. From Silvermine Bay, the first ferry for Hong Kong departs around 6.15 am and the last is around 10 pm daily.

Monday to Saturday, adult fares are HK$6 deluxe class (HK$10 after 12 noon on Saturday) and HK$4 ordinary class. Sunday and public holidays, adult fares are HK$10 deluxe class and HK$6 ordinary class.

MA WAN
Ma Wan is a low wooded island off the north-eastern tip of Lantau. It was once famous as the 'Gate to Kowloon,' where foreign ships would collect before entering Chinese waters. There are two beaches where swimming is possible – Tung Wan and Tung Wan Tsai. Paths from the ferry pier lead to the beaches across the island. Bathing from other beaches on the island is either messy or dangerous; there is pollution in the north and dangerous currents on the west that swirl up to the notorious Kap Shau Man, 'rapid water gate.'

Getting There
You can get to Ma Wan on the Tai O ferry which hops along the north coast of Lantau from Tai O to Sha Lo Wan and Tung Chung, before heading to Tuen Mun in the New Territories via Ma Wan. Check the ferry times; they are not frequent like the Silvermine Bay service.

Peng Chau

This quiet little island, a bit under a square km in area, is inhabited by people who earn a living from fishing, farming and making matches, furniture and metal tubes. There are also two ornamental porcelain-processing works here. There are no cars on Peng Chau and you can walk around it with ease in an hour. There's been a drift of middle-class Hong Kong Chinese towards this island, much as there has been a drift of westerners to Cheung Chau and Lamma. Peng Chau is also a popular jumping-off spot for the Trappist Monastery on Lantau. The monastery's boat meets every ferry and takes passengers over the short stretch of water to Lantau.

Getting There
Ferries to Peng Chau leave from the Outlying Districts Pier on Hong Kong Island. The first ferry departs Hong Kong around 7 am and the last around 11.15

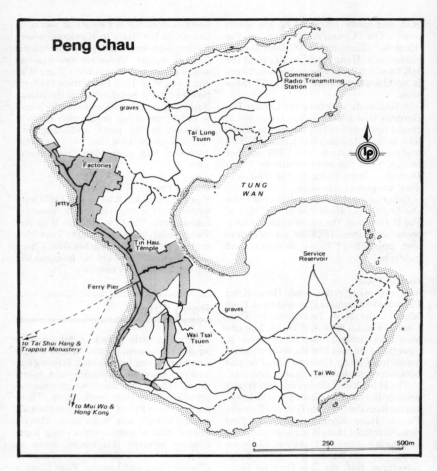

Peng Chau

graves

Factories

jetty

Tin Hau
Temple

Ferry Pier

to Tai Shui Hang &
Trappist Monastery

to Mui Wo &
Hong Kong

Commercial
Radio Transmitting
Station

Tai Lung
Tsuen

TUNG
WAN

Service
Reservoir

graves

Wai Tsai
Tsuen

Tai Wo

0   250   500m

pm, with about 16 ferries per day Monday to Saturday and a couple less on Sunday and public holidays. The first ferry from Peng Chau to Hong Kong departs at around 6.35 am and the last at about 10.20 pm. Monday to Saturday adult fares are HK$3.50 ordinary class and HK$6 deluxe class (HK$10 after 12.30 pm on Saturday). On Sunday adult fares are HK$5 ordinary class and HK$10 deluxe class. A few ferries go from Hong Kong to Cheung Chau via Peng Chau; check with the HKTA or HYF for details.

Po Toi

A tiny island south-east of Hong Kong, Po Toi has a population of 200 or so. It is almost completely abandoned by the original inhabitants who went to the big smoke to seek their fortune, so it's practically untouched and a popular excursion spot on weekends. Rumour has it that there are 3500-year-old carvings at a place called Ghost Rock – said to be of Khmer, Burmese or Indian origin.

Apart from these mysterious carvings the island is beautiful and virtually deserted with great views across to Lamma and Hong Kong from its heights. It's good for walking; there are the odd dirt tracks but they're overgrown and occasionally peter out. Most of the island is covered in short grass so you won't have to bush-bash.

The one settlement on the island has a number of small Chinese restaurants by the harbour serving cheap food. The *King Kee Restaurant* hands out its own little maps of the island – but they're in Chinese.

Getting There

Ferries to Po Toi leave from the Government Pier in Hong Kong Central. There are a couple of ferries per day, and they go via Sok Kwu Wan on Lamma Island.

You could go to Po Toi in the morning, spend a few hours on the island, then go to Sok Kwu Wan where you could have a meal in one of the many seafood restaurants before returning on the ferry to Hong Kong Central or on the *kaido* or ferry to Aberdeen.

Other Islands

In the far north of the colony, in Mirs Bay, is **Ping Chau**. Literally a stone's throw from the China coast, it used to be one of the best-known destinations for people who wanted to leave China by swimming – braving the sharks and Mao's patrol-boats for a life in the factories of Hong Kong! The island's highest point is only about 30 metres, but it has unusual rock layers in its cliffs which glitter after a night of rain. Ping Chau is a good place for beachcombing, especially on Lai Tau Wan where you can pick up colourful seashells from the white, sandy beach. The island is also good for swimming though some of the beaches are slate. There may be a HYF ferry to Ping Chau on Saturday, leaving from Tai Po Kau in the New Territories and returning to Tai Po Kau the following day.

Another remote island in Mirs Bay is **Kat O**, inhabited by about 2000 or so Hoklo fisherpeople, distinguishable by their traditional black costumes. Like Ping Chau, it was once a destination for swimmers fleeing China. Kat O is a pretty little island with good, clean water though the beaches require walking to and sometimes only appear at low tide. It's overgrown and hard to walk around in the summer.

Nearby **Ap Chau** is a mere speck, but has a population of over 500 people. They're all members of the True Jesus Church which has its headquarters in Taiwan: speaking-in-tongues and shaking-in-ecstasy-type religious service.

Tap Mun is at the mouth of Long Harbour in Mirs Bay and is inhabited by fisherpeople. It's noted for its Tin Hau Temple whose altar makes whistling sounds when easterly winds roar. In the Tap Mun Cave on the other side of the island, it is said the sound of drums and gongs beaten inside the temple can be heard.

The **Soko Islands** are a group of sparsely populated islands to the south of Lantau. Most of the inhabitants live on Tai A Chau. There are about 200 people here, their ancestors having arrived about 150 years ago.

Shek Kwu Chau is a small island near Cheung Chau. Like **Hei Ling Chau**, which is north of Cheung Chau, it's restricted to the public since it's used as a drug treatment and rehabilitation centre.

Places to Stay

Hong Kong is no bargain basement when it comes to finding somewhere to sleep for the night. The exorbitant price of land translates into expensive beds – but there's no shortage of people willing to pay for them. The hotel situation is exacerbated by Hong Kong's general housing shortage. Hundreds of hotel rooms are inhabited for months at a time by company and government employees waiting for an apartment to turn up somewhere.

The Hong Kong Tourist Association publishes a brochure, updated every six months, that lists hotels of all prices plus a few hostels and guest houses. The HKTA also runs a hotel booking counter at the airport, and though they won't find you a rock-bottom doss-house, they will do their best to get you something. This can be especially useful if you arrive at night since the cheapies are more likely to be full by then and it's no joy carting your luggage around the streets looking for elusive beds at midnight. Many won't open the door at that hour even if they have got a bed.

BOTTOM END

Cheap accommodation can be found, but not at the level available in other parts of South-East Asia. There are no family-run *losmen* down every side-street with beds for US$2 a night such as you can find in Indonesia. Resign yourself to the fact that if you can get a bed for HK$20 to $25 a night or a box for HK$40 you're doing very well indeed!

Most of the cheap or budget-priced accommodation is around Tsimshatsui in Kowloon, with some in Wanchai on the Hong Kong side. The hostels run by the International Youth Hostel Association are also cheap, and the YMCAs and the YWCAs have cheap dormitory accommodation (but expensive rooms). If you stay in any proper hotels or guest houses you will find a 10% service charge and a 5% government tax added to your bill. You won't get troubled with either in the cheap places.

Chungking Mansions

As much as I would like to avoid mentioning this place, the centre of dirt-cheap accommodation in Hong Kong is *Chungking Mansions*, a vast high-rise dump on Nathan Rd, Tsimshatsui, rubbing shoulders with the Holiday Inn and facing the Hyatt Regency. Chungking Mansions contains countless cheap (or cheapish) guest houses, a few of them relatively upmarket. At the time of writing this place was cited for demolition, or failing, that renovation – in any case by the time you get to Hong Kong it either won't be there or by some miracle it may have been cleaned up, the stairways unclogged and the rats chased away. Unfortunately, perhaps because it gets such a prominent write-up in these books people seem to get sucked into this place as if there was no alternative; there is, in fact, quite a few.

The entrance to Chungking Mansions is a shopping arcade fronting Nathan Rd. The arcade meanders around a few corners to make a rectangle of sorts. Wander around and you will find lifts labelled A to E. The lifts are in pairs – one does the even floors and one the odd floors – only two tiny lifts for each 16-storey block! Signs above the lifts will tell you which floors the various hotels are on.

Despite the state of the building itself, most of the little hotels are OK – generally clean and often quite comfortable, if not exactly spacious. The Mansions is a good place to eat cheaply too, with a number of low-priced restaurants, many of them run by Indians and Pakistanis. Some of these hotels seem to cater only to Chinese or Indians, others to Pakistanis or westerners.

Top: Po Lin monastery, Lantau (AS)
Left: A rope-drawn boat at Tai O village, Lantau (AS)
Right: At a Trappist monastery, Lantau (AS)

Top: Pak Tai temple, Cheung Chau (AS)
Left: Fishing junks in the harbour of Cheung Chau (AS)
Right: Statue in Pak Tai temple (AS)

Some places give you the cold shoulder, others are very friendly and will take anybody. Whole floors have been taken over by some hotels and several places in different blocks may be run by the same person. Some blocks, by the way, are cleaner and less crowded than other blocks.

The places listed below are just a sample of what's available in Chungking Mansions. There are far too many hotels to list them all, and every month new ones open and old ones close. Prices are only a guide and vary with the season (peaking in June-September), length of stay and the degree to which the owner is willing to bargain. If you want to find other hotels, look for the signs above the elevators in each block.

A Block

Travellers' Hostel (tel 3-682505), 16th Floor, is the place lots of western shoe-string travellers head for. It has mixed dormitory accommodation for HK$20 a bed, and rooms from HK$60. Although this place has been expanding its money-making activities over the last few years (acting as an agent for China visas, selling film and Lonely Planet guidebooks – you name it, they do it), the one thing they haven't put much effort into is improving the standard of accommodation. So how about it guys? We give you a pretty good plug in these books, so how about reciprocating by cleaning up and repainting the rooms, installing some air-conditioning and solid bunks that don't shake every time someone turns a toe over in the night, adding thicker mattresses, and maybe even relocating the TV set away from the bedrooms?

Otherwise, Travellers' Hostel is a good place to meet people and to pick up information, and has some of the cheapest rates on China visas as well as some of the cheapest accommodation in Hong Kong. I'd hate to see the place lose any business but I get too many harsh words about it (and about Chungking Mansions in general)

to give an unqualified recommendation. They also have a dormitory and rooms on the 13th floor – quieter and cleaner than those on the 16th. Simple breakfasts on the 16th go for around HK$10 – gets you eggs, bacon, toast, spaghetti and coffee.

Park Guest House, 15th Floor. Singles about HK$60 and doubles around HK$70-80.

New International Guest House, 11th Floor. Singles HK$65 and doubles HK$70 including TV and air-conditioning. Little rooms into which you slot the bed and yourself, but it is clean and friendly.

Welcome Guest House, 8th Floor, is the one I'd probably go for in this block. Run by a very friendly man, rooms are HK$50 a single and about HK$70 a double. He has more rooms on the 15th floor. Dormitory beds are HK$20. One person was so taken with the place that 'when I got back from China and found them all full, I took a bed next to the entranceway just so I could stay there.'

Chungking House (tel 3-665362) 4th & 5th Floor. A respectable place with a large number of rooms, some with TV, telephone and air-conditioning. Singles from HK$140 and doubles from HK$180 to $220. Rooms can be booked at the HKTA office at Kai Tak Airport.

Lee Garden Guest House (tel 3-7232805) 3rd Floor. A cheap place, clean and definitely worth a look. Also seems to be popular with travellers.

B Block

Asia Guest House, 17th Floor. Singles HK$50, doubles HK$70 and thundering TVs. It caters mainly to Indians but will take westerners. Both the 16th and 17th floors of this block seem to be an Indian enclave (in much the same way the 16th floor of A block has been taken over by westerners)

Carlton Guest House, 15th Floor. Singles HK$75, doubles HK$100. Very clean, very tidy place and friendly people. It caters mainly to a Pakistani clientele, but will take westerners.

New Washington Guest House, 13th Floor and the *Shanghai Guest House*, 8th Floor, are run by the same person. Singles HK$60 and doubles from HK$90. Doubles for HK$120 with air-conditioning and bath. I'd recommend these places, though some people find the rooms far too claustrophobic for the price.

Columbia Guest House, 12th Floor. A quiet and clean place but the people who run it are consistently unfriendly towards westerners. Nevertheless worth trying if you can't find something else.

Hong Kong Guest House, 11th Floor. Singles HK$50, doubles HK$70. One traveller wrote:

They pulled a real fast one on me; they offered me a 'great deal' on a room HK$30 for a single, if I paid a week's rent. They did advise me the rent was non-refundable, in case I checked out sooner, but they didn't tell me, and I soon found out, that the room is adjacent to the TV room and due to paper-thin walls sleep was impossible. When I asked to be moved to another room, they said they could do this but it would cost me another HK$30 per night. Unless you are an insomniac, give this place a miss.

A more recent letter noted: 'Forget it, a persistent tout and surly people; one night there and I left.'

Travellers Friendship Hostel 6th floor, has mixed dormitory accommodation at HK$20 per night. It's rather cramped (to say the least) but popular with travellers.

C Block

Tom's Guest House, 16th Floor. Singles HK$50, doubles HK$70 to $80. Friendly manager.

Kowloon Guest House, 10th Floor. An OK place with singles for HK$70 and doubles HK$120.

D Block

Lee's Guest House, 16th Floor. Looks like a clean, comfortable place, but the owners don't seem very friendly nor in the least bit enthused about foreigners. You'd probably be looking at around HK$100 for a single or double (try bargaining), but I think you'd be wasting your time coming here.

Peking, 14th Floor. Singles HK$70 and doubles HK$80 – some rooms have fans and air-conditioning. The people who work here are really friendly.

Boston (tel 3-680081) 10th Floor. Singles HK$45, doubles HK$65. Little boxes for rooms but each has a fan, and though it's a rather rundown-looking place it should be OK. Also try the *Paris Guest House* next door.

Princess Guest House (tel 3-673101), 3rd floor. Singles HK$40, doubles HK$60 with fan. The people who work here are very friendly and the place is not bad for the price, though the rooms are very small. Nevertheless, it gets good reports from travellers. You can leave excess luggage here if you are going to the outer islands, Macau or China.

E Block

Sheraton Guest House 3rd & 14th Floor. Rooms on the 14th floor (tel 3-7220090) are small but it's a very decent place with singles around HK$90 and doubles about HK$140. Rooms on the 3rd floor (tel 3-687981) are more basic but also cheaper; singles HK$50 and doubles HK$70. The manager is friendly and you should be able to find him on the 3rd floor.

Hoover Guest House (tel 3-668166), 9th Floor, has singles and doubles for about HK$80. Very bare and basic but should be OK.

New World Guest House, 7th Floor. Single boxes here for HK$50 (and I mean boxes!). Rather less claustrophobic doubles for HK$130 with TV, fan and air-conditioning.

The Ys

The Ys in Hong Kong don't have quite the same level of cheap accommodation they have elsewhere, but by Hong Kong standards they're still good value.

The *YMCA* (tel 3-692211) on Salisbury

Rd, Kowloon is the most popular. It rivals Chungking Mansions and many travellers prefer it as it's clean and less claustrophobic – although it's nowhere near as cheap as it was a few years ago. Like Chungking Mansions, it's well situated, just a few minutes' walk from the Star Ferry. In fact its location is so envied by hoteliers that there have been rumours for years that the Y would be pulled down to make way for something else. The Y also has a swimming pool, gymnasium, sauna, tennis courts, library, restaurant (unexciting but cheap meals), bookshop, barber, left-luggage room, lockers and passport photo machine. Dormitory accommodation for both men and women is HK$40 per night. Single rooms run from HK$120 and doubles from HK$150. It seems you can book rooms in advance but not dormitory beds. Air-conditioned singles go for HK$160 and doubles for HK$180.

There's also the *YMCA International House* (tel 3-319111) at 23 Waterloo Rd, Kowloon. It's got singles (men only) from HK$40 to $50; with air-conditioning, HK$70. Doubles (men and women) with air-conditioning run from HK$220. The place is close to the Waterloo MTR Station, or take Bus No 7 or 7A from the Kowloon-side Star Ferry Terminal.

The *YWCA Guest House* (tel 3-7139211) is conveniently located at 5 Man Fuk Rd (Waterloo Rd Hill) in Kowloon. Single rooms run from HK$110 and doubles from HK$250. Cheaper rooms may be available. Take Bus No 7 or 7A from the Kowloon-side Star Ferry Terminal.

On the Hong Kong Island side there is the *YWCA Headquarters Hostel* (tel 5-223101) at 1 MacDonnel Rd. They only take women and couples – no single men. Rooms for women start from HK$60 a single and HK$90 a double. Rooms for couples start at HK$130. To get there take Bus No 12A from in front of the shops adjoining the Star Ferry Terminal. This takes you straight past the YWCA and drops you off on MacDonnel Rd just a few minutes walk away.

Other Cheapies

There are a few privately run hotels and hostels of the Chungking genre, mostly in the streets near Chungking Mansions. The Hong Kong Student Travel Bureau may also be able to get cheaper rates in some hotels for visiting students, but don't expect too much help for real rock-bottom accommodation. Some cheap hotels are strictly short-time places where you rent by the hour, and bring a friend not your suitcase; others are brothels or double as brothels; and others are good alternatives to staying in the Chungking Mansion sweat-box!

Foreign Youth Service Centre (otherwise known as the Hong Kong Hostel) (tel 3-678952) is on the 11th floor at 230 Nathan Rd, Kowloon. It's near the Jordan Rd subway station and is only a short walk from Salisbury Rd. Dormitory beds go for HK$20. A decent place, it's rather less cramped than Travellers' Hostel in Chungking Mansions. Lockers and cooking facilities are available.

Also recommended is the *International Youth Accommodation Centre* (tel 3-663419), 6th floor, 21A Lock Rd, Kowloon. It's clean and cheap and popular with travellers. Dormitory beds go for HK$22. Another is the *Grand View Mansion* at 119 Chatham Rd, Kowloon, with dorm beds for HK$20.

Around the corner from Chungking Mansions is the *Garden Hostel* on Mody Rd, Tsimshatsui; turn right as you come out of the main entrance to the mansions and then right at the first street. Then, on the left side of the street, go through the photo stand to the 3rd floor. Accommodation is HK$22 in a dorm, clean and air-conditioned. A double room with fan is HK$70.

Also try the *Hong Hey House* (tel 3-7216775) on the 8th floor, Block B, Champagne Court, 16 Kimberley Rd, Tsimshatsui. Kimberley Rd runs off Nathan Rd, opposite Kowloon Park and only a short walk up from Chungking Mansions.

The *Hong Kong Student Travel Bureau* (tel 3-7213269) in Room 1021, Star House, Tsimshatsui, Kowloon, runs a hostel for travellers in Tsimshatsui. Apparently it's only got four people per room, and the rooms have air-conditioning. The catch is that it costs HK$70 per person per night! Inquire at the HKSTB office.

The *Soldiers & Sailors Home* is at 22 Hennessy Rd on the the Hong Kong Island side, and gets good reports from travellers. The rooms are big – singles HK$55 and doubles HK$100. There's a restaurant on the ground floor which serves fairly cheap though not particularly memorable meals.

Youth Hostels

The International Youth Hostel Association has a number of hostels in Hong Kong. Their office is in Room 1408, Block A, Watson's Estate, 4-6 Watson Rd, North Point, Hong Kong Island (tel 5-700985 and 5-706222).

The hostels charge about HK$8 a night for a dormitory bed. They close between 10 am and 4 pm, and it's lights-out at 11 pm. Advance booking is required for some hostels and this can be done by either writing, telephoning or going to the head office. If you don't already have a YHA card, it will cost you HK$80 to get one, but the card is worth it if you are going to be staying a while. Although there is a hostel on Hong Kong Island, and one near the Po Lin Monastery on Lantau Island, others

are located in remote areas – and if that's where you want to go then they're definitely worth investigating. The hostels are:

Ma Wui Hall (tel 5-875715) on top of Mount Davis, Hong Kong Island. Everyone who stays here invariably raves about the place. It's a bit out of the way, but quiet and in a beautiful location. There are cooking facilities but you'll have to bring your own food supplies. The hostel has over 100 beds. It closes between 10 am and 4 pm. To get there take Bus No 5B from the Central Bus Terminus going to

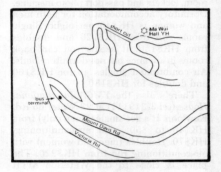

Felix Villas at Minden Plaza, Causeway Bay. Get off at the terminus and walk back 100 metres. Look for the YHA sign and follow the unnamed motorable road – there is a short-cut (with a sign) halfway up the hill. The walk from the bottom up to the hostel takes about 20 to 30 minutes. If you come from the airport, get a harbour tunnel bus No 101 (southbound) outside the airport to Kennedy Town terminus, then change to the 5B bus or take a taxi direct to the hostel.

Bradbury Hall (tel 3-282458), Check Keng, Sai Kung Peninsula, New Territories. The easiest way to get there would be to take the ferry from Ma Liu Shui (adjacent to University Railway Station) to Chek Keng.

Cambrai Lodge, Nim Wan, Laufaushan, New Territories. This is only open on

weekends and holidays. Take Bus No 50 from the Jordan Rd Terminus, or No 260 from the Star Ferry to Yuen Long. Then take a 'green line' minibus from Tai Fung St to a place called Pak Lai. Get off and follow the access road for about half an hour. You'll see a YHA sign at a road junction; both roads run to Nim Wan village but the longer route is straightforward, while the short-cut meanders through vegetable fields and farm houses.

S G Davis Hostel (tel 5-9857610) at Ngong Ping, on Lantau Island, is in a beautiful setting just around the corner from the Po Lin Monastery. Take a ferry from the Outlying Ferry Pier to Silvermine Bay on Lantau, and then go by bus to Ngong Ping. For more details, see the Lantau Island section in this book.

Pak Sha-O Hostel (tel 3-282327) Pak Sha-O, Jones Cove, Sai Kung Peninsula. The best way to get here is to take the ferry from Ma Liu Shui (adjacent to University Railway Station) to Lai Chi Chong. Then walk for an hour from Lai Chi Chong to the hostel.

Sze Lok Yeun Hostel (tel 0-988188), Tai Mo Shan Rd, Tsuen Wan, New Territories. Take the No 51M bus at Tsuen Wan MTR Station, alighting at Tai Mo Shan Rd. Follow the Tai Mo Shan Rd, and after walking for about 45 minutes, turn onto a small concrete path on the right-hand side which leads directly to the hostel.

Wayfoong Hall (tel 0-6568323), Plover Cove, Ting Kok Rd, Tai, New Territories. Take the train from Kowloon (Hunghom) Railway Station to Tai Po Railway Station. Take Bus No 75K from Tai Po to Tai Mei Tuk village and follow the access road with the fishpond on one side and the sea on the other.

Jockey Club Mong Tung Wan Hostel (tel 5-9841389), Mong Tung Wan, Lantau Island. Take a ferry from the Outlying Islands Ferry Pier to Silvermine Bay, and then take a bus to Pui O. Walk along the road to Ham Tin, and at the junction of Chi Ma Wan Rd and the temple take a footpath to Mong Tung Wan – a 45-minute walk.

Campsites

Tent camping is permitted at a number of the Youth Hostels – check with the YHA for details. Campers who are members of the YHA are charged HK$8 per night per person, and that entitles you to use of the hostel toilets and washrooms. There are a number of government and independently run campsites on Lantau Island – the HKTA has a printed leaflet listing them.

MID-RANGE

As you move upmarket the availability and standard of rooms improves markedly. There are many hotels with rooms starting at around HK$200 a single and HK$300 a double, and a few even cheaper than that.

Kowloon

Lytton House Inn (tel 3-673791) is in Lytton House, Mody Rd, Tsimshatsui, Kowloon. Rooms here are like caves – miniscule, dingy cubicles with attached shower and toilet for HK$120 single or double. It might be very quiet though.

The *Sky Guest House* (tel 3-854010) on the 14th floor of the building on the corner of Nathan and Jordan Rds, Kowloon, has singles and doubles from HK$100, with TV, air-conditioning and attached bathroom. If you can afford something slightly upmarket then this is a fine place.

Green Jade Hotel (tel 3-677121), 1st floor, 29-31 Chatham Rd, Kowloon. Singles HK$150, doubles HK$200. Despite the cost the rooms are small and cramped and very dingy, only vaguely better than some of the places in Chungking Mansions – the only advantage being that you're not actually in Chungking Mansions. If they've got better rooms then they didn't go out of their way to show them to me!

On the same road is the *Baccarat Hotel* (tel 3-665922), on the 11th floor, Windsor Building, at Nos 29-31. Singles and doubles here are HK$250. The rooms are of moderate size with double beds and attached bathroom, and the staff is friendly. If you're looking for something mid-range then this is a good place to try.

Probably better, though, is the *Ritz Hotel* (tel3-692282) nearby at 122 Austin Rd, Kowloon. Singles run from HK$240 and doubles from HK$320, plus 5% tax and 10% service charge.

Some other places on the Kowloon side include:

Astor (tel 3-667261), 11 Carnarvon Rd. Singles/doubles HK$240/$320.
Bangkok Royal Garden (tel 3-679181), 2 Pilkem St, Yaumati. Singles/doubles HK$155/$190.
Carlton (tel 3-866222), Tai Po Rd. Singles/doubles HK$250/$300.
Fortuna (tel 3-851011), 355 Nathan Rd. Singles/doubles HK$250/$330.
Galaxie (tel 3-307211), 30 Pak Hoi St. Singles/doubles HK$190/$220.
Grand Hotel (tel 3-669331), 14 Carnarvon Rd. Singles/doubles HK$280/$330.
Imperial (tel 3-662201), 32-34 Nathan Rd. Singles/doubles HK$265/$295.
International (tel 3-663381), 33 Cameron Rd. Singles/doubles HK$180/$250.
Kings (tel 3-301281), 473 Nathan Rd. Singles/doubles HK$175/$210.
Nathan (tel 3-885141), 378 Nathan Rd. Singles/doubles HK$240/$300.
Shamrock (tel 3-662271), 223 Nathan Rd. Singles/doubles HK$180/$210.

Hong Kong

On the Hong Kong Island side there's the *Star Bridge (Sing Kiu) Guest House* at the corner of Fenwick St and Lockhart Rd in Wanchai (enter from the Fenwick Rd side). Singles and doubles from HK$200. Other places include:

Caravelle (tel 5-754455), 84-86 Morrison Hill Rd. Singles/doubles HK$280/$320.
Harbour (tel 5-748211), 116-122 Gloucester Rd, Singles/doubles HK$200/$300.
Hong Kong Cathay (tel 5-778211), 17 Tung Lo Wan Rd, Causeway Bay. Singles/doubles HK$240/$280.
Harbour Hotel (tel 5-748211), 116-122 Gloucester Rd, Wanchai. Singles/doubles HK$200/$300.
Luk Kwok (tel 5-270721), 67 Gloucester Rd, Wanchai. Singles/doubles HK$200/$240. This, by the way, is one of Hong Kong's more famous hotels, immortalised as the 'Nam Kok Hotel' in Richard Mason's *The World of Suzie Wong*. It's huge, old-fashioned and comfortable.
Singapore (tel 5-272721), 41-49 Hennessy Rd. Singles/doubles HK$250/$310.

TOP END

Luxury hotels and other nearly luxury or merely first-class accommodation is easy to find in Hong Kong, so if that's what you're after you don't really need to read this. The HKTA leaflet lists all major hotels, and their airport booking office will find you a room if you haven't already booked one. And if you wander down to Tsimshatsui or Hong Kong Central you'll trip over a luxury skyscraper at just about every corner.

However, even luxury hotels are not sacred in Hong Kong. Once upon a time there were plans to demolish the *Peninsula Hotel* and build a new one. The old colonial *Repulse Bay Hotel* was pulled down a few years ago – and though another apartment block was going to be shoved up on the site at the time of writing, nothing had been built at all.

The premium on space in Hong Kong has presented a challenge to hotel architects who strive to outdo each other in squeezing as many people as possible into a small space. Some of the later hotels seem to have been built on the shoehorn principle, so you either lie down or stand up because chairs don't fit into the plan, and if you want more space than that you pay extra for it. Lower ceiling heights add to this claustrophobia. If you're paying good money for a bed you might at least get some elbow room, so go for a slightly older place if you get a choice.

At the top end of the scale, a suite of high-ceilinged spacious splendour at the Peninsula Hotel will cost you a mere HK$2200 to $3200. A room is HK$900 to

$1200. Mind you, if you're going to pay for a suite they'll probably send a Rolls-Royce from the fleet to pick you up from the airport, so at least you'll save the bus fare. I could go on endlessly regurgitating top-end hotels, but a few of the main ones where the other half can be found are listed below:

Kowloon

Ambassador (tel 3-666321), corner Nathan and Middle Rds. Singles/doubles HK$320/$390.

Empress (tel 3-660221), 17-19 Chatham Rd. Singles/doubles HK$350/$450.

Golden Mile Holiday Inn (tel 3-693111), 46-52 Nathan Rd. Singles/doubles HK$440/$620.

Harbour View Holiday Inn (tel 3-7215161), 70 Mody Rd. Singles/doubles HK$550/$630.

Hong Kong Hotel (tel 3-676011), Canton Rd. Singles/doubles HK$410/$590.

Hyatt Regency (tel 3-662321), 67 Nathan Rd. Singles/doubles HK$570/$620.

Marco Polo (tel 3-7215111), Harbour City, Canton Rd. Singles/doubles HK$450/$640.

Miramar (tel 3-681111), 134 Nathan Rd. Singles/doubles HK$450/$640.

New World (tel 3-694111), 22 Salisbury Rd. Singles/doubles HK$340/$360.

Park (tel 3-661371), 61-65 Chatham Rd. Singles/doubles HK$350/$390.

Peninsula (tel 3-666251), Salisbury Rd. Singles and doubles from HK$900. Hong Kong's most illustrious hotel.

Regal Meridien (tel 3-7221818), 71 Mody Rd. Singles/doubles HK$550/$660.

Regal Meridien Hong Kong Airport (tel 3-7180333), Sa Po Rd. Singles/doubles HK$430/$460.

Regent (tel 3-7211211), Salisbury Rd. Singles and doubles from HK$750.

Royal Garden (tel 3-7215215), Tsimshatsui East. Singles/doubles HK$440/$490.

Shangri-la (tel 3-7212111), 64 Mody Rd, Tsimshatsui East. Singles/doubles HK$650/$700.

Sheraton (tel 3-691111), 20 Nathan Rd. Singles and doubles from HK$800.

Hong Kong

Excelsior (tel 5-767365), 281 Gloucester Rd, Causeway Bay. Singles/doubles HK$600/650.

Furama Inter-continental (tel 5-2555111), 1 Connaught Rd, Central. Singles/doubles HK$600/660.

Hilton (tel 5-233111), 2 Queen's Rd, Central. Singles/doubles HK$570/630.

Lee's Garden (tel 5-767211), Hysan Avenue, Causeway Bay. Singles/doubles HK$530/600.

Mandarin (tel 5-220111), 5 Connaught Rd, Central. Singles and doubles from HK$930.

Plaza (tel 5-7901021), 310 Gloucester Rd, Causeway Bay. Singles/doubles HK$480/520.

LONG-TERM ACCOMMODATION

Living in Hong Kong is something of an enigma. For some travellers it means three months penance teaching English to the locals, and heading back in the evening to suffocate in a shoebox in Chungking Mansions or sleep on a bunk in Travellers' Hostel, before they can leave for China or Thailand – or Australia for those with loftier aspirations. Others find themselves stalled in Hong Kong like the crew of Odysseus's ship in the land of the Lotus Eaters: ' . . . those who ate this honeyed plant, the Lotus, never cared to report, nor to return: they longed to stay forever, browsing on that native bloom, forgetful of their homeland.'

Those who adopt the lotus-eater attitude don't care whether they're making a fortune or living on the poverty line. Those who come here to make money out of casual labour have got problems if they also expect to live too high a lifestyle (and maybe any lifestyle at all for that matter). The basic problem is that the cost of living in Hong Kong is high – especially for westerners determined to live as such. But *gwailos* willing to experiment with the traditional western lifestyle and take advantage of Hong Kong's cheap side can cut the cost of existence considerably, and even travellers can make enough money out of the place to keep on travelling.

The biggest item in the monthly budget is rent. The vast majority of the colony's property is rented. Rents are high because space is short – the problem became so critical that legislation had to be introduced to stop the price of flats shooting beyond even the executive pocket.

Places to Live

The most popular areas to live on Hong Kong Island are the Mid-Levels, the Peak, and the south side of the island, but apartments are available in other areas.

Mid-Levels covers the long strip of hillside area from Conduit and Robinson Rds at the western end of the island to Jardine's Lookout in the centre of the island. Most of the flats throughout the Mid-Levels have harbour views, from partial to spectacular. Rents also vary enormously, from partially reasonable by Hong Kong standards to the spectacularly expensive. A two-bedroom flat in Mid-Levels could cost you from around HK$6000 to $7000 per month for something modest, not to say HK$30,000 or more for a luxury apartment. Many westerners who can afford such accommodation don't pay for it; their company does. Clearly, Mid-Levels is not for you.

Some westerners moved out to the New Territories towards Castle Peak, Shatin and Clearwater Bay. The problem here is the traffic. Congestion is appalling during the rush hour and is a factor to be considered if you work office hours and are looking for a place to live. The search for economic rent also drove a lot of *gwailos* out to the islands, where they've found the bonus of peaceful village life, sea and sand. Cheung Chau has the largest western community among the islands, and even has its own village pub and a couple of cafés catering to the western clientele. The ferry service to most of the major outer islands is good and makes for easy commuting to work in Hong Kong Island or Kowloon. Rents are no longer as rock-bottom as they were a decade ago, but they're still cheaper than on Hong Kong Island. Lamma is the other island with a sizeable western community.

An important factor in determining the cost of rent is the age of a building. Usually the newer the apartment block the higher the rents. Since even moderate Hong Kong rents are still high by international standards, most single people share flats with other people. On the Kowloon side, Waterloo Hill and Homantin Hill cost about the same, but you will pay less if you head out for somewhere rather less popular like Kowloon Tong, Happy Valley or North Point. Stanley and Repulse Bay are fashionable and pricey. Moving up both in altitude and cost, there's always the Peak, which you will never be able to afford.

Flats in Hong Kong are generally rented exclusive of rates and unfurnished. However, rattanware and household effects are cheap and flats can be furnished inexpensively.

Leave Flats

If you are stuck for accommodation, 'leave flats' are worth investigating. Employees on contract are rewarded every couple of years with long holidays, and they usually rent their flats out while they go back home to see the folks. The usual duration is three months, during which time you are responsible for the rent and the wages of the amah (servant). Occasionally people even offer the flat rent-free with just the amah's wages to pay, in order to have someone keep an eye on the place. Nice work if you can get it, but this doesn't happen often. Leave flats are listed under a separate heading in the classified advertisements of the *South China Morning Post*.

Where to Look

The best place to look for flats is in the classified sections of the *South China Morning Post* or the *Hong Kong Standard*, the two morning papers.

Then of course there's the real estate agents: Harriman's Realty Company (5-249191), Hutchison Properties Ltd (5-213241) and Riggs Realty (5-284548) are among the biggest real estate owners in town and you can put yourself on the waiting list if they don't have something straight away.

If you're lucky enough to be moving to Hong Kong on a contract you'll probably have your hotel room paid for you while you flat-hunt. That's the custom in Hong Kong and if that isn't in your contract then you haven't negotiated very well. But if you're left to your own devices, the 'Places to Stay' section in this book lists a number of hotels of different prices and respectabilities. Some hotels may offer discounts for longer stays.

Other Considerations

Presuming, of course, that you've got the money to have a choice, weather is also something to consider when renting a flat. The humidity causes two problems during the summer, namely condensation and mildew. Some flats have 'hot cupboards' to store things like leather goods, cameras and so on which are particularly susceptible to mildew. Many people install dehumidifiers or low-consumption bar heaters in wardrobes to protect clothes and shoes. If you're furnishing a flat, the best advice is not to have a closed-in wardrobe but to have a simple rail with a curtain around it — definitely the best way to beat mildew.

At the opposite end of the scale, you'll find that the first two months of the year can be extremely chilly – cold enough for winter woolies and a coat. A biting winter monsoon blows in from China, the days are overcast and often drizzly, and the thermometer drops to 15°C. Since Hong Kong's winter is short, the apartments are built with the heat in mind. If you're not prepared for them, those two winter months can be one long shiver.

As for typhoons, when the warning signal goes out don't forget to clear your balconies and terraces of potted plants, furniture and anything else that could blow off their perches and conk somebody.

Some people have amahs (servants), who are employed either part time or as live-in-help. Part-time amahs (negotiable on pay, hours and duties) generally come in to clean up once or twice a week, while full-time amahs do the housework, cook and look after the kids. A number of Filipino housemaids work in Hong Kong, usually coming over on two-year contracts arranged through employment agencies. They get a monthly wage plus board and lodging, and you also have to provide a ticket for them back to the Philippines at the end of their contract. Servants from the People's Republic are also employed in Hong Kong now, imported through agencies in China.

Places to Eat

You can eat American, Korean, Australian, Indonesian, Indian, Malaysian, Japanese, Spanish, Swiss, Jewish, Mexican, Hungarian, British, maybe Russian, and yes, even Chinese food in Hong Kong. Unfortunately it is a sad fact of life that eating out at a Chinese restaurant in Hong Kong is no longer cheap – not in the old sense of the word anyway. Even the *dai pai dongs*, the food stalls in the street, don't have the rock-bottom prices they used to 10 years ago. However, you can still get a big, steaming bowl of noodles, roast pork, vegetables and bean curd for around HK$8, so there's not much to complain about.

Only about 2% of Hong Kong's work force is involved in either agriculture or fishing, yet they manage to provide the colony with 90% of its fish, about 50% of its poultry, 30% of its fresh vegetables, about 20% of its pigs, and a small quantity of rice. The rest is imported, mainly from China.

Most of the food is sold fresh in markets, with residents making their shopping trips once in the morning and again in the afternoon – the Chinese simply won't live anywhere far from a fresh food market. While there are numerous western fast-food chains and several supermarkets selling imported, packaged and processed food, they play a minor role in the scheme of things.

There are over 30 pages of restaurants listed in the Hong Kong telephone book, and a guesstimated total of 30,000 eating places of one description or other in the colony – a couple of them are listed below. If you want to do some more exploring, a useful book is the *Post Guide to Hong Kong Restaurants* compiled by Barry Girling and published by the *South China Morning Post*. It lists a whole range of eating houses of different cuisines and prices, including a number in Macau, and is available from

most of the major bookshops for around HK$45. Also useful is the *Visitor's Guide to Chinese Food in Hong Kong* published by the Hong Kong Tourist Association, which lists a large number of dishes in English and in Chinese characters. The HKTA booklet *The Official Guide to Shopping, Eating Out & Services in Hong Kong* has a short listing of restaurants of various cuisines. The *A-O-A Dining & Night-Life Guide* is useful for the touristy upmarket restaurants.

DIM SUM

Dim sum is the Cantonese way of eating both breakfast and lunch. The name means 'light or savoury snack' but literally translated the Chinese characters mean 'to touch the heart' – after all, the way to someone's heart is through their stomach. Dim sum crosses all barriers and occasions. Boat people eat it on the quayside to start the day. Rich *tai-tais* (housewives) linger over it at lunchtime to spin out their gossip and businesspeople clinch deals over it.

Dim sum are tiny delicacies – dumplings, meat balls, spring rolls, buns and spareribs. *Gwor ching chung*, for example, is a large glutinous rice dumpling, filled with duck, preserved egg yolks and mushrooms, and wrapped in lotus leaves. *Guon tong gau* is a steamed dumpling stuffed with minced pork and chicken soup. *Fung jau* is deep-fried chicken feet. These courses are followed by sweets like *daan tat* (tasty custard tarts) and *nor mai chi* (coconut snowballs). Dim sum dishes are said to number over a thousand in all.

Dim sum restaurants in town are usually very large – some seating thousands – and they get packed at lunchtime so tables can be difficult to get. To some people dim sum is any time after 4 am; in Hong Kong it's usually available in the restaurants from about 7 or 7.30 am up until 3 pm.

The food comes in small round bamboo baskets or in wooden pots. These are stacked on trays or trolleys which are brought round to the tables. As the waitresses do the rounds they call out the name of the dish and if you like what you see, try it. Dim sum dishes cost a few dollars per container and the bill is reckoned by tallying the empties on your table at the end of the meal.

Yum cha, strictly speaking, is what you do with dim sum – it means to drink tea. It also means to have dim sum – the two go together. A pot of tea will be brought, and when you need more, just take the lid off the pot and you'll get a refill. In the traditional dim sum houses wonderful (often vintage) teas are served. In Hong Kong there are three types of black tea: *keemun* from the north, *oolong* from the south and orange *pekoe*. There are also green and sweet-scented jasmine teas.

The HKTA publishes a useful little booklet called *Your Guide to Some Dim Sum Delights in Hong Kong*. Despite the bozo title it lists a number of dim sum dishes with both their English and Chinese names and Chinese characters – each accompanied by a colour picture of the dish. It costs only HK$5. Also useful for its dim sum listings – with illustrations – is the *A-O-A Dining & Night-Life Guide*.

There are a large number of places in Hong Kong serving dim sum, although most of the traditional tea houses are now gone. One, the *Luk Yu* (tel 5-246029), remains at 24-26 Stanley St, Central. It opened some 50 years ago in Wing Kut St but eventually moved to Stanley St. It still has the traditional stained-glass panels on the walls, mahogany and blackwood tables and straight-backed chairs, and wooden ceiling fans. For years *gwailos* who strayed into its hallowed interior were ignored or else admitted only under sufferance. Today the Luk Yu will serve westerners, and if you wander in for early morning dim sum (from about 7.30 am onwards) you'll find it patronised by sober-suited Chinese businesspeople

Some popular dim sum include:

har kau	淡水鮮蝦餃	shrimp dumpling
shiu mai	蟹黃乾蒸賣	meat dumpling
pai kwat	豉汁蒸排骨	steamed spare ribs
ngau yuk mai	乾蒸牛肉賣	steamed beef balls
tsing fun kuen	雞絲蒸粉卷	steamed shredded chicken
kai bao tsai	香菰雞飽仔	steamed chicken bun
cha siu bau	蠔油叉燒飽	steamed barbecued pork bun
tsing ngau yuk	荷葉蒸牛肉	steamed beef ball in lotus leaf
cha chun kuen	炸雞絲春卷	fried spring roll
wook kok	蜂巢香芋角	fried taro vegetable puff
ham sui kok	軟滑咸水角	fried dumplings
fun gwor	鳳城蒸粉果	steamed dumplings filled with vegetables & shrimps
daan tart	千層雞蛋撻	custard tart
ma tai go	炸馬蹄糕條	fried water chestnut sticks
ma lai go	欖仁馬拉糕	steamed sponge cake
ma yung bau	蛋黃椰蓉飽	steamed sesame bun
yeh chup go	鮮奶椰汁糕	coconut pudding
shui tsung kau	雪耳水晶餃	white fungus sweet dumpling
chien tsang go	蛋黃千層糕	1000 layer sweet cake with egg yolk filling
tse chup go	爽滑蔗汁糕	sugar cane juice roll

pondering their morning newspapers. Tea is served to you by the most sombre-faced waiters in Hong Kong. Your tea bowl is placed in a metal bowl and tea is first poured over it to allow the tea bowl to heat up. All told, it's a rather expensive place to have breakfast – dishes are about HK$5 to $6 each – but it's definitely worth visiting at least once!

In Tsimshatsui, Kowloon, there's the *Capital Restaurant*, 2nd floor, Block A, Chungking Mansions, 40-44 Nathan Rd. It's cheaper than the Luk Yu, brighter than a circus, reminiscent of a school canteen – but dim sum here is probably as good as anywhere else. Dishes start from about HK$4 each, plus a bit extra for tea.

A number of other dim sum places in Tsimshatsui are: *Gold Wheel*, 172 Nathan Rd; *Golden Crown*, 66 Nathan Rd; *Oceania*, Shop 281, Ocean Terminal; and *Orchid Garden*, 37 Hankow Rd.

In Central try: *Blue Heaven*, 38 Queen's Rd; *City Hall*, top floor, Edinburgh Place; *Lychee Village*, 15D Wellington St (telephone first as they may only serve dim sum on Sunday – the number is 5-245618); *State*, 9th and 10th floors, Li Po Chun Chambers (opposite Macau Ferry Pier), Des Voeux Rd; and *Yung Kee*, 32 Wellington St.

Other dim sum restaurants on the Hong Kong side include: *Kin Kwok*, Leighton Centre, Happy Valley; *Pearl City Nightclub*, 22 Paterson St, Causeway Bay; *Orchid Garden*, 481 Lockhart Rd, Causeway Bay; and *Glorious*, East Town Building, 41 Lockhart Rd, Wanchai.

CHINESE FOOD

Chinese cooking is famine cooking. The Chinese will eat anything and everything that moves, and no part of an animal or plant is wasted. What we now regard as Chinese culinary exotica is really a product of the need to make the most of everything available, salvaging the least appetising ingredients which wealthy nations reject as waste, and making them into appetising food. The people's long history of poverty, overpopulation and repeated famine has led to some interesting dishes: fish heads, ducks' feet, dog and cat meat, bird saliva, fish lips and eyeballs, to name a few. Even the method of cooking is a consequence of the shortage of fuel; cutting the food into small pieces and stir-frying it in a wok is more fuel-efficient than baking or spit-roasting. Pigs and chickens have always been a feature of the cuisine because they have unchoosy eating habits and can be raised on very small areas of land.

Plan of Attack

There are a few ground rules for eating Chinese food. The general plan of the campaign is to order one dish per person plus one more. Restaurants which cater to western whims may serve you the soup first, but it's more common as far as Chinese are concerned to wash their food down with it at the end.

The Chinese eat rice with their daily meals, shovelling it in with chopsticks with the plate held up to the lips, so don't feel self-conscious about doing the same. At banquets, though, rice is used to fill up the gaps; to eat a lot of it implies you are still hungry and is an insult to your host.

Small dishes in the middle of the table are soya sauce and chilli. Use the china spoon to take the food from the large serving plates to your bowl. The other small bowl is for tea. The bill, in Chinese, is *mai daan*.

Chopsticks

Chinese chopsticks are blunt at the end, unlike those in Japan, which are pointed. The best way to learn to use chopsticks is to be very hungry in a place which doesn't have forks. Hold the chopsticks between the thumb and the forefinger, resting them on the index finger, and move them up and down in a pincer fashion. Hunger will perfect the technique and the following diagram may help:

Using chopsticks

Place first chopstick between base of thumb and top of ring finger. (Bend fingers slightly.)

Hold second chopstick between top of the thumb and tops of middle and index fingers.

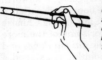

Keeping the first chopstick and thumb still, move the other one up and down by middle and index fingers.

Don't worry about making a mess on the table – everyone does. Raise the bowl right up to your lips and shovel in the rice – though it will probably take a lot of practice to master the shovelling process.

Sauces

As with western cuisine, Chinese food is accompanied by, or dipped into, various complementary sauces. When your food is served it will usually arrive with small bowls of sauces – some sweet, others salty or spicy depending on the dish. Steamed chicken is usually eaten with minced ginger, scallion or peanut oil; roast goose is served with tart plum sauce; shark's fin soup is accompanied by vinegar; and dried fried oyster uses peppercorn-flavoured salt.

Drinks

The obligatory pot of Chinese tea accompanies all Chinese meals. There are three main types of tea: green or unfermented; *bo lay* fermented, also known as red tea; and *oolong*, which is semi-fermented. Within these main categories there are many varieties, in much the same way as there are many varieties of western wines. Chinese teas are often scented using jasmine, chrysanthemum, rose and narcissus petals. It is always drunk straight, without milk or sugar. If the pot of tea is empty simply half open the lid and a waiter will refill it. Hong Kong has only one tea plantation – at Ngong Ping on Lantau Island. It is open to tourists.

Chinese wines are really not wines in the western sense of the word, since most of them are actually spirits distilled from rice, millet and other grains, herbs and flowers. Tonics are made by mixing various traditional health-giving ingredients into rice– and grain-based wines. *Siu hing* is a rice-based wine; the fiery *go leung* and *mao tai* are distilled from millet and have an alcohol content of 70%; and *ng ka pay* is a sweet herbal wine.

Although brandy is supposed to be the most popular alcoholic drink with the Hong Kong Chinese, on the other side of the border beer seems to have taken first place – and by any standards beer from the PRC is great stuff. The best-known is *Tsingtao*, made with a mineral water which gives the beer its sparkling flavour. It's really a German beer since the town where it's made, Tsingtao, was once a German concession. A brewery established there by the Germans was inherited by the Chinese once the foreigners were booted out of China. Local brews are found in all the major cities of China and are of varying quality but are almost always very good. (Chinese women, by the way, don't drink or smoke, but it's considered permissible for western women.)

Banquets

Chinese banquets progress a little differently from ordinary meals. A formal dinner usually lasts about 1½ hours and is preceded by 10 or 15 minutes of tea and polite conversation. The host presides at the head of the table and high-ranking guests are seated to his left or right. Dishes are served in sequence, beginning with cold appetisers and continuing to 10 or more courses, with soup usually served after the main course, and used to wash the food down.

Sometimes the host will serve the guest, as is the Chinese custom. If not, use the small china spoon to take food from the large serving plates to your own bowl. The usual rule is to serve everyone too much; empty bowls imply that the host hasn't served a sufficient quantity of food, so if you see a bit left in a bowl then leave it there. Similarly, though rice may be the staple, at banquets it is used only as a filler; to consume great quantities is to imply that you're still hungry and is considered an insult to your host.

In a formal setting it is impolite to drink alcohol alone; toasts are usually offered to neighbours or to the whole table. It is appropriate for the leader of the guests to offer a toast to everyone at the table, and the Chinese host usually begins the toasts after the first course. Avoid excessive toasting since inebriation is frowned upon. There are usually three glasses per person on the table: one for soft drinks, one for beer and another for toasts. Toasts are often made with the fiery mao-tai and the expression 'Gan bei!' which literally implies 'Empty the cup!' In the course of a banquet there may be several 'gan bei' toasts, but custom dictates that you need only drain your glass on the first one. Subsequent toasts require just a small sip – the Chinese are *not* great drinkers. The Han Chinese don't clink their classes when toasting. Don't be late for a formal banquet; it's considered extremely rude. The banquet ends when the food and toasts end – the Chinese don't linger after the meal.

In China, visiting delegations, cultural groups, etc, are usually given a welcoming banquet by their host organisation. At the very highest levels there'll be formal invitations and a detailed seating plan based on rank and higher algebra. At lower levels it's a simpler affair, though the ritual and etiquette are much the same. You may find yourself being applauded when you enter an official function, such as a large banquet. This is a Chinese custom which is used as a greeting or indicates approval – the correct response is to applaud back!

Eater's Rescue Vocabulary

The HKTA *Visitor's Guide to Chinese Food in Hong Kong* mentioned above has useful lists of Chinese dishes in both Chinese and Roman script. Though many Hong Kong restaurants have menus in both Chinese and English, it's worth getting some of these books and leaflets if you really want to get into eating Chinese food – particularly for some of the more unusual dishes. In the *dai pai dongs* and small restaurants, pointing is as good a way as ordering as any, though you may find the following list useful:

chicken	鸡	rice	米饭
jī		mǐ fàn	
pork	猪肉	dumplings	饺子
zhū ròu		jiǎo zi	
beef	牛肉	soup	汤
niú ròu		tāng	
duck	鸭		
yā		tea	茶
frog	青蛙	chá	
qīng wā		water	水
snake	蛇	shuǐ	
shé		beer	啤酒
prawn	虾	pí jiǔ	
xiā			
squid	鱿鱼	bean curd	豆腐
yóu yú		dòu fù	
octopus	章鱼	vegetables	蔬菜
zhāng yú		shū cài	
crab	蟹	pepper	胡椒
xiè		hú jiāo	
eel	鳝鱼	mushrooms	蘑菇
shàn yú		mó gū	
fish	鱼		
yú			

Cooking Styles

Traditional Chinese food can be divided into four major categories: Beijing (sometimes called Mandarin) and Shandong; Cantonese; Shanghainese and Jiangzhenese; and Szechuan (Sichuan). All four types can be tried in Hong Kong. There are also a number of lesser-known styles including Chiu Chow and Hakka.

Cantonese This is southern Chinese cooking – lots of steaming, pot-boiling and stir-frying. Cantonese is the most widely eaten Chinese food in Hong Kong and anywhere else where the Chinese takeaway has become part of the culture. It's also the cheapest to eat, and is the best of the bunch if you're worried about cholesterol and coronaries, as it uses the least amount of oil. It's lightly cooked and not as highly spiced as the other three main styles. It includes lots of vegetables, roast pork, chicken, steamed fish and fried rice. *Congee* is a thick Cantonese rice porridge.

Specialities are abalone, shark's fin soup (very expensive), roast pig and a snake dish known as 'dragon's duel tiger' which is a combination of wild cat and snake meat. Pigeon is a Cantonese speciality; there are a number of different ways to eat it, including with lemon or oyster sauce, but the gourmet's delight is plain roast. Since the Cantonese live next to the sea and Hong Kong is surrounded by water there's also plenty of seafood.

Incidentally, you do not find fortune cookies in Cantonese or any other real Chinese cuisine; they are a foreign invention. Thousand-year-old (also known as hundred-year-old) eggs are a Cantonese speciality – these are duck eggs soaked in a solution which includes tea, lime, alum, soda and salt for several days (not a thousand years). This turns the white of the egg green and the yolk a greenish-black. The egg should be eaten with a slice of pickled ginger.

One of the best places for eating seafood – and patronised by the Chinese, not flooded out with tourists – is the evening food stalls on Temple St in Kowloon. On the Hong Kong side the Wanchai district has some good fish restaurants. The traditional place for tourists to eat seafood has always been the floating restaurants at Aberdeen, on the southern side of Hong Kong Island, but that's now a very impersonal, expensive tourist extravaganza. Eating on a *sampan* in the Causeway Bay typhoon shelter used to be the sort of clever thing that only people in the know did, but that too has joined the tourist trip/trap list. You'll find the sampan women opposite the Excelsior Hotel.

For excellent, inexpensive seafood you can't beat the island restaurants, particularly on Cheung Chau, Lantau and Lamma. Of all the touristy venues, Sok Kwu Wan on Lamma Island – visited in the evening by an endless relay of boats bringing in customers from Hong Kong Island – is probably the best, and not a bad way to finish off a day-trip to the island. It's not for those who think that all God's creatures have souls and suffer like the rest of us. You pick your fish from a tank while it's merrily swimming around and 20 minutes later it's on your table.

If you visit the New Territories, don't forget Laufaushan with its famous oysters. There are numerous restaurants in the village.

Beijing & Shandong cooking styles come from one of the coldest parts of China and use heaps of spices and chilli to warm the body up. Bread and noodles are often used instead of rice. The chief speciality is Beijing duck, of which the crisp skin is the prized part. To achieve this crispiness the duck is air-dried and then coated with a mixture of syrup and soya sauce before roasting. The skin is carved off and is served wrapped in thin pancakes with spring onions or leeks, cucumber, turnip and plum sauce. The remainder of the duck meat is sauteed with bean sprouts, and the bones are used to make a soup with the addition of a Chinese cabbage.

Another chicken speciality is beggar's chicken, supposedly created by a beggar who stole the emperor's chicken and then had to bury it in the ground to cook it. The chicken is stuffed with mushrooms, pickled Chinese cabbage, herbs and onions, and is then wrapped in lotus leaves, sealed in clay and baked all day in hot ashes. It's actually supposed to have originated in Zhejiang Province in the Yangtze River region.

Some good Beijing dishes include: chicken or pork with soya-bean sauce; bean curd with pepper sauce; fried shredded beef with chilli sauce; stewed mixed vegetables; barbecued chicken; fried shrimp eggs and pork pancakes.

Another speciality is Mongolian barbecue – assorted barbecued meats and vegetables mixed in a hotpot. Try it at the *Poor Man's Nightclub*, outside the Macau Ferry Wharf; it's good and cheap. If you want more salubrious surroundings for your hotpot (or any other Beijing meal) then try the *Mongolian Barbecue*, 58 Leighton Rd, Causeway Bay.

For a relatively cheap meal with good food try the inappropriately named *American*, 18 Lockhart Rd, Wanchai; or the *New American* at 179 Wanchai Rd, Wanchai. Also try the *Manhattan*, 301 Hennessy Rd, Wanchai; dishes start at HK$25 but it's a great restaurant with friendly staff – they even have bears' paws on the menu. Try the fried shrimp in toasted sesame.

If you book into the *Peking Garden* in the Excelsior Hotel Shopping Arcade, Causeway Bay, you can dine off bears' paws and watch nightly displays of noodle-making. Other dishes include beggar's chicken or snake soup (they'll skin the snake at your table if you like).

Shanghainese & Jiangzhenese cooking styles are noted for their use of seafoods. The cuisine is heavier and oilier than either Beijing or Cantonese, and uses lots of chilli and spices. Eels are popular and so is drunken chicken – the bird is cooked in *shaoshing*, a potent Chinese wine which tastes a bit like warm sherry. Other things to try are the cold meat and sauce dishes,

ham and melon soup, bean curd with brown sauce, braised meatballs, deep-fried chicken, and pork ribs with salt and pepper.

The big speciality of Shanghainese food is the strange, hairy crab which arrives in September or October and keeps the gourmets happy for three months or so. The crabs are eaten for the roes and are beyond the price of most shoestring travellers. Jiangzhe cooking specialises in poultry and seafood, which are cooked in their own juices to preserve their original flavour.

For eels or drunken chicken it's the *Great Shanghai*, 26 Prat Avenue, Kowloon. For good value and good food try the *Yat Pun Heung*, 12 Kai Chiu Rd, Causeway Bay (hard to identify because there's no English name outside). Also try the *Sanno*, 46 Wellington St, Central.

Szechuan (Sichuan) This is the hottest of the four categories and is characterised by heavy use of spices and peppers. Specialties include frogs' legs and smoked duck. The duck is cooked in peppercorns, marinated in wine for 24 hours, covered in tea leaves and cooked over a charcoal fire.

Other dishes to try are shrimps with salt and garlic; dried chilli beef; vegetables and bean curd; bears' paws braised in brown sauce; fish in spicy bean sauce and aubergines in garlic. Sichuan food also features noodles and beautiful, warm bread.

Reasonably priced Szechuan restaurants include the *Kam Kong*, 60-60A Granville Rd, Kowloon, which serves the type of spicy dishes which bring tears to the eyes. On the same street is the *Fung Lam* at No 23.

No prizes for guessing the speciality of the *Red Pepper* at 5 Lan Fong Rd, Causeway Bay. At the *Sze Chuen Lau* (tel 5-8918795), 466 Lockhart Rd, Causeway Bay, they do a special winter dish of Sichuan pork which must be ordered ahead.

Chiu Chow is the name of a fisherpeople who made their home around the port of Swatow (Shantou) in south-eastern China. Chiu Chow food is also known as Swatow. This cooking uses a lot of different sauces and is inclined to be a bit oily so congee is used to counteract this.

As fisherpeople, the Chiu Chow developed a cuisine in which seafood figures prominently. Since it's been influenced by Cantonese cooking, vegetables are used abundantly. Chiu Chow cuisine is best known for its shellfish dishes, especially steamed lobster, deep-fried shrimp balls, crabmeat balls and steamed eel.

Goose is a speciality, especially soyed goose, traditionally served with pieces of fried goose blood – which can be a bit hard to take if you haven't been brought up on this sort of thing. If that doesn't turn you on, try grey mullet or oysters.

Chiu Chow meals start and finish with a small cup of a dark, bitter tea known as 'iron Buddha' – one to get the stomach ready, the other to calm it down. It's a type of *oolong* tea and is thought to aid digestion. It's also known as the 'Iron Goddess of Mercy' or Tit Kwun Yum.

There are a couple of Chiu Chow restaurants in Hong Kong. Try the *Chiu Chow Restaurant* on 463 Queen's Rd West – it's on the Hong Kong side heading west from Central towards Kennedy Town. Also check if the *Chiu Chau* at 485 Lockhart Rd, Kowloon, is still running.

Hakka cuisine is a mixture of Cantonese and Shanghainese developed by the Hakka peasants who have been farming the New Territories since long before Queen Victoria's day. Hakka women in the New Territories can be recognised by their distinctive, wide-brimmed, spliced-bamboo hats with a black cloth fringe. The Hakka were originally northern Chinese who migrated south over the centuries, hence the amalgam of styles in their cooking.

The Hakkas' efforts to use every part of the animal results in such delicacies as chicken blood soup and braised fish lips. Stuffed duck (deboned through the neck and stuffed with rice, lotus seeds and chopped meat) is a Hakka speciality.

Good value is *Home*, 19 Hanoi Rd, Kowloon where there are a large number of main courses starting from HK$22 to $25. Soups are around HK$17. Also try the *Kowloon Tsui King Lou*, 7 Saigon St, Yaumati, Kowloon.

Vegetarian

Hong Kong – believe it or not – is a good place for vegetarian Chinese food. Even if you are not a vegetarian it is worth giving one of the excellent vegetarian restaurants a try.

Vegetarian food is based on soya-bean curd – but the Chinese do some miraculous things with it. A 'fish' can be made by layering pieces of dried bean curd, or fashioned from mashed taro root. Not only do they make it taste like any food you could think of, they make it look like it as well. *Lo lun chai* is a delicious mixed vegetable dish, a meal in itself. Try also the noodle and bean curd dishes, congee, fried spring rolls, sweet-and-sour *wun tun* and sweet corn soup.

On the Kowloon side there's the sizeable *Choi Kun Heung Vegetarian Restaurant*, 219E Nathan Rd, conveniently located near the main tourist district.

One of the best-known vegetarian restaurants in Hong Kong is the *Wishful Cottage* at 336 Lockhart Rd, Wanchai. It does delicious vegetarian dim sum at lunchtime. One soup plus a main dish is enough for two people here. The building in which this place is housed has an incredibly ornate exterior – makes it look like a Chinese temple.

Vagi Food Restaurant (that's Vagi, not Vegi), 8 Cleveland St, Causeway Bay, has good food – if you can ignore the overstated signs at the entrance and put up with some of the gimmicky names on the menu.

If you want a non-meat option and eat in

style, the lunchtime buffet at the *Hilton Hotel* includes a good selection of well-cooked vegetarian dishes. Even the coffee shop in the hotel serves vegetarian food.

Some of the Taoist temples serve vegetarian food and there are a number of Buddhist Association restaurants in the colony. Unfortunately, they are not sign-posted in English and are therefore hard to find. If you stay at the *Po Lin Monastery* on Lantau Island you will eat vegetarian food, though a lot of people find it very bland.

Other Chinese Restaurants

If you're after roast suckling pig then the multi-storied and imposing *Yung Kee Restaurant*, 36-40 Wellington St, Central is the place to go. Roast suckling pig is sold by the pound; a portion serving six to eight people would cost around HK$70, so if you're with a group it's not as expensive as it may sound.

For the sharp, salty, rich taste of Yunnan ham there's the *Sun Tung Lok Restaurant*, 78 Morrison Hill Rd, close to the Happy Valley Racetrack. The ham is usually cooked with seafood, chicken or other meats and costs around HK$50 per dish.

And the snake restaurants? To find these, go down past Wing Sing St in the western district of Hong Kong, to where Queen's Rd curves around to the left and becomes Queen's Rd West. Continue straight ahead, not to the left, and you will be on Bonham Strand East. Veer left opposite Kwong Yuen St for Jervois St. Down here and along Hillier St are the snake shops.

Cheap Chow

For atmosphere, value and food quality, nothing beats the *dai pai dongs* – the Chinese food stalls. Many of the clutches of food stalls were cleared away years ago from the streets of Central and some other areas, but you can still find them else-where.

The best thing to do in these places is

wander around, see what's cooking and point. You'll find fish balls, roast pork, chicken, bean curd, shrimps, mussels, prawns, fishheads and shellfish. Noodles come in two shapes: the large, wide flat ones (*fun*) are fried, and the thin ones like spaghetti (*mean*) are cooked in soup. Rice, in Chinese, is *fan* and a couple of rice and noodle dishes include: *char siu fan* (rice with roast pork); *guy fan* (chicken rice); *yuu dan fun* (fish balls and noodles); *ngau yuk yuen mean* (beef meatballs and noodles); *hau fun wun tun* (soup of noodles with shrimp, pork, prawn, mushroom dumplings). To ask for 'one plate' say *yat deep*.

Best spots are the *Night Market* at the northern end of Temple St, Kowloon; and the *Poor Man's Nightclub* by the Macau Ferry Terminal. You'll also find them off Hennessy Rd, Wanchai, around North Point on Hong Kong Island, and at Yaumati and Mongkok in Kowloon.

In the Tsimshatsui tourist enclave you'll find *dai pai dongs* and small restaurants along Hau Fuk St, immediately to the east of Nathan Rd – particularly good at night when the restaurant tables spill over into the streets. Many of the restaurants along here have aquariums full of live crabs, squid, eels, fish, and shellfish, and there are also chickens, ducks and other skinned and roasted animals dangling in the front windows. Watch them dish up some frog soup for you: the frog is sliced across the back of the neck with a cleaver and the insides are adeptly pulled out in one lump and carved up. HK$12 or so gets you a bowl of rice, frog and fish soup. A big bowl of steamy noodles, bean curd and chicken pieces goes for HK$8. A wok-fried combination of prawns, squid, bamboo shoots and rice would cost you around HK$10 to $12. Top it off with a small bottle of beer for an additional HK$3.

Some cheapish restaurants in the Tsimshatsui region include the *Hoe Hoe Restaurant* at 37C Carnarvon Rd; the *Siu Lam Kung Seafood Restaurant* at 22

Hanoi Rd; and the *Wing Wah Restaurant* at 21A Lock Rd, which is popular with Chinese.

On the Hong Kong Island side in Causeway Bay, between the World Trade Centre and Victoria Park, what was once Houston St has been transformed into a canopied pedestrian mall complete with gushing fountains, and has been renamed Food St. Here and in the adjoining streets it's nothing but restaurants in different styles and nationalities, with cute names and shiny facades. This is not so much a tourist trip as one for the locals, and gets packed on Sundays with Chinese. The food, while good, is not exactly cheap, but a few places offer good value. Among those worth looking in on is the *Boil & Boil Wonderful* – the name refers to the bubbling pots. The food is Cantonese and pretty good. Also Cantonese is the *Riverside* (no, there's no river). They have an English menu as well, which includes braised brisket of beef and roast suckling pig. The *Houston Restaurant* serves a mixture of cuisines from satay to toasted savouries to spaghetti. For noodles, worth a try would be *Nanking Noodles* and *Phoenix Noodles* – the latter for good *congee* (rice porridge). There are also pizzarias and grill houses – and more places around the corner in Cleveland and Paterson Sts.

OTHER ASIAN FOOD

Hong Kong is one big Asian hotpot and just about any cuisine within a 5000-km radius of the place can be found here. Good value are the numerous Pakistani and Indian restaurants, as well as many of the Malaysian places.

Indonesian

For Indonesian food try the *Java Rijsttafel* at 38 Hankow Rd, Kowloon; or the *Shinta*, 1st floor, Kar Yau Building, 36 Queen's Rd East, Wanchai. Both are good and offer a set-price lunch each day where you can stuff yourself on a *rijsttafel* – literally 'rice table.' Also try the *Indonesia Padang Restaurant*, 85 Percival St, Causeway Bay.

The *Indonesia Satay House* in the Lytton Building, 34-38 Mody Rd, Tsimshatsui is moderately priced and a most pleasant place in which to eat. Gado gado is HK$18. You'd probably be looking at around HK$25 to $30 per person for a full meal.

Japanese

Hong Kong has quite a few Japanese restaurants, so if you like eating on the floor with your shoes off (optional – most have chairs too) then there are a number to choose from.

Somewhat upmarket is the *Osaka Japanese Restaurant* at 14 Ashley Rd, Tsimshatsui. There's also the *Ozeki*, which once had the distinction of having a chef licensed to prepare the notorious and potentially lethal fugu fish, but the local authorities said no, so you'll have to settle for more mundane Japanese delights instead. The Ozeki is in Basement 2, New World Centre, Tsimshatsui.

The *Yagiu*, 13 Stanley St, Central is another recommended place, very pleasant and relaxed. Dishes start at HK$35. Sushi dishes also cost from HK$35.

Korean

For some reason Korean cuisine has never been regarded as one of the world's greats, but after a trip or two to a barbecue-style Korean restaurant you may end up raving about it. The legendary ginseng is featured on many menus, especially in ginseng chicken (serves four, order in advance). Chicken and beef are cheapest; prawns are dearer.

The place to head in Kowloon is the *Manna*, which has three branches: 83B Nathan Rd; Lytton Building, 32B Mody Rd; and 6-6A Humphrey's Rd. They give you the ingredients and you barbecue them on little table-top gas cookers. A sample of prices: deer HK$36, frogs' legs HK$31; chicken HK$26 – and the helpings are very large. Japanese beer is HK$10 a bottle, sake HK$10 a bottle and ginseng HK$10 per glass.

Filipino

The *Little Manila* on 9 Minden Avenue, Tsimshatsui, Kowloon has a large range of moderately priced main courses around HK$17 to $20 each. It also serves European food. On the same street at No 11 is the *Mabuhay Restaurant*, which serves Spanish and Filipino food. On Mody Rd, at the intersection with Minden Avenue, is the Lytton Building where you'll find the *Barrio Fiesta* Filipino restaurant.

On the ground floor of the Chungking Mansions shopping arcade, hidden away in one of the back corners, is the *Chungking Café* which serves up good, cheap Filipino food in sizeable quantities.

Vietnamese

Since the end of the Vietnam War Hong Kong has permitted over 14,000 people from Indo-China to settle in the territory. At least one consequence has been the establishment of a number of Vietnamese restaurants.

In Kowloon these include the *Golden Bull*, 9 Hart Avenue, Kowloon which has a number of main courses around HK$20 to $25 and soups and snacks from HK$10.

Worth trying is the *May King Café*, 335 Lockhart Rd, Wanchai. A nifty little place is the *Saigon Beach Restaurant*, 66 Lockhart Rd, Wanchai, where main courses start at HK$16. It serves Vietnamese pizza.

Malaysian

The *Kuala Lumpur Restaurant* at 12 Observatory Rd, Kowloon, serves Malay dishes plus European and Chinese food. A good place and well worth visiting is the *Nam Ah*, 23 Ashley Rd, Tsimshatsui, where main courses of curried vegetables and rice start at just HK$13.

On the Hong Kong side is the *Malaya Restaurant*, 15B Wellington St, Central, where most dishes cost between HK$18 to $24. European food is served too but is much more expensive.

A variation on the noodle is the 'Singapore' variety – threadlike strands of rice noodles stirred with vegetables, chicken and shrimp in a hot curry sauce. They serve them up at the *Nam Ah* mentioned above, and also at the *King Bun*, 158 Queen's Rd, Central. Main courses at the latter start from around HK$30 to $40 and then just go up and up and up . . .

Indian & Pakistani

The greatest concentration of cheap Indian and Pakistani restaurants is in Chungking Mansions, Nathan Rd, Kowloon. A meal of curry with chappatis and dahl will cost maybe HK$15 to $20 per person. Some of these places include *Nanak Mess* (11th floor), which is good and cheap and has friendly people; and *Umar-E-Khayam* (7th floor). Both are in Block A. *Deep Mess* of Block B is one of my favourites. *Mumtaj Mahal* (12th floor) and *Islamabad Club* (4th floor) are in Block C. *Sher I Punjab* (8th floor) is another favourite. It is in Block D with *Halal Southern Indian* (3rd floor) and *New Humphrey's Apartments* (3rd floor). *Cholia Mess* (7th floor) and *Karachi Mess* (3rd floor) are in Block E.

On the ground floor shopping arcade of Chungking Mansions are two places distinguished only by their colour schemes, *Kasmiri Food* and *Lahore Fast Food*. You can get dishes of curried mutton or chicken with rice and chappati for around HK$10. Both open early in the morning so they're good for breakfast. Behind Chungking Mansions at 8 Minden Avenue is the *Woodlands*, an Indian vegetarian restaurant.

On the Hong Kong Island side there's the *Mohammadi Mess*, 2nd floor, 28A Stanley St, Central. It's a Pakistani place run by friendly people, and is cheap and much the same standard as those in Chungking Mansions. Large helpings of curry run from around HK$14. A similar place is the *Indian Club Maharani Mess* at

40 Wyndham St. Somewhat upmarket is the *Siddharth Club* at 57 Wyndham St, Central, which serves north Indian food; chicken tandoori is around HK$40 and it's enough for two people.

Thai

For Thai food there's a small restaurant in the *Bangkok Hotel*, 2 Pak Hoi St (behind the London Theatre), Kowloon. Another restaurant can be found on the 1st floor of *King's Hotel*, 473 Nathan Rd, Kowloon. Thai food can be searingly hot, especially the shrimp soup, but there are other less devastating dishes too. Prices are similar to those in modest Cantonese restaurants.

WESTERN

There are numerous good-quality French, Italian and international restaurants in Hong Kong. Most of them tend to be quite expensive and you'll pay at least as much as you would for a similar meal in other countries. The HKTA *Official Guide Book* lists many of them.

Italian

When your stomach cries for pizza, lasagna, cappuccino or other Italian food, try *La Bella Donna*, 51 Gloucester Rd, Wanchai. The house wines are OK too. Another good place is *Rigoletto's* at 16 Fenwick St, Wanchai. If you're staying at the Soldiers & Sailors Home on Hennessy Rd, try the *Spaghetti House* just a few doors down.

On the Kowloon side there's the *Spaghetti House* at 3B Cameron Rd, where spaghetti dishes range from about HK$11 (spaghetti done in garlic butter sauce) to HK$22 (spaghetti with cuttlefish, shrimp, garoupa and crab in a mushroom onion sauce). They also serve pasta and pizzas (about HK$18 for a regular size) as well as submarine sandwiches.

Also Italian is *La Taverna* at 36-38 Ashley Rd, Tsimshatsui. Pizzas are served at *Café Pizza* in the Shamrock Hotel, 223 Nathan Rd. *Pizza Hut* has dug its heels into Hong Kong along with the other fast-food chains. One of their branches is in the New World Centre, Tsimshatsui; as fast-food goes they're not bad.

German

For German food try the upmarket *Old Heidelberg Restaurant/Bar* at 24-30 Ashley Rd, Tsimshatsui.

American

For American-style giant sandwiches there's *Lindy's*, 1st floor, 57 Peking Rd, Tsimshatsui. Sandwiches (on rye, white, toasted or plain) range from HK$20 for a grilled ham-and-cheese to HK$32 for a steak sandwich. It also serves meals. The lunch menu includes a wide range of sandwiches but the dinner menu isn't nearly as extensive or cheap.

The *Beverley Hills Deli* in the New World Centre, Tsimshatsui does kosher-style food but it's not cheap. If you want strict kosher they've got it pre-packed.

Rick's Café is in a basement in the Enterprise Centre at 4 Hart Avenue, Tsimshatsui. You descend the steps under the gaze of a stuffed camel. The café serves oddly named sandwiches and drinks as well as Mexican-style snacks.

The *San Francisco Steak House*, Barnton Court, Harbour City, Tsimshatsui, might be worth a try. Steak and lobster is accompanied by a baked potato, jumbo onion rings and toasted garlic bread. On the Hong Kong side try the *Texas Rib House*, Victoria Centre, Watson Rd, Causeway Bay.

Mexican

Also upmarket but serving really good Mexican food is *La Tortilla*, 28 Cameron Rd, Kowloon. Main courses are about HK$32 to $45 so a decent meal with beer and dessert would cost you around HK$70 – but it's worth it. On the Hong Kong side there's the *Casa Mexicana*, Victoria Centre, 15 Watson Rd, Causeway Bay.

British & Australian Pub Food

If you yearn for home-style cooking but don't want to spend a fortune, try some of the bars and nightclubs. For Australians suffering pie'n'sauce withdrawal symptoms there's *Ned Kelly's Last Stand*, 11A Ashley Rd, Kowloon, where you can get fresh pies or other Australian suburban dishes like stew, sausages or steak. The *Stoned Crow* at 12 Minden Avenue, Kowloon, has a similar clientele, but is more of a restaurant as well as a bar. A proper meal will cost around HK$30. Also on Minden Avenue the *Blacksmith's Arms* is at No 16.

The English pub has come into vogue in a big way and these days you can find Tudor beams all over the place. *The Brewery* in Ocean Centre is one of the best for good British fare like steak-and-kidney pudding or plates of beef, but it's an expensive place. There are many pubs on the Hong Kong side though, and a typical meal of steak, eggs and chips would be around HK$20. Try the *Horse & Groom*, 126 Lockhart Rd, Wanchai; the *Elephant's Castle* next door; and a few doors along, the *Hunter's Castle Pub*.

Other Western Restaurants

For a basic meal of meat, chips and two vegetables I'd recommend the *YMCA* on Salisbury St, Tsimshatsui. A decent meal would be around HK$25 to $30. Breakfasts run about HK$15 to $20, although they do have a set breakfast for HK$16. A bit more expensive but a good alternative to the YMCA is the restaurant in the *Mariner's Club*, just around from the Sheraton Hotel in Tsimshatsui.

The *Brewery Restaurant & Bar* on the 3rd floor of the Ocean Centre, Tsimshatsui is run by the same bunch that runs the adjoining *Self Service*. They have a lunchtime 'farmer's buffet' for around HK$60 on weekdays, and HK$70 on weekends and public holidays.

A number of hotels have a set-price menu for lunch. Best of these is the Squire Luncheon at *Gaddi's*, a French restaurant in the Peninsula Hotel; it's also one of the most expensive restaurants in Hong Kong. On a more modest scale, set-price breakfasts and lunches are available at some of the top end hotels. The *Holiday Inn* on Nathan Rd, next to Chungking Mansions, has had a buffet breakfast going for several years now. It used to be fairly cheap and popular with travellers, but it now stands at HK$50 per head and isn't good value for money anymore. Worth trying are the vegetarian meals at the *Hilton* on the Hong Kong side.

For those on starvation budgets who want to drink as well as eat cheaply, take yourself into some of the bars and tourist hotels during happy hour – normally between 5 and 7 pm. To attract patrons some of these lay on small chow like meatballs and peanuts, which are free with half-price drinks.

Fast Foods

Fast-food outlets abound in Hong Kong these days, especially in the busy commercial and tourist areas where the traditional Chinese *dai pai dongs* have been forced off the street. Fast food is by no means out of keeping with the Chinese way of doing things. All over China and South-East Asia the Chinese are experts at dishing up a ready meal off a wok and a campfire from their streetside stalls. But while market-bought fresh food is the mainstay of the Hong Kong diet, the Chinese have also shown a seemingly unbounded enthusiasm for western-style fast foods. Most of the time it's not tourists you see queuing for hamburgers but Chinese.

As much as you can equate fast food with junk food, the fast-food venues can actually be a boon to travellers looking for a cheap meal – and you'll very likely find yourself eating a Big Mac more often than you expected when you left home to see the world. The fast-food chains also have a curious pull if you've just returned from a lengthy stay in China and can't stand the sight of one more noodle or bowl of rice.

The ubiquitous *McDonald's* is in force of course, with a dozen outlets, including those at the Hang Chong Building, 5 Queen's Rd, Central near the City Hall; the Yu To Sang Building, 37 Queen's Rd, Central; across from Chungking Mansions at 12 Peking Rd, Tsimshatsui; and further north near the corner of Nathan and Gascoigne Rds. No better, no worse than back home. A basic hamburger is HK$3.30, a Big Mac is HK$7.40 and something called a 'World Famous Meal' is HK$8.30.

The local chain is *Maxim's*, which offers sit-down restaurants as well as fast foods, either to take away or eat. They do a quick breakfast for HK$12 which gives you a main course of eggs (fried or pulped) with either two slivers of bacon or two sausages about the diameter of a pencil – liberally doused in oil. Unless you're starving, give it a miss. One of their branches is on the 1st floor, Ocean Centre, Tsimshatsui.

In much the same vein as Maxim's is *Self-Service*, 3rd floor, Ocean Centre, Tsimshatsui. It's easy to see why it's called Self-Service; after Maxim's I wouldn't ask anyone to serve this stuff up to a dog. A full breakfast gropes down your throat for HK$9, a full American breakfast for HK$12.50. The difference between a full breakfast and a full American breakfast is that you get a cup of orange juice and a croissant with the latter. But what I'm still pondering over is the 10% service charge added to the bill.

Other places serving vinyl imitation food include *Orange Julius* and *Burger King*. The latter's 'real American flavour' is much the same price as McDonald's. There are a few *Wendy's* fast-food restaurants around, with super salad bars.

Apart from these big names, there are countless other fast-food shops – sometimes lurking behind a cake shop. The windows and front counters will be filled with untold varieties of exotic cakes and biscuits while the hamburgers and suchlike are at the back of the shop. *Cherik-off Cakes & Fast Foods*, 184 Nathan Rd,

Kowloon, is a typical example. Prices are usually lower than those at the big names. The Cherik-off, by the way, is pretty good for cakes and bread, and upstairs they have occasional specials like borscht or cream soup, shredded beef with rice, and tea or coffee for just HK$11.

If you just want a coffee, call into one of the *Dairy Farm* ice-cream parlours. There is one close to Chungking Mansions at 74-78 Nathan Rd. Coffee and tea cost about HK$2. Ice cream ranges from HK$6 for a cup to HK$12 for a banana boat.

Markets

It has always been the determined eaters of western food who complain about the cost of food in Hong Kong. Western ingredients have to be imported and are therefore expensive. The Hong Kong or China-grown vegetables and other foods are cheap and very good, and if you are living in Hong Kong it's worth taking full advantage of the markets. If you're travelling down from hyper-expensive Japan (where an apple costs over US$1), you'll find that the pleasantly low cost of Hong Kong fruit seems like a better bargain than any stereo gear or cameras!

The biggest market is the one in Queen's Rd, Central. It has three floors of fresh fish, poultry, meat and vegetables. The day's prices are posted on a huge noticeboard which is a handy guide. In fact, you will seldom have cause to question the price. Regulars bargain in a subtle fashion by fingering the produce gently and grimacing or smiling alternatively when the price is given. Incidentally, it is generally acknowledged that you will do better shopping in markets, regardless of what you are buying, if you can ask the price in Chinese. There are markets scattered throughout the colony, including one on Queen's Rd East, Wanchai.

Vegetables, meat and other purchases are parcelled up neatly in paper and twine. They are weighed in *leung*, which is the equivalent of 1¼ oz or 37.5 gm; or in *catty*, where one catty is 1¼ lbs or about half a kg; or simply by the dollar's worth. The *South China Morning Post* has a daily listing of market prices for meat, poultry, fish, crabs, lobsters and vegetables, with prices given in dollars per catty.

Supermarkets

If you want to buy and cook food yourself, apart from the markets you've got quite a number of supermarkets selling imported, processed foods to choose from.

Close to Chungking Mansions is *Dairy Lane*, which is inside the Dairy Farm Creamery (ice-cream parlour) at 74-78

Nathan Rd. Across the road is the *Swing Supermarket* at 23-25 Nathan Rd.

The *Oceanways Supermarket* is in the basement of the Ocean Terminal near the Star Ferry Pier, Kowloon. On the 2nd floor of the Ocean Terminal is the *Park n' Shop Supermarket* (open 8.30 am to 8 pm).

Also try the *Welcome Supermarket* on Waterloo Rd, Kowloon, just near the corner with Nathan Rd. It's particularly convenient if you're staying in the Waterloo Rd YMCA.

Shopping

Hong Kong's reputation as a shopper's paradise continues to flourish despite the fact that it's not all it used to be. True, there is no duty and sales tax in Hong Kong, and this accounts for the main savings on a lot of goods, but escalating rents, rising wages, and rises in commodity prices throughout the world have pushed up the prices of some goods considerably. The locals may tell you that you have to live in Hong Kong to get a real bargain, but this needn't deter you from buying something you want if the price is right for you.

GROUND RULES

Visitors have traditionally left Hong Kong laden with cameras, watches, stereo equipment and jewellery. You only have to look round the departure lounge of Kai Tak Airport to know they still do. Even if the savings aren't what they were a few years ago, they're possible if you know what you want and if you know the value of what you are buying.

Hong Kong comes into its own in areas other than electronics and jewellery. It produces a large slice of the world's denim market, so you can get denim jeans, skirts or dresses for a quarter of the price back home. Goods from the People's Republic of China can be bought much more cheaply in Hong Kong than they can in the west. Strange little souvenirs and curios you can't get anywhere else (or before you can get them anywhere else) can be picked up for a couple of dollars – like digital egg-timers and musical birthday cards. While this all sounds like fun, there are some things about shopping in Hong Kong you should be aware of.

Information

The HKTA publishes a handy little booklet called *The Official Guide to Shopping, Eating Out, & Services in Hong Kong* which gives you a complete list of goods available in Hong Kong and the names and addresses of a number of shops where you can buy these goods. Shops which are members of the HKTA display the HKTA sign on their door, generally offer better service, and are less likely than other shops to rip you off or do the hard sell.

The HKTA leaflet *Arts & Crafts Museums* lists a number of places where you can buy various goods including brassware, carpets, Chinese lanterns, temple rubbings, ceramics and reproductions of temple wall paintings (especially door gods) – even places to buy local beer and mahjong sets.

There's a plethora of other books on shopping in Hong Kong, but a couple of good ones include *New Shoppers Guide* (Lincoln Green Publishing, Hong Kong, 1983) by Claudia Cragg, and *The Complete Guide to Hong Kong Factory Bargains* by Dana Goetz. New ones pop up and fade away all the time so it's hard to recommend any specific book. These two are worth getting; they'll tell you much more then we can possibly fit in here.

Duty-Free Goods

Hong Kong is a duty-free port. The only imported goods on which duty is paid are alcohol, tobacco, perfumes, cosmetics, cars and a number of petroleum products. This often makes many other goods cheaper than back home, but you'll still have to know your prices at home to know a bargain in Hong Kong. Also, it may be that the difference in price is so small it's not worth the worry and the hassle of buying on the other side of the world – Hong Kong is no longer the great bargain basement it once was.

Guarantees

Be careful when buying things in Hong

Kong. There are too many cases of visitors being sold defective equipment. Many retailers won't honour warranties and there is substantial pirating of brand names. Some dealers offer a local guarantee card and occasionally an international one for better brands of goods. As a general rule, things bought in Hong Kong are not returnable and deposits are not refundable.

Every guarantee should carry a complete description of the item (including model and serial numbers) as well as the date of purchase, the name and address of the shop it was purchased from and the shop's official stamp.

If you buy goods like cameras and electronics at discount prices, then make sure – if you really do need the latest model – that the model hasn't been superseded. Also find out whether the guarantee is affected by the discount. The agent or importer can tell you this; the HKTA *Official Guide to Shopping, Eating Out & Services in Hong Kong* lists the names and telephone numbers of the agents for a large number of goods sold in Hong Kong. Contacting the agents is a good way of getting a detailed explanation of what each model actually does, rather than relying on the shopkeeper's advice.

Always check prices in a few shops, take your time, and return to the shop a number of times if necessary. Don't buy anything expensive in a hurry and always get a manufacturer's guarantee that is valid worldwide. When comparing prices – on cameras for example – make sure you're comparing not only the same camera body but also the same lenses and any other accessories. And make sure, if you buy something like a video system, that it's compatible with your stuff back home.

Bargaining

Everyone who has any sense bargains in Hong Kong, but some people turn it into an exercise in east-west relations, a test of one-upmanship and the continuing

superiority of the white race. I've seen wealthy tourists who, after bargaining for an hour and cutting the price by half, walked out of a shop without the thing they wanted because the shopkeeper refused to drop the price a few dollars more. Don't bother bargaining in department stores – prices are fixed there – but bargain in all other shops and in the markets.

Shipping Goods

Goods can be sent home by post, and some stores will package and post the goods for you by sea or air. If you take the goods out of Hong Kong with you in your luggage, be warned that Hong Kong airport is strict about size and weight limitations. If your bags are overweight they'll charge you for excess baggage. Cabin baggage must also stay within a certain size – if the bag doesn't fit through the hole in the board behind the check-in desk then you can't take it with you in the cabin. (You can only have one piece of cabin baggage small enough to fit under your seat in the aircraft.)

Refunds & Rip-offs

If you're worried about being ripped off, take some of these hints. Don't shop alone – it's easier to defraud a single person; get a written receipt before handing over the money; check the receipt and make sure the goods are working and are not incomplete or secondhand, and then take the goods into your possession immediately or they may be switched; beware of 'kind' offers to box the goods; don't pay until you're holding the item and about to leave the shop. If you're defrauded, the police can't help, but you should call the Consumer Council.

One ploy of dishonest shopkeepers is to sell you attachments and fittings that should have been included with the goods in the first place (such as connecting cords between the amplifier and cassette deck of a stereo; or a camera case at a nominal charge – most new cameras come with their cases) and thus get back their 'generous' discount. Another ploy is to pack your purchases for you to collect later, removing all attachments and fittings that can be resold. The chances are you won't unpack the stuff until you get home, and by then it's too late. Just a few experiences of dissatisfied customers:

Took deposit and demanded extra $800 for camera when I came for delivery . . . use abusive language and start fist fights.

Signed a receipt for US$200 disc player. They had another receipt underneath first one, and produced a $30 record player when they went to put disc player in box. So ended up with $30 record player which cost $200 – and receipt for record player (switched!).

Bait and switch. False prices. Bad attitude!

Couldn't be worse. They try to provoke you! To start a fight . . . .

If you feel you've got a raw deal, you should return immediately to the shop, taking the goods with you plus the receipt, and try and get a refund or an exchange. If you have serious problems, you might try contacting either the Hong Kong Tourist Association on the 35th floor of the Connaught Centre (tel 5-244191) or the Hong Kong Consumer Council at 6 Heard St, ground floor, Wanchai, Hong Kong (tel 5-747388). We've had no feedback on whether either of these organisations can really do anything for you, but they may be worth a try. The Consumer Council is an independent consumer group – they have been known to publish names of rip-off shops in the papers and to name them on radio and TV, so even if you can't save your own money maybe you'll help save someone else's.

Fake Goods
The other thing to watch out for is fakes – and not just fake labels (eg: Pierre Cardin or some other famous brand) on Hong Kong-made jeans, but electronic goods which look indistinguishable from the real

INSTANT CLASS – Pierre Cardin labels sold on Temple Street...

thing. Sometimes the quality is the same as the real thing and you get it at a much cheaper price; sometimes the quality is much poorer. Almost anything you care to name is counterfeited in Hong Kong, from cigarette lighters to perfumes, Gucci leather goods, luggage and clothes. Obviously there's more risk buying electronic goods than buying clothes or luggage.

Fake watches, both digital and conventional, are a prime example. It's unwise to lay out on what appears to be a Girard-Perregaux being sold for a rock-bottom price on a street corner. Watches have a habit of falling off the backs of trucks in Hong Kong, and when they do their expensive Swiss innards are taken out and sold while their cases are filled with highly inferior local substitutes. Cameras passed off as new may actually be second-hand or faulty. Both the lens and the camera body must have one of those little gold stickers on them which says 'passed' – if they don't then the camera or lens is a factory reject right from the start. Antiques and jewellery are also problem areas – see below for details.

PLACES TO SHOP
The two big touristy shopping areas are Tsimshatsui in Kowloon and Central on the Hong Kong Island side. Besides the

shops and stores on the streets, many of the large hotels in these areas have their own shopping arcades jammed with stereo and camera shops, jewellers, antique dealers and expensive fashion boutiques. The centrepiece is Nathan's Rd, named after a former governor and once called 'Nathan's folly' because such a wide boulevard was deemed unnecessary at the time it was built. The trees that once lined the street are gone, but some would say that the folly has remained.

Opening Hours

There are no hard and fast shopping hours in Hong Kong, but generally speaking, shops in the four main shopping areas stay open as follows: Central and Western districts 10 am to 6 pm; Causeway Bay and Wanchai 10 am to 9.30 pm; Tsimshatsui, Yaumati and Mongkok 10 am to 9 pm; Tsimshatsui East 10 am to 7.30 pm. Another major shopping district is Taikoo Shing on Hong Kong Island.

Most shops are open seven days a week, although a few of the larger department stores are closed on Sunday. Some of the Japanese department stores are open Sunday and to make up for this are closed on a given weekday. Street markets are open every day and well into the night (with the exception of the Jade Market in Kowloon which is open only for a few hours of each day). Lots of shops close down for two or three days during the Chinese New Year holiday period.

Shopping Complexes

Large complexes like the *Ocean Terminal* and the *New World Centre* – both in Tsimshatsui – house dozens and dozens of shops on several floors under one roof. Hotel shops can be expensive but don't be put off buying things in the shopping complexes – you can often get a bargain in the Ocean Terminal or New World Centre just as easily as you would elsewhere. Big shopping and commercial buildings have also been built in Tsimshatsui East.

Western, Hong Kong Chinese & Japanese Department Stores

Hong Kong's original western-style department store is *Lane Crawford*, which has one branch on Nathan Rd and another one in Queen's Rd, Central. They sell British and American goods.

There are local department stores like *Wing On*, also in Queen's Rd; and *Dragon Seed* in the Connaught Centre, by the Hong Kong Star Ferry concourse.

Japanese department stores in the colony include *Daimaru*, *Matsuzakaya* and *Mitsukoshi* in Causeway Bay; *Isetan* and *Tokyu* in Kowloon; and *Da Da* in Kowloon and Wah Fu Estate.

Some department stores such as the Wing On and the Daimaru have food and drink sections.

Chinese Stores

The Chinese government runs large department stores in Hong Kong which sell almost everything that China exports, from antiques to chopsticks to do-it-yourself acupuncture kits (I'm not kidding!). You'll get a greater variety and often cheaper prices than you can in China itself! If you're going to China it's a good idea to have a look around these stores to get some guidelines on range and price. There are two types of stores: 'China Products' and 'China Arts & Crafts.'

The China Products stores sell the ordinary, domestic, down-market end of merchandise like cloth, garments, household goods and furniture as well as extravagantly embroidered silk kimonos, short happi coats, negligees, magnificently embroidered bedspreads and fabulously gaudy satin pillowcases. You can buy cheap silk by the yard and have it made into shirts and blouses. Stroll around the food section too. You'll see jars and bottles of the most amazing-looking foods and a huge selection of teas in beautiful boxes at incredibly cheap prices. The stores have their own pharmacies which sell all the old Chinese cures and medicines as well as dried seafood and deer antlers.

The Arts & Crafts stores sell the artsy/crafty, curio/antiquity stuff (but for cheap little souvenirs, stick to the Products stores). These places are like Aladdin's Cave – the porcelain departments alone stock every type of traditional Chinese teapot and cup, porcelain dishes, tiny ornaments, snuff bottles, pots and pans – all at surprisingly low prices. The toy department's worth a look too; it has beautiful kites worth buying to put on a wall even if you never fly them, lovely pencils, and painting kits.

The best of the China Products stores is the one opposite Central Market in Queen's Rd, Central. There's a combination China Products and Arts & Crafts store at 233-239 Nathan Rd, Kowloon – though it's quite a small shop. Another good China Products store is at the corner of Percival St and Hennessy Rd in Causeway Bay.

The Arts & Crafts stores are all in Tsimshatsui on the Kowloon side: in the New World Centre, Salisbury Rd; at 30 Canton Rd, near the corner of Haiphong; and in Star House, Salisbury Rd. The one in Star House is probably the most touristy of the lot.

Many of Hong Kong's small shops also sell China products. If you see a small 'made in China' stamp it's worth checking the price at China Products or Arts & Crafts first. Occasionally there will be a few cents difference and sometimes a lot more. Prices in a tourist shop, for instance, will be considerably higher than in the Chinese government stores.

The other place to find what's coming out of China is the *Hong Kong Exhibition Centre* on the 3rd and 4th floors of the low block and on the 5th floor of the main block of the China Resources Building at 26 Harbour Rd, Wanchai (open 10 am to 7 pm) opposite the Wanchai Ferry Pier. Their exhibitions have included Chinese food products, books and electronics as well as goods from some of the more distant northern provinces like Shaanxi and Xinjiang. Goods manufactured in

Hong Kong and from other countries are also exhibited in the Exhibition Centre. The *China Resources Artland* on the ground and 1st floors (open 10 am to 7 pm) sells just about every variety of artwork from China, including paintings, porcelain, jewellery and silk.

Chinese Arts & Crafts Villages

In some places village handicrafts are made and sold before your very eyes – all in the air-conditioned comfort of a modern multi-storey commercial building. Or as one tourist brochure puts it, 'See skilled artisans practising traditional Chinese arts and crafts in surroundings as authentic as China itself . . . .'

One of these places is *Peak Tower Village*, 2nd floor, Peak Tower, Victoria Peak, Hong Kong Island. You can consult a fortune-teller here (President Nixon did) and dress up in Chinese costume to have your photo taken. *Chi Fu Village* is in the Chi Fu Commercial Centre, Chi Fu Yuen, Pokfulam, Hong Kong Island. *Yee Tung Village* is in the Excelsior Hotel Shopping Arcade, 2nd floor, Causeway Bay, Hong Kong.

Factory Outlets

A number of jewellery and clothes wholesalers open their factories to customers. These might be worth checking out.

The HKTA produces a free handout listing factory outlets which are members of the Association. These and other places advertise on the back page of the classified section of the *South China Morning Post*. A very useful book available in Hong Kong is *The Complete Guide to Hong Kong Factory Bargains* by Dana Goetz, which costs around HK$40 and lists all sorts of factory outlets as well as provides useful advice on how to buy.

A wide range of goods is available from these outlets, like jewellery (including jade and opals), leatherware, silks, shoes, handbags, knitwear, woollen garments, antiques, ceramics and imitation antiques. Most of the shops are open from 9 am to 6

a slow night in the snake oil business

pm six days a week, though some close earlier on Saturday, and a few are open on Sunday.

Ivory and jade carving factories can be visited and you can see jewellery being manufactured. Just get a copy of the HKTA leaflet on arts and crafts which lists the factories which will show visitors around. The same applies to carpet, furniture and camphorwood chest factories.

Local Shops & Markets

The little hardware stores in places like Causeway Bay and the Western District on Hong Kong Island, as well as on the outer islands, are worth investigating for souvenirs. You'll find lots of odd things that make great presents – for yourself and other people.

Basketware is always good value – unfortunately the large flat rice-shakers and fruit baskets are too big to pack easily. There are still small baskets and intriguing little things like cricket cages. Or cart home armfuls of Chinese cooking stuff – woks which could knock the bottom out of the frying pan market, kitchen knives and implements.

You can also buy this sort of thing at the various markets around the colony. All the New Territory towns have markets. Cheung Chau has a morning and night market which sets up on the quayside, as well as the permanent covered one in the centre of Cheung Chau village (hardly a village now but a small town). Stanley on Hong Kong Island has a permanent market which is good for clothes, including imitation designer jeans.

The night markets of Temple St in Kowloon and the Poor Man's Nightclub near the Macau Ferry Terminal also sell clothes, cassettes, watches, ballpoint pens with built-in digital clocks, radios, knives, cheap jewellery, naughty postcards, potions, lotions and false teeth, among hundreds of other items. Local *gwailos* tend to belittle the night markets, reckoning that anything bought there has a life-expectancy of about two weeks, and that for a few dollars more you can buy infinitely better stuff – say from a little backstreet jeweller in Kowloon. Still, the best feature of the night markets is their entertainment value. Just walk around for a while and watch palmists and fortune-tellers with their caged birds; the man building a denture one tooth at a time; food stalls with their soup, noodles and satays; and the roar of mahjong tiles. The Kowloon City Market on Lion Rock Rd should also be worth checking out. Take Bus No 1 from the Kowloon Star Ferry Terminal.

CLOTHES MARKETS, SHOPS & TAILORS

Now we come to the alleys: the reason why Hong Kong women look so chic despite the fact that many of them get peasant wages. You can buy just about anything in the fashion/drapery line from a button upwards in the alleys.

The clothing alleys run between Queen's Rd and Des Voeux Rd in Central. One sells buttons and zips. Wing On St, known to the locals as 'Cloth Alley' sells materials. Li Yuen St sells costume jewellery, belts, scarves and shoes. Another street is devoted almost exclusively to handbags and luggage, and yet another to sweaters, tights, underwear and denims.

The streets between Nathan and Chatham Rds, Kowloon, and those in Causeway Bay are also good for cheap clothes: sweaters, trousers, skirts. You'll see lots of little boutiques and street hawkers. Good, cheap leather handbags are a great buy, as are Chinese padded jackets, silk scarves, real-looking fake gold jewellery and well-cut jeans. Cheap tights and underwear too. On the Kowloon side there's the Temple St night market

mentioned above, and numerous places along Granville Rd.

The night markets and alleys will have cheaper prices than the shops, but you may find that because of the largely Chinese clientele the sizes are mainly small – and you can't try things like the pants on before you buy. You're also taking a chance on quality – as you'll discover when the dyes run and run. A lot of the time you can ignore the monogram on the article – Hong Kong is monogram-mad and makes excellent reproductions of fashion luggage, handbags and clothes along with copies of the label.

Tailors exist in profusion in Hong Kong – there are about nine pages worth in the yellow pages of the telephone directory. Some require that you buy material from them, while others will let your bring your own. The more time you give the tailor, the more fittings you get and the better the outcome is likely to be.

Hong Kong does a great line in fake classy shoes. Any one of the numerous shoe shops in Wong Nei Chong Rd, Happy Valley will run you up a little pair of imitation Jourdans or Diors for a very reasonable price. Ready-to-wear shoes are available too, at good prices. Italian labels are part of the faking process.

If you are tempted to buy non-Hong Kong fashion goods, you will find they're expensive. Despite being nominally duty-free, this stuff is extremely expensive since it caters to the wealthy Hong Kong Chinese.

ANTIQUES & CURIOS

Another problem area is buying antiques – how do you tell a real Ming vase from a fake when the cracks and chips and age discolouration have been cleverly added to fool you? The New Territories teem with little factories quite legitimately turning out 'antique' carvings and porcelain with the best possible intentions. Many dealers state when a piece is a reproduction; some even restrict their sales on them. Others don't particularly feel the necessity to tell customers/suckers. You might like to know that the Tang Dynasty ran from 618 to 906 AD, the Song from 960 to 1279, the Ming from 1368 to 1644 and the Qing from 1566 to 1911. So a Qing vase need only be 75-odd years old, which in western terms would hardly qualify as an antique. Basically, if you don't know what to look for or who to buy from, the serious purchase of antiques is not for the tourist on a stop-over!

There are still many beautiful things to buy in Hong Kong, including fine examples of Chinese art and craft – not necessarily antique, which doesn't matter as long as you are not paying antique prices. Cat and Ladder Sts, behind Queen's Rd, used to be the happy hunting ground for antiques and curios but the little shops and hawkers have been cleared away. Nowadays the place to look is in the junk shops on nearby Hollywood Rd where there's a brisk trade in porcelain, bronzes, cloisonné and the like. Many of the shops which used to be in Cat and Ladder Sts have moved here. True, this street has probably been gone through with a fine comb, but there are interesting curios to pick up, like old postcards, or picture magazines of the glorious Nippon troops issued by the Japanese army during the occupation of China.

If you want to take one good piece of Chinoiserie back – carving, figurine or whatever – then it would probably be best to stick to the Chinese government Arts & Crafts Stores mentioned above. Here at least you'll know you're getting exactly what you pay for. They have good antique departments with scrolls, paintings, jade, porcelain and old carvings. They also have good supplies of camphorwood chests – a favourite buy for foreigners – and beautiful carpets made in China.

For the serious antique buyer, two Hong Kong auction houses – *Lammert's* and *Sotheby Parke Bernet* – hold regular sales. There is also an annual International Asian Antiques Fair held in Hong Kong.

JEWELLERY

Much the same ground rules for antiques apply to jewellery. If you don't know what to look for then you can expect the same lack of success – and there's plenty of fake stuff around.

There are large numbers of jewellery shops in the streets of Tsimshatsui and in the large hotels and shopping arcades. You can buy any precious stone here, including sapphires from Burma, rubies from Ceylon, opals from Australia and Mexico, and emeralds from the Soviet Union. Green transparent agate – shipped in from Burma – is indistinguishable from emerald to the tourist's naive eye. Other stuff turns up in shops under exotic names: plain old garnet, pretty as it is, becomes 'Arizona ruby'; yellow quartz is flogged off as topaz; speckled quartz becomes 'Indian jade'; and so on.

Jade

Jade is another problem. The deep green colour associated with some jade pieces can be achieved with a dye-pot, as can the white, green, red, lavender and brown of other pieces. Also, green soapstone and plastic can be passed off as jade. Most 'Chinese' jade sold in Hong Kong comes from overseas, from South Africa, New Zealand, Australia and the US. One trick of jade merchants is to sell a supposedly solid piece of jade jewellery which is actually a thin slice of jade backed by green glue and a quartz.

It is said that the test for jade is to try scratching it with a steel blade; real jade will not scratch. Another test is to put water on the jade. If it is genuine, the water will stay in droplets.

One of the main places where locals buy jade in Hong Kong is the jade market at the junction of Reclamation and Kansu Sts under the flyover in the Yaumati district in Kowloon, about 250 metres away from the old site in Canton Rd.

Ivory

Ivory tusks do reach Hong Kong, and ivory

jewellery and ornaments are a big seller. Whether you want to keep the elephant killers in business is up to you. Once again, ivory can be artificially aged and the dye-pot is in constant use to produce the uniformity of colour which sells so well. Camel bone, walrus and plastic are used to produce fakes.

Tsimshatsui is full of ivory but you might do better to try the Stanley/Wellington Sts areas in Central which are packed with ivory shops used by Chinese as well as *gwailos*.

Some countries – like the USA and Australia – prohibit the import of ivory. If you want to check if that rule applies to your own country, you can contact your embassy or consulate in Hong Kong, or telephone the Hong Kong Government Trade Department (the ivory section is at 3-7222491).

Diamonds

The Diamond Importers Association, Room 10, 8-10 Duddell St, Central (tel 5-235497), will give you a list of members who give a fair price and guarantee. If you just want to look, they might be able to make an appointment for you with a retailer or cutting factory.

Gold & Gems

Hong Kong has a reputation for being a cheap place for gems and gold, although this probably isn't true. What is cheap is the labour which makes turning the gems and gold into wearable jewellery. The cost of gold is tied to world markets and fluctuates accordingly. The marking of gold items is *not* mandatory in Hong Kong, the only legal requirement being that any marking should be accurate. The HKTA requires its members to mark any gold or gold-alloy item they display or sell with the fineness of the gold or gold-alloy, and with the identity of the manufacturer or retailer.

Nightlife

Sitting in your hotel room or lying on your dormitory bed has many things to recommend it, not least of which is it's cheap. Unfortunately it's also very dull. There is much more to Hong Kong nightlife than vegetating in front of the television set in Travellers Hostel, familiar as the American and British cartoons may be. Yes, it costs money to go out – far less money than it cost you to get to Asia in the first place – and if you're philosophical about it you can spend your money having a good time in Hong Kong and save some in China where most of the streets are dead and everything is boarded up by 9.30 pm. You needn't necessarily think in terms of pubs, discos, bars and other venues that require money; some cultural shows in Hong Kong are free. Just walking through a street lined with *dai pai dongs* is more entertaining than the Bar City Disco any night, and there's often the added bonus of whole Cantonese opera ensembles performing on the sidewalk.

HAPPY HOUR

A useful phrase to remember in Hong Kong is 'happy hour' – the local custom designed to drag in drinkers at off-peak time. During happy hour, drinks in clubs, bars and hotels are half price. The binge actually lasts anywhere between two to four hours, some time between 5 and 9 pm, so if you get involved in a drinking session watch out for the end of happy hour when prices leap or measures plummet. Girlie bars and clubs will offer you a straight half-price drink. The more expensive hotels offer their own version of the custom, which is a double for the price of a single – and they often lay on small chow, which with a little discreet application you can turn into a complete frayed-shoestring budget meal while you are very slowly sipping your cut-price drink.

Drink prices vary considerably in Hong Kong according to surroundings and services offered. In the girlie bars you can buy a beer for yourself but you're expected to buy drinks for the women. They won't want beer – instead they'll drink orangeade or 7UP for which you'll be charged the price of a screwdriver or champagne. Still, if it's company you want you'll just have to pay for it by the book. You can try sitting on your own, but unless you are a regular whose foibles are accepted you won't get a very warm reception.

Discos and nightclubs are the most expensive places in which to drink. Most have an entry charge which includes the price of the first one or two drinks. The cost of eating there varies – in the more expensive places you could be up for a couple of hundred dollars for a meal.

PUBS & BARS

If the girlie bars are not for you but you still want to drink – especially if you want to drink in mixed company – then head for one of the ethnic bars which have sprung up in the last decade. British and Australian-style pubs abound. Drinks are cheaper than in the girlie bars – but not cheap – though you can usually get a reasonably priced meal. Some places have singers and bands while others have no distinguishable culture at all.

British pubs started shooting up like mushrooms in the mid-70s. They offer imported British beers and serve all the standard British fare like ploughman's lunches, pies and fish 'n' chips.

Highly recommended is the *Godown* in the basement of Sutherland House, Chater Rd, Central – this place started it all and became the unofficial Hong Kong & Shanghai Bank social club. A jazz band performs every Wednesday night from 8.30 pm to 12.30 am.

The *Mad Dogs Pub* at 33 Wyndham St,

Central, is a marvellously reproduced Australian pub – some people say it's a marvellously reproduced British (or more specifically Scottish) pub. It takes up two floors. Serves light fillers but not meals.

The *Jockey Pub* is in Swire House, Central (in between Connaught and Chater Rds, next to the Mandarin Hotel). It doubles as an English pub and a disco in the evening. Further east, the *Bull & Bear*, ground floor, 10 Harcourt Rd, Central, is a rowdy, friendly place.

The *Dickens Bar* in the Excelsior Hotel, Gloucester Rd, Causeway Bay, does good food and has music most nights. A resident jazz band plays every Sunday afternoon from 3 pm.

The real pub-crawl is in Lockhart Rd, Wanchai, where barely a page from this book can be wedged between the spaces that separate the line-up. The *Bell Inn* is at No 94; *Old China Hand Tavern* is at No 104; *Hunters Castle Pub* is at Nos 114-120; *Horse & Groom* is at No 126; *Elephants Castle Pub* is next door at 128; and *Kangaroo Lounge & Pub* is at No 180. Opening hours vary but something is bound to be open from about 11 am or noon through to the early hours of the morning. Most serve up traditional British pub food like bacon, eggs and chips for around HK$18 a serve.

In Tsimshatsui a typical British pub is the *Blacksmith's Arms* at 16 Minden Avenue, behind Chungking Mansions. The *White Stag* at 72 Canton Rd, Kowloon, has an imitation Tudor-style interior.

For a return to down under, Aussies head for *Ned Kelly's Last Stand* at 11A Ashley Rd, Tsimshatsui. There's lots of bushranger memorabilia around the walls. Meat pies, steak and other Australian delicacies can be had at reasonable prices, and jugs of imported beer run from around HK$60. They have a nightly jazz band – you can jam with them if you can play. The pub's casual atmosphere makes it a good place for meeting other travellers. You may find Americans and Canadians outnumber Australians by 10 to one!

Also in Tsimshatsui, the *Waltzing Matilda Arms* is a gay pub at 22 Cameron Rd. Its cousin the *Waltzing Matilda Inn* at 9 Cornwall Avenue is a basic bar, no frills.

All the major hotels have numerous bars of course, some with bands (like the Dickens Bar in the Excelsior Hotel, mentioned above). There are too many to name all of them and anyway they're not hard to find, but if you like drinking in plush surroundings you could drop into: the *Sky Lounge* on the 18th floor of the Sheraton, corner Nathan and Salisbury Rds, Tsimshatsui (not cheap but a good view); the *Camelot Bar* in the Merlin Hotel, 2 Hankow Rd, Tsimshatsui; *Yum Sing Bar* in the Lee Gardens Hotel (jazz band most nights), Hysan Avenue, Causeway Bay; *Dragonboat Bar* in the Hilton, Queen's Rd, Central.

GIRLIE BARS

The World of Suzie Wong and its girlie bars is a persistent image of Hong Kong – even if the movie of the book dates way back to 1960 (and the book itself to 1957). The image is rather faded now, but the girlie bars are still operating in Suzie's old territory in Wanchai on the Hong Kong Island side, and also in Tsimshatsui on the Kowloon side. However, the main concentration of straight-out brothels is no longer in Wanchai but in Kowloon's Mongkok district.

Suzie would find Wanchai a bit quiet now. Lockhart Rd used to be the golden girlie strip during the Vietnam War, where war-weary soldiers would knock off Chinese women in between knocking off Vietnamese peasants. It's still worth a look but the bright lights are not so dense anymore. In the less pretentious places the entertainment is just juke-box music, the drinks cheaper. Others have bands, usually Filipino musicians who can make perfect replicas of any sound in the world.

Bunched together on Lockhart Rd, Wanchai, are a number of topless and girlie bars: the *Mermaid* at No 90, the *Washington* at 102, the *Butterfly* at 100, the *Carnival* at 112, and diagonally across the road you'll find the *Panda*, *Popeye* and *San Francisco* – among many others!

One of the better-known topless bars – where you pay extra to have your drink served by a woman dressed only in her knickers – is the appropriately named *Bottoms Up* at 14 Hankow Rd, Tsimshatsui, run by a former Windmill woman. Despite the bare flesh it has a cosy 'nice girls' atmosphere and a regular clientele who seem to treat it like a local, at least until 9 pm when happy hour ends and prices double. It gets its share of groups of women having a night out. Also in Tsimshatsui: the *Red Lips Bar* at 1A Lock Rd; the *Red Lion* at 15 Ashley Rd; and *Four Sisters Inn* at 1 Minden Row. *Club Casanova* is at 1A Mody Rd, opposite the Holiday Inn; and the *Playboy* (bar, nightclub, bunnies and floorshow) is in Peking Rd.

There's any number of other topless places in the side streets of Tsimshatsui and down Lockhart Rd, Wanchai. Some girlie bars, hostess clubs or whatever you want to call them don't exactly encourage women customers. If you're male you're expected to drink with the establishment's women. Some topless bars are more than happy to serve women – perhaps it reinforces the look-don't-touch atmosphere of these places.

NIGHTCLUBS & DISCOS

Disco is a big thing in Hong Kong – and getting bigger every year across the border in China too. Many Hong Kong discos are in the top tourist hotels – and all of them are expensive. To get in you'll be looking at anything from HK$60 to $70, but this usually includes the first one or two drinks. Prices rise on Friday and Saturday nights, and a few places charge well over HK$100 entrance fee.

Nightspots favoured by western expatriates in Hong Kong include the *Godown*, basement of Sutherland House,

Chater Rd, Central; and the *Frontpage*, 175 Lockhart Rd, Central.

Top-priced hotel discos include the *Hollywood East*, Hotel Regal Meridien, Mody Rd, Tsimshatsui East. A bit less expensive is the *Talk of the Town*, top floor, Excelsior Hotel, Gloucester Rd, Causeway Bay. Lower down on the price ladder try the *Eagle's Nest* in the Hilton Hotel, Queen's Rd, Central, which also has a Chinese restaurant ('Guests may don Mandarin robes for their Chinese banquet and dance the tango to the nostalgic tunes of our house orchestra'). *Another World Disco* is in the basement of the Holiday Inn, Nathan Rd, Tsimshatsui. *Good Earth Disco* is in the Sheraton Hotel, corner Nathan and Sheraton Rds, Kowloon.

Other hotels with discos and/or nightclubs include the *Mandarin*, Connaught Rd, Central; the *Harbour* and Luk Kwok, both on Gloucester Rd, Wanchai; and the *Plaza* on Gloucester Rd, Causeway Bay. In Tsimshatsui try the *Ambassador*, corner Nathan and Middle Rds; the *Holiday Inn*, Nathan Rd; the *Peninsula*, Salisbury Rd; the *Regent*, Salisbury Rd; and the *Shangri-La*, Mody Rd.

Other discos on the Hong Kong Island side include the well-established *Disco Disco* at 40 D'Aguilar St, Central, noted for its gay clientele; the giant-size *Today's World* with tomorrow's prices at 443 Lockhart Rd, Wanchai; and the *Makati Inn*, Luard Rd, Wanchai.

In Tsimshatsui try the *New York New York Discoclub* in the New World Centre; and in the same building the memorable *Bar City*, a conglomeration of eight bars and discos in eight tasteless decors – each room has a different theme including 'Country and Western' (with mechanical bull) 'Cutty Sark' (an imitation boat) and the 'World of Suzie Wong' (imitation Hong Kong). Another disco is *Spats* at 26 Hankow Rd, Kowloon.

If you like your nightlife rather more elegant and less frenetic, you can dine between courses when you dine at *Gaddi's*, the Peninsula Hotel's exclusive restaurant and one of the most expensive in Hong Kong. Down the road at the New World Centre there's *Cabaret*, where there's a band and on some nights a floor show. The *Capital Restaurant*, 2nd floor, Chungking Mansions, is done up in a sort of circus-*cum*-McDonald's decor and has nightly Chinese floor shows.

Many of the top hotels have nightspots with imported entertainment. They sometimes run under the name of 'supper clubs' or something similar, and tend to be fairly formal places requiring jacket and tie for men and glad rags for women. 'Nightclub' can be a misleading term; many high-class places call themselves nightclubs – as do some sordid little bars which are girlie bars under another name, and where the floor show may be a couple of people or more doing simulated sex acts.

CONCERTS & CULTURE

Programmes of Chinese instrumental music, opera, puppetry, folk songs and dancing, lion dances, acrobatics and kung-fu are presented by the HKTA, the Arts Centre and the Urban Council. Lists of what's happening can be obtained from the Arts Centre or the HKTA offices.

The HKTA has a monthly leaflet listing cultural shows at a number of venues. Also ask for their leaflet *Chinese Festivals & Special Events* which lists all sorts of events throughout the whole year – anything from the go-cart Grand Prix (no kidding), film and music festivals, and religious celebrations to the annual Miss Hong Kong meat parade. The *South China Morning Post* has a daily 'What's on Today' column which lists events at the Arts Centre and City Hall, as well as library opening times.

The Hong Kong Arts Centre (tel 5-271122) is at 2 Harbour Rd, Wanchai, Hong Kong. It offers Chinese film shows and music as well as western films, music and other cultural events. Bookings can be made at the Arts Centre; or at some of the MTR Ticketmate kiosks, including

those at Tsimshatsui and Jordan stations and at Old Mercury House, 3 Connaught Rd, Central. Book by phone at 5-280626. Art exhibitions are also held at the Arts Centre.

There are two arts festivals a year. The Asian one is in October and the western one is in January/February. Details can be obtained and seats booked at HKTA offices in Australia, Europe, the States and elsewhere overseas. Held about the same time as the arts festival is the Hong Kong fringe festival. An international film festival is held around March and April, and an exhibition of photographs and posters is held each April.

Chinese cultural shows and events – like Fujianese string puppets, Chinese folk songs and dances, acrobatics and magic – are held in the Ocean Terminal Concourse and the New World Centre, Tsimshatsui; and in the City Hall and Landmark Building on the Hong Kong Island side.

Chinese cultural shows are also held every Thursday between 1 and 2 pm at the City Plaza Shopping Centre, King's Rd, Tai Koo Shing, Hong Kong Island (Tai Koo Shing is just east of Causeway Bay). Once again, enquire at the HKTA about what's on. City Plaza even has an ice-skating rink. It's easy enough to get to; there's a free bus every hour on the hour from 10 am onwards from the Star Ferry terminal on the Hong Kong Island side; alternatively, the Shaukiwan tram passes the main entrance or you can take the MTR to Taikoo Station.

Pop concerts are usually staged at the Lee Theatre on Leighton Rd in Happy Valley, or at the City Hall. Check the local papers for names of performers. Hong Kong has a number of classical orchestras – again, check with the HKTA or the newspapers.

CINEMAS

Hong Kong is full of fanatical cinema-goers. There are about 90 to 100 cinemas in the colony and they're always packed. A large proportion of them show US or British films while the rest show mainly locally made kung-fu epics, comedies and melodramas, with the sound at full volume and preceded by equally loud advertisements and trailers. Hong Kong's leading movie companies are Shaw Brothers with its huge Movietown studios on Clearwater Bay Rd in the New Territories; and Golden Harvest, which started the Bruce Lee kung-fu movies.

All movies shown in Hong Kong have to be approved by the government Panel of Film Censors. According to the Hong Kong Year Book, the censorship standards are 'drawn from ascertained community views, and a panel comprising 90 members of the public assists the Panel of Film Censors in reflecting community views.' Democracy Hong Kong-style. Western films generally get chopped, but less so by the censors than by the avaricious cinema managers who want to cram as many showings as possible in one day. Non-box-office smashes often have a short run – like one performance – and are taken off without notice. Other films have been known to get chopped in an effort to remove anything regarded as offensive to the People's Republic, and some have even been banned from being shown in Hong Kong for the same reason (this has been going on for many years).

Check the daily papers for screenings. Shows usually start at around 12.30, 2.30, 5.30, 7.30 and 9.30 pm (the two-hour slot thus making chopping necessary), with special or late shows on holidays and at weekends. Ticket prices for the main cinemas start at around HK$15.

Cultural associations like the Alliance Française and the Goethe Institute also show films, open to the public. There are a couple of film societies in Hong Kong, of which the best known is Studio One. If you like films – foreign, local, commercial, experimental – they'd be worth contacting at the Hua Hsia Building, Gloucester Rd, Wanchai, tel 5-202282.

GAMBLING

Apart from a few licensed lotteries and horse-racing there is no other *legal* gambling in Hong Kong. If you want to lose your money then go to the casinos in Macau.

FREEBIES & CHEAPIES

For a good time without paying for it – or paying as little as possible for it, you stingy bastard – there are a couple of possibilities.

As mentioned above, sidewalk performances of Cantonese opera are sometimes held amidst the night markets – try the top end of Temple St on a busy night. Chinese opera performances are also held at Kowloon's Lai Chi Kok Amusement Park and you can then wander around the park itself. To get there, take Bus No 6A from the Kowloon-side Star Ferry Terminal to the end of the line. There's a small admission fee to the park, and it's open daily 11 am to 11 pm (an hour earlier on Sunday and public holidays).

Personally, I'd rather watch the Chinese gut frogs then endure another Madonna record. If you can't afford/stand discos, the night markets like Temple Street on the Kowloon side and the Poor Man's Nightclub near the Macau Ferry Terminal on the Hong Kong side are great entertainment value – as are the palm readers and assorted fortune-tellers. Or head to the horse-races every Wednesday night (September to May) at Happy Valley or Shatin (more details in the Hong Kong Island chapter).

If you want to know what it would feel like to be an extra in *Metropolis*, try a late-night promenade along the almost-deserted elevated walkways of very high-rise Central – this will give you an awesome sense of your own puniness. Take the Peak Tram to the peak, or a top-deck tram ride from Kennedy Town to Shaukiwan perhaps – Hong Kong by night is a very different experience from Hong Kong by day. There are also night-time harbour cruises (see the section on Tours in the Getting Around chapter of this book for details), which could be a pleasant way to spend a few hours. If you wonder why Hong Kong has no flashing neon lights, it's because of the city's proximity to the airport – amidst all those other lights the pilots need some way to tell the difference between Nathan Rd and the runway.

TELEVISION

If all else fails, there's always the English-language television. It's almost indistinguishable in form, content and standards from Australian TV: a mish-mash of mind-bogglingly stupid American and British veggie-coms, old movies featuring dead actors, live actors in dead movies, Dukes of Hazzard re-runs, and James Bond jerking off in Kowloon. The best thing I've ever seen on Hong Kong TV was a People's Republic documentary about an operation to remove a rudimentary second mouth from the side of some guy's head. English and Chinese-language TV and radio programmes are listed in the *South China Morning Post* and the *Hong Kong Standard* daily newspapers; Macau television programmes are also listed.

TEA DANCES

Before the rollicking days of R & R, tea dances were the thing. Charles Grey started the habit in Shanghai in the 1930s and it was soon imported into Hong Kong, where it quickly caught on since both tea and women were plentiful. Twenty years ago the colony had hundreds of ballrooms and there were a few left several years ago. The best-known was the *Tonnochy* in Tonnochy Rd, Wanchai, with strictly 1930s decor right down to the long couch on which the women sat, and the ornate goldfish tank. It was a demure place where about 200 hostesses, smartly and quietly dressed, sipped tea or danced sedately with sober-suited businessmen. A tea dance would start at 5.30 pm. A dance ticket costing a few dollars enabled a man to pick a girl from the stable and dance, drink tea (served with melon seeds or dried beef to chew on), or talk for the space of one *chung* – two pieces of music or around eight minutes. After 9 pm the price of a ticket went up but the chung lasted for four numbers (around 15 minutes). Despite its western origins the tea dance became a Chinese pursuit of pleasure. Whether such dances are still held in Hong Kong I have no idea.

Macau

Macau

Only 65 km from Hong Kong but pre-dating it by some 300 years, Macau is the oldest surviving European settlement in Asia, a city of cobbled side streets, baroque churches, Portuguese fortresses, Chinese temples, half a dozen casinos, five-star hotels, unpronounceable Portuguese street names, decaying colonial villas, the final resting place of numerous European seamen and soldiers, and a hybrid of Portuguese and Chinese culture, cooking and people.

Macau is an oddity which has managed to cling to the Chinese coast – despite attempts by the Chinese, the Spanish and the Dutch to brush it off – since the middle of the 16th century. For over a hundred years previously the Portuguese had been pushing down the west African coast in their search for a sea route to the Far East, delayed by the immediate attractions of slaves and gold from Guinea which brought immediate material rewards, and by their ambition to find the mysterious Christian king Prester John who would join them in a crusade against the Moslems.

When Vasco da Gama's ships rounded the southern cape of Africa and arrived in Calicut in India in 1498, the Portuguese suddenly got a whiff of the enormous profits to be made from the Asian trade – and since the trade was almost exclusively in the hands of Moslems they had the added satisfaction (and excuse) that any blow against their commercial rivals was a blow against the infidels. In practice there was never any real intention of conquering large tracts of territory, colonising foreign lands or converting en masse the native populations to Christianity; trade was always first and foremost in Portuguese minds. To this end a vague plan was devised to bring all the important Indian Ocean trading ports under Portuguese control as well as to establish whatever fortifications were needed to protect their trade.

Thus the capture of Malacca on the Malay peninsula in 1511 (their first ships having arrived there in 1509) followed the capture of Goa on the west coast of India, and preceded the Portuguese attempt to subdue the 'Spice Islands' of the Moluccas in what is now Indonesia and thus control the lucrative spice trade. The Portuguese never did manage to monopolise the trade. As the years rolled by their determination and ability to do so declined and by the end of the 16th century their efforts were brought to a close by the arrival in Indonesia of powerful Dutch fleets also bent on wresting control of the spice trade.

More encouraging for the Portuguese was the trade with China and Japan. On their earliest voyages to India the Portuguese had heard of a strange, light-skinned people called the 'Chin' whose huge ships had once visited India (from 1405 to 1433 the second Ming Emperor Yong Le had dispatched several enormous maritime expeditions which had made contact with many parts of Asia and Africa) but whose voyages had suddenly ceased. When the Portuguese arrived in Malacca in 1511 they came upon a number of junks with Chinese captains; realising now that the Chins were not a mythical people, and concluding that they had come from the 'Cathay' of Marco Polo's travels, a small party of Portuguese were sent northwards to find out what they could and possibly open trade with the Chinese. The first Portuguese to set foot on Chinese soil did so in 1513 at the mouth of the Pearl River, near what is now Macau and Hong Kong. The first Portuguese arrived in Japan in 1542 by accident, their ship having been blown off course.

By and large, initial Portuguese contact

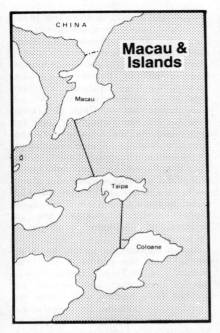

CHINA

Macau & Islands

Macau

Taipa

Coloane

apparently in return for ridding the area of marauding pirates who plagued this stretch of the coast, though the peninsula was never formally ceded to the Portuguese.

Macau grew rapidly as a trading centre, largely because the Chinese wanted to trade with foreign countries but were forbidden to go abroad on penalty of death. The most lucrative trade route of the Portuguese was the long circuit from the west of India to Japan and back, with Macau as the essential link. Acting as agents for the Chinese merchants, they took Chinese goods to the west coast of India, exchanging them for cotton and textiles which they then took to Malacca. In Malacca they sold the cottons to local merchants in exchange for spices and aromatic woods. They then continued to Japan, where they sold their Malacca cargo for Japanese silver, swords, lacquerware and fans, returning to Macau to exchange them for more Chinese goods.

With the Japanese forbidden to enter Chinese ports, the Arabs displaced by the Portuguese, the trade of other Asian nationalities with China largely insignificant, and no other Europeans yet on the scene, somewhat by accident the Portuguese had become the carriers of all large-scale international commerce with China and Japan. By the beginning of the 17th century Macau supported several thousand permanent inhabitants, including perhaps a thousand Portuguese. The rest were Chinese Christian converts, mixed-race Christians from Malacca, and Japanese Christians as well as a large number of African, Indian and Malay slaves. Large numbers of Chinese citizens worked in the town as hawkers, labourers and servants. There were many Chinese traders as well.

Trade was the most important activity of the new town, but Macau was also fast becoming a centre of Christianity in the Far East. Priests and missionaries accompanied Portuguese ships, though the attack was not jointly planned and the

with China did not go well, and for years their attempts to gain a permanent trading base on the China coast met with little success. In the early 1550s they came to some sort of agreement with Cantonese officials to settle on Sanchuang, a small island about 80 km to the south-west of the mouth of the Pearl River. In 1553 the Portuguese abandoned Sanchuang due to its exposed anchorage, moving to another island closer to the Pearl River. To the north-east was a peninsula of land where the Portuguese also frequently anchored. It had two natural harbours – an inner one on the West River, and an outer one in a bay facing the Pearl River – and to its south were some sheltering islands. Around 1556 or 1557 the Portuguese and some Canton officials made an agreement which allowed the Portuguese to rent this peninsula of land – known variously as Amagao, Amacon, Aomen and Macau –

interests of traders and missionaries frequently conflicted. Among the earliest missionaries was Francis Xavier (later canonised) of the Jesuit order, who had spent the years 1549 to 1551 in Japan attempting to convert the heathens there before turning his attention to China. Xavier made it as far as Sanchuang – having been stalled by other Portuguese who feared the consequences of his meddling in Chinese affairs – where he died in December 1552. However, in the years to follow it was Jesuit missionaries, not traders, who were able to penetrate China beyond Macau and Canton.

The Portuguese who stayed in Macau, along with their Macanese (mixed-blood) descendants, succeeded in creating a home away from home with luxurious rococo houses and splendid baroque churches – paid for with the wealth generated by their monopoly on trade with China and Japan. These structures included the Basilica of Sao Paulo, hailed as the greatest monument to Christianity in the East. Apart from traders and priests, this odd little colony also attracted a number of colourful adventurer-madmen, artists and poets. Among them was the 16th-century poet Luis de Camoes, who was banished from Portugal to Goa and then to Macau. He is said to have written at least part of his epic poem Os Lusiadas, which recounts the voyage of Vasco da Gama to India, in Macau – although some say he was never in the colony at all. British artist George Chinnery spent a quarter of a century in Macau from 1825 until his death in 1852 and is remembered for his paintings of the place and its people.

The Portuguese decline was as rapid as its success. In 1580 Spanish armies occupied Portugal. Then, in the early years of the 17th century, the Dutch began making their presence felt in the Far East. In response, the Portuguese at Macau began building fortresses in anticipation of Dutch attacks. The Dutch made several forays on Macau – including major but

unsuccessful attacks in 1607 and 1627. Then the Japanese became suspicious of Portuguese (and also Spanish) intentions, and began persecuting Japanese Christians, eventually closing the country to foreign trade in 1637. In 1640 the Dutch took Malacca by force. Although Portugal regained its independence in 1640, all trade connections with China and Japan were cut off. The Portuguese could no longer provide the Chinese with the Japanese silver they wanted in exchange for their silk and porcelain, nor with spices since the spice trade was now in the hands of the Dutch. Macau was no longer of any use to the Chinese and by 1640 they had closed the port of Canton to the Portuguese. Macau rapidly deteriorated into an impoverished settlement in danger of extinction.

Macau managed to survive by other means. From the middle of the 18th century – as the French, Dutch, Danes, Swedes, Americans and Spanish all profited from trading with China via Canton – restrictions and regulations concerning non-Portuguese residing in Macau were lifted and the colony in effect became an outpost for all of Europe in China, a position which it held until the British got Hong Kong in 1841 and other Chinese ports were forced open to foreign trade in the years that followed. Until the middle of the 19th century the history of Macau is a long series of incidents – incitement, standoffs, threats, disputes and attacks involving the Portuguese, Chinese and British – as the Portuguese attempted to maintain their grasp on Macau. The Portuguese even made plans around 1850 to attack Canton as the British had done during the Opium Wars, so that they could dictate a Chinese-Portuguese treaty. A series of disasters (including the intended flag-ship of the fleet blowing up off Taipa Island) meant that this plan never came to fruition and the Portuguese were once again forced to settle their differences with China through negotiation. However, it was not until

1887 that a treaty was signed in which China effectively recognised Portuguese sovereignty over Macau. As for the problem of keeping Macau financially afloat, that had been more or less solved by Governor Isidoro Francisco Guimaraes (1851-1863), who introduced what has become the best-known feature of the colony – licensed gambling.

Macau had turned into something of a decaying back-water town by the late 19th century, though it continued to serve as a place of refuge for Chinese fleeing war and famine in the north. When the Sino-Japanese War erupted in the 1930s, the population swelled to a formidable 500,000. Europeans also took refuge here during WW II because the Japanese honoured Portuguese neutrality and did not take Macau as they did Hong Kong. More people came in 1949 when the Communists took power in China. Macau was also a destination for the Vietnamese boat people from 1978 until about 1980. Somehow the tiny place managed to contain them all.

Macau's last great convulsion occurred in 1966, when China's Cultural Revolution spilled over into the colony. Macau was stormed by Red Guards and there were violent riots. A few Red Guards were shot dead by Portuguese troops. The then-governor reportedly proposed that the troubles could be ended if Portugal simply left Macau forever – but fearing loss of foreign trade that was carried on through Macau and Hong Kong, the Chinese backed off. In 1974 a military coup in Portugal brought a left-wing government to power which proceeded to divest Portugal of the last remnants of its empire (including Mozambique, Angola and East Timor), yet the Chinese told the Portuguese that they preferred to leave Macau as it was. The future of Macau can only be guessed at. The same solution to the Hong Kong problem might be applied, or the colony could go on much as it has been for decades to come.

Today the Portuguese government officially regards Macau as a piece of Chinese territory under Portuguese administration. It has a governor who is appointed by the president of Portugal. In theory, the main governing body is the Legislative Assembly of 17 members – six of them are elected by a suffrage of some 51,000 registered voters, five are appointed by the governor and six are selected by what may be termed 'economic interest groups.' Municipal affairs are handled by the *Leal Senado* or 'Loyal Senate.' Portuguese is the official language, though Cantonese is – obviously – more widely spoken. English is regarded as a third language though it's more commonly spoken then Portuguese. Macau includes two islands – Taipa and Coloane – within its boundaries, and covers a total area of just 15½ square km. The population consists of about 95% Chinese and about 3% Portuguese and other Europeans; the rest are from other regions. In all, something like 350,000 to 400,000 people live in the colony.

Macau's main industry, gambling, is run by a syndicate of Chinese business-people trading under the name of STDM – Sociedade de Turismo e Diversoes de Macau (Macao Travel & Amusement Co). This group made a bid for, and won, monopoly rights on all licensed gambling in Macau in 1962. About a third of government revenue comes from gambling, another third from direct and indirect taxes, and the rest from land rents and service charges. The colony has various light industries – fireworks, textile and garment production, for example – and wages are much lower than in Hong Kong.

Tourism has been getting a shot in the arm in recent years, with a number of large luxury hotels being built on the mainland and on the islands. Yet apart from the Chinese gamblers, the majority of tourists who go to Macau spend just a few whistle-stop hours there. Many who go to Hong Kong don't bother going to Macau at all – a misfortune because it is one of those curious places where something new can be found on every visit.

Incidentally, Macau means the 'City of God.' It takes its name from A-Ma-Gau, the Bay of A-Ma. At Barra Point stands the A-Ma Temple which dates back to the early 16th century. According to legend, A-Ma, a poor girl looking for a passage to Canton, was refused by the wealthy junk owners but a fisherman took her on board. A storm blew up and wrecked all the junks except the boat carrying the girl. When it landed in Macau, the girl disappeared, only to reappear later as a goddess on the spot where the fisherman built her temple.

VISAS

For many visitors all that's needed for Macau is a passport. Visas are not required of Portuguese citizens, and Brazilian citizens do not need them for stays of up to six months. Citizens of Australia, Austria, Belgium, Canada, Denmark, France, Greece, Italy, Netherlands, New Zealand, Norway, Spain, Sweden, the UK, the USA and West Germany, plus a few Asian countries, do not require visas for stays of less than 90 days. British Commonwealth subjects who are residents of Hong Kong do not require visas for visits of up to seven days. Other residents of Hong Kong don't need visas for visits of up to three days.

If you do need a visa they're available on arrival in Macau. They cost M$52 and are valid for 20 days in Macau or two visits within 20 days. You can also get visas from Portuguese consulates abroad. The Portuguese consulate in Hong Kong is in Room 1405, Central Building, 3 Pedder St, Central (tel 5-231338). A visa stamp could make an interesting souvenir once the People's Republic takes over the colony.

If you enter Macau from China via the border town of Gongbei you may find there are no visa or customs formalities on the Macau side (but there are on the Chinese side).

CUSTOMS

Customs formalities are few – it's unlikely you'll be bothered by them. You're allowed to bring in a reasonable quantity of tobacco, alcohol and perfumes; and like Hong Kong, Macau customs takes a *very* dim view of drugs. There are no export duties on anything bought in Macau, and that includes antiques, gold, jewellery, radios and cameras. However, Hong Kong authorities will allow one bottle of wine or spirits plus 50 cigarettes into Hong Kong duty-free from Macau, and when you come back from Macau they may check your bags. They're also very touchy about people bringing in fireworks.

MONEY

The Macau unit of currency is the pataca, usually written as M$, and which comprises 100 avos.

The pataca is worth slightly less than the Hong Kong dollar, with a permissible variation of up to 10%. For convenience the two currencies are interchangeable, at least in Macau where both Hong Kong notes and coins are accepted. In practice, Macau currency is not accepted in Hong Kong except at the banks – where the exchange rate is truly dreadful!

Coins come as 10, 20 and 50 avos and one and five patacas. Notes are five, 10, 50, 100 and 500 patacas. Commemorative gold $1000 and silver $100 coins have been issued along the way, though it's hardly likely you'll see them used as currency.

Changing Money

Foreign currency and traveller's cheques can be changed at the banks in Macau. There are a number of Portuguese and foreign banks in the colony as well as branches of major Hong Kong banks. They also be changed with the money-changers (they operate 24 hours a day in the casinos) or at the big hotels, if that's where you're staying.

The Seng Heng Bank is conveniently at 142 Avenida Almeida Ribeiro and is

Macau Banknote

another place that will change foreign currency and travellers' cheques. They will give you Hong Kong dollars if you ask for them. There appears to be no money-changer at the ferry wharf, so before you leave Hong Kong, exchange some Hong Kong currency for Macau currency. You'll need it for the buses which don't accept Hong Kong money.

Try and use up all your Macau currency before leaving. You can exchange the leftover currency at the moneychangers and banks in Hong Kong, but the rate is

Macau Banknote

dreadful; you'll lose almost a third of your money.

Credit Cards
Many major hotels, restaurants and shops accept credit cards issued by one, two or all of the following: American Express, Carte Blanche, Diners Club, Master-Charge, Overseas Trust Bank and Visa.

INFORMATION
There's an excellent Macau Tourist Office in Hong Kong, at Room 1729, Star

House, Salisbury Rd, Tsimshatsui, Kowloon. They stock lots of books, leaflets and other tourist paraphernalia and are well worth dropping in on to see what's available before you go to Macau.

In Macau the Tourist Office (tel 77218) is at No 1 Travessa do Paiva, just back from the Praia Grande and around the corner from Government House. They're friendly, helpful people. The office is open weekdays 8.40 am to 1 pm and 3 to 5 pm; and Saturday 8.40 am to 1 pm.

The office's standard guide to the colony is the free *Macau Guidebook* which fills you in on visas, customs, climate, etc, and gives a rundown on the major sights and things to do. One of their best leaflets is called *The Heritage of Macau Building Sites*, a list of important buildings still standing in the colony. Many of these are either hidden away in the back streets – like the Moneylender Tower on Rua Camilo Pessanha – or in obscure corners where tourists are unlikely to venture. If you want a rundown of just how much is left of old Macau, get this leaflet. A number of the Tourist Office's other leaflets list churches, gardens and temples – worth picking up for some more background information. In addition, good maps of Macau – in both English and Chinese – are available free from them.

The Tourist Office's *Travel Trade Handbook* is oriented towards travel agents, although you may find it useful if you spend some time in Macau. *Macau Travel Talk* (also available at the office) is a tourist newspaper which seems to be directed mainly to people in the travel business but does carry interesting articles about the colony. The Hong Kong tourist newspapers *Orient* and *Hong Kong* (both available free from the HKTA in Hong Kong) are other sources of articles and information about Macau.

Overseas Tourist Offices

Outside of Macau and Hong Kong there are a number of Macau Tourist Information Bureau offices, including:

Australia
   Suite 604, 6th floor, 135 Macquarie St, Sydney (tel 02 241-3334)
Britain
   13 Dover St, London WIX 3PH (tel 01-629 6828)
Canada
   475 Main St, Vancouver, BC, V6A 2T7 (tel 604 687-3316)
   700 Bay St, Suite 601, Toronto, Ontario, Canada M5G 1Z6 (tel 416 593-1811)
Germany
   c/o Portugiesisches Touristick Amt, Kaiserstrasse 66,6000, Frankfurt/Main (tel 06 11/23 24 93)
Japan
   4th floor, Toho Twin Tower Building, 5-2 Yurakucho 1-Chome, Chiyoda-ku, Tokyo (100) (tel 03 501-5022/5023)
Philippines
   Suite 209, Manila Midtown Hotel, M Adriatico St, Ermita, Manila (tel 521-95-11)
Singapore
   Room 07-06, Afro-Asia Building, 63 Robinson Rd, Singapore 0106 (tel 2250022)
USA
   3133 Lake Hollywood Drive, Los Angeles, California 90068 (tel 213-851-3402)
   Suite 201, 170 Broadway, New York, New York 10017 (tel 212 608-3910)

CLIMATE

The same as in Hong Kong – for details, see the Hong Kong section of this book.

HEALTH

Vaccinations and inoculation certificates are not normally required unless cholera has been detected in Hong Kong or Macau or if you're coming in from an infected area. Accident treatment in Macau's Government Hospital on Estrada de Sao Francisco is free.

READING

There are a couple of useful books on Macau. A good standard text is *A Macao Narrative* (Heinemann Asia, Hong Kong, 1978) by Austin Coates. Another is *Macau* (Oxford University Press, Hong Kong, 1984) by Cesar Guillen-Nuñez.

One of the more evocative books

written on Macau is *Historic Macao* (Oxford University Press, Hong Kong, 1984) by C A Montalto de Jesus. The book was first published in 1902 as a history of the colony. In 1926 the author added extra chapters in which he suggested that the Portuguese government cared so little about the colony and did so little to meet its needs that it would be better if Macau was administered by the League of Nations. The Portuguese government was so outraged that copies of the book were seized and destroyed; few originals remain today. The book can be bought at the Luis de Camoes Museum in Macau.

Also in English is *The Fortifications of Macau* by Jorge Graca, which gives an account of the numerous forts, batteries and bulwarks built to protect the city. It's available from the Tourist Office in Macau.

There are a couple of books useful for exploring the colony. John Clemen's *Discovering Macau* (MacMillan, Hong Kong, 1983) is updated every so often and is available from the Macau Tourist Office in Hong Kong. It contains lots of background information and details of things to see and do in the colony.

Since gambling is so important to Macau it's worth reading up on. Some of the games – like Jai-Alai and a couple of Chinese games – are explained later on, but for deeper explanations get a copy of the *Macau – AOA Gambling Handbook*, a humorous little book available from the Macau Tourist Office in Hong Kong for HK$10 and worth buying in itself even if you never go to Macau. For an interesting rundown on gambling in Macau there's *Gambler's Guide to Macao* (South China Morning Post, 1979) by B Okuley and F King-Poole, which tells you how it all began and how some of the money can be accounted for. Although it's a few years old, it makes interesting reading.

POST & COMMUNICATIONS

The General Post Office is in Leal Senado Square on Avenida de Almeida Ribeiro.

Overseas phone calls can be made from here. Larger hotels also provide facilities for postal services, phone calls and cables. There are post offices in Taipa and Coloane villages, and overseas calls can be made from them. Local telephone calls from private or hotel phones are free. They're 30 avos in a public phone box – put the money in before you lift the receiver.

GENERAL INFORMATION
Emergency
In case of an emergency, phone 333 for the police, 3300 for an ambulance.

Electricity
Electricity is supplied to the 'old' section of Macau at 110V AC 50 Hz. The 'new' section and Taipa and Coloane Islands are supplied with 220V AC 50 Hz. Power supplied to the hotel rooms is normally 220V AC 50 Hz, but it's wise to check before plugging in your appliances.

Water
Macau's water supply is pumped directly from China and is purified and chlorinated. Distilled water is supplied in all the big hotel rooms and in the better restaurants. However, some of the water supply might be pumped up straight from the Pearl River – worth keeping in mind.

Maps
Free from the Macau Tourist Offices in Hong Kong and Macau is the *Tourist Map*, which lists the major sights, hotels, etc in Portuguese, English and Chinese characters.

More detailed is the *Macau Map*, available for M$4 and published by the Wai Hung Stationery Company. The street names on this map are all in Chinese characters and there's a key on the back with their corresponding Portuguese names. It shows the bus routes too, so you may find it worth getting if you spend some time in Macau. It's sold by some of the shops and sidewalk newspaper vendors.

Also get the *AOA Orientation Map Macau*, which comes as a supplement to the *AOA Pictorial Guide* to Macau. The map's well worth having; the sights and large hotels are all clearly marked and there are side maps showing the bus routes. The main streets are marked with both their Portuguese names and in Chinese characters. The accompanying picture book makes a nice souvenir.

FESTIVALS

The Chinese in Macau celebrate the same religious festivals as their counterparts in Hong Kong, but there are a number of Catholic festivals and some Portuguese national holidays as well. The tourist newspaper *Macau Travel Talk*, available from the Macau Tourist Offices, has a regular listing of events and festivals in Macau.

Most important of the Catholic festivals is the Feast of Our Lady of Fatima, when the Fatima image is removed from San Domingo Church and is taken in procession around the city. Another important day is the Procession of Our Lord of Passion, held in February.

Other Catholic religious events include the Feast of Corpus Christi in June. The Feast of St Anthony of Lisbon, also held in June, celebrates the birthday of the patron saint of Lisbon. A military captain, St Anthony receives his wages on this day from a delegation of city officials, and a small parade is held from St Anthony's church. Another June event is The Feast and Procession of John the Baptist, the patron saint of Macau. The Feast of the Immaculate Conception is held in December.

25 April marks the Anniversary of the Portuguese Revolution, a commemoration of the overthrow of the Michael Caetano regime in Portugal in 1974 by a left-wing military coup. This is a public holiday. Portuguese Republic Day is in October, and Portuguese Independence Day is on 1 December.

GETTING THERE

Macau is 65 km to the south-east of Hong Kong. You can get there from Hong Kong by jetfoil, jetcat, hydrofoil, hoverferry and high-speed ferry. With the exception of the hoverferries, all these depart from the massive new Macau Ferry Terminal on Connaught Rd, Central, Hong Kong Island. The terminal is a favourite for pickpockets – Macau-bound gamblers tend to carry lots of cash. Children over one year of age pay full fare on the various Macau transports.

When you buy your ticket to Macau, the Hong Kong government departure tax of HK$15 (per adult) is automatically added to the price. Luggage on the jetfoils and hydrofoils is limited to 20 lbs (about 9 kg) per person, mainly because of lack of space – all luggage has to be carried on board with you.

It's wise to book a return ticket if you have to be back in Hong Kong by a certain time (weekends in particular are heavily booked). However, if you get to the wharf in Macau early in the morning you shouldn't have any trouble getting a ticket back – except perhaps during the Macau Grand Prix when the colony is packed out with visitors. If you can't book a seat for the day you want, try doing a 'standby,' as the craft may have empty seats despite being fully booked.

Jetfoil

This amazing machine is not found in many places in the world. Powered by a submerged jumbo jet engine, the craft skims the water at 80 kmph, giving a very smooth ride even in heavy seas. Some of them now have radar which allows them to make trips at night. They take a bit less than an hour to make the trip from Hong Kong to Macau.

Upper-deck fares are HK$66 on weekdays, HK$72 on weekends and public holidays, and HK$88 at night. Lower-deck fares are HK$57 on weekdays, HK$63 at weekends and public holidays, and HK$77 at night.

Ferry Ticket

Jetcat

The Hong Kong & Macau Hydrofoil Company has a couple of these jet-propelled catamarans. They carry over 200 passengers each and take about 70 minutes to make the trip from Hong Kong to Macau. Fares are HK$46 on weekdays and HK$58 at weekends and public holidays.

Hydrofoil

This is marginally slower than the jetfoil and not quite as stable – the advantage is that you can stand out at the back of them and take photos if you want. The hydrofoils are run by the Hong Kong & Macau Hydrofoil Company and take 75 minutes to make the trip to Macau. Fares are HK$46 on weekdays and HK$58 at weekends and public holidays.

Hoverferry

Sealink Ferries Company Ltd (the British cross-channel company) operates hoverferries from the pier at Sham Shui Po in Kowloon to Macau. They take just over an hour to make the trip. Fares are HK$45 on weekdays and HK$56 at weekends and public holidays.

High-Speed Ferry

By the time you read this, Macau's new high-speed ferries should be making regular runs between Macau and Hong Kong. Fares should be about HK$35 in economy class, HK$45 in first class and HK$55 in the VIP cabins. There are no evening or weekend surcharges. These ferries will have a capacity of about 650 passengers each, and include an open deck area with deck chairs. They take about 1½ hours to make the crossing and will probably replace the slower ferries on the route, but check when you get to Hong Kong.

Helicopter

For people really in a hurry there are plans for a helicopter service between Hong Kong and Macau. These plans have been around for years; so far nothing has come of them and it looks like nothing ever will.

Ticket Outlets – Hong Kong

In Hong Kong, tickets for the jetfoils, jetcats, hydrofoils and ferries can be bought at the Macau Ferry Terminal (tel 5-457021); at the Macau Travel Service Counters at 230 Tung Choi St, Mongkok, Kowloon (tel 3-807193); and at 201 Cityplaza, Taikoo Shing, Hong Kong Island (tel 5-678173).

Tickets for the jetfoils can also be bought at the Hong Kong Wharf Office, New World Centre, Tsimshatsui, Kowloon; at the Ticketmate kiosks in the Tsimshatsui and Jordan Rd MTR stations; and at the Cables & Wireless Office, Old Mercury House, Connaught Rd, Central.

Tickets for the hoverferries can be bought from several places including: the Kowloon Macau Ferry Terminal, Shamshuipo, Kowloon (tel 3-7291221); HYFCO Travel Agency at the Central Harbour Services Pier on Hong Kong Island (tel 5-423428); China Travel Service Offices at 77 Queen's Rd, Central (tel 5-259121); and 1st floor, 27-33 Nathan Rd, Tsimshatsui (tel 3-667201).

Ticket Outlets – Macau

In Macau, tickets for the jetfoils, jetcats, hydrofoils and ferries can be bought at: the Hotel Lisboa; the Outer Harbour Ferry Terminal on Avenida da Amizade;

and the STDM office opposite the Floating Casino on Rua das Lorchas.

You can make advance bookings for the ferries, jetfoils, jetcats and hydrofoils at the Hotel Lisboa and the STDM office, but it seems the Ferry Terminal only sells tickets for immediate departure.

Tickets for the hoverferry can be bought from: China Travel Service, Hotel Metropole, 63 Rua da Praia Grande (tel 88499); Sintra Tours, Hotel Sintra, Avenida de Amizade (tel 85111); and the Outer Harbour Ferry Terminal on Avenida da Amizade (tel 566621, 78467).

GETTING AROUND

Macau is such a small place that walking is a very feasible way to see a good deal of it – at least around the mainland peninsula. You will, however, need transport to get to the islands and also to the extremities of the mainland peninsula.

Taxi

Taxis in Macau are black with cream-coloured roofs. All have meters. Flagfall is M$4 for the first 1½ km; thereafter it's an additional 50 avos (M$0.50) for every 1/4 km. Each piece of luggage carried in the trunk costs an additional M$1. A surcharge of M$5 is added for journeys to Taipa, and a surcharge of M$10 for trips to Coloane. There is no surcharge if you are making a return trip from the islands to the mainland. Few taxi-drivers speak English so it helps to carry a bilingual map with you. A taxi from the Outer Harbour Ferry Terminal to the Floating Casino will cost about M$7.

Bus

Public buses run from 7 am until midnight, and until 11 pm on Taipa and Coloane Islands. On all five routes within the city, the fare is a flat 50 avos per journey. Double-decker buses will take you from the mainland to Taipa and Coloane Islands. Privately run minibuses also ply various routes around the mainland peninsula. Whatever you do, try to avoid taking the buses during peak hour; they are jam-packed like sardine tins!

Several maps showing the bus routes are available – see the above Maps section for details. It gets too long and confusing to describe the routes here, so do yourself a favour and outlay a few dollars for the maps. A couple of important buses are:

Bus No 3 – this will take you from the Outer Harbour Ferry Pier down the Avenida da Amizade, around the back of the Hotel Lisboa, down Avenida de Joao IV, and right into Avenida do Infantes and Avenida de Almeida Ribeiro all the way to the western shore. It terminates just north of the Floating Casino. On the return journey it follows the same route except that it travels along the short stretch of Rua da Praia Grande rather than the Avenida de D Joao IV.

Bus No 5 – picks up passengers from the stop just a minutes walk south of the Border Gate with China. It takes you past the Canidrome and the Kun Iam Temple, heading southward to Avenida do Infantes where it turns right and carries on to the end of Avenida de Almeida Ribeiro. It then heads south along the shorefront and terminates at the Ma Kok Temple near the tip of the southern peninsula. Heading from the city centre to the Border Gate, you may find that this bus doesn't go the whole way (it confused me too). In that case you'll have to get off at the Canidrome and walk the last stretch.

Bus No 1 – starts from the Ma Kok Temple, follows the shorefront most of the way to the Lin Fung Temple, and then circles round the Canidrome, taking the same route back to the Ma Kok Temple.

For details on buses from the mainland to the islands, see the section on Taipa and Coloane Islands below.

Bicycle

Cycling can be a good way of getting around parts of the colony. There is a bicycle hire shop at the top end of the Avenida de D Joao IV, not far from the

Hotel Lisboa. They charge M$4 per hour and a day rate could be bargained – no security or deposit is required. You can also hire bikes at a place on Coloane Island – see that section for details.

Once you get off the cobblestone lanes, Macau streets are quite terrifying. There's very little space between you and the cars so a bicycle helmet could be worth bringing! Even a Macau policeman's motorcycle helmet – which leaves the ears exposed and is often sold in the local shops – would be preferable to having your bare skull hurled into the bitumen. Bicycles are not allowed on the bridges to Taipa and Coloane Islands.

Car

Self-drive mokes can be rented as soon as you step off the ferry pier. Macau Mokes Ltd (Tel 78851) has its office in Room 202, 1st floor, Macau Ferry Terminal Building. Or you can book beforehand at Macau Mokes Ltd (tel 5-434190), 1701 Hollywood Centre, 233 Hollywood Rd, Hong Kong Island.

Drivers must be a minimum of 23 years of age and must have held a driver's licence for not less than two years – you'll probably need both your home driver's licence and an international licence. (Hong Kong driver's licence holders must get an international licence to drive in Macau.)

Mokes can be hired Monday to Friday for HK$240 per day, and on weekends and public holidays for HK$270 per day. If you can afford it, this is probably the best way of seeing both the mainland and the islands in a short time. Some of the larger hotels offer chauffeur-driven cars.

Walking

Macau is small, but not that small! Walking will do you for getting around the end of the mainland peninsula if you're not in a hurry – but that's about all. The islands are much too big to get around on foot and if you don't have a moke or bike you'll need buses to help you get around.

Pedicab

Pedicabs are bicycle-drawn rickshaws. You may see the odd motor-driven one, but most operate on pedal-power. They're not so cheap either and it's probably not worth the hassle of trying to bargain with drivers. Look at about M$5 for a single short journey and about M$25 to $30 for an hour of sightseeing. Some of them hang around outside the ferry terminal, but most seem to congregate outside the Hotel Lisboa.

Tours

There are numerous tours of Macau starting either in the city itself or from Hong Kong, including visits to the main sights, shops and casinos. The latter take you across to Macau and back to Hong Kong on the hydrofoil. A typical day and evening tour costs around HK$500.

A number of agencies around Macau organise tours of the city and/or the islands. City tours last a couple of hours and include most of the main sights like the Kun Iam Temple, the Sao Paulo Cathedral and the Jai Alai Stadium. Island tours last about two hours and take you to Taipa and Coloane. Bus and minibus city tours cost around M$60 to $70 per person including lunch; island tours cost around M$15 per person without lunch. For a list of agencies offering tours, ask at the Macau Tourist Offices in Macau or in Hong Kong. Sintra Tours (tel 86394), Hotel Sintra, Avenida da Amizade offers daily 2½ hour tours of the city using a tape-recorded commentary – costs about M$22 per person.

There are also tours of Macau which include a trip across the border to China, with visits to the border town of Gongbei and the former residence of Dr Sun Yat-sen in Cui Heng village. Typical price for a one-day combined Macau and China tour starting from Hong Kong is around HK$420. All sorts of other tours of Macau and China are available in Hong Kong, including four-day trips to Macau, Canton, Foshan and Zhaoqing for around HK$1500

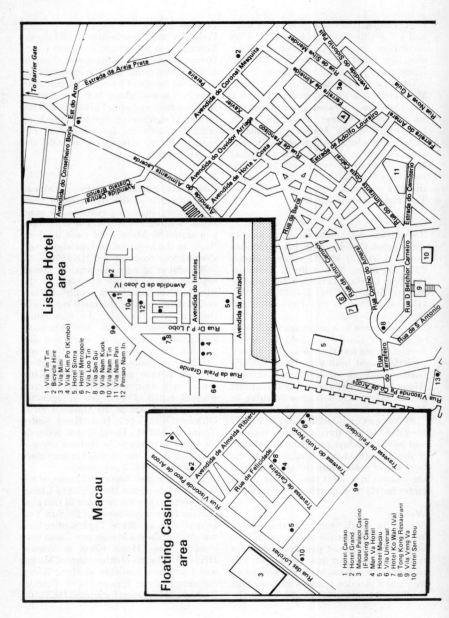

Macau

Lisboa Hotel area

1 Vila Tin Tin
2 Bicycle Hire
3 Vila Mini
4 Vila Kim Po (Kimbo)
5 Hotel Sintra
6 Hotel Metropole
7 Vila Loo Tin
8 Vila San Sui
9 Vila Nam Kuok
10 Vila Nam Tin
11 Vila Nam Pan
12 Pensao Nam In

Floating Casino area

1 Hotel Cantao
2 Hotel Grand
3 Macau Palace Casino (Floating Casino)
4 Man Va Hotel
5 Hotel Macau
6 Vila Universal
7 Hotel Ko Wah (Va)
8 Tong Kong Restaurant
9 Vila Veng Va
10 Hotel San Hou

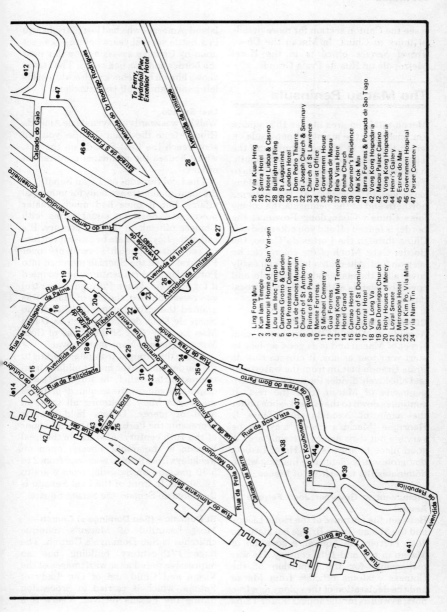

1 Ling Fong Mui
2 Kun Iam Temple
3 Memorial Home of Dr Sun Yat-sen
4 Lou Lim Ieoc Temple
5 Camoes Grotto & Garden
6 Old Protestant Cemetery
7 Luis de Camoes Museum
8 Church of St Anthony
9 Ruins of Sao Paulo
10 Monte Fortress
11 S Michael Cemetery
12 Guia Fortress
13 Hong Kong Mui Temple
14 Hotel Grand
15 Cantao Hotel
16 Church of St Dominic
17 Central Hotel
18 Vila Long Va
19 San Domingos Church
20 Holy Houses of Mercy
21 Leiral Senado
22 Metropole Hotel
23 Vila Kim Po, Vila Mini
24 Vila Nam Tin
25 Vila Kuan Heng
26 Sintra Hotel
27 Hotel Lisboa & Casino
28 Bullfighting Ring
29 St Augustines
30 London Hotel
31 Dom Pedro Theatre
32 St Joseph Church & Seminary
33 Church of St Lawrence
34 Tourist Office
35 Government House
36 Pousada de Macau
37 Bela Vista Hote
38 Penha Church
39 Governor's Residence
40 Ma Kok Mui
41 Barra Fortress & Pousada de Sao Tiago
42 Vong Kong Hospedaria
42 Macau Palace Casino
43 Vong Kong Hospedaria
44 Henri's Gallery
45 Estrela do Mar
46 Government Hospital
47 Parse Cemetery

– see the Canton section for more details of tours to China. In Macau the *China Travel Service* office is in the Hotel Metropole on Rua de Praia Grande.

The Macau Peninsula

Macau totals an area of just 15½ square km, including the mainland peninsula on which the city of Macau is built and the islands of Taipa and Coloane to the south. A two km bridge connects the peninsula to Taipa, which is in turn linked by a long causeway to Coloane. At the extreme northern end of the peninsula the colony joins China's Guangdong Province; the border is fenced off and you enter and exit China through the Portas do Cerco, the Border Gate. Much of the colony can be seen on foot. Alternatively, you can easily cover all of the mainland on a bicycle, and cover the islands with the help of the local buses.

CENTRAL MACAU

Avenida de Almeida Ribeiro is the main street of Macau and is as good a place to start your tour as any. It crosses Rua da Praia Grande just up from the waterfront and effectively divides the narrow southern peninsula of Macau from the rest. It continues down to the Hotel Lisboa under the name of Avenida do Infante D Henrique (Macau's streets may not be very big but their names certainly are). A good place to start is the Hotel Lisboa, that grotesquely distinctive building which dominates the waterfront of Macau.

Monument to Governor Joao Ferreira de Amaral

Between the entrance of the Hotel Lisboa and the Macau-Taipa Bridge is a statue to Joao Ferreira de Amaral, a governor of Macau in the mid-19th century. He was responsible for the expulsion of the Chinese customs officials from Macau and the declaration of the colony as a free port, as well as for the annexation of Taipa

Island. Amaral – who had lost his right arm in a battle several years before – was set upon by Chinese assassins one day near the border and was beheaded. The statue shows him on horseback with a whip in his left hand fighting off the attackers.

Leal Senado

Walking westwards up Avenida de Almeida Ribeiro from the Praia Grande, you will soon reach the Leal Senado on the left, which houses the municipal government offices.

The Leal Senado, or 'Loyal Senate,' is the main administrative body for municipal affairs, but it once had much greater power and dealt on equal terms with Chinese officials in the last century. It's called the Loyal Senate because it refused to recognise Spanish sovereignty over Portugal when the Spanish marched into Portugal in the 17th century and occupied it for 60 years. When Portuguese control was re-established, the city of Macau was granted the official name of 'Cidade do Nome de Deus de Macau, Nao ha Outra Mais Leal' or 'City of the Name of God, Macau. There is None more Loyal.'

Above the wrought-iron gates leading to the garden, inside the main building, is an interesting bas-relief, the subject of some dispute. Some say the woman depicted is the Virgin Mary sheltering all those in need of mercy. Others hold that it represents the Portuguese Queen Leonor of the 16th century. Also inside the Leal Senado is the public library, open on weekdays from 9 am to noon and from 2 to 5.30 pm, and on Saturday from 9 am to 12.30 pm. In front of the Leal Senado is the Largo do Senado, the Senate Square.

St Dominic's (San Domingo's) Church

Most beautiful of Macau's baroque churches is San Domingo's Church. The huge 17th-century building has an impressive tiered altar with images of the Virgin and Child and of Our Lady of Fatima, which is carried in procession during the Fatima festival. There is a small museum at the back full of church regalia, images and paintings. The church is only open in the afternoons. To get in, ring the bell by the iron gates at the side. It is on Rua do Sao Domingos, at the northern end of Largo do Senado.

Money-Lender Tower

Continuing west along Avenida de Almeida Ribeiro, brings you to a small street called Rua Camilo O Pessanha. Here you'll find the 'money-lender' tower, a multi-storey tower built in the 19th century in which the possessions of rich Chinese families were stored.

Luis de Camoes Museum

A block or two along from Rua Camilo O Pessanha is Rua Cinco de Outubro. Here you turn right and right again at Rua do Tarrafeiro, which brings you out in front of the Church of St Anthony – a modern building. The church is memorable for having been burnt to the ground three times.

To the left is the entrance to the Luis de Camoes Museum, a historically interesting building and once the headquarters of the British East India Company in Macau. The museum has an extensive collection that includes early Chinese terracotta, enamelware and pottery; paintings; old weapons; religious objects; and a collection of sketches and paintings of old Macau and Canton. However, the building itself – which dates back to the 18th century – is of the most interest. It's open from 11 am to 5 pm daily, except Wednesday and public holidays. Admission is M$1.

Camoes Grotto & Gardens

Behind the museum in the Camoes Grotto and Gardens is another memorial to Luis de Camoes, the 16th-century Portuguese poet who has become something of a local hero though his claim is not all that strong. He is said to have written his epic *Os Lusiadas* by the rocks here, but there is no firm evidence that he was ever in Macau at all. There is a bust of him in the gardens,

looking rather better than the original, so it is said. A pleasant, cool and shady place, the gardens are popular with the local Chinese and you may find old men sitting here playing checkers; they don't mind an audience. There are good views from the top of the hill.

Old Protestant Cemetery

Beside the Camoes Museum is the Old Protestant Cemetery, resting place of numerous non-Portuguese who made their way to Macau. The cemetery was needed because ecclesiastical law forbade the burial of Protestants on Catholic soil – which meant the whole of Macau, at least inside the city walls. Beyond the walls was Chinese soil, and the Chinese didn't approve of foreigners desecrating their pitch either. The unhappy result was that Protestants had to bury their dead either in the nearby hills and hope the Chinese wouldn't notice, or else beneath the city walls, a sort of no man's land. Finally the governor allowed a local merchant to sell some of his land to the English East India Company – despite a law forbidding foreign ownership of land – and the cemetery was at last established in 1921. A number of old graves were then transferred there, which explains the earlier dates on some of the tombstones. The gate shows the date 1814, which was when the cemetery committee was set up.

Among the better-known people buried here is artist George Chinnery, noted for his portrayals of Macau and its people in the first half of the 19th century. Then there's Robert Morrison, who was the first Protestant missionary to China and who, as his tombstone records, 'for several years laboured along on a Chinese version of the Holy Scriptures which he was spared to see completed.' Morrison is buried beside his wife Mary who became one of the cemetery's first burials after dying in childbirth – 'erewhile anticipating a living mother's joy suddenly, but with a pious resignation, departed this life after a

Portuguese monk in Macao

Rua de Santo Antonio to the ruins of the Cathedral of St Paul (Sao Paulo), said by some to be the greatest monument to Christianity in the east. The cathedral was finished sometime in the first decade of the 17th century, and the crowned heads of Europe competed to present it with its most prestigious gift. Built on one of Macau's seven hills, it was designed by an Italian Jesuit and built by early Japanese Christian exiles. Today all that remain are the facade, the magnificent mosaic floor and the impressive stone steps leading up to it. The church caught fire during a disastrous typhoon in 1835.

The facade has been described as a sermon in stone, recording some of the major highlights of Christianity in the various carvings. At the top is the dove, representing the Holy Spirit, surrounded by stone carvings of the sun, moon and stars. Beneath the dove is a statue of the Infant Jesus surrounded by stone carvings of the implements of the crucifixion. In the centre of the third tier stands the Virgin Mary, with angels and two types of flowers – the peony representing China and the chrysanthemum Japan. The fourth tier has statues of four Jesuit saints.

To get to the cathedral direct from the Leal Senado, walk up the Largo do Senado away from Avenida de Almeida Ribeiro, and then turn left up the steep Rua da Palma, which takes you to the ruins. Alternatively, you can approach it from the rear by walking up Estrada do Cemiterio from Rua do Campa Avenida do Conselheiro, passing the cemetery and continuing up Rua Horta da Companhia.

short illness of 14 hours, bearing with her to the grave her hoped-for child.' Also buried here is Lord John Spencer Churchill, an ancestor of Sir Winston Churchill.

Other inscriptions on the tombstones indicate that ship's officers and crew are well represented here. Some died from accidents aboard, like falling off the rigging. Others died more heroically, like Lieutenant Fitzgerald, 'from the effects of a wound received while gallantly storming the enemy's battery at Canton.' Captain Sir Humphrey Le Fleming Senhouse died 'from the effects of fever contracted during the zealous performance of his arduous duties at the capture of the Heights of Canton in May 1841.'

Ruins of Sao Paulo
From the Camoes Museum you walk down

Old Monte Fortress
The citadel of Sao Paulo do Monte is on a hill overlooking the ruins of Sao Paulo and was built by the Jesuits around the same time. The first Portuguese settlers in Macau built their homes in the centre of the peninsula, and the fort once formed the strong central point of the old city wall of Macau. Cannons on the fort are the very ones that dissuaded the Dutch from

further attempts to take over Macau. One cannon ball landed on a powder keg atop one of the invader's ships, which exploded, blowing the Dutch out of the water in 1622. Since this event occurred on 24 June, St John the Baptist's Day, he was promptly acclaimed the city's patron saint.

Today the old building is used as an observatory and a museum. From it there are sweeping views across Macau. Enter the fort from a narrow cobbled street leading off Estrada do Repouso near Estrada do Cemiterio. There is also a path from the fortress down to the ruins of Sao Paulo.

THE SOUTH

There are a number of interesting sights on the peninsula – once known to the Chinese as the 'Water Lily Peninsula' – to the south of Avenida de Almeida Ribeiro. A good way to start exploring this region is to walk up the steep Rua Central near the Leal Senado.

Dom Pedro V Theatre

To the right off Rua Central is the Dom Pedro V Theatre, a cream-coloured, colonnaded building which dates back to 1872.

Church of St Augustine

Around the corner from the Dom Pedro Theatre, in the Largo de Santo Agostinho, is the Church of St Augustine, which has foundations dating from 1586 though the present church was built in 1814. Among the people buried here is Maria de Moura, who in 1710 married Captain Antonio Albuquerque Coelho after he had lost an arm through an attack by one of Maria's unsuccessful suitors. Unfortunately Maria died in childbirth and is buried with her baby and Antonio's arm.

Church of St Lawrence

Heading back down to and continuing along Rua Central, you'll find yourself on Rua de S Lourenco. On the right is the Church of St Lawrence with its twin square towers. Stone steps lead up to the ornamental gates, but if you want to go in, use the side entrance. The original church is thought to have been built on this site at the time the Portuguese first settled in Macau, but the present one only dates from 1846.

Seminary of St Joseph

Behind the Church of St Lawrence on Rua Do Seminario is the Church & Seminary of St Joseph. Enter the church through the seminary and across the courtyard. The church dates from the mid-18th century and has a central dome, three altars and an arched corridor which leads to a pleasant courtyard. A gallery of religious art in the seminary is also planned.

Harbour Office

Rua de S Lourenco leads into Rua da P E Antonio and Calcada da Barra. Near the end of Calcada da Barra is the peculiar Harbour Office, originally built in 1874 to accommodate Indian troops – thus the distinctive arches.

Ma Kok Miu (A-Ma Temple)

At the end of Calcada da Barra is the Ma Kok Miu at the base of Penha Hill. It is otherwise known as the A-Ma Temple and is dedicated to the goddess A-Ma (or 'Mother'). A-Ma is more commonly known by her Hong Kong pseudonym Tin Hau, which means Queen of Heaven.

The original temple on this site was probably already standing when the Portuguese arrived, although the current building may only date back to the 17th century.

A-Ma became A-Ma-gao to the Portuguese and they named their colony after it. The temple consists of a number of shrines dating from the Ming Dynasty. The boat people of Macau come here on pilgrimage each year in April or May. The temple is actually a complex of temples, some dedicated to A-Ma and others to Kun Iam.

There are several stories about A-Ma, one of which is related in the Religion section of the Facts About the Country chapter – but in Macau the tale goes that she was a beautiful young woman whose presence on a Canton-bound ship saved it from disaster. All the other ships in the fleet, whose rich owners had refused to give her a passage, were destroyed in the storm.

Barra Fortress

From the Ma Kok Miu you can follow Rua de S Tiago da Barra around to the Barra Fortress at the end of Avenida da Republica. This fortress once had great strategic importance when it was built in 1629, as ships entering the harbour had to come very close to the shore. The Pousada de Sao Tiago Hotel has been built within the walls of the fortress and is worth seeing even if you can't afford to stay there.

Along the Waterfront

Avenida da Republica continues round the coast and turns into Rua sa Praia do Bom Parto, which in turn becomes Rua da Praia Grande.

On the way it takes you past the pink **Governor's Residence**, built in the 19th century as a residence for a Macanese aristocratic family.

Further along is the **Bela Vista Hotel**, Macau's equivalent of the Singapore Raffles, built at the end of the 19th century.

On a hill above the Bela Vista is the **Bishop's Residence** and **Penha Church**. From here you get an excellent view of the Pearl River and across to China. In front of the church is a replica of the Grotto of Lourdes.

Continuing along Rua da Praia Grande brings you to **Government House**, pink like the Governor's Residence. Originally built for a Portuguese noble in 1849, it was acquired by the government at the end of the 19th century.

At the corner of Rua da Praia Grande and Avenida da Amizade is the **Jorge Alvares monument**. Alvares is credited with being the first Portuguese to set foot on Chinese soil when he and his party landed on the island of Lin Tin, halfway between Macau and Hong Kong.

THE NORTH

Beyond the Camoes gardens and museum and the ruins of Sao Paulo are a number of attractions. The best way to get around to them all is with a bicycle, since this area is far too spread out to do much walking.

Lou Lim Loc Gardens

From the ruins of Sao Paulo you can head up Estrada do Cemiterio and turn left into Avenida do Conselheiro, which becomes the Ferreira de Almeida. Here you'll find the restful Lou Lim Loc Gardens. They and the ornate mansion with its columns and arches, now the Pui Ching School, once belonged to the wealthy Chinese Lou family. The gardens are a mixture of European and Chinese, with huge shady trees, lotus ponds, pavilions, bamboo groves, grottoes and strangely shaped doorways. The twisting pathways and ornamental mountains are built to represent a Chinese painting and are said to be modelled on those in the famous gardens of Suzhou in eastern China.

Avenida Conselheiro Ferreira de Almeida

If you turn right instead of left out of Estrada do Cemiterio into this street, you'll come to a line-up of renovated buildings which date back to the beginning of the 1920s, and which will give you some idea of what the city looked like in those days.

Memorial Home of Dr Sun Yat-Sen

Around the corner from the Lou Lim Loc Gardens, at the junction of Avenida da Sidono Pais and Rua de Silva Mendes, is the Memorial Home of Dr Sun Yat-Sen. Sun practised medicine in Macau for some years before turning to revolution and seeking to overthrow the Qing Dynasty.

A rundown on Sun's involvement with the anti-Qing forces and later with the Kuomintang and Communist parties is given in the chapter on Canton. The memorial house in Macau was built as a monument to Sun and contains a collection of flags, photos and other relics. It replaced the original house which blew up while being used as an explosives store. The house is open every day except Tuesday. Hours are Monday, Wednesday, Thursday and Friday from 10 am to 1 pm; and Saturday and Sunday from 10 am to 1 pm and 3 to 5 pm.

Kun Iam Temple
From the Sun Yat-sen Memorial Home, carry on up Rua de Silva Mendes and turn left into Avenida do Coronel Mesquita.

Here you'll find the Kun Iam Temple. It's really a complex of temples, the most interesting in Macau, and is dedicated to the goddess Kun Iam (Kuan Yin), the Queen of Heaven and the Goddess of Mercy. The temple dates back some 400 years, though the original temple on the site was probably built more than 600 years ago.

This was also the place where the first treaty of trade and friendship between the USA and China was signed in 1844. These days it's a place for fortune-telling rather than treaties and gets many visitors.

Lin Fung Miu (Lotus Temple)
From the Kun Iam Temple you can continue up Avenida do Coronel Mesquita and turn right at Avenida do Almirante Lacerda. Pass the Canidrome and the Old Fortress of Mong Ha (still used by the military – entry is prohibited) and turn right into Estrada do Arco, where you'll find the Ling Fung Miu or Lotus Temple. The main hall of this temple is dedicated to Kun Iam. Another shrine is for A-Ma the Goddess of Seafarers, and another is for Kuan Ti the God of War, Riches, Literature and Pawnshops. The temple complex probably pre-dates the arrival of the Portuguese at Macau.

Portas do Cerco
Once a popular tourist spot, the Portas do Cerco is the gate between Macau and China. Like Lok Ma Chau in Hong Kong, many visitors went there simply because it was the border, and that was as close as anyone ever got to China. There's really nothing of interest here, but if you want to see it then head straight up Istmo Ferreira do Amaral from the Ling Fung Temple.

The Eastern Perimeter
From the Portas do Cerco you can loop back down to the Hotel Lisboa along the eastern perimeter of the city. Head east along Avenida de Venceslau de Morris. At its extremity by the sea is the **Temple of Macau-Seac**. From here you can head south along the twisty road that runs beside the reservoir (Reservatorio de Agua) and overlooks the giant **Jai-Alai Palace**.

Further down and on the hill above you to the right is the highest point in Macau, known as the **Guia Fortress**. The 17th-century chapel here is the old hermitage of Our Lady of Guia. The lighthouse is the oldest on the China coast, first lit in 1865.

At the junction of Estrada de Cacilhas and Estrada de Sao Francisco is the **Parsee Cemetery**. Opposite it is the **Precious Blood Building** which was built at the end of the second decade of this century for a wealthy Macanese lawyer. Next to it and built about the same time is the palatial **Leng Nam School**.

From here you can continue down to the Hotel Lisboa, or take a short detour westwards along Calcada do Gaio to see the **Vasco da Gama monument**. Da Gama's was the first Portuguese fleet to round the southern cape of Africa and make its way to India. Then continue down Calcada do Gaio, turn left into Rua do Campo and follow it round to the Hotel Lisboa. Just before you reach the hotel you'll see the **Military Club Building**, built in 1872 and one of the oldest examples of Portuguese architecture still standing in the colony.

Behind it are the **Sao Francisco Barracks**, which house a military museum. The museum is open to the public daily from 2 to 5 pm.

PLACES TO STAY

There's not much bargain-basement accommodation to be found in Macau – in fact, there's even less than in Hong Kong. There are cheap hotels around, but some of them look upon westerners with revulsion. Females may have a better chance of finding a room in these places than large, hairy, threatening-looking western males. You'll add to your problems if you go at the weekend, when they have clientele to spare. Fortunately there are a large number of hotels to choose from in Macau, and the place has its fair share of friendly hotel keepers, so you shouldn't have too many problems getting a room. If you're looking at upmarket accommodation, there is no shortage of top-class hotels – some of them tourist attractions in their own right.

Bottom End

The cheap and mid-range hotels are congregated mainly in two areas: in the streets around the back of the Hotel Lisboa, and in the streets in the vicinity of the Floating Casino on the other side of the peninsula. The places mentioned below are only a sample of what's available. New places open up and others close down all the time, while some get demolished. So if one place is gone, look for another. Hotels in Macau usually have signs above the footpath, so they're not hard to find.

The streets in the vicinity of the Floating Casino are probably the best happy hunting ground for cheap accommodation. One of the cheapest is *Hotel Cantao*, which is just back from Avenida de Almeida Ribeiro around to the side of the Hotel Grand. It's a very basic hotel; wall partitions are thin and you may get a lot of noise from neighbouring tenants. Nevertheless I've found it a pleasant

enough and conveniently located place. Singles and doubles M$34.

Opposite the Floating Casino on Rua das Lorchas is the *Macau Hotel*. It's a bare and basic place but rooms are cheap with singles from M$30 and doubles from around M$50. They will take foreigners. Also opposite the Floating Casino is the *Hospedaria Nam Ko*, which is very basic but is run by friendly and amiable people. Singles with washroom and fan go for around M$24.

Heading south along Rua Das Lorchas, you'll come to Praca Ponte E Horta. The *Vila Kuan Heng* (tel 573629) is on the 3rd floor at No 6D Praca Ponte E Horta. It's a clean, decent place with medium-sized rooms with double beds. The people who work here are friendly and the place will probably be fairly quiet – I'd definitely recommend it! Singles and doubles from M$50.

Diagonally opposite the Vila Kuan Heng is the *Vila Lucky Seven* (tel 83418) at No 10 Praca Ponte E Horta. You have about as much hope of getting a room here as you have of getting a camel through the eye of a needle!

Head down Avenida de Almeida Ribeiro back towards the Hotel Lisboa. The *Vila Long Va* (tel 76541) is on the 8th floor of the Wing Hang Bank, 21 Avenida de Almeida Ribeiro. It's another place with a distinct antipathy to foreigners. Women might find trying for a room worthwhile. As for men, the last I heard the rich man was still trying to get into heaven.

At Rua da Praia Grande, Avenida de Almeida Ribeiro becomes Avenida do Infante D Henrique. Right near the corner with Rua da Praia Grande is the *Vila Kimbo (Kim Po)* (tel 81353) on the 1st floor, 57A Avenida do Infante D Henrique. It's an OK place with singles and doubles from around M$50 to $60, but they may not take you. Could be worth a try but I wouldn't go out of my way to come here. Next to the Vila Kimbo is the *Vila Mini* – a decent little place and your chances of getting a room here are even smaller.

Running between Rua Dr P J Lobo and Avenida de D Joao IV is Rua do Commandante Mata E Oliveira, and running southwards off this is a small street where you'll find the *Vila Tin Tin* (tel 89669). It's a clean, fairly quiet, bright place with singles and doubles for M$60.

Mid-Range

Hotel Bela Vista (tel 573821) on Rua Comendador Kouhoneng 8 overlooking the waterfront is one of Macau's old colonial bastions. Singles run from M$90 and doubles from M$120. The more expensive second-floor rooms have private balconies and overlook the sea. This is Macau's crumbling version of Hong Kong's Peninsula or Singapore's Stanley Raffles, and is the most famous hotel in the place. It's an old colonial-style building, over 100 years old, with views over the bay and down the road to the governor's residence. Like much of Macau, it has an air of colonial decadence gone to seed, which you either love or hate. Those who do like the Bela Vista like it just the way it is, and the place is often heavily booked, especially in summer months and around Christmas and Chinese New Year. Even if you don't stay here, it's a good place to go for a meal or a drink on the verandah terrace, which gives you a sort of detached ringside view of Macau. There's even a short book about the hotel by local historian Father Manuel Teixeira. It may be available from the Macau Tourist Office.

There are a number of medium-priced hotels on the western side of the peninsula, in the vicinity of the Floating Casino. On the shorefront is the *Grand Hotel* (tel 2741), at the corner of Avenida de Almeida Ribeiro and Rua Visconde Paco de Arcos. Singles run from around M$70 and doubles from M$110.

Close by, running southwards off Avenida de Almeida Ribeiro, is Travessa de Caldeira, where you'll find the clean and neat *Man Va Hotel* (tel 88656) with singles for M$115 and doubles for M$150.

chinese Priest

The streets immediately to the west of the Hotel Lisboa – in the area bounded by Rua da Praia Grande, Avenida de D Joao IV and Avenida do Infante D Henrique – is another good hunting ground. There are many small streets here with a number of cheap or medium-priced hotels, and new ones pop up all the time.

The *Vila Mini* and the *Vila Kimbo* have already been mentioned above; both are on Avenida do Infante D Henrique.

Head up Rua da Praia Grande. At No 74 A-1 is the *Choi Un Inn* (tel 972423). It's a nice, clean place with bright rooms and the people here are reasonably friendly. Singles and doubles M$70. Also on the Praia Grande is the *Vila Nam Kuok*, where I literally got the toe of my thong in the door before being waved off! At No 44 is the *Va Lai Villa*, which looks a decent place but is also unlikely to take you.

Cutting through Travessa de Caldeira is Rua de Felicidade. On this street is the *Hotel Ko Wah (Va)* (tel 75599) with singles and doubles from M$100. Next to it at No 73 is the *Vila Universal* (tel 573247) with singles at M$100 and doubles at M$130.

From the Rua de Felicidade you can head down Travessa do Auto Novo to the *Vila Veng Va* on Travessa das Virtudes (upstairs, 2nd floor), which has singles and doubles for M$85. They also have rooms for four people for M$110. It looks like a good place and should be worth trying.

My pick of the medium-priced hotels (apart from the Bela Vista) is the *London Hotel* (tel 83388) on Praca Ponte E Horta, which runs eastward off Rua das Lorchas. Singles run from M$80 and doubles from M$100 – more on weekends. The rooms are small but they're clean and comfy with attached toilet and bathroom, and many of them have air-conditioning.

Also good is the *Hotel Central* (tel 77700), 26-28 Avenida Almeida Ribeiro. Singles run from M$80, doubles from M$90, plus 15% service charge and government tax. All rooms are air-conditioned.

There are a couple of places in the vicinity of the Hotel Lisboa. At No 10 Avenida de D Joao IV is the *Vila Nam Pan* (tel 572289) which, despite the forbidding-looking stairway up from the street, is a nice place with clean rooms, comfy beds and air-conditioning (although rooms do not have attached bathrooms). Friendly people too. Singles and doubles M$100.

On Rua Dr P J Lobo is the *Vila San Sui* (tel 572256), which gives its address as 28-38 Rua da Praia Grande though you enter off Rua Dr P J Lobo. Singles M$100 and doubles M$120. It's got medium-sized rooms with air-conditioning and attached bathrooms and is quite a decent place. In the same building is the *Vila Loo Tin*, with slightly tacky singles and doubles for M$90 with attached bathroom. Try and avoid the noisy front rooms.

Running parallel and immediately to the north of Rua do Commandante Mata E Oliveira is Travessa da Praia Grande. At No 4 you'll find the *Vila Nam Tin* (tel 81513), a bright, airy place with friendly people. Rooms have attached bathrooms. Singles and doubles are M$90. At No 3 is the *Pensao Nam In* (tel 81002), which has somewhat run-down, tacky rooms, but they do have air-conditioning and attached bathroom. Generally it's an OK place; singles are M$90 and doubles M$100.

On Avenida de Lopo Sarmento, at the rear of the Hotel Lisboa, is the *Vila San Vu* which probably won't take you, and next to it the *Vila A Pak* (tel 76466) with singles and doubles from around M$90 to $100 – also unlikely to take you. One street back is the *Vila Hoi Pan*, a decent place with singles for M$100 and doubles for M$160.

Heading further out from the Hotel Lisboa up Estrada de Sao Francisco just past the Government Hospital, you'll see the *Vila Chung Tou* (tel 78018) and the *Vila Mekado* (tel 77193) – both in the same building and charging around M$120 for singles and doubles. They're a bit overpriced considering that the rooms don't have their own bathrooms.

Top End

With the push for tourism and business, quite a few top-end hotels have sprouted up in Macau in the last few years, like the massive *Hyatt Regency* on the waterfront of Taipa Island, and the *Macau Excelsior*, which is the giant slab near the ferry and hydrofoil terminal. Some of them are listed below. All of them tack on an extra 10% service charge and a 5% government tax. Some hotels offer only double room rates. However, you can often get large discounts – sometimes as much as 40% – on room rates at many top-class hotels on weekdays.

Hotel Lisboa (tel 77666) Avenida de Amizade. Singles M$180, doubles from M$300. This is the large orange-and-white tower dominating the waterfront

Top: One of Macau's many decaying Portuguese villas (AS)
Left: The facade of Sao Paulo – a sermon in stone and Macau's most famous landmark (TW)
Right: The Hotel Lisboa casino – a sermon in bad taste and Macau's 2nd most famous landmark (AS)

Top: Monument to Amaral, a former governor of Macau (AS)
Left: Statues in the temple of Ling Fong, Macau (AS)
Right: Statue of earth god Tou-Tei in the United Chinese Cemetery, Taipa (AS)

which you see as you come into Macau on the ferry or hydrofoil. Rumour has it that the architect's brief was to create something memorable – and that he certainly has.

Hotel Excelsior (tel 567888), Avenida da Amizade. Singles M$450, doubles M$650.

Hotel Presidente (tel 71822), Avenida da Amizade. Doubles from M$300.

Sintra (tel 85111), Avenida de D Joao IV. Doubles from M$240, 40% discount on weekdays (except public holidays).

Pousada de Sao Tiago (tel 78111), Avenida da Republica. Doubles from M$500. A tourist attraction in itself, this hotel is actually built within the walls of the 17th-century Barra Fortress and is worth going down to see even if you don't stay here. It's also within a short walk of the Ma Kok Temple.

Metropole (tel 88166), Rua da Praia Grande 63-63A. Singles M$200, doubles from M$290.

Matsuya (tel 75466), Calcada de S Francisco 5. Singles M$200, doubles from M$250. Owned by the People's Republic.

Royal (tel 78822), Estrada da Vitoria. Singles M$300, doubles M$380.

The *Hyatt Regency* (tel 27000), is on Taipa Island. Singles and doubles from M$400. They have a shuttle-bus service to take you between the hotel and the city.

Pousada de Coloane (tel 28144), Cheoc Van Beach, Coloane Island. Doubles from M$250. Good restaurant and terrace bar. The entire hotel may disappear in the new residential/tourist complex being built at the beach.

PLACES TO EAT
However devoted you are to dim sum, you will find eating and drinking in Macau even more of a must. Its food is an exotic mixture of Portuguese, African and Chinese cooking – they've coined it 'Macanese.'

The most famous dish is African chicken baked with peppers and chillis. *Bacalhau* is cod, served baked, grilled,

stewed or boiled; the cod is imported and rather salty. Sole – a tongue-shaped flatfish – is another Macanese delicacy. Then there's ox tail and ox breast, rabbit prepared in various ways, and soups like *caldo verde* and *sopa a alentejana* made with vegetables, meat and olive oil. The Brazilian contribution is *feijoadas*, a stew made of beans, pork, potatoes, cabbage and spicy sausages. The Goanese contribution, from the former Portuguese enclave of Goa on the west coast of India, is spicy prawns.

Since Macau is a Portuguese colony, you can wash your meal down with plentiful and cheap quantities of imported Portuguese red and white wines, port and brandy, as well as accompany it with warm bread rolls. Wines are cheap; Mateus Rose is the most famous and you can buy it for around M$20 a bottle in the wine shops. You can get a bottle of red or white

Blind Beggar

from about M$15 – drinkable for those not heavily into chateaux. Spirits and beer are cheaper in Macau than in Hong Kong and many people leave the place with a bottle of Mateus tucked under their arm. Cognac and the like are also cheaper in Macau than in Hong Kong – even cheaper than at duty-free stores. In the restaurants half-bottles of wine are around M$16 to $20 and full bottles M$30 to $45 (although some restaurants may be considerably cheaper than others).

Apart from cod, there's other seafood aplenty – shrimp, prawns, crab, squid and white fish. You won't find Macau's baked crab or huge grilled and stuffed king prawns anywhere else. There are lots of little seafood restaurants where you pick your meal out of the tank in the front of the shop.

If you're going for a meal, it's worth remembering that people eat early in Macau – around 8 pm. You can find the dining room clear and the chef gone home by 9 pm. The Macau Tourist Office publishes a useful free leaflet called *Eating Out in Macau* which lists the more established restaurants in the city. Their *Macau Travel Trade Handbook* is also handy. Barry Girling's *Post Guide to Hong Kong Restaurants* (South China Morning Post Ltd, 1984) has a section on Macau restaurants which is worth having if you want to do more exploration of the colony's restaurants.

Portuguese & Macanese

For both the food and the *dolce vita* (ambience to Californians), eat at the *Bela Vista*, which has the bonus of beautiful views and an open terrace to eat on. The hotel restaurant serves mainly snacks (Spanish omelettes, shrimp toast, jam pancakes and the like) and a set meal for lunch and dinner. A meal of ox-tail soup, stewed chicken, mixed fruit and coffee or tea will cost just M$22 per person, and a couple of bottles of wine will send dinner sprawling late into the evening.

Not far from the Bela Vista is *Henri's*

Palace at 4 G-H Avenida da Republica. Also known as *Henri's Gallery*, this place serves African chicken and spicy prawns and could be well worth checking out. Tables and chairs outside let you take in the view across to the islands.

For good, cheap Portuguese/Macau food, the *Estrala do Mar*, on the Travessa do Paiva off the Rua da Praia Grande, is the place to go. Also the *Solmar* at 11 Rua da Praia Grande – not just a reasonably priced restaurant but a meeting place for the Portuguese community. Seafood is the speciality.

Fat Siu Lau (House of the Smiling Buddha) does Portuguese cuisine despite its name. It's at 64 Rua da Felicidade, which was once the old red-light 'Street of Happiness.' Turn left opposite the Central Hotel in Avenida de Almeida Ribeiro. It's supposed to be the oldest restaurant in Macau – or at least the oldest Macanese restaurant in the colony, dating back to 1903 – and roast pigeon is the speciality.

A great place to eat is the *Café Safari* at 14 Pateo do Cotovelo, near the Senate Building. It's good for Macanese and coffee-shop-type dishes, and is popular for breakfasts.

Chinese

Not bad is the *Restaurant Long Kei* on Leal Senado Square, with dishes starting from around M$16. It's a fairly straight-forward Chinese place with bright over-head lights and sparse surroundings, but the waiters are amiable and a full meal here will only set you back about M$30 – probably much less if you eat in a group.

The *Jade Restaurant*, a minutes walk west of Leal Senado Square at 30 Avenida Almeida Ribeiro, is a large, ostentatious place with a good reputation for daytime dim sum.

There are a couple of restaurants in the streets in the vicinity of the Floating Casino. They're all pretty standard seafood places, and though probably nothing to rave about, they are worth trying. For eels go to the *Restaurant Tong Kong* at the corner of Travessa de Caldeira and Rua de Felicidade, where your meal is swimming in the tanks at the front windows. The waiters here are most enthused about being tipped. Across the road is the *Restaurant Lei Kong Kei*, which has shrimp, eels and fish in the tanks at the front window. The *Floating Casino* has a restaurant but it's bland and boring and surprisingly expensive for what you get!

A good place for cheap eats is the *Café Ieng Keng Tsing* at 13 Rua Cinco de Outubro, a minutes walk from the Hotel Cantao. It's got reasonably priced meals (with breakfast around M$10), decent coffee, and a menu in English, Chinese and Portuguese.

Dai Pai Dongs

For the cheapest eats in Macau, try the *dai pai dongs*. Good seafood can be had at the ones along Estrada Do Arco, not far to the south of the Barrier Gate. A big plate of rice noodles, vegetables, sea snails and a big bottle of Tsingtao beer will only set

you back about M$16. The idea with the sea snails is to use two toothpicks (provided in a container on the table) in a pincer-like motion to roll the whole organism out of its shell in a single piece, dip it in some spicy sauce and devour.

Many evening foodstalls are open until after midnight in front of the Floating Casino on Rua das Lorchas. Another collection of *dai pai dongs* can be found alongside the sports field on Avenida da Amizade near the Hotel Lisboa. They're set up in the evening in the laneway which runs along the eastern side of the sports field. Most of them serve seafood and vegetable combinations – and it's a good place if you want to try fishheads.

At the bottom end of the range, there are innumerable small Chinese restaurants and noodle shops everywhere in Macau. A big bowl of noodle soup and veggies goes for around M$7.

NIGHTLIFE & OTHER ENTERTAINMENT
The casinos are where Macau's nightlife

Keno players
LISBOA CASINO - MACAO

carries on. The spin of the wheel and the toss of the dice are – for a large number of visitors – what Macau is all about. It certainly is for the majority of gambling-addicted Chinese from Hong Kong, where the passion is officially limited to the horseraces at Shatin and Happy Valley, and to a couple of lotteries.

Banish from your mind any images you may have of immaculately clad Chinese James Bond types and ritzy women dripping with diamonds. Macau's casinos are functional fruit-machine palaces with all the sophistication and glamour of a church bingo session. As in Las Vegas, the croupiers look no less bored, the clientele no better dressed.

All the casinos are owned and operated by a company known as the Sociedade de Turismo e Diversoes de Macau (Macao Travel & Amusement Company, STDM to its many friends) – a small syndicate of wealthy Chinese businesspeople. *Hotel Lisboa* has the main casino which attracts the tourists, but there are several others. Although Macau has had a reputation for centuries as a gambling centre, casino gambling only got underway in 1934 when a Chinese syndicate called the Tai Hing obtained monopoly rights from the colonial government to start operating casinos. Monopoly rights came up for renewal every five years and the monopoly went to whichever company would pay the government the most in tax. The story goes that the original owners of the Tai Hing were able to pay a puny sum in tax to the government, but held on to the monopoly by paying off their competitors. It wasn't until after the death of the two founders of the Tai Hing that the STDM gained a monopoly on the gambling industry. The STDM introduced western gambling games into the casinos, built the Hotel Lisboa, introduced the hydrofoils and jetfoils and shared in the building of the harness-racing track on Taipa Island.

You can bet on roulette, Chinese dominoes, boule, blackjack, baccarat, craps, fan tan, keno, dai-sui or two flies crawling up a wall. If your lucky numbers don't come up, you could also try the harness-racing track, the greyhound track and the massive Jai-Alai Indoor Stadium. For people like me who have found themselves dumbfounded at the sight of all these cards and dice chucked around tables:

Blackjack is also known as '21' – a card game in which each card counts for a particular number of points. The object of the game is to draw cards so that you get 21 points or closer to 21 points than the dealer. Should you 'bust' by going over 21, you lose even if the dealer, playing the house hand, also busts – which is the factor that gives the casino the advantage in the game.

Craps is played with a pair of dice rolled across a table. When a two, three or 12 is tossed on the first roll, it is a loss for the shooter and the term 'craps' is used. If a seven or an 11 results, it means the shooter won. If any of the other possible totals result from the initial roll, this is called a point. The shooter continues to roll the dice until he or she wins by rolling that point again, or loses by rolling a seven before making the point . . . and so on. Bets are made on the results of each shot.

Baccarat is where the bigger money is spent – but exactly why this game has attracted the wealthy no one seems to know. Macau's minimum bet is M$100. This is another card game in which a pair of two-card hands – the 'player' hand and the 'bank' hand – are dealt and the one which scores closest to nine points is the winner. Again, different cards count for different points. Neither hand is the house hand, and players can place wagers on either hand. The casino makes its money by deducting a commission on each winning wager on the bank hand.

Jai-Alai and a couple of Chinese games are explained below. For more information on games and casinos contact the STDM at 2B Avenida Almeida Ribeiro, Macau; ask at the Macau Tourist Offices; or get the books mentioned in the Reading section at the start of this chapter.

Hotel Lisboa

The Hotel Lisboa has two floors of gambling, catering to all and offering everything from fruit machines (slot machines, one-armed bandits or 'hungry tigers' as the Chinese call them) up to M$1000 stakes on baccarat. The bigger money crosses the tables upstairs, where there's no shortage of people placing that sort of bet, and plenty more putting M$10 chips on the roulette wheel. If you get hungry there's no shortage of restaurants – you need only walk a few steps from the gaming rooms to get a sandwich. The slot machines work on Macau 50c coins and Hong Kong $1, $2 and $5 coins. Some take tokens.

Macau Palace (Floating Casino)

This is the Chinese baroque extravaganza floating off the waterfront on Rua das Lorchas. There are several floors of gaming rooms here, ranging from a bare one for people with only small quantities of money to more luxurious surroundings for the wealthier folk. Bus No 3 down Avenida Almeida Ribeiro comes out almost opposite the Floating Casino.

Kam Pek Casino

The Kam Pek is just off the same street and caters to a Chinese clientele addicted to the Chinese games of *Fan Tan* and *Dai-Sui*. If you want to give gambling a try and have some fun, try *Fan Tan*. Porcelain buttons are pulled from a pile in a cup and counted out in fours. You bet on how many will be left after the last complete four has been taken out.

Dai Sui (big and small) is played with three dice. They are thrown under a covered glass cannister and you have to guess what numbers come up. The game is also known as *Sik Po*, which means 'dice treasure.' Less commonly, it's known as *Cu Sik* or 'guessing dice.'

Keno is another Chinese game. It's basically a lottery in which the object is to pick some of the 20 winning numbers out of 80 possible selections. The minimum ticket costs only M$5.

Jai-Alai Palace

Opposite the hydrofoil pier is the home of *Jai Alai* (pronounced 'Hie-a-lie'), a cross between squash and lacrosse and reputed to be the world's fastest ball game – you also see it played in Mexico and a few other countries. It's not a casino game, but in Macau it's been turned into another gambling opportunity and is played in the massive HK$60 million Jai-Alai Palace, which can seat 4000 people.

The playing court is 55 metres long by 16 metres wide. The ball has a rubber core covered in nylon and cotton threads and an outer surface of goatskin. It is three-quarters the size of a baseball and harder than a golf ball. Each player alternatively catches it and throws it with his 'pletora' – an elongated wicker basket with an attached leather glove that is strapped to his wrist.

The object of the game is to use the pletora to throw the ball against the front wall with such speed and force that your opponent can't return it before it has bounced twice on the floor (it can bounce off the side and/or back walls as well as once on the floor). A number of bets can be made on the game, including which team will win or place second. Even if you're not into gambling and if you've never seen Jai-Alai played, it's worth taking a look in here!

The Jai-Alai Palace is opposite the ferry wharf. Bus Nos 3 and 3A will take you along Avenida Almeida Ribeiro to the Hotel Lisboa, and then up Avenida Do Dr Oliveira Salazar to the wharf and the Jai-Alai Palace.

Macau Excelsior Hotel Casino

Macau's fifth and newest casino – also run by the STDM – is in the Macau Excelsior Hotel. You can play both western and Chinese gambling games here.

Canidrome

For dog-racing enthusiasts there is a canidrome – yes, that's what they call it – now run by the STDM which took it over in late 1984. It's off t Avenida do Almirante Lacerda, leading to the Barrier Gate. Greyhound racing is held every Saturday and Sunday night, and on the second and fourth Wednesday night in summer from 8 pm. Admission is M$2 in the public stand, and M$5 in the members'. Bets start at just M$1. To get there take Bus No 5 from Avenida de Almeida Ribeiro – it drops you off right outside the track.

Harness-Racing Track

There is a harness-racing track on Taipa Island, operated by the Macau Trotting Club. Admission is M$3. Transport on race days is by bus from the stop outside the Lisboa Hotel near the statue of Governor Ferreira do Amaral. The cost is M$4 one way, but this includes the admission price.

Other Entertainment

Apart from the casinos and the racing tracks, at first glance there doesn't seem to be much other entertainment in Macau apart from watching Chinese throttle frogs in the *dai pai dongs*.

The tourist newspaper *Macau Travel Talk* (available from the Macau Tourist Offices) lists cultural events and shows in the colony, including concerts and performances of Portuguese folk-dancing, religious celebrations and art exhibitions.

Discos have started to boom in Macau. There's one on the third floor of the new wing of Hotel Lisboa. The *Green Parrot* disco is in the Hyatt Regency.

Or there's the nightly Crazy Paris Show hosted by the Hotel Lisboa, where you can watch a dozen or so European girls take their clothes off. The only thing crazy about it is the admission price of M$90. One visitor who saw the show concluded that the performers are transsexuals . . . Macau never ceases to come up with something new.

Macau Grand Prix

One event which could be worth catching is the annual Macau Grand Prix – it's been going for over 30 years now and is held each November. As in Monaco, the streets of the town make up the racetrack. The six-km circuit starts near the Hotel Lisboa and follows the shoreline along Avenida da Amizadé, going around the reservoir and back through the town to the Lisboa.

There are actually two Grand Prix – one for cars and one for motorcycles – and both races have attracted a lot of international contestants from Japan, Australia, the USA, Britain and Europe. Pedicab races are included as a novelty event.

Some 50,000 people flock to see the racing each year, so have fun trying to find accommodation. Be sure to book a return ticket on the hydrofoil or jetfoil if you have to get back to Hong Kong. If you don't, you may still be able to squeeze on board one of the ferries. Certain areas in Macau are designated as viewing areas for the races. Streets and alleyways along the track get blocked off, so it's unlikely you'll be able to get a free view without difficulty.

The Islands

Due south of the mainland peninsula are Taipa and Coloane Islands, once the haunt of pirates – the last raid being as recent as 1910. A bridge connects Taipa to the mainland, and there is another bridge between Taipa and Coloane. Together the islands make a worthwhile day-trip, with several interesting temples, shipbuilding yards and fireworks factories. Some of the largest tourist and commercial developments in Macau – like the harness-racing track – have been built on these islands.

Getting There

From the Macau mainland you catch Bus No 21 to Taipa and Coloane. The bus runs

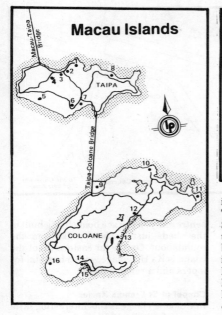

Macau Islands

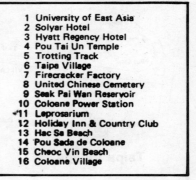

1 University of East Asia
2 Solyar Hotel
3 Hyatt Regency Hotel
4 Pou Tai Un Temple
5 Trotting Track
6 Taipa Village
7 Firecracker Factory
8 United Chinese Cemetery
9 Seak Pai Wan Reservoir
10 Coloane Power Station
*11 Leprosarium
12 Holiday Inn & Country Club
13 Hac Sa Beach
14 Pou Sada de Coloane
15 Cheoc Vin Beach
16 Coloane Village

island. The bus puts you off at the Largo Tamagnini Barbosa (Tamagnini Barbosa Square). There are several attractions in the village, and from here you can walk or bus to other places of interest on the island or catch a bus to Coloane Island. Despite the developments taking place in Macau, the fringes of Taipa village are lined with slums – you can see them on the outskirts of town on the road to Coloane.

Taipa Village
The chief attraction in Taipa village is the Tin Hau Temple, adjacent to the bus station. Notice the large, ornate altar in front of the main shrine containing the image of the goddess. The temple was built 170 years ago and part of it is now used as a school. Around the corner from the bus station is the sizeable Pak Tai Temple on the Largo de Camoes.

There are several fireworks factories in the village. One is the Kuong Un on the road to the United Chinese Cemetery.

Taoist & United Chinese Cemeteries
From Taipa village you can walk to the United Chinese Cemetery on the north coast of the island. On the way you pass a large Taoist cemetery. The United Chinese Cemetery spreads across a steep hill facing the sea; it's presided over by a gross 30 metre-high statue of Tou Tei, the Earth God.

down Avenida Almeida Ribeiro, across the Macau-Taipa bridge, and then along the west coast of Taipa. It takes you past the harness-racing track, through Taipa village and across the second bridge to Coloane Island. The bus skirts the west coast of Coloane Islands and terminates at the roundabout in Coloane village. From here you can take buses to Hac Sa Beach, Cheoc Van Beach and other parts of the island.

Fares are: Macau to Coloane village M$1.50; Coloane village to Taipa village M$0.50; Macau to Taipa village M$1. Apart from the stops along Avenida Almeida Ribeiro you can pick up the bus from the stop by the statue in front of the Hotel Lisboa.

TAIPA ISLAND
From the Macau mainland you can take a bus across the Macau-Taipa bridge to Taipa village, the main settlement on the

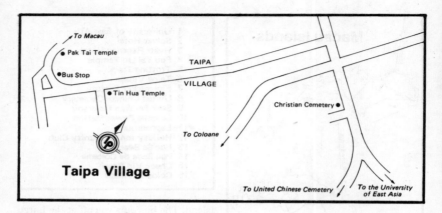

To Macau
Pak Tai Temple
Bus Stop
TAIPA
Tin Hua Temple
VILLAGE
Christian Cemetery
To Coloane

Taipa Village

To United Chinese Cemetery
To the University of East Asia

Pou Tai Un Temple

This is the largest temple on the island. It's a modern building in the usual Chinese joss-house design and is situated in the north-west corner of the island. The Him Son Fireworks Factory is next door to the temple.

Harness-Racing Track

You'll see the Macau Trotting Club's raceway from the bus on the way from the mainland to Taipa village.

Other

With the mainland covered head to foot in buildings, developers have been moving out to the vacant land on Taipa and Coloane. Two of Macau's top hotels, *Hotel Solyar* and the *Hyatt Regency Macau* – built only within the last few years – are near the trotting track. The latter was built in Alabama and was shipped in components to Macau for assembly! The recently completed University of East Asia is also in this area.

COLOANE ISLAND

This is the larger of the two islands. The bus from Taipa takes you to Coloane village, where you can bus, walk or bicycle to several places of interest around the island. The village is a junk-building

centre and you can see boats being built in the sheds just a short walk from the roundabout. On the far eastern tip of the island is Ka Ho village, with a hospital for lepers and a refugee camp.

Chapel of St Francis Xavier

In Coloane village is this interesting little chapel, built in 1928 in honour of St Francis Xavier who died on nearby Shang Ch'an Island in 1552. Xavier had been a missionary in Japan and followed up his successes there by coming to the China coast. The chapel houses a piece of his right arm bone in a glass display case (other pieces of Saint Francis can be found in southern India). The bone fragment stands beside several boxes of bones of the Portuguese and Japanese Christians who were martyred in Nagasaki in 1597, of Vietnamese Christians killed in the early 17th century, and of Japanese Christians killed in a rebellion in Japan in the 17th century. Outside the chapel is a monument surrounded by cannonballs commemorating the defeat of pirates by local forces in 1910.

Temples

There are several temples worth a look in Coloane village. The Sam Seng Temple is just past the bank (Banco Commercial de

Macau) as you head towards the junk-building yards.

Near the Chapel of St Francis, tucked away in a back street, is a small temple for Kun Iam – a tiny shrine within a small walled compound.

The main temple of interest is the Tam Kong (Tam Kung) Temple. Its chief attraction is a metre-plus whalebone carved into a model of a ship, with a wooden dragon's head and a crew of brightly painted little men with Chinese hats. For more details on Tam Kung, see the section on religion at the start of this book.

Beaches

Cheoc Van Beach is the most popular one on the island. It's very small – only about 200 or 300 metres long – but it's not bad as far as beaches in this part of the world go. At least it's not bad for the moment. By

the time this book is out, work will be well under way on a massive hotel and residential complex; and by the time they're through with it, you won't recognise the place.

Hac Sa Beach is bigger than Cheoc Van, and the sand here is a natural grey – it's not dirty. Ka Ho Beach is a rather ugly place with shanties and an oil-storage site on a nearby hill.

Places to Stay & Eat

The *Pousada de Coloane* (tel 28144) overlooks Cheoc Van Beach. Doubles run from M$250. It has a good restaurant and terrace bar too. The whole hotel may disappear in the new residential/tourist complex being built at the beach.

There are several restaurants around the roundabout in Coloane village, like the *Fat Kei*, *Alam Mar* and *Choi Un Kei*. A number of cheaper noodle shops line the

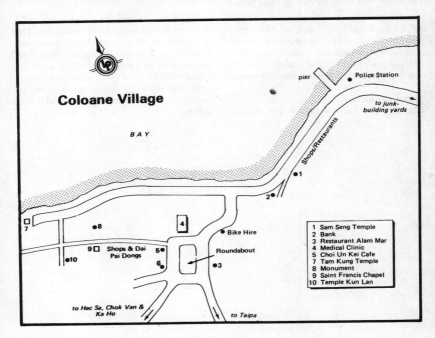

Door God, Tam Kong temple, Coloane Island

small side street that leads to the Chapel of Saint Francis as well as the street leading to the junk-building yards. Some of the restaurants are quite expensive – ask the prices first or you could be in for an unpleasant surprise when the bill comes!

Getting Around
One of the best ways to get around Coloane is on bicycle. You can't ride bicycles across the bridges connecting the mainland and the islands, but you can hire a bike in Coloane village. Near the roundabout is a little shop with a row of bikes outside. The rate is M$6 per hour, and you have to leave some form of security – an ID card or a hydrofoil ticket will do.

Canton

Canton

Known to the Chinese as 'Guangzhou', Canton is one of the oldest cities in China, the capital of Guangdong Province and for over a thousand years one of the main gateways to China. It was the people of Guangdong Province who first made contact (often unhappy) with both the merchants and the armies of the modern European states, and it was these people who spearheaded the Chinese emigration to America, Australia and South Africa in the mid-19th century. The move was spurred by gold rushes in those countries, but it was mainly the wars and growing poverty of the century which induced the Chinese to leave in droves. The image of a 'Chinatown' most Westerners have today is based on Canton. Cantonese food is eaten and the Cantonese dialect is spoken among the Chinese populations from Melbourne to Toronto to London.

The history of the Guangdong region over the last 2000 years is known to us in outline. While the Chinese were carving out a civilisation centred on the Yellow River region in the north, the south remained a semi-independent tributary peopled by native tribes, the last survivors of whom can be found today as minority groups. It was not until the Qin Dynasty (221-207 BC), when the Chinese states of the north were for the first time united under a single ruler, that the Chinese finally conquered the southern regions. However, revolts and uprisings were frequent and the Chinese settlements remained small and dispersed among a predominantly aboriginal population.

Chinese emigration to the region began in earnest around the 12th century AD. The original native tribes were killed by Chinese armies, isolated in small pockets or pushed further south – like the Li and Miao peoples who now inhabit the mountainous areas of Hainan Island off the southern coast of China. By the 17th century the Chinese had outgrown Guangdong. The pressure of population forced them to move into adjoining Guangxi Province and into Sichuan, which had been ravaged and depopulated after rebellions in the mid-17th century.

As a result of these multiple migrations, the people of Guangdong are not a homogeneous group. The term 'Cantonese' is sometimes applied to all people living in Guangdong Province. More commonly, it refers to those who shared the language and culture of a grouping of counties during the last imperial dynasties. Other inhabitants of Guangdong are distinguishable from the 'Cantonese' by their language and customs – like the Hakka people who started moving southward from the northern plains around the 13th or 14th centuries.

What the migrants from the north found beyond the mountainous areas of northern and western Guangdong was the Pearl River Delta, cutting through a region which is richer than any in China except the regions around the Yangtze and Yellow rivers. The Pearl River Delta lies at the south-east end of a broad plain stretching over both Guangdong and Guangxi provinces. Because of their fertility, the delta and river valleys could support a very large population. The abundant waterways, heavy rainfall and warm climate allowed wet-rice cultivation, and two crops a year could be grown (although in the past century the growth of the population and its heavy concentration in the Canton area was more then Guangdong could sustain, so grain had to be imported).

The first town to be established on the site of present-day Canton dates back to the Qin Dynasty, coinciding with the conquest of southern China by the north. Close to the sea, Canton became an outward-looking city. The first foreigners to come here were the Indians and the Romans, who visited the city as early as the 2nd century AD. By the time of the Tang Dynasty 500 years later the Arab traders were coming here regularly and a sizeable trade with the Middle East and South-East Asia grew up.

Initial contact with modern European nations was in the early 16th century, when the Portuguese were allowed to set up base downriver in Macau in 1557. Then the Jesuits came and aroused the interest of the Imperial Court with their scientific and technical knowledge (mainly through their expertise in astronomy, which permitted the all-important astrological charts to be produced more accurately; others worked as makers of fountains and curios or as painters and architects, but overall the Jesuit influence on China was negligible) and in 1582 were allowed to establish themselves at Zhaoqing, a town north-west of Canton, and later in Beijing itself. The first trade overtures from the British were rebuffed in 1625, but the Imperial government finally opened Canton in 1685.

British ships began to arrive regularly from the East India Company bases on the Indian coast, and the traders were allowed to establish warehouses ('factories') near Canton as a base from which to ship out tea and silk. In 1757 an new imperial edict restricted all foreign trade to Canton, an indication of just how little importance was placed on trade with the western barbarians. Canton was always considered to exist on the edge of a wilderness, far from Nanjing and Beijing, which were the centres of power under the isolationist Ming (1368-1644) and Qing (1644-1911) dynasties.

In the 19th century the Cantonese sense of independence, aided by the distance from Beijing, allowed Guangdong to become a cradle of revolt against the north. The leader of the anti-dynastic Taiping Rebellion, Hong Xiu-quan (1814-1864), was born in Huaxian to the north-west of Canton, and the early activities of

the Taipings centred around this area. Later Canton was a stronghold of the Republican forces after the fall of the Qing Dynasty in 1911; Sun Yat-sen, the first president of the Republic of China, was born at Cuiheng village south-west of Canton. Sun headed the Kuomintang (Nationalist) Party in Canton in the early 1920s, from which he and later Chiang Kai-shek mounted their campaigns against the warlords who controlled the north. At this time Canton was also the centre of fledgling Communist Party activities.

The events around Canton in the 19th century were nothing new. Centuries before, the southerners had gained a reputation for thinking for themselves, and rebellions and uprisings were a feature of Canton right from its foundation. As early as the 10th century it became independent along with the rest of Guangdong Province. The assimilation of southern China was a slow process, reflected in the fact that the southerners refer to themselves as men of Tang (of the Tang Dynasty of 618 to 907 AD), while the northerners refer to themselves as men of Han (of the Han Dynasty of 206 BC to 220 AD). The northerners regarded their southern compatriots with disdain. As one 19th-century northern account put it, 'The Cantonese . . . are a coarse set of people . . . . Before the times of Han and Tang, this country was quite wild and waste, and these people have sprung forth from unconnected, unsettled vagabonds that wandered here from the north.' The traditional stereotype of the Cantonese – five million of whom live in the city of Canton and its surrounding suburbs – is of a proud people, frank in criticism, lacking in restraint, oriented to defending their own interests, and hot-tempered. They are also regarded as shrewd business-people and as quick, lively and clever in catching on to new skills, which for the most part are those of small traders and craftspeople.

Of all the Chinese, the Cantonese have probably been the most influenced by the outside world. Part of this stems from Canton's geographical position – the Cantonese live a mere 111 km from Hong Kong and 2313 km from their national capital. Almost everyone in southern Guangdong has relatives in Hong Kong who for years have been storming across the border loaded down with the latest hairstyles and gifts of cooking oil, TV sets or Sony cassette recorders – goods which the average Chinese either can't afford or which are in short supply in the People's Republic. Despite attempts to tear down their TV antennas, many Cantonese can receive Hong Kong's transmission of the latest bourgeois/subversive episodes of shows like *Dallas*, long considered ruinous influences on their moral and ideological uprightness.

However, ideology is not what China is all about today. Economic progress, modernisation, free enterprise and private business – things which were anathema little more than a decade ago when Mao was alive – is the path that China is now taking. Where better to see these changes than in Canton, which has for centuries been one of the centres of Chinese capitalism?

China's economic policies have undergone a radical change since the death of Mao Zedong and the fall of the so-called 'Gang of Four' led by his wife Jiang Qing. Under Mao, China had largely isolated itself from the economy of the rest of the world, apprehensive that economic links with other countries would make China dependent on them. The Cultural Revolution of the 1960s put an end to even the most basic forms of private enterprise – free markets, simple food stalls and privately owned restaurants, all regarded as bourgeois capitalism. All aspects of the economy – from restaurants to steel mills to paddy fields – came under state ownership and rigid state control.

Mao died in 1976, and within a few years, under the leadership of Deng Xiaoping, China turned away from the narrow path of self-reliance, centralised planning and state ownership and control of all facets of the economy which characterised the Maoist era. The usual label applied to the new economic policies is the 'Four Modernisations' – the modernisation of industry, agriculture, defence, and science and technology. The Chinese government's intention is to turn China into a modern state by the year 2000, to quadruple production of everything, and to boost dramatically the average annual income of the people.

Today the PRC's centrally planned economy has moved to a three-tiered system. On the highest rung is the state, which continues to control consumer staples (such as grains and edible oils) and industrial and raw materials. On the second rung come services and commodities, which can be purchased or sold privately within a price range set by the state. At the low end is rural and urban 'free marketing', where prices are established between buyer and seller, except that the state can step in if there are unfair practices. Modernisation of the country is to be achieved mainly by two means: increasing production in both industry and agriculture by turning over the responsibility to the workers and peasants; and import of sorely needed foreign technology and expertise.

The 'Four Modernisations' (which are, on the whole, a continuation of policies instituted by Deng and President Liu Shao-qi in the early 1960s but cut short by Mao's Cultural Revolution, which purged both of them) manifest themselves in great and small ways. Perhaps their most obvious mark in Canton are the giant hotels built there in the last few years: the China Hotel, New Garden and White Swan. Designed to rake in foreign exchange, they cater to every whim of the business-person and upmarket tourist, providing swimming pools, saunas, bowling alleys, discos, revolving restaurants and armies of bow-tied waiters unobtrusively pampering dollar-bearing capitalists with duck terrine and white chocolate mousse. You trip over a hotel like this on every street corner in Hong Kong, but the point is that 10 years ago such hotels did not exist in China!

At the other end of the economic ladder are the free markets and small private enterprises which have been established in Canton and elsewhere in China. Take a walk along Zhongshan Lu one night: a hawker squats on the footpath with a piece of cloth laid out before him covered with zips, tacky sunglasses and key-rings; next to him a man with a scale and measuring stick charges a fee to measure the height and weight of passersby; and up the road a line up of female shoe-repairers can be found. The street peddlers may not seem so extraordinary – you see them all over Asia – but in China what makes them so remarkable now is that little more than 10 years ago during the Maoist era, they were not to be seen.

Today private enterprise takes every form. Cooks, maids and nannies are becoming commonplace in the homes of middle and upper income families. At least one Chinese company in Canton has, since mid-1984, been exporting cooks and cleaning women to Hong Kong. There are numerous privately run inns, hotels, restaurants and rickshaw drivers, and even prostitution is once again noticeable (if it ever was suppressed during the Maoist era). Canton and neighbouring industrial zones like Shenzhen are hardly representative of the rest of China; most Chinese cities and towns are much greyer and far less prosperous. However, Canton is an indication of the direction in which the rest of China seems to be heading. You'll get at least a glimpse of some of the successes, pitfalls, fallacies and curious results of the new economic policies.

VISAS

The only people automatically excluded from entering China are holders of South Korean, South African and Israeli passports. Otherwise, visas for individual travel to China are readily available in Hong Kong. Don't worry if you have a Taiwanese visa in your passport – it doesn't turn heads anymore, and in any case plenty of Taiwanese citizens now visit the People's Republic.

In Hong Kong several agents issue the visa, most in as little as 24 hours. Some issue it the same day. If you're prepared to wait a few days, the cost of the visa is reduced. Generally the agents offer a choice of a visa by itself, or a package deal including visa fee and the cost of transport to China. You'll normally be issued a one-month visa but that varies. Some people get two months, and even three is not unheard of – don't be surprised if three months is the norm by the time this book is out! The cost of visas and the type of package deals you get change frequently, so use this information as a rough guide to what's available.

Visa applications require two passport-sized photos and must be written in English. The application asks you to specify your itinerary of travel and your means of transport, but you can deviate from this as much as you want. You *don't* have to leave from the place you specify on the form. You're advised to have one entire blank page in your passport for the visa. Some of the agents who issue visas include:

Travellers Hostel, 16th floor, Block A, Chungking Mansions, Nathan Rd, Tsimshatsui, Kowloon (tel 3-687710 or 3-682505). A popular place to get visas, partly because theirs are cheap and partly because many travellers stay here. One-month visa issued in two days for HK$70; one-month visa issued same day for HK$110 to $140. Package deals are also available.

Wah Nam Travel, 3rd floor, Eastern Commercial Centre, 397 Hennessy Rd, Wanchai, Hong Kong Island (tel 5-8911161). There is a second office at Room 602, Sino Centre, 582-592 Nathan Rd, Kowloon (tel 3-320367). Another good place to get a

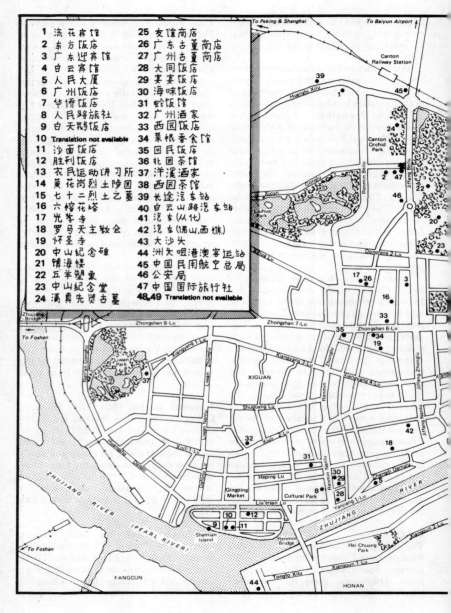

1 流花宾馆
2 东方饭店
3 广东迎宾馆
4 白云宾馆
5 人民大厦
6 广州饭店
7 华侨饭店
8 人民路旅社
9 白天鹅饭店
10 Translation not available
11 沙面饭店
12 胜利饭店
13 农民运动讲习所
14 黄花岗七十二烈士陵园
15 七十二烈士之墓
16 六榕花塔
17 光孝寺
18 罗马天主教会
19 怀圣寺
20 中山纪念碑
21 镇海楼
22 五羊塑象
23 中山纪念堂
24 满真先贤古墓
25 友谊商店
26 广东古董商店
27 广州古董商店
28 大同饭店
29 美美饭店
30 海味饭店
31 蛇饭馆
32 广州酒家
33 西园饭店
34 菜根香食馆
35 回民饭店
36 北园茶馆
37 泮溪酒家
38 西园茶馆
39 长途汽车站
40 白云山路汽车站
41 汽车(从化)
42 汽车(佛山,西樵)
43 大沙头
44 洲头咀港澳客运站
45 中国民用航空总局
46 公安局
47 中国国际旅行社
48,49 Translation not available

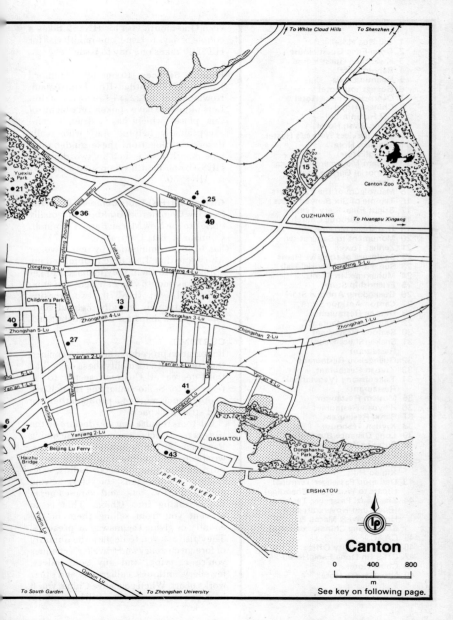

Canton

0   400   800
         m
See key on following page.

visa. One-month visa for HK$80 takes a couple of days to issue; one-month visa for HK$200 takes one day to issue.

Phoenix Services, Room 603, Hanford House, 221D Nathan Rd, Tsimshatsui, Kowloon (tel 3-7227378 or 3-7233006). Lots of people have spoken very highly of this place, which has a friendly and exceptionally helpful staff who really deserve a plug from these guidebooks! One-month visa issued in two days for HK$70; one-month visa issued same day for HK$250.

Guangdong (HK) Tours Company Ltd in the Seaview Commercial Building (diagonally opposite the New Macau Ferry Terminal), Connaught Rd, Central (tel 5-497194), has been recommended by one traveller who wrote that 'Last time I submitted my application to them they managed to get me a three-month visa – straight and at no additional cost (HK$70, two working days). Extremely friendly, helpful staff, lots of useful maps for free distribution.'

CUSTOMS
Immigration procedures are so streamlined they're almost a formality these days. The third-degree at Customs seems to be reserved for Seiko-smuggling Hong Kong people, much more of a problem than the odd stray backpacker.

Customs require that you declare on the 'Baggage Declaration for Incoming Passengers' the number of cameras, wristwatches, recorders (including multi-purpose combination sets), radios, calculators, electric fans, bicycles, sewing machines, TV sets and cine-cameras you're taking into China. This is to prevent you from selling them in the country or giving them away as presents. They also ask you to declare the quantity of foreign currency and traveller's cheques you're carrying, and any gold, silver, jewellery, antiques, calligraphy and other works of art. When you leave China, you'll be asked to show that you still have all the items listed. Don't lose the declaration form!

You're allowed to import 600 cigarettes or the equivalent in tobacco products, four bottles of alcohol, 3000 feet of movie film (8mm only) and a maximum of 72 rolls of still film. Importation of fresh fruit is prohibited. It's illegal to import any printed material, film or tapes 'detrimental to China's politics, economy, culture and ethics', but don't get paranoid about what you take to read. One thing which the Chinese really are touchy about is the import of bibles, mainly Chinese-language bibles. If you've got them and they do search your bag (unlikely), they'll probably confiscate them.

Cultural relics, handicrafts, gold and silver ornaments, and jewellery purchased in China have to be shown to Customs on leaving. You'll also have to show your receipts; otherwise the stuff may be confiscated. Receipts for articles bought in cultural relics stores and in Friendship Stores must be stamped 'Paid in Foreign Exchange Certificates' (this indicates that the article was bought with foreign currency). Cultural relics must have their attached red seal intact or a certificate from the authorities.

Customs usually only check that you've still got your Walkmans and your camera with you and that you're not departing with large doses of Chinese currency. If you lose the form but have all the goodies a foreigner is expected to be carrying, you probably won't be hassled, but if you have no form and no goodies then there could be problems. Sometimes Customs doesn't even bother to check the form.

MONEY

The basic unit of Chinese currency is the yuan, which is divided into jiao and fen. Ten fen make up one jiao, and 10 jiao make up one yuan. Most Chinese use the term 'mao' instead of 'jiao.' There are, in fact, two types of currency in use in China: renminbi and Foreign Exchange Certificates.

Renminbi

RMB or 'People's Money' is issued by the Bank of China. Paper notes are issued in denominations of one, two, five and 10 yuan; one, two and five jiao; and one, two and five fen. Coins are in denominations of one, two and five fen. The one-fen note is a small yellow note, the two fen is a small blue note and the five fen is a small green note. The larger-denomination notes have pictures of workers and peasants and the like on them.

Foreign Exchange Certificates

FECs or 'tourist money' have been issued in China for use by foreign tourists, diplomats, overseas Chinese and Chinese from Hong Kong and Macau. FECs come in six denominations: 50 yuan, 10 yuan, five yuan, one yuan, five jiao and one jiao. There are no coins. Apparently there's a 100-yuan note but I've never seen it.

You're meant to use FECs in places which serve foreigners only, such as Friendship Stores, hotels and foreign trade centres. They're also supposed to be used for payment of through-train fares to Hong Kong or ship fares to Hong Kong or Macau; international and domestic airfares; international telecommunications charges and parcel post; and imported goods. In practice, it's a very confused situation out there; sometimes you can pay in RMB or FEC, sometimes in both, and sometimes they insist on payment with FEC. The general trend is towards tightening up the rules and enforcing the use of FECs where they're supposed to be used.

At the time of writing there are rumours that the Chinese government is going to abolish the Foreign Exchange Certificates (such rumours occasionally pop up) – perhaps in an effort to curb the black market, perhaps for other reasons. There is also talk of introducing a separate currency altogether for use in the Shenzhen Special Economic Zone bordering Hong Kong.

Happy Cantonese Banknote

Changing Money

Foreign currency and travellers' cheques can be changed at the main centres of the Bank of China or its branch offices in the tourist hotels, at some shops such as the Friendship Stores, and at some of the big department stores. In Canton you can change cash and traveller's cheques at the banks in the White Swan, the Dong Fang and the Liu Hua hotels.

You'll be issued FECs and small change will be made up of the RMB one-, two-and five-fen notes and coins. Entry and exit points for China – such as the train station at Shenzhen at the border with Hong Kong, or the Customs Building at Gongbei at the border with Macau – are equipped with banks at which you can change foreign currency into Chinese money, or reconvert FECs to foreign currency on exiting China. If you're taking the express train from Canton to Hong Kong you must reconvert your Chinese yuan at the train station in Canton; the train does not stop at the border.
Foreign currency and traveller's cheques can be changed at the main centres of the dollars; pound sterling; Hong Kong dollar; most West European currencies; and a number of major Asian currencies. Traveller's cheques from most of the world's leading banks and issuing agencies are now acceptable in China – stick to the

major companies such as Thomas Cook, American Express, Bank of America and so on, and you'll be OK.

The exchange rate usually hovers around two yuan for one US dollar, but when the US dollar skyrocketed in 1984 and 1985 the rate crept close to three yuan per dollar, and by April 1986 the rate had hit 3.2 per dollar. The rates listed below were current when the US dollar was particularly strong. The prices given in the book are those when the exchange rate was around Y2.80 to one US dollar.

Australia		Sweden	
A$1	= Y2.22	SKr1	= Y0.42
Canada		Switzerland	
C$1	= Y2.28	SF1	= Y1.54
Germany		UK	
DM1	= Y1.30	£1	= Y4.57
France		USA	
FF1	= Y0.42	US$1	= Y3.20
Japan		Hong Kong	
Y1000	= Y1.57	HK$1	= Y0.41

Reconverting Chinese Currency

When you change hard currency to FECs in China, you're given an exchange receipt recording the transaction. If you've got any leftover Chinese currency when you leave the country and want to reconvert it to hard currency you will require those vouchers – not all them, but at least equal to the amount of Chinese currency you want to change. FECs can be taken in and out of the country as you please, but RMB is not supposed to be taken out. Unless you're definitely going back to China, change the whole lot to hard currency since Chinese yuan are useless outside the country.

It used to be the case that so long as you had exchange receipts you could also change RMB back to hard currency. This may still be the case at some exit points, but the rules have been tightened up and you may find that banks at some exit points (like the one at the border with Macau) won't do it anymore. So if you change money on the black market, make sure you use up all your excess RMB before leaving the country. If you do get stuck with a heap of RMB, ask around at the travellers' hang-outs in Hong Kong, as someone who's going to China may buy it. The Liu Hua Hotel in Canton will change FECs to foreign currency if the original transaction was done there.

Credit Cards
In general, credit cards are gaining more acceptance in China for use by foreign visitors in the major cities and tourist centres. Federal Card, Visa, MasterCard, American Express and Diners Club can all come in useful in Canton, but beware of hefty commissions charged on any transactions!

Black Market
Naturally, with this sort of dual-money system the black market is also a booming industry in China. In Canton there is a whole tribe of change-money men and women plying their trade around the tourist hotels (particularly around the Liu Hua Hotel across the road from the railway station). They will change FECs for RMB at a premium. Otherwise, you could try changing money in some of the small shops and restaurants around the Liu Hua Hotel. Some Chinese may ask

you to buy goods from the Friendship Stores for them. Other dealers buy the goods with the FECs they've bought from you and then re-sell them to Chinese customers at a mark-up. In mid-1985 the black market exchange rate in Canton was around 160 to 170 RMB for 100 FECs, but the rate will probably fluctuate. It may have been particularly high because the US dollar was booming and because of more rumours that the dual-money system was going to be done away with.

INFORMATION
CITS (China International Travel Service) is the Chinese government organisation which deals with China's foreign tourist hordes, though mainly with organising and making travel arrangements for group tours. CITS will buy train and plane tickets for you (and some boat tickets); reserve hotel rooms; organise city tours; get tickets for the cinema, opera, acrobatics and other entertainment; organise trips to communes and factories; and provide vehicles (taxis, minibuses) for sightseeing or transport.

CITS has two offices in Canton. The main one is in Room 2366 in the old wing of the Dong Fang Hotel (tel 62427 or 69900, ext 2366). The office is open daily from 8.30 am to 8.30 pm. They've had a sordid reputation for years, being for the most part either unwilling or unable to answer enquiries from tourists who are not part of a group, and seemed to spend most of their time hiding behind the screens they've put up around the front desk. The only way you could get anything out of them was to stick your fingers down their throats. However, things seem to have improved here lately and they do have a number of interesting books and magazines for sale as well as maps of Canton, Foshan, Zhaoqing and a few other spots in Guangdong Province.

There's a friendlier CITS office at 179 Huanshi Lu (tel 63233 or 61451) right next to the CAAC building – you'll see it on your left as you come out of the railway station. Opening hours are the same as for the Dong Fang Hotel office. They now have English-speaking staff here and it's become popular with travellers.

CTS (China Travel Service) is mainly concerned with tourists from Hong Kong, Macau and Taiwan, and with those foreign nationals of Chinese descent (that is, overseas Chinese) who visit China in groups or individually. CTS tends not to deal with western tourists, but in Hong Kong, where they speak English, you can use their services to book trains, planes, hovercraft and other transport to China, and they issue China visas.

HEALTH
Vaccinations against cholera are required if you arrive within five days of leaving an infected area. Yellow fever vaccinations are required if you're arriving within six days of leaving an infected area. If you're coming from a 'clean' area, inoculations against cholera, yellow fever, typhoid and smallpox are not necessary.

Although Hong Kong is free of malaria, it's still a problem in southern and southeastern China where transmission of the malarial parasite occurs year-round. Malaria is spread by mosquitoes, which transmit the parasite that causes the disease. Protection is simple: either a daily or weekly tablet which kill the parasites if they get into your bloodstream. You usually have to start taking the tablets about two weeks before entering the malarial zone and must continue taking them for several weeks after you've left it. Resistance to two types of anti-malarial tablets, chloroquine and fansidar, has been reported in China. There is little information on the extent of the resistance, but Guangdong Province has been reported as one of of the chloroquine-resistant areas. You should also try to avoid getting bitten in the first place. Take some rub-on mosquito repellent and coils with you, and sleep under the nets provided by many Chinese hotels. Rubbing on Tiger Balm keeps mosquitoes away too.

The best advice regarding water in China is not to drink it from the tap, unlike water in Hong Kong and despite the fact that getting sick from drinking the water is less of a problem in China than it is in other Asian countries. Even the cheap hotels provide vacuum flasks of boiled water in their rooms and dormitories.

Hospitals
If you get sick, you can go to one of the hospitals or clinics which deal with foreigners. The medical clinic for foreigners is the Guangzhou No 1 People's Hospital, 602 Renmin Beilu (tel 33-090). The consulting room of the *Yu Xiu* Overseas Chinese Hospital is in Room 2220, North Building, Liu Hua Hotel. The Foreign Guest Medical Room in Canton's Dong Fang Hotel is open daily from 8 am to 10 pm.

Pharmacies
There are lots of well-stocked pharmacies in China selling both western and Chinese medicines, but if you really need something you'd be better off bringing it with you. One of the problems of buying medicines in China is that the labels on the bottles are in Chinese and you may have trouble figuring out what the right dose is. It's recommended that you bring your own aspirin, medicine for diarrhoea and medicine for relief of cold symptoms. You should definitely bring your own prescription medicines.

LANGUAGE
Canton is a very straight-forward city; it's familiar with and caters well for tourists. In the tourist hotels and at the CITS offices there will almost always be someone around who speaks at least communicable English. Hong Kongers are usually very friendly and helpful despite their reputation in Hong Kong itself. Reading place names or street signs is not difficult; usually the name in Chinese characters is accompanied by the pinyin form. The thing to do is get yourself a phrasebook, a

bilingual map of the city, and a map with the bus routes on it – and you shouldn't have too many problems.

The Cantonese speak the same language as their relatives across the border in Hong Kong and Macau. However China uses a system of simplified characters, as well as a different system for writing Chinese characters with Roman letters called the 'pinyin' system – see the Language section at the start of this book for details.

Below are a number of phrases which should come in useful, together with their pinyin forms. Remember though that the pinyin pronounciation is based on Mandarin pronounciation, not on Cantonese pronounciation – so even if you do get the pinyin pronounciation right you may not be understood by Cantonese-speakers. Also remember that the phrases below are in simplified Chinese characters – they are meant to be used in China and may not be understood in Hong Kong or Macau where the old style characters are still used.

The best way to use these phrases is to copy out the appropriate characters onto a separate piece of paper and show it to the Chinese. This stops them from taking the book and reading it end to end (no joking) and also means you don't have to rely on getting the pronunciation of this tonal language right – a nearly hopeless task without some tuition.

Tones

The four basic tones used in the pinyin system are indicated by the following marks:

— ´ ˇ `
high level rising falling-rising falling

An unmarked syllable is unstressed and is pronounced lightly and quickly with no particular tone.

Places

Public Security Bureau
  gōng ān jú 公安局

China International Travel Service
  zhōng gúo gúo jì lǚ xing shè 中国国际旅行社

CAAC
  zhōng gúo mín yòng háng kōng zǒng jú 中国民用航空总局

Main Train Station
  hǔo chē zǒng zhàn 火车总站

Post Office
  yóu jú 邮局

Long Distance Bus Station
  cháng tú qì chē zhàn 长途汽车站

Airport
  fēi jī chǎng 飞机场

Hotels

guest house
  bīnguǎn 宾馆

hotel
  lǚguǎn 旅店

I want a single room
  wǒ yào yí jiān dān rén fáng 我要一间单人房

I want a double room
  wǒ yào yí jiān shuāng rén fáng 我要一间双人房

I want a dormitory bed
  wǒ yào yí zhāng chuáng wèi 我要一张床位

How much is it per night?
měi wǎn zhè jiān duō shǎo qián?

每晚这间多少钱？

Is there anything cheaper?
yǒu pián yi yì diǎn ma?

有便宜一点的吗？

Toilets

toilet
ce suo

厕所

men
nan

男

women
nu

女

Transport

train
huǒ chē

火车

plane
fei ji

飞机

bus
gōng gòng qì chē

公共汽车

hovercraft
qì diàn chúan

气垫船

boat
chúan

船

I want to go to . . .
wǒ yào qù . . .

我要去…

I want to buy one/two/three tickets to . . .
wǒ yào yī/èr/sān zhāng qù . . . de piào

我要一/二/三张去…的票

Could you buy a ticket for me?
kě yi tì wǒ mái yí zhāng piào ma?

可以替我买一张票吗？

What time does the train leave?
huǒ chē ji diǎn zhōng kāi?

火车几点钟开？

What time does the bus leave?
qì chē ji diǎn zhōng kāi?

汽车几点钟开？

What time does the boat leave?
chuan ji diǎn zhōng kāi?

船几点钟开？

When does the plane leave?
fei ji ji diǎn zhōng qi fei?

飞机几点钟起飞？

When is the first bus?
tóu bān qì chē ji diǎn zhōng kāi?

头班汽车几点钟开？

When is the last bus?
mò bān qì chē ji diǎn zhōng kāi?

末班汽车几点钟开？

When is the next bus?
xià yì bān qì chē ji diǎn zhōng kāi?

下一班汽车几点钟开？

How much is a hard seat?
yìng xi duō shǎo qián

硬席多少钱？

How much is a soft seat?
ruǎn xi duō shǎo qián?

软席多少钱？

Train number
che hǎo

车号

From which platorm does the train leave?
. . . huǒ chē cóng nǎ ge zhàn tái chū fā?

…火车从哪个站台出发？

How long does the trip take?
zhè cì lǚ xíng yào duō jiǔ?

这次旅行要多久?

Where is the first class waiting room?
tóu děng hòu wū zài nǎr? Where is the baggage room?
xíng li wū zài nǎr?

头等候室在哪儿?

行李室在哪儿?

I want to return this ticket
wǒ yào tùi zhè zhāng piào

我要退这张票

Where can I buy a bus map?
zài nǎr néng mǎi dào qì chē lù xiàn dì tú?

在哪儿能买到汽车路线地图?

Bicycles

I want to hire a bicycle
wǒ xiǎng zū yí liàng zi xíng chē

我想租一辆自行车

How much is it for one day?
yì tiān duō shǎo qián?

一天多少钱?

How much is it for one hour?
yí gè xiǎo shí duō shǎo qián?

一个小时多少钱?

Time

tonight
jīn wǎn

今晚

today
jīn tiān

今天

tomorrow
míng tiān

明天

the day after tomorrow
hòu tiān

后天

in the morning
zǎo shàng

早上

in the afternoon
xià wǔ

下午

Post Office

I want to send this letter to . . .
wǒ yào jì zhè fēng xìn dào . . .

我要寄这封信到...

letter
xìn

信

package
bao guǒ

包裹

air mail
háng kōng

航空

surface mail
píng yóu

平邮

Countries

Australia
aòdàlìyà

澳大利亚

USA
měiguó

美国

Germany
déguó

德国

France
fǎguó

法国

Switzerland
ruìshì

瑞士

Sweden
ruìdiǎn

瑞典

New Zealand
xīnxīlán

新西兰

Britain
bùlièdiān

不列颠

Canada
jiānádà

加拿大

Buying

How much does it cost? (lit. How much money?)
duō shǎo qián?

多少钱?

That's too expensive
tài gùi le

太贵了

Is there anything cheaper?
yǒu pián yi yì diǎn de ma?

有便宜一点的吗?

Numbers

one *yī* 一	seven *qī* 七	twenty *èr shí* 二十	
two *èr* 二	eight *bā* 八	thirty *sān shí* 三十	
three *sān* 三	nine *jiǔ* 九	one hundred *yī bǎi* 一百	
four *sì* 四	ten *shí* 十	one hundred and ten *yī bǎi yī shí* 一百一十	
five *wǔ* 五	eleven *shí yī* 十一	one hundred and twenty *yī bǎi èr shí* 一百二十	
six *liù* 六	twelve *shí èr* 十二	two hundred *èr bǎi* 二百	

two hundred and twenty-one
èr bǎi èr shí yī 二百二十一

General Phrases

yes
shì 是(的)

no
bù 不(是)

I cannot read or write Chinese
wǒ bù huì shuō huò xiě zhōng wén

我 不会说或写中文

Street Names & Nomenclature

Chinese streets are usually split up into sectors. Each sector is given a number or – more usually – labelled according to its relative position to the other sectors according to the compass points. For example *Zhongshan Lu* (Zhongshan Road) might be split into an east and a west sector; the east sector will be designated *Zhongshan Donglu* and the west sector will be *Zhongshan Xilu*.

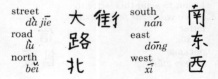

street *dà jiē* 大街	south *nán* 南
road *lù* 路	east *dōng* 东
north *běi* 北	west *xī* 西

READING

China is changing so fast that any book on the country quickly goes out of date. There are a couple of interesting books on Canton, but you really need to do some background reading on China first to get the city – and the Chinese – into some sort of perspective. Michael Buckley and I co-wrote Lonely Planet's *China – A Travel Survival Kit*, which attempts to put the country's first 5000 years into an 820-page nutshell. Not only will it point you in a few more directions in Guangdong Province and the rest of China, it will give you an overview of Chinese history, politics and other background. Some books specifically on Canton are listed below.

An interesting account of early western contact with China comes from the Jesuit priest and missionary Matteo Ricci, who was permitted to take up residence at Zhaoqing near Canton in the late 16th century, and in Beijing in 1601. An English translation of his diaries has been published under the title of *China in the*

16th Century – the Journals of Matteo Ricci 1583-1610. Some poignant comments on the Jesuit influence in China are made by Jonathan Spence in his book *To Change China – Western Advisers in China 1620-1960* (Penguin, 1980).

Another old account is *Kwang Tung or Five Years in South China* (Oxford University Press, London, 1982) by the English Wesleyan minister Reverend John Arthur Turner, who worked as a missionary in China from 1886 to 1891. His book was originally published in 1894.

A personal account of Canton in the early days of China's Republican period comes from American academic and Sinologist Earl Swisher, published as *Canton in Revolution – The Collected papers of Earl Swisher, 1925-1928* (Westview Press, USA, 1977).

Ezra F Vogel's *Canton Under Communism* (Harvard University Press, 1969) covers the history of the city from 1949 to 1968.

To Get Rich is Glorious (Pantheon Books, 1984), by American journalist and many-times China traveller Orville Schell, is a concise and easy-to-read overview of the major changes in China's economic policies and political thinking over the last few years. If you want to get some idea of the path that China is now taking and what the country might be like in the 21st century, this is the book to get.

Phrasebooks

A phrasebook will come in handy for even a brief trip to Canton. Lonely Planet's *China Phrasebook* includes common words, useful phrases and word-lists in English, simplified Chinese characters, and putonghua. Although putonghua uses the Mandarin pronunciation, the Chinese script is universal and is understood by all.

A good phrasebook you can find in Hong Kong is the *Speechless Translator*, which has columns of Chinese characters (and English translations) that you simply string together to form sentences, no talking required. It's already very popular among travellers.

Journals & Newspapers

China publishes various newspapers, books and magazines in a number of European and Asian languages. The papers you're most likely to come across are *China Daily*, the English-language daily newspaper which began publication in mid-1981; *Beijing Review*, a weekly magazine on political and current affairs; and *China Reconstructs*, a monthly magazine.

Some western journals and newspapers are sold in the major tourist hotels in the main cities. The *Herald Tribune* and the Asian edition of the *Wall Street Journal* are all sold in Canton. *Time*, *Newsweek* and *Reader's Digest* (the latter has given up knocking Chinese Communists and has devoted its bitching to the Russians and Vietnamese) have wide distribution. *Time* and *Newsweek* sell for around Y3 to Y3.50 each.

Maps

A number of good maps of Canton are readily available. Hawkers outside the railway station sell excellent bus maps in Chinese. Across the road in the Liu Hua Hotel you can get a good tourist map (in English) at the shop on the ground floor of the south building. A similar map is available free from the CITS office in the Dong Fang Hotel.

POST & COMMUNICATIONS

As well as the local post offices, there are branch post offices in just about all the major tourist hotels in Canton. You can send letters through them as well as packets and parcels containing printed matter. Centrally located is the post office in the Dong Fang Hotel, open daily from 7.30 am to 9 pm.

If you're posting other parcels overseas, you have to go to the post office by the side of the railway station. It's the large building with the SEIKO sign on top. Here you have to get the parcel contents checked and fill out a customs form for it. The international postal service is efficient, and airmailed letters and postcards will probably take around five to 10 days to reach their destinations. There is also an International Express Mail Service now operating in many Chinese cities. If possible, write the country of destination in Chinese, as this should help speed the delivery.

The tourist hotels have telex and long-distance telephone facilities, and again the service is quite efficient. Lines are a bit faint but OK and you usually won't have to wait more than half an hour before you're connected. The Liu Hua Hotel, across the road from the railway station, has a direct-dial service to Hong Kong which is quite cheap.

GETTING THERE

You can get to Canton from Hong Kong by ferry, express or ordinary train, hydrofoil or plane. The one rule to remember is avoid going on weekends and (even more so) at holiday times like Easter and Chinese New Year! At those times everything is booked out and the crowds pour across the border from Hong Kong, trampling backpackers in their wake. Avoid taking the local train from Kowloon to the border on weekends; queues of Hong Kong people are miles long!

Some of the main ways of getting to Canton are listed below. Useful Chinese phrases which may help you buy tickets for transport out of Canton are given in the language section. Long-distance bus stations and the train stations in Canton have left-luggage rooms – fee is about 60 fen per piece.

Ferry

The Pearl River Shipping Company runs two ships between Hong Kong and Canton. They are the *Tianhu* and the *Xinghu*. One ship departs Hong Kong daily from the Tai Kok Tsui Wharf in Kowloon at 9 pm and arrives in Canton the following morning at 7 am. In Canton the other ship departs at 9 pm and arrives in Hong Kong at 7 am. The overnight ferry is one of the best and most popular ways of getting to Canton. The vessels are large, clean and very comfortable – but bring a light jacket because the air-conditioning is fierce!

To Canton For ferries to Canton you can book tickets at the China Travel Service offices at 77 Queen's Rd, Central, Hong Kong Island (tel 5-259121) or at the office on the 1st floor, 27-33 Nathan Rd, Kowloon (tel 3-667201) (entrance on the Beijing Rd side). Some of the agencies that issue China visas will also make bookings on this boat for you. There are no ferries on the 31st of each month. The fares per person are listed below, but you may find them a bit cheaper if you buy them at the wharf itself and not from an agent:

	Xinghu	Tianhu
2-person cabin	HK$180	HK$160
4-person cabin	HK$150	HK$120
Dormitory bunk	HK$100	HK$100
Seat only	HK$70	not available

If you can't get a cabin or a bunk then buy a seat ticket, and as soon as you get on board go to the purser's office. The purser distributes leftover bunks and cabins, but you should get in quick if you want one.

If you come in from Hong Kong on the ferry, there's a bus which goes directly from the wharf to the railway station via the Renmin Daxia Hotel and the Dong Fang Hotel. It costs Y1, but is well worth it. Otherwise, there are taxis, but the drivers are starting to pounce on people as they emerge from the Customs office.

To Hong Kong Ferries (and some of the hovercraft) to Hong Kong depart from Canton's Zhoutouzi Wharf. This is in the Honan area on the south side of the Pearl River. To get to it you have to cross

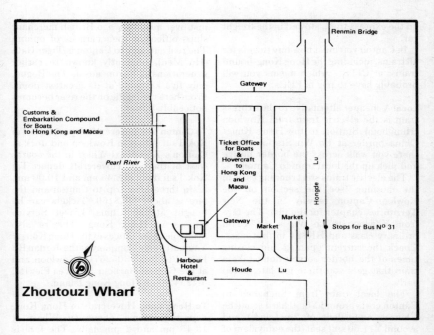

Customs &
Embarkation Compound
for Boats
to Hong Kong and Macau

Pearl River

Renmin Bridge

Gateway

Ticket Office
for Boats
&
Hovercraft
to
Hong Kong
and
Macau

Hongde Lu

Gateway

Market

Market

Stops for Bus Nº 31

Harbour
Hotel
&
Restaurant

Houde   Lu

Zhoutouzi Wharf

Renmin Bridge and continue straight ahead down Hongde Lu until you come to Houde Lu – look for a blue and white sign in English and Chinese which says 'Zhoutouzi Pier.' It hangs on the side of a building on the corner of Hongde and Houde Lu. Turn down Houde Lu – follow the map in this book to the wharf.

The ticket office for ferries and hovercraft to Hong Kong and Macau is at the gateway to the wharf. You may find that this office only sells tickets for same-day departure. Bookings can be made at the office next to the Overseas Chinese Hotel in Haizhu Square.

Bus No 31 (not trolley bus No 31) will drop you off just near Houde Lu. To get from the wharf to the railway station walk up to the main road, cross to the other side and take Bus No 31 all the way to the station; cost is 15 fen.

Rail

Express The express train between Hong Kong and Canton is a comfortable and convenient way of entering China. Adult fare is around HK$120 one way. Timetables change, so check departure times when you're in Hong Kong. There's usually three express trains per day – there's usually one train early in the morning and two more in the early afternoon. More will probably be put on during the holiday periods. The whole trip takes a bit less than three hours.

In Hong Kong, tickets can be booked up to seven days before departure at the CTS office at 24-34 Hennessy Rd, Wanchai, and at 62-72 Sai Yee St, Tak Po Building, Mong Kok, Kowloon. Tickets for the day of departure can be bought from Kowloon Railway Station. Return tickets are also sold, but only seven to 30 days before departure. You're allowed to take bicycles on the express train, stowed in the freight car.

In Canton you must now buy tickets for all trains, including the Hong Kong-bound trains, at CITS – which means you will probably have to pay in FECs.

Local A cheaper alternative to the express train is the electric train from Kowloon (Hunghom) Station to the Hong Kong/China border at Lo Wu Station. From there you walk across the border bridge and pick up the local train to Canton.

The electric trains start running early in the morning (see the section on the Kowloon-Canton railway in the New Territories chapter for details). The fare from Kowloon to Lo Wu is HK$12 in ordinary class and HK$24 in first class. Check the current opening and closing times of the border so you don't take a train that gets you there too late or too early.

The local train from Shenzhen to Canton costs around Y5.50 hard seat (the Chinese equivalent of 2nd class) and around Y11.50 soft seat (the equivalent of first class). There are several trains per day from Shenzhen to Canton, but the schedules change so often that they're hardly worth quoting here. The trip from the border to Canton takes about 2½ to three hours. Extra trains may be put on during the holiday periods like Easter and Chinese New Year, when people from Hong Kong scramble across the border.

Once you've been through Customs at the Shenzhen train station, you usually have to wait for the Canton-bound train. The waiting hall in Shenzhen station is always packed, but there are two large restaurants upstairs if you want to eat, and it's worth taking the opportunity to wander around in the town.

Hovercraft
The route taken by the hovercraft is the same as that used by the earliest navigators in these waters. At the mouth of the Pearl River (Zhu Jiang) is Lintin Island, where

just over a century ago British merchant ships offloaded their cargoes of opium. The real gateway to Canton is Tiger Gate (Hu Men), popularly known to earlier generations of Europeans as The Bogue, only five km wide at its greatest point. From here the traffic on the river becomes noticeably busier.

To Canton The hovercraft depart from Tai Kok Tsui Wharf in Kowloon and dock at Canton's Zhoutouzi Wharf in the southwest of the city. Hovercraft depart Tai Kok Tsui daily at 8.45 am and 10.00 am; it's a three-hour trip to Canton and the fare is about HK$160. Tickets can be bought at the China Travel Service Offices in Hong Kong. They're also available at the offices of the Hong Kong & Yaumati Ferry Company at the Jordan Rd Ferry Pier (tel 3-305257) in Kowloon, and at the Central Harbour Services Pier (tel 5-423428) on Hong Kong Island.

To Hong Kong Hovercraft to Hong Kong depart Canton's Zhoutouzi Wharf at 12.45 pm and 2 pm daily. The fare is around Y37. Tickets for the hovercraft can be bought from the CTS office (tel 61112) at 40 Kiu Kwong Rd in Haizhu Square and at the Liu Hua Hotel service desk. You should also be able to buy them at the wharf, though it may be a good idea to book beforehand.

Air
The Civil Aviation Administration of China (CAAC) operates direct flights between Hong Kong and six Chinese cities, including Canton. There are a couple of flights a day to Canton. The fare is HK$297 economy class (Y87 in the other direction) and the flight takes about 35 minutes.

In Hong Kong, flights can be booked at the CAAC office on the ground floor of Gloucester Tower, Des Voeux Rd, Central, Hong Kong Island (tel 5-216416). The office is open Monday to Friday 9 am to 1 pm and 2 to 5 pm, and Saturday 9 am to 1 pm. It is closed on Sundays and public holidays.

The free baggage allowance on the flights for an adult passenger is 20 kg in economy class and 30 kg in first class. You are also allowed five kg of hand luggage, though this is rarely weighed. Hong Kong airport tax is payable on this flight, and if you fly from Canton to Hong Kong there is an airport tax of Y10.

In Canton, CAAC is at 181 Huanshi Lu, to your left as you come out of the railway station. It's open 8 am to 8 pm daily. Canton's Baiyun Airport is in the northern suburbs, 12 km away from the city centre. Your air ticket entitles you to free transport on the CAAC bus from the CAAC office to the airport, and from the airport to the CAAC office when you arrive at the other end. Alternatively, you can take a taxi to the airport, but you will have to pay for that yourself.

At the time of writing plans were in the pipeline to break CAAC up into a number of separate airlines. These new airlines were to include the Beijing-based Air China, which would handle international and major domestic services, presumably including Shanghai, Canton and Hong Kong; and the Canton-based China Southern Airways. So sometime in the life-span of this book you might find yourself flying to China on an airline other than CAAC.

Bus

The Chinese are constructing a highway from Hong Kong to Canton to Zhuhai – so watch out for the opening up of bus services between Hong Kong and Canton. This will probably change the schedule and frequency of a lot of the other forms of transport currently used to get up to Canton. The new highway also means that possibly quite soon you'll be able to bring your own car or motorcycle across from Hong Kong to China.

To Shenzhen Currently there is a bus service from Hong Kong to Shenzhen,

operated by *Citybus*. Also try the *Motor Transport Company of Guangdong & Hong Kong Ltd* at the Canton Rd Bus Terminus, Kowloon. Already cars are allowed to drive across the border from Hong Kong to Shenzhen.

To/from Macau On the other side of the border from Macau is the Chinese town of Gongbei, a sort of mini-Shenzhen. From the Gongbei bus station, which is opposite the Customs building, you can catch buses to Canton and other parts of Guangdong Province.

Alternatively, *Kee Kwan Motors* across the street from the floating casino sells bus tickets to Canton for M$31. One bus takes you to the border at Gongbei, and a second bus takes you from there to Canton two hours later. The trip takes about five hours in all. On weekdays buy your ticket the evening before departure. If you have fresh fruit with you, eat it before getting to the border, as you cannot take it into China.

There are several buses per day from Canton's long-distance bus station on Huanshi Xilu (a short walk west of the railway station) to Gongbei. The fare is Y8 in an air-conditioned minibus or about Y4 in the local bus – the ride to the border takes five hours. There are also buses to Macau leaving around 6.30 am daily from the Overseas Chinese Hotel in Haizhu Square, though the fare is Y13.50; get tickets from the booking office next to the hotel, open 8.30 to 11.30 am and 2 to 5.30 pm. You'll be checked at Customs on the Chinese side but you probably won't have any checks on the Macau side.

Tours

If your time is limited then the brief tours from Hong Kong are worth considering – expensive, but if you have to whip around the country then a tour is a good way of doing it. One thing you will never be able to complain about on a tour is not being shown enough. Itineraries are invariably jam-packed with as much as can possibly be fitted into a day, and the Chinese expect stamina from their guests.

There are innumerable tours you can make from Hong Kong or Macau. The best people to go to if you want to find out what's available are the Hong Kong travel agents, the Hong Kong Student Travel Bureau or China Travel Service. Also worth trying is the August Moon Tour & Travel Agency (tel 3-693151) at Shop 4, Ground Floor, Ambassador Hotel Shopping Arcade, 26 Nathan Rd, Kowloon. They keep a pretty good stock of leaflets and information on a whole range of tours to China. You should book tours in advance.

I could go on endlessly regurgitating all the tours to China now available, but those to the border town of **Shenzhen** are probably the most popular. These are usually daily except on Sundays and public holidays, and the price hovers around HK$300 to $320 for visa, transport and lunch. The tour includes visits to the Shenzhen Reservoir (from which Hong Kong gets most of its water), the Shenzhen art gallery, a kindergarten, commune, and the local arts and crafts shop. Some trips also include the adjacent **Shekou** district just to the west of Shenzhen.

You can take day-trips from Hong Kong to **Zhongshan**, another Special Economic Zone north of Macau. Cost is around HK$420 and you're taken by hydrofoil to Macau and then by bus over to Zhongshan. These tours include a visit to Cui Heng village, the birthplace and former residence of Sun Yat-sen. One-day tours to Canton are available for around HK$630 – you go by hovercraft to Canton in the morning and return by train in the evening. The trips include visits to the major sights and to handicraft shops. There are also tours of a couple of days' length which include Canton, Zhongshan, Shiqi, Zhaoqing and Foshan for around HK$1500 to $1700; and three-day tours to Canton and Foshan for around HK$1300. Then there are combined Hong Kong New Territories and Canton tours, and combined Macau and Canton tours . . . .

Essentially the same tours can be booked in Macau. If you're in that city and want to book a tour, it's probably best to do so at the China Travel Service Office (Metropole Hotel, Rua de Praia Grande) or with the travel agents in the large tourist hotels – they'll have employees who speak English.

An enthusiastic one-day visitor described her tour as follows:

The tour starts in Macau at 9.30 am at the Mondial Hotel. Chinese customs are no problem . . . . Our whole bus group (about 20 people) crossed the border in just 15 minutes.

The programme then was a 20-minute visit to the Dr Sun Yat-sen Memorial Middle School followed by a half-hour visit (with a tea break) to the late founder of the Republic of China's residence. We had an excellent 1½-hour lunch in Shaqi with prawns, fish soup, chicken, pork, duck and real beer . . . . We then had a half-hour walk around Shaqi, a short visit to a farmer's house in a small village and tea back at the border before we crossed into Macau.

The Chinese guide would stop the bus while we were driving through the country if we wanted to take pictures. He was very well-informed, and to me he seemed very open. It was a well-organised, friendly and helpful tour – money well spent.

– Marian Yeuken

GETTING AROUND

Canton proper extends for some 60 square km, with most of the interesting sights scattered throughout, so seeing the place on foot is impractical. Just the walk from the railway station to the Pearl River is about six km – not recommended for beginning each day's sightseeing.

Bus

Canton has an extensive network of motor and electric trolley buses which will get you just about anywhere you want to go. The problem is that they are almost always packed. If an empty bus pulls in at a stop, a battle for seats ensues and a passive crowd of Chinese suddenly turns into a stampeding herd. Even more

Top: The ubiquitous bicycles of China crowd the streets of Canton (JH)
Bottom: The Pearl river from Renmin Bridge, Canton (AS)

Top: Mausoleum of the 72 Martyrs, Canton, includes an Egyptian obelisk and the Statue of Liberty (AS)
Left: Pre-revolution architecture on Shamian Street, Canton (AS)
Right: Post-revolution schoolroom, near Canton (JH)

aggravating is the speed at which this mobile pile of humanity moves, accentuated by Chinese drivers' peculiar habit of turning off their motors and letting the bus roll to the next stop. You just have to be patient, never expect anything to move rapidly and allow lots of time to get down to the railway station to catch your train. Sometimes you may find you'll just give up and walk. One consolation is that buses are cheap; you'll rarely pay more than 15 fen per trip, and more usually only five or 10 fen.

When you get on a bus, point to where you want to go on the map, and the conductor (who is seated near the door) will be able to sell you the right ticket. They usually tell you where you have to get off. Once upon a time, in the early days of individual travel to China, it was common for Chinese to offer their seats to foreigners. Sorry, but the novelty has worn off and these days you'll stand like everybody else.

Good maps of the city in Chinese – together with the bus routes – are sold by hawkers outside the railway station and at some of the tourist hotel bookshops. Get one! There are too many bus routes to list here but a couple of important ones are:

Bus No 31 – runs along Hongde Lu just to the east of Zhoutouzi Wharf, across Renmin Bridge and straight up Renmin Lu to the main railway station at the north of the city.

Bus No 30 – runs from the main railway station eastwards along Huanshi Lu before turning down Nonglin Xialu to terminate in the far east of the city. This is a convenient bus to take if you want to go from the railway station to the Baiyun and New Garden hotels.

Bus No 5 – from the main railway station, this bus takes a similar route to Bus No 31, but instead of crossing over Renmin Bridge it carries on along Liuersan Lu, which runs by the northern side of the canal separating the city from Shamian Island. Get off here and walk across the small bridge to the island.

Taxi

Taxis are available from the major hotels 24 hours a day. You can also catch them outside the railway station or hail them in the streets – which is a first for China. Demand for taxis is great, particularly during the peak hours: mornings from 8 to 9 am, and lunch and dinner hours.

Flagfall is Y2.10 with the red taxis and Y2.40 with the blue taxis. The meter ticks over about Y1 per km, so a ride from the Dong Fang Hotel to the Bai Yun Hotel, say, will cost about Y3.50. You can hire taxis for a single trip or on a daily basis. The latter is definitely worth considering if you've got the money or if there's a group of people who can split the cost.

Minivan

Minivans which seat about a dozen people ply the streets on set routes. If you can find out where they're going, they're a good way to avoid the crowded buses.

Bicycle

Canton has finally got at least one place to rent bicycles, and no doubt other rental shops will follow. The Happy Bike Rental Station is on Shamian Island, near the White Swan Hotel and across the road from the Government Services Workers' Hostel.

Canton City

Canton is situated at the confluence of the Pearl and Zengbu rivers, much of the city lying on the north bank of the Pearl and bounded to the west by the Zengbu. As you look out from the upper storeys of the Zen Hai Tower, the city appears a nondescript jumble of drab buildings stretching into the haze.

Canton was originally three cities. The inner city was enclosed behind sturdy walls and was divided into the new and old cities. The outer city was everything outside these walls. The building of the walls was begun during the 11th century and completed in the 16th. They were 15 km in circumference, eight metres high and five to eight metres thick. The two main thoroughfares of today, Jiefang Lu (Liberation Rd) and Zhongshan Lu, running north-south and east-west respectively, divided up the old walled city. They met the walls at the main gates.

The city in its present shape began to take form in the early 1920s. The demolition of the walls was completed, the canals were filled in and several km of motorways were built. This paralleled an administrative reorganisation of the city government that produced China's first city municipal council.

Outside the city walls to the west lies the *xiguan* (western quarter). Wealthy Chinese merchants built their residences the same distance from the centre of the city as the foreign enclave of Shamian Island. The thoroughfare still known as Shihbapu became the street of millionaires in the 19th century and remained the exclusive residential district of the well-to-do class. It was these people who patronised the famous old restaurants of the area.

In the north-east of the city is the *xiaobei* (little north) area. During the late dynastic times it was inhabited mainly by out-of-town officials, as it was close to the offices of the bureaucracy. It was later developed into a residential area for civil servants, which it remains today.

At the western end of Zhongshan Lu is a residential district built in the 1930s, using modern town-planning methods. It's known as Dong Shan (East Mountain). Part of the Dong Shan residential area is called Meihuacun (Plum Blossom Village). It is a 'model village' laid out in the 1930s with beautiful residences constructed for high-ranking officials.

Before the Communists came to power, the waterfront on the south side of the Pearl River was notorious for its gambling houses and opium dens. The area became increasingly integrated into the city with the completion of the first suspension bridge in 1932. It was then developed as a site for warehouses and factories.

Although Canton may first strike you as a traffic-clogged city, you only have to side-step off the main streets and down the alleyways to find the residences of the Cantonese: dimly lit houses, men playing cards under a 40-watt light bulb, Chinese pop songs wafting through the evening air. Although it tends to pale in comparison with Hong Kong, Canton remains one of the liveliest towns in China, and it's not hard to imagine that this could have been what Hong Kong looked like before the skyscrapers sprouted. In summer the older areas make interesting walking and there are a number of sights worth checking out, including temples, churches, revolutionary pilgrimage spots, mosques and parks.

REVOLUTIONARY MONUMENTS

There are a number of monuments in memory of the Communists massacred here by the Kuomintang in 1927, and one interesting memorial to an early anti-Qing revolt.

At the turn of the century secret societies were being set up all over China and by Chinese abroad. They were aimed at bringing down the crumbling Qing Dynasty. In 1905 several of these merged to form the Alliance for Chinese Revolution, headed by the Cantonese Dr Sun Yat-sen.

The Qing Dynasty fell in 1911 when the court announced the nationalisation of the railways. The move was viewed by provincial governors and wealthy merchants as an attempt to restrict their autonomy. An army coup in Wuhan in central China seized control of the city and the heads of many other provinces declared their loyalty to the rebels. By the year's end, most of southern China had repudiated Qing rule and given its support to Sun Yat-sen's Alliance. On 1 January 1912 he was proclaimed president of the

Dr. Sun Yat-Sen

Chinese Republic, but it was a republic in name only since most of the north was controlled by local military leaders – warlords – left over from the Qing Dynasty.

In the wake of these events China underwent an intellectual revolution, as the country's intelligentsia searched for a new ideology which could solve the country's social problems, end the warlordism and prevent further encroachments and demands on the Chinese by the foreign powers. Study groups and other political organisations sprang up everywhere – among their members were people like Zhou En-lai and Mao Zedong – and in 1921 several Chinese Marxist groups banded together to form the Chinese Communist Party (CCP).

By then Sun Yat-sen had managed to secure a political base in Canton, setting up a government made up of surviving members of the Kuomintang, the party which had emerged as the dominant revolutionary political force after the fall of the Qing. In shaky alliance with the Communists, the Kuomintang began training a National Revolutionary Army under the command of Chiang Kai-Shek, who had met Sun in Japan some years before. Sun died in 1925 and by 1927 the Kuomintang was ready to launch its 'Northern Expedition' – a military venture under the command of Chiang designed to subdue the northern warlords.

However, Chiang was also engaged in a power struggle within the Kuomintang, and as the NRA moved in on Shanghai (then under the control of a local warlord, but whose strength had been undermined by a powerful industrial movement organised in the city by the Communists) he took the opportunity to put down both the Communists and his enemies in the Kuomintang. Supported by the Shanghai industrialists who were worried about the trade union movement, and foreigners who feared the loss of trade and privileges, Chiang let loose a reign of terror against the Communists, Communist sympathisers and anyone who advocated revolutionary change in China. With the help of Shanghai's underworld leaders, money from Shanghai bankers and the blessings of the foreigners in Shanghai, Chiang armed hundreds of gangsters, dressed them in Nationalist uniforms, and launched an overnight surprise attack which wiped out the Communists in the city. This was quickly followed by the massacre of Communists and other anti-Chiang factions in Canton, Changsha and Nanchang. By the middle of 1928 the Northern Expedition had reached Beijing and a national government was established with Chiang holding the highest political and military positions. Those Communists who survived the massacres retreated to the Jinggang Mountains on the Hunan-Jiangxi border and into other mountainous areas of China – from where they began a war against the Kuomintang which lasted just over 20 years and which ended in victory for the Communists in 1949.

Peasant Movement Institute

Canton's Peasant Movement Institute was founded in 1924 on the site of a Ming Dynasty Confucian temple. The institute was used by the fledgling Communist Party as a school to train peasant leaders from all over the country. It was set up by Peng Pai, a high-ranking Communist leader who believed that if a Communist revolution was to succeed in China then the peasants must be its main force. Mao Zedong – of the same opinion – took over as director of the institute in 1925 or 1926. Zhou En-lai lectured here and one of his students was Mao's brother, Mao Zemin. Peng was executed by the Kuomintang in 1929, and Mao Zemin was executed by a warlord in Xinjiang Province in 1942.

The buildings were restored in 1953 and they're now used as a revolutionary museum. There's not a great deal to see at the institute: a replica of Mao's room, the soldiers' barracks and rifles, and a number of photographs. The institute is at 42 Zhongshan 4-Lu. It is open daily from 8.15 to 11.30 am and 2.30 to 5.30 pm.

Memorial Garden to the Martyrs

This memorial is within walking distance of the Peasant Movement Institute, eastwards along Zhongshan Lu. It was officially opened in 1957 on the 30th anniversary of the December 1927 Canton uprising.

In April 1927 Chiang Kai-shek had ordered his troops to massacre Communists in Shanghai and Nanjing. On 21 May the Communists led an uprising of peasants on the Hunan-Jiangxi border, and on 1 August they staged another in Nanchang. Both uprisings were defeated by Kuomintang troops.

On 11 December 1927 the Communists staged yet another uprising in Canton, but this was also bloodily suppressed by the Kuomintang. The Communists claim that over 5700 people were killed during or

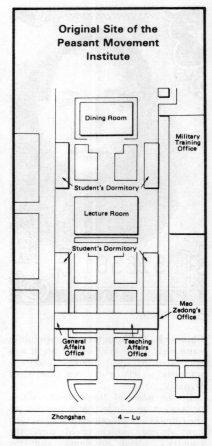

after the uprising. The memorial garden is laid out on Red Flower Hill (Honghuagang), which was one of the execution grounds.

There's nothing of particular interest here, though the gardens themselves are quite attractive. Here you'll also find the Pavilion of Blood-Cemented Friendship of the Sino-Soviet Peoples and the Pavilion of Blood-Cemented Friendship of the Sino-Korean Peoples.

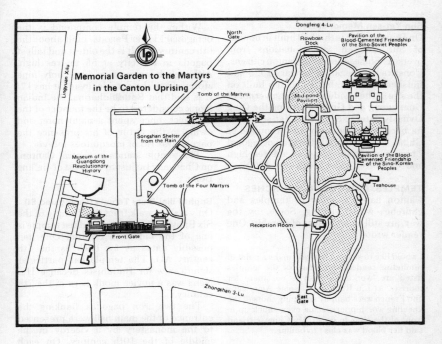

Memorial Garden to the Martyrs in the Canton Uprising

North Gate

Lingyuan Xilu

Tomb of the Martyrs

Songshan Shelter from the Rain

Museum of the Guangdong Revolutionary History

Tomb of the Four Martyrs

Front Gate

Dongfeng 4-Lu

Rowboat Dock

Pavilion of the Blood-Cemented Friendship of the Sino-Soviet Peoples

Mid-pond Pavilion

Pavilion of the Blood-Cemented Friendship of the Sino-Korean Peoples

Teahouse

Reception Room

Zhongshan 3-Lu

East Gate

Mausoleum of the 72 Martyrs & Memorial of Yellow Flowers

This memorial was built in memory of the victims of the unsuccessful Canton insurrection of 27 April 1911. (It was not until October of that year that the Qing Dynasty collapsed and a Republic of China was declared in the south of the country.) The uprising had been organised by a grouping of Chinese organisations which opposed the Qing and which had formally unified at a meeting of representatives in Tokyo in August 1905, with Sun Yat-sen as leader.

The memorial was built in 1918 with funds provided by Chinese from all over the world, and was the most famous revolutionary monument of pre-Communist China. It's a conglomeration of architectural symbols of freedom and democracy from all over the world, since the outstanding periods of history in other countries of the world were going to be used as a guide for the new Republic of China.

What that really means is that it's an exercise in architectural bad taste. In front, a small Egyptian obelisk carved with the words 'Tomb of the 72 Martyrs' stands under a stone pavilion. Atop the pavilion is a life-sized replica of the Liberty Bell in stone. Behind it stands a miniature imitation of the Trianon at Versailles, with the cross-section of a huge pyramid of stone on its roof. To top it all off is a miniature bronze replica of the Statue of Liberty. The Chinese influence can be seen in the bronze urns and lions on each side.

The monument stands on Yellow Flower Hill (Huanghuagang) next to Xianlie Lu, to the east of the Baiyun and New Garden hotels.

Sun Yat-sen Memorial Hall

On Dongfeng Lu is this hall built in honour of Sun Yat-sen with donations from overseas Chinese and from Canton citizens. Construction began in January 1929 and finished in November 1931. It's built on the site of the residence of the governor of Guangdong and Guangxi during the Qing Dynasty, later used by Sun Yat-sen when he became president of the Republic of China. The Memorial Hall is an octagonal Chinese monolith some 47 metres high and 71 metres wide; it can seat 4000.

TEMPLES, MOSQUES & CHURCHES

Canton has a number of temples and churches worth visiting. Some, by the way, are still active places of worship. One reader wrote:

I would like to suggest that you make a point of reminding readers that many of the temples listed are 'working' – they're not there for tourists. At Liu Rong Si ... some Americans and French were happily snapping shots of the kneeling worshippers; some even snuck up in front of the altar to do so. My Chinese friend said her blood was close to boiling.

Temple of the Six Banyan Trees (Liu Rong Si)

The history of the temple is vague. It seems that the first temple on this site, called the 'Precious Solemnity Temple,' was built during the 6th century AD but was ruined by fire in the 10th. The temple was rebuilt at the end of the 10th century and was renamed the 'Purificatory Wisdom Temple' since the monks worshipped Hui Neng, the sixth patriarch of the Zen Buddhist sect. Today the temple serves as the headquarters of the Guangzhou Buddhist Association.

The temple received its name from Su Dongpo, a celebrated poet and calligrapher of the Northern Song Dynasty who visited the temple in the 11th or 12th century. He was so enchanted by the six banyan trees growing in the courtyard (no longer there) that he inscribed the two large characters for 'Six Banyans' on the temple.

Within the temple compound is the octagonal Flower Pagoda, built about the 6th century AD. It is the oldest and tallest pagoda in the city at 55 metres high. Although it appears to have only nine storeys from the outside, inside it has 17. It is said that Boddhidharma, the Indian monk considered to be the founder of the Zen sect, once spent a night here, and owing to the virtue of his presence the pagoda was rid of mosquitoes forever.

The temple stands in central Canton, on Chaoyang Lu just to the west of Jiefang Beilu.

Bright Filial Piety Temple (Guangxiao Si)

Only a short walk from the Temple of the Six Banyan Trees, this Buddhist temple is one of the oldest in Canton. One hall possibly dates as far back as the 4th century AD. The temple has particular significance for Buddhists because Hui Neng was a novice monk here in the 7th century.

The two iron pagodas flanking the entrance to the main hall were presented to the monastery by a viceroy in the middle of the 10th century. On each pagoda are thousands of miniature representations of the Buddha. The temple buildings are of much more recent construction, the original buildings having been destroyed by fire in the mid-17th century.

The temple is on Hongshu Lu, just to the west of the Temple of Six Banyan Trees. It appears to be closed to tourists, or at least to individuals. A section of the temple complex is now used as the Guangdong Antique Store.

Five Genies Temple (Wuxian Guan)

This is a Taoist temple held to be the site of the appearance of the five rams and celestial beings in the myth of the foundation of the city – see section below on Yuexiu Park for the story.

The stone tablets flanking the forecourt commemorate the various restorations undergone by the temple. The present buildings are comparatively recent. The earlier buildings that dated from the Ming Dynasty were destroyed by fire in 1864.

The large hollow in the rock in the temple courtyard is said to be the impression of a celestial being's foot; the Chinese refer to it by the name of 'Rice-Ear Rock of Unique Beauty.' The great bell which weighs five tonnes was cast during the Ming Dynasty – it's three metres high, two metres in diameter and about 10 cm thick, probably the largest in Guangdong Province. It's known as the 'calamity bell,' since the sound of the bell, which has no clapper, is a portent of calamity for the city.

The temple is at the back of a laneway off Xianyang 4-Lu, which runs westwards off Jiefang Zhonglu.

Roman Catholic Church

This impressive edifice is known to the Chinese as the 'house of stone,' as it is built entirely of granite. Designed by the French architect Guillemin, the church is an imitation of the Gothic structures prevalent in Europe in the Middle Ages. Four bronze bells suspended in the building to the east of the church were cast in France. The original coloured glass was also made in France, but almost all of it is gone.

The site was originally the location of the office of the governor of Guangdong and Guangxi provinces during the Qing Dynasty, but the building was destroyed by British and French troops at the end of the Second Opium War in the 19th century. The area was leased to the French following the signing of the Sino-French 'Tianjin Treaty,' and construction of the church began in 1863. It was completed in 1888.

The Roman Catholic church stands on Yide Lu, nor far from the riverfront. It's normally closed except on Sunday, when masses are said. All are welcome.

Huaisheng Mosque

The original mosque on this site is said to have been established in 627 AD by the first Moslem missionary to China, possibly an uncle of Mohammed, though the present buildings are of recent construction. The name of the mosque means 'Remember the Sage' in memory of the prophet. Inside the grounds is a minaret, which because of its flat, even appearance has come to be known as the 'Guangta' or 'Smooth Tower.' The mosque stands on Guangta Lu, which runs eastwards off Renmin Zhonglu.

Mohammedan Tomb & Burial Ground

Situated in Orchid Garden at the top of Jiefang Beilu, this is thought to be the final resting place of the Moslem missionary who built the original Huaisheng Mosque. It is not the only ancient Moslem tomb in China. There are two others outside the town of Quanzhou on the south-east coast of China, thought to be the tombs of missionaries sent to China by Mohammed together with the one now buried in Canton.

The Canton tomb is in a secluded bamboo grove behind the Orchid Garden. Continue past the entrance to the garden through the narrow gateway ahead, and take the narrow stone path on the right. Behind the tomb compound are individual Moslem stone graves as well as a large stone arch. The tomb came to be known as the 'Tomb of the Echo' or the 'Resounding Tomb' because of the noises that reverberate in the inner chamber.

THE RIVERFRONT

The northern bank of the Pearl River is one of the most interesting areas of Canton. Filled with people, markets and dilapidated buildings, it contrasts with the tidy greyness of the modern northern region of the city.

Liuersan Lu

Just before you reach the end of Renmin Lu, Liuersan Lu leads off westwards. 'Liu er san' means 'six two three,' referring to 23 June 1925, when British and French troops fired on striking Chinese workers during the Hong Kong-Canton Strike of that year.

Qingping Market

A short walk down Liuersan Lu takes you to the second bridge which connects the city to the north side of Shamian Island. Directly opposite the bridge, on the city side, is Qingping Market on Qingping Lu – one of the best city markets in the whole country yet one of Canton's lesser-known attractions.

If you want to buy, kill and cook it yourself, this is the place to come, since the market is more like a take-away zoo. Near the entrance you'll find the usual selection of medicinal herbs and spices, along with such delectables as dried starfish, snakes, lizards and deer antlers. Further up you'll find the live ones waiting to be butchered: sad-eyed monkeys rattle at the bars of their wooden cages; tortoises crawl over each other in shallow tin trays; owls sit perched on boxes full of pigeons; half-alive fish swim around in tubs while being squirted with jets of water to keep them aerated. You can also get pangolins, dogs and raccoons, either alive or in a variety of positions resulting

from recent violent death – which may just swear you off meat for the next few weeks.

The market spills out into Tiyun Lu, which cuts east-west across Qingping Lu. Further north is another area supplying vegetables, flowers, potted plants and goldfish.

Shamian Island

Liuersan Lu runs parallel to the northern bank of Shamian Island. The island is separated from the rest of Canton by a narrow canal to the north and east, and by the Pearl River to the south and west. Two bridges connect the island to the city. At the side of the bridge leading to the island in the east stands a monument to the martyrs of the Shaji Massacre (as the 1925 massacre was known).

'Shamian' means 'sand flat,' which is all the island was until foreign traders were permitted to set up their warehouses (factories) here in the middle of the 18th century. Land reclamation has increased its area to its present size: 900 metres from east to west, and 300 metres from north to south. The island became a British and French concession after they defeated the Chinese in the Opium Wars,

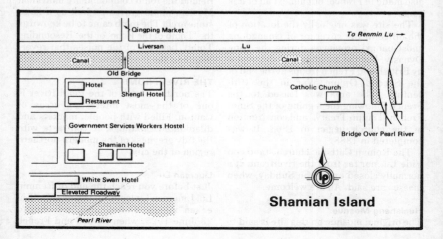

Shamian Island

and is covered with decaying old colonial buildings which housed the trading offices and the residences of the foreigners. Today, most of these are used as offices or apartment blocks and the area retains a quiet residential atmosphere, detached from the bustle just across the canals.

Another 30,000 square metres of land was added to the south bank of the island for the site of the 35-storey White Swan Hotel which was built here in the early 1980s. It's worth a walk along the north bank of Shamian Island to get a view of the houses on Liuersan across the canal. They're all seedy-looking three- and four-storey terrace houses, probably dating to the 1920s and 1930s, but a pretty sight in the morning or evening sun. A few buildings of much the same design survive in the back streets of Hong Kong Island.

Cultural Park

This park has its main entrance on Liuersan Lu. It opened in 1956 and is the Chinese equivalent of Coney Island. Inside are fairground amusements like merry-go-rounds and swirling planes, a roller-skating rink, exhibition halls, an aquarium which exhibits aquatic products from Guangdong Province, and theatres for film and opera. It's usually open until 10 pm – not a bad place to drop into.

Shisanhang Lu

The Cultural Park backs on to Shisanhang Lu. 'Shisanhang,' which means '13 Factories,' is a reminder that this is where the infamous opium warehouses were located. Nothing remains of the original buildings, which were completely destroyed in 1857, and the area was developed into a busy trading centre. By the 1930s it housed the leading banks and exchange houses, and so became known as Bankers Street.

Riverboat Trip

A tourist boat-ride down the Pearl River runs daily from 3.30 to 5 pm and costs Y10. Boats leave from the pier just east of Renmin Bridge. They take you down the river as far as Ershatou and then turn around and head back to Renmin Bridge.

Haichuang Park & Ocean Banner Monastery

Renmin Bridge stands just to the east of Shamian Island and runs over the Pearl River to the area of Canton known as Honan, the site of Haichuang Park. This would be a nondescript park but for the remains of what was once Canton's largest monastery, the Ocean Banner. It was founded by a Buddhist monk in 1662, and in its heyday the grounds covered 2½ hectares. Soon after 1911 the monastery was used partly as a school and partly as a soldier's barracks. It was opened to the public as a park in the 1930s. Though the three colossal images of the seated Buddha have gone, the main hall remains.

The entrance to the park is on Xiangqun Lu. The large stone which decorates the fishpond at the entrance is considered by the Chinese to look like a tiger struggling to turn around. The stone came from Lake Tai in Jiangsu Province, some 1800 km north of Canton. During the Qing Dynasty the wealthy used these rare, strangely shaped stones to decorate their gardens. Many are found in the gardens of the Forbidden City in Beijing, though none as large as this one, which was brought to Canton by a wealthy Cantonese merchant in the last century. The Japanese took Canton in 1938 and plans were made to ship the stone to Japan, though this did not happen. After the war, the stone was sold to a private collector for five million yuan and disappeared from public view. It was finally returned to the park in 1951.

PARKS & GARDENS

Chinese make a great thing of their parks and gardens, decorating them with pavilions and bridges. Many of them can be quite disappointing as scenic attractions, but as places to see the Chinese at their most relaxed, they're always worth a look in on. Along with films and restaurants, parks are a major source

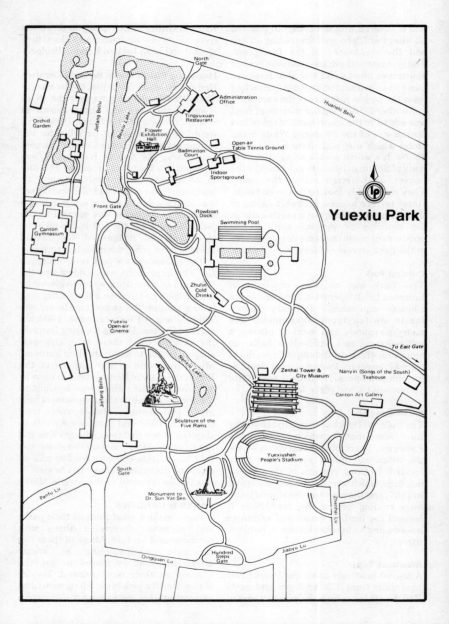

North Gate

Administration Office

Tingyuxuan Restaurant

Flower Exhibition Hall

Badminton Court

Open-air Table Tennis Ground

Indoor Sportsground

Orchid Garden

Jiefang Beilu

Beixiu Lake

Huanshi Beilu

LP

Yuexiu Park

Front Gate

Rowboat Dock

Swimming Pool

Canton Gymnasium

Zhulin Cold Drinks

Yuexiu Open-air Cinema

Nanxiu Lake

To East Gate

Zenhai Tower & City Museum

Nanyin (Songs of the South) Teahouse

Canton Art Gallery

Jiefang Beilu

Sculpture of the Five Rams

Yuexiushan People's Stadium

South Gate

Monument to Dr. Sun Yat-Sen

Zhenhai Lu

Panlu Lu

Hundred Steps Gate

Qingquan Lu

Jiaoyu Lu

of leisure for the Chinese. It's worth getting up early (around 7 am) to see the young and old exercising. Jogging, tai-chi and calisthenics are the usual activities, but you'll often find old women swinging on tree branches (no kidding) and old men running slower than they could walk. Others walk their pet birds, carrying them in wooden cages. The parks are sites for minor exhibitions of painting, photography or flowers (notably chrysanthemums in December).

Yuexiu Park

This is the biggest park in Canton, covering about 93 hectares. Here you'll find the Zenhai Tower, the Sun Yat-sen Monument and the large Sculpture of the Five Rams.

The Sculpture of the Five Rams – erected in 1959 – is the symbol of Canton. It is said that long ago five celestial beings, wearing robes of five colours, came to Canton riding through the air on rams. Each carried a stem of rice, which they presented to the people as an auspicious sign from heaven that the area would be free from famine forever. Guangzhou means 'broad region,' but from this myth it takes its other name, City of Rams, or just Goat City.

The Zen Hai Tower, also known as the Five Storey Pagoda, is the only part of the old city wall that remains. From the upper storeys it commands a view of the city to the south and the White Cloud Hills to the north. The present tower was built during the Ming Dynasty, on the site of a former structure. Because of its strategic location it was occupied by the British and French troops at the time of the Opium Wars. The 12 cannon in front of the tower date from this time (five of them are foreign, the rest were made in nearby Foshan). The tower now houses the City Museum, with exhibits which describe the history of Canton from neolithic times until the early part of this century.

The Sun Yat-sen Monument is south of the Zenhai Tower. This tall obelisk was constructed of granite and marble blocks in 1929, four years after Sun's death, on the site of a temple to the goddess Kuan Yin (Guanyin). There's nothing to see inside, though a staircase leads to the top where there's a good view of the city. On the south side of the obelisk, the text of Dr Sun's last testament is engraved in stone tablets on the ground:

For 40 years I have devoted myself to the cause of national revolution, the object of which is to raise China to a position of independence and equality among nations. The experience of these 40 years has convinced me that to attain this goal, the people must be aroused, and that we must associate ourselves in a common struggle with all the people of the world who treat us as equals. The revolution has not yet been successfully completed. Let all our comrades follow the principles set forth in my writings 'Plans for National Renovation,' 'Fundamentals of National Reconstruction,' 'The Three Principles of the People' and the 'Manifesto of the First National Convention of the Kuomintang' and continue to make every effort to carry them into effect. Above all, my recent declaration in favour of holding a National Convention of the People of China and abolishing unequal treaties should be carried into effect as soon as possible.

This is my last will and testament.

(Signed) Sun Wen
11 March 1925

West of the Zenhai Tower is the Sculpture of the Five Rams. South of the tower is the large sports stadium with a seating capacity of 40,000. The park has its own roller-coaster as well as three artificial lakes: Dongxiu, Nanxiu and Beixiu. You can hire rowboats in Beixiu for 40 fen per hour plus a Y5 deposit, which is refunded when you sail safely back into port.

Canton Orchid Park

Originally laid out in 1957, this pleasant little park is devoted, as the name suggests, to orchids – over a hundred varieties. The Y1 admission fee includes tea, which you can have in the rooms by the small pond. Except Wednesday, the park opens daily from 7.30 to 11.30 am and 1.30 to 5 pm. This is also the site of an ancient Moslem tomb – see above for details. The orchid park is at the northern end of Jiefang Beilu, not far from the main railway station.

Other Parks
The enormous Liuhua Park on Renmin Beilu contains the largest artificial lake in the city. It was built in 1958, a product of the ill-fated Great Leap Forward. There is an entrance to the park on Renmin Beilu.

Just east of Beijing Lu, on the north side of Zhongshan 4-Lu, is a Children's Park where parents bring their tiny tots to play on swings and slides.

The Canton Zoo was built in 1958 and is one of the better zoos you'll see in China. It's on Xianlie Lu, north-west of the Huanghuagang Mausoleum of the 72 Martyrs.

AND MORE
Guangdong Provincial Museum is on Yanan 2-Lu, on the south side of the Pearl River. It houses exhibitions of archaeological finds from Guangdong Province.

On the same road is Zhongshan University, which houses the Lu Xun Museum. One of China's great modern writers, Lu Xun (1881-1936) was not a Communist though most of his books were banned by the Kuomintang. He taught at the university between January and September 1927.

Down the road from the city, Canton's first commercial nuclear power reactor is being built by foreign firms on the Leizhou Peninsula near Daya Bay. Daya Bay is just north-east of Mirs Bay, which borders Hong Kong's New Territories; the plant will also provide power for Hong Kong.

Footnote If there's one area of economics and finance that the Chinese are still stumbling around in, it's advertising and marketing for the foreign market. The Chinese have come up with such bizarre brand names as 'Flying Baby' and 'White Elephant,' and one factory gave a new ginseng product the fatal name of 'Gensenocide.' The disco in Canton's new China Hotel is called 'Checkmates' and an alarm clock was once marketed under the name 'Golden Cock.' A perusal of the billboards along Canton's Renmin Beilu comes up with such space-age products as

1 Broadcasting Room		17 Yak	
2 Baboon, Mandrill		18 Lion Hill	
3 Gorilla		19 Hippopotamus	
4 Goldfish		20 Restaurant	
5 Boa House		21 Monkey Hill	
6 Snakes		22 Lesser Panda	
7 Reptiles		23 Panda	
8 Birds		24 Kangaroo	
9 Smaller Animals		25 Mexican Dog	
10 Gibbon		26 Asian Elephant	
11 Lynx		27 Giraffe	
12 Bear		28 Bactrian Camel	
13 Leopard		29 Zebra	
14 Bear Hill		30 Bear	
15 Tiger Hill		31 Deer	
16 Herbivores			

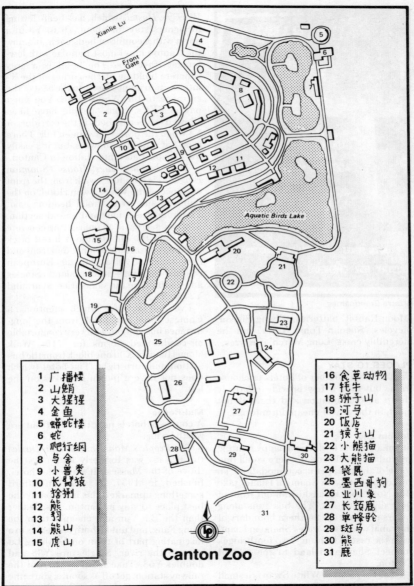

Xianlie Lu

Front Gate

Aquatic Birds Lake

Canton Zoo

1	广播楼
2	山鹋
3	大猩猩
4	金鱼
5	蟒蛇楼
6	蛇
7	爬行纲
8	鸟舍
9	小兽类
10	长臂猿
11	捡猁
12	熊狗
13	熊山
14	熊山
15	虎山

16	食草动物
17	牦牛
18	狮子山
19	河马
20	饭店
21	猴子山
22	小熊猫
23	大熊猫
24	袋鼠
25	墨西哥狗
26	亚川象
27	长颈鹿
28	单峰驼
29	斑马
30	熊
31	鹿

Bizarre Brandnames

'Moon Rabbit' batteries, 'Flying Pigeon' bicycles, 'Shaolin Tonic Water' and the incredibly crass 'Long March' car tyres.

PLACES TO STAY

Canton has a number of hotels to choose from, but only a few provide relatively cheap accommodation and there is not much in the way of cheap dormitories.

Bottom End

Shamian Island is almost a happy hunting ground for hotels and it's here you'll find some of the cheaper accommodation. To get to the hotels on Shamian Island, take Bus No 5 from Huanshi Xilu out front of the railway station. The bus runs along Liuersan Lu on the northern boundary of the canal which separates Shamian Island from the rest of Canton. Two footbridges connect Shamian Island to the rest of Canton.

Near the massive White Swan is a small place called the *Government Services Workers Hostel*, which has been letting foreigners stay for about Y6 to Y8 in a dorm with a couple of beds each. It's now the Canton hotel most popular with low-budget travellers. The hotel is a grey concrete building on the corner of the T-intersection immediately to the east of the entrance to the White Swan. You must pay in FECs. Some people have been allowed to sleep on beds in the corridor for Y4 when the dorms have been full. There is no hot water for showers, but it's easily the cheapest accommodation in Canton.

The *Shamian Guest House (Shamian Binguan)* is a minutes walk from the front entrance of the White Swan Hotel, on the opposite side of the road heading east. The hotel has a new and an old section. The new section is an uninspiring concrete block, but the old section is a red brick building with ornate colonnaded front and iron railing, typical of the European colonial buildings on the island. Singles and doubles are the same price, at around Y27 to Y32.

I've had a letter which mentions a Chinese hotel one block from the long-distance bus station, with very comfortable air-conditioned dorms for Y10: 'Walk along Huanshi Xilu one block from the bus station and turn right. The hotel (which does not have a pinyin name) is on the left.'

Mid-Range

A couple of hotels near the riverfront are worth trying:

The *People's Mansions (Renmin Daxia)* (tel 61445) was formerly known as the 'Love of the Masses.' It's an older hotel, finished in 1937. If you can afford something upmarket, this is probably the best place to stay in Canton. It's cleaner than the Bai Yun and cheaper than the Dong Fang, and unlike both of them is in a fascinating part of town on Yanjiang Lu next to the river. Singles are Y38 and doubles Y58. Take Bus No 31 from the railway station, get off as soon as you come to the river, turn left and walk up Yanjiang

Lu for about 10 minutes. You can't miss the hotel, which is a big white tower. From the upper storeys it offers great views across the city or across the Pearl River.

The *Guangzhou Guest House (Guangzhou Binguan)* (tel 61556) is at Haizhu Square, east of the Renmin Daxia. Singles and doubles run from Y63. Bus No 29 from the front of the railway station goes straight past the hotel. Haizhu Square is a big roundabout with a giant statue in the middle; you can't miss it.

The *Overseas Chinese Mansion (Huaqiao Dasha)* (tel 61112) is on Haizhu Square just near the Guangzhou Guest House. Single and double rooms start from Y20 but they won't take westerners. A very few people have managed to get into the dormitory, which costs Y6 per bed, but you'll probably be wasting your time.

The *Kwantung Guest House (Kwantung Binguan)* is at 655 Jiefang Lu, in between Dongfeng Lu and Zhongshan Lu. At time of writing this place had shut its doors and seemed to be up for renovation, but whether it will reopen as a hotel, I don't know. Rooms used to go for about Y40 and it was a pleasant place with friendly staff, though the location was a bit out of the way.

Top End

The *Liu Hua Hotel (Liu Hua Binguan)* (tel 68800 or 34304) is a large tourist hotel directly across the road from the railway station. It's easily recognisable by the big 'Seagull Watch' sign on the roof. There are no single rooms, but double rooms range from Y48 to Y62 and are very comfortable – though the cheaper ground floor rooms can be very noisy. The ground floor even has a whole room full of dodgem cars!

The *White Cloud Guest House (Bai Yun Binguan)* (tel 67700) on Huanshi Donglu is a large tourist hotel east of the railway station. A lot of foreign tour groups get put up here. Singles run from Y45 and doubles from Y75. The hotel is in an exceptionally dull part of town, and you'd

be better off staying somewhere else – it's convenient for the Friendship Store but that's about all. 'Bai' is pronounced 'bye' and the vowel in 'Yun' is a short 'o' as in 'book.' The hotel is named after the White Cloud Hills (Bai Yun Shan) to the immediate north. Bus No 30 from the railway station goes straight past the hotel.

The *Dong Fang Hotel* (tel 69900, 32644 or 32810) is directly across from the Trade Fair building. The Dong Fang mainly caters to business people and foreign tour groups. Single rooms run from Y65 and doubles from Y70. 'Fang' is pronounced 'fung' to rhyme with 'hung.' It's about a 15-minute walk from the railway station, or take Bus No 31.

Right next to the Dong Fang Hotel is the gleaming *China Hotel (Zhongguo Dajiudian)* (tel 66888), which boasts a disco (admission Y15, open daily 9 pm to 2 am) and bowling alley. Rooms start from Y120 a single and from Y130 a double – plus 10% service charge and 5% tax. It's another Hong Kong venture, this time under the auspices of New World Hotels International.

Canton's newest and most spectacular hotel is the *Garden Hotel (Huayuan Jiudian)* (tel 73388) at 368 Huanshi Donglu, opposite the Bai Yun Hotel. It's a member of Hong Kong's Peninsula group of hotels and is built on a scale which would only be possible with cheap socialist labour at hand. Room prices are surprisingly low: singles and doubles are the same price and range from Y100 to Y250. The hotel is topped by a revolving restaurant.

The *White Swan Guest House (Baitiane Binguan)* (tel 86968) is the huge white tower on the south-eastern shore of Shamian Island. It's also got a first for China – a waterfall in the lobby! There are no single rooms, but doubles range from Y100 to Y140 plus 10% service charge and 5% tax. The more expensive rooms face the river.

PLACES TO EAT

There is an old Chinese saying that to enjoy the best that life has to offer, one has to be 'born in Suzhou, live in Hangzhou, eat in Canton and die in Liuzhou.' Suzhou is renowned for its beautiful women, Hangzhou for its scenery, and Liuzhou for the finest wood for making coffins. I have not been to Suzhou, I was not all that impressed by Hangzhou and I have no wish to die in China, but as Chinese food goes, Canton ain't a bad place to stuff your face.

There are dozens of famous old establishments in this city along with heaps of smaller places, so eating out is not to be passed up. All the restaurants of any size have private rooms or partitioned-off areas, if you want to get away from the hoi-polloi – and since restaurants tend to be crowded this is a distinct advantage. The Chinese just don't go in for the western fashion of eating in dimly lit, intimate surroundings. In fact, they have a word renao which is the flip-side of privacy and intimacy; literally it means 'hot and noisy,' suggesting the pleasure that Chinese find in getting together with a large group of friends and relatives for a meal in a noisy, brightly lit room, chopsticks clicking and everyone talking.

Ordering Meals If you can speak Chinese, you can book tables over the phone. If there's a group of you with no particular preference in what you eat, then you could try stipulating how much you want to pay and let the staff do the rest, though this doesn't always work out well. If you can't speak Chinese, you need a phrasebook which lists dishes in Chinese characters. At the end of this section is a list of the dishes mentioned here in English, pinyin and Chinese characters. Failing that, the best way to order a meal is to point at something that somebody else already has.

Opening Hours Normal service hours in Canton's restaurants are usually around 5 to 9 am for breakfast, 10 am to 2 pm for lunch and 5 am to 8 pm for dinner. Several places have longer hours, but remember that China wakes up early and goes to sleep early. No use wandering into a restaurant late at night and expecting to be served.

Chinese Food

There are a couple of worthy places close to the riverfront. Foremost is the *Datong Jiujia (Great Harmony Restaurant)* (tel 86396 or 86983) at 63 Yanjiang Lu, just around the corner from Renmin Lu. It occupies all of an eight-storey building overlooking the river. The sixth floor has the cheaper dining rooms. Specialities of the house are crisp fried chicken and roast suckling pig. The skin of the pig is the delicacy, crisply roasted, dipped in bean sauce, salt and sugar, and served with a spring onion in a steamed roll.

Close to the Datong Restaurant is the *Yan Yan Restaurant*. It's on a side street which runs east from Renmin Lu; look for the pedestrian overpass which goes over Renmin Lu just up from the intersection with Yanjiang Lu – the steps of the overpass lead down into the side street and the restaurant is opposite them. It is easily recognisable by the fish tanks in the entrance; get your turtles and catfish as well as roast suckling pig here. The place is fantastically well air-conditioned.

The *Seafood Restaurant* (sign in English) is at 54 Renmin Lu and serves what appear to be giant salamanders around 80 cm long and about 20 cm wide.

One of the city's best-known restaurants is the *Guangzhou* (tel 87136 or 87840) at 2 Xiuli 2-Lu on the corner with Wenchang Lu. It boasts a 70-year history and in the 1930s came to be known as the 'first house in Canton.' Its kitchens were staffed by the city's best chefs and the restaurant was frequented by the most important people of the day. The four storeys of dining halls and private rooms are built around a central garden courtyard, with potted shrubs and flowers and landscape paintings designed to give the feeling (at least to the people in the dingy ground-floor rooms) that you're 'eating in a landscape.' Anyway, the food at this self-proclaimed illustrious restaurant ain't bad and ordinary dishes are quite cheap. Specialities of the house include shark fin soup with shredded chicken, chopped crabmeat balls and braised dove.

A couple of places on Zhongshan Lu in the section between Renmin Lu and Jiefang Lu are worth a try. The *Huimin Fandian (Moslem Restaurant)* is at 326 Zhongshan Lu, on the corner with Renmin Lu – look for the Arabic letters above the front entrance. It's an OK place, but go upstairs since the ground floor is dingy. The *Xiyuan* is further up and on the other side of the road at No 46. It's OK for basic food, but nothing amazing. Eat upstairs, since the ground floor is just a grotty canteen.

North of Zhongshan Lu is Dongfeng Lu, which runs east-west across the city. At No 320 Dongfeng Beilu is the *Beiyuan Jiujia (North Garden Restaurant)* (tel 33365 or 32471). This is another of Canton's 'famous houses' – a measure of its success being the number of cars and tourist buses parked outside. Inside is a courtyard and garden from which the restaurant takes its name. Specialities of the house include stewed pork, roast duck, barbecued chicken liver, steamed chicken in huadiao wine, stewed fishhead with vegetables, fried crab, steamed fish, fried boneless chicken (could be a first for China), fried snow-white shrimp and stewed duck legs in oyster sauce.

In the west of Canton, the *Banxi Jiujia (Banxia Restaurant)* (tel 85655 or 88706) at 151 Xiangyang 1-Lu is an enormous place and the biggest restaurant in the city. It's noted for its dumplings, stewed turtle, roast pork, chicken in tea leaves and a crabmeat-shark fin consommé. This place is also famed for its dim sum, served from 5 to 9.30 am, at noon and again at night. Dim sum includes fried dumplings

stuffed with shrimp, chicken gizzards, pork and mushrooms – even shark fins! Or you could try egg rolls stuffed with chicken, shrimp, pork, bamboo shoots and mushrooms, all fried crispy brown. The main-course menu includes monkey brains; these are first steamed with ginger, scallions and rice wine, and then steamed again with crab roe, eggs and lotus blossoms.

Off in the same general direction is the *Taotaoju (Abode of Tao Tao)* (tel 87501) at 288 Xiuli 1-Lu. Originally built as a private academy in the 17th century, it was turned into a restaurant in the late 19th century. Tao Tao was the name of the wife of the first proprietor. Dim sum is the speciality here; you choose sweet and savoury snacks from the selection on trolleys that are wheeled around the restaurant. Tea is the preferred beverage and is said to be made with Canton's best water, brought from the Nine Dragon Well in the White Cloud Hills.

Not far from the Taotaoju is a mooncake bakery, the *Lianxiang Lou (Lotus Fragrance Pavilion)*. Traditionally, mooncakes were eaten at the mid-autumn festival when the moon was brightest. The soft, golden crusts are stuffed with sweet and savoury fillings like fruit, nuts, lotus seeds and red beans. They're also used for weddings and receptions and are exported to Hong Kong.

Beijing Lu has two of Canton's other 'famous' restaurants. The *Yeweixiang Fandian (Wild Animals Restaurant)* (tel 30997) is at No 247. This is where you can feast on dogs and cats, deer, bear paws and snake. Once upon a time they even served tiger. *Taipingguan Canting (Taiping Restaurant)* (tel 35529) at 344 Beijing Lu serves both western and Chinese food. The roast pigeon here is supposed to have been a favourite of no less a personage than Zhou En-lai.

When the missiles start firing, you can eat your way into oblivion at Canton's underground restaurant, the *Diaxia Canting*, a short walk from the Dong Fang

Hotel down Jiefang Lu. From the street, only a concrete archway topped by a green neon sign is visible. The entrance is through the archway and along the lane. This structure was originally built as a bomb shelter, but today some of the corridors are hung with exhibits of local artwork, while the rooms have been turned into game rooms and dining halls. The place is very popular with Canton's youth and was one of the first of its kind in China (bomb-shelter restaurants are now a common sight there). The restaurant is open for lunch and dinner and the fried rice is excellent.

A few other restaurants worth mentioning include the *Xiyuan (West Garden) Teahouse* on Dongfeng 1-Lu. It's popular with the more well-heeled young people. The teahouse is set in a large garden with lots of bonsai on display.

The *Nanyuan Jiujia (South Garden Restaurant)* (tel 50532 or 51576) is at 120

Qianjin Lu. Their specialities include pigeon in plum sauce and chicken in honey and oyster sauce. Qianjin Lu is on the south side of the Pearl River. To get to it you have to cross over Haizhu Bridge and go down Yuejin Lu. Qianjin Lu branches off to the east.

Snake Restaurants

Just to the west of Renmin Lu at 43 Jianglan Lu is the *Shecanguan (Snake Restaurant)* (tel 23424). They display their selection of snakes in the window. The restaurant was originally known as the 'Snake King Moon' and has a history of 80 years. To get to the restaurant you have to walk down Heping Lu, which runs west from Renmin Lu. After a few minutes you come to Jianglan Lu; turn right and follow the road around to the restaurant, which is on the left-hand side of the road. The Chinese believe that snake meat is effective in curing diseases. It is supposed

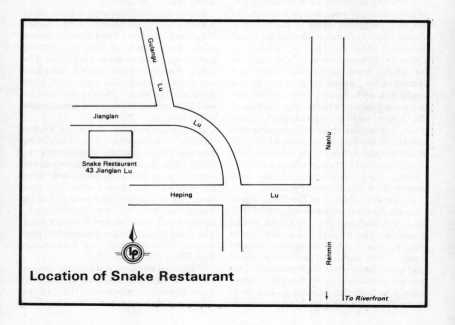

Location of Snake Restaurant

to be good for dispelling wind and promoting blood circulation, and is believed to be useful in treating anaemia, rheumatism, arthritis and asthenia. Snake gall bladder is supposed to be even more effective in dispelling wind, promoting blood circulation, dissolving phlegm and soothing one's breathing. Way back in the 1320s the Franciscan Friar Odoric visited China and commented on the snake-eating habits of the southern Chinese. 'There be monstrous great serpents likewise, which are taken by the inhabitants and eaten. A solemn feast among them without serpents is thought nothing of.' Creative snake recipes include fricasseed assorted snake and cat meats, snake breast meat stuffed with shelled shrimp, stir-fried colourful shredded snakes, and braised snake slices with chicken liver.

Fast food shop

Vegetarian

There's at least one vegetarian restaurant in Canton, the *Tsaikenhsiang* at 167 Zhongshan Lu. It's dingy and depressing downstairs but upstairs is OK. They have private rooms too.

Overall, China is hell for vegetarians. Some people carry notes in Chinese that say things like 'I am a vegetarian; I do not eat *any* meat' and pass it on to the waiter in the hope that somehow the message will get through to the person in the responsible position in the kitchen. Sometimes it works and sometimes it doesn't.

Cheap Eats

There are innumerable *dai pai dongs* open at night in the vicinity of the Renmin Daxia Hotel. If you walk around the streets, and particularly along Changdi Damalu on the north side of the hotel, you'll find quite a few culinary delights, including such delectables as frogs, toads and tortoises kept in buckets on the side of the road. At your merest whim these will be summarily executed, thrown into the wok and fried. It's a bit like eating in an *abattoir*, but at least there's no doubt about the freshness.

A couple of restaurants on Shamian Island are OK for a meal. There is an excellent restaurant a short walk from the White Swan Hotel. Turn right from the entrance of the White Swan, and then left at the first T-intersection. The restaurant is two streets up on the right-hand side of the road. The staff is friendly and the food is good and cheap. The *Shengli Hotel* on the north bank of the island has an OK restaurant.

Good though fairly mundane food is served in the little restaurants in the laneway (Zhanqian Lu) alongside the Liu Hua Hotel. A few of these places are marginally better than the others; look around until you see something you like. Some of the restaurateurs have an aggravating habit of trying to snatch you off the street, and some charge ridiculous prices, like Y1 for a small bowl of soupy noodles, but in general, you should be able to get a sizeable helping of meat, rice and veggies with beer for a few yuan. Try to avoid the Double Happiness brand beer which is commonly sold here; it tastes like a sickly-sweet soft drink.

Fast Food

Perhaps the most telling feature of the direction in which China is heading is the China Hotel's *Hasty Tasty Fast Food* shop which opens out onto Jiefang Beilu. It looks and tastes exactly like any Hong Kong or American fast-food venue, with banks of neon lights implanted in the ceiling and laminex tables. A jumbo burger will knock you down Y3, a hot dog Y1.80 and a fruit jelly Y1. It's not the only western-style fast-food outlet in China; as if to prove that the Chinese are no less adverse to adopting the worst from the west as any other Third World country, there should be several more fast-food venues in Beijing by the time this book is out. None other than than Donald Duck leads the french fries and hamburger revolution's advertising campaign. Be grateful for small mercies – it could have been Mickey Mouse.

Some popular dishes served in Canton's restaurants include:

man tan xiang	满罈香	an elaborate stewed pork dish
pian pi gua hu ya	片皮挂炉鸭	roast duck
guei hua xiang zha	桂花香扎	barbecued chicken liver
hua diao ji	花雕鸡	steamed chicken in hua diao wine
jiao wai yo tou	郊外鱼头	stewed fish head with vegetables
xiang zhih chao xie	香汁炒蟹	fried crab
song zi yu	松子鱼	steamed fish
gan jian ji fu	干煎鸡甫	fried boneless chicken
yu zha xia re'r	油炸虾仁	fried snow white shrimp
hao yu ya	蚝油鸭掌	stewed duck legs in oyster sauce
cui pi zha zi ji	脆皮炸子鸡	crisp fried chicken
shao ru zhu	烧乳猪	roast suckling pig
lao hu rou	老虎肉	tiger meat
she	蛇	snake
xiong zhang	熊掌	bear's paws
mao rou	猫肉	cat meat
gou rou	狗肉	dog meat

Some other useful words:

炒饭	fried rice	龙井茶	long jing (dragon well) tea
炒面	fried noodles	杭菊茶	Hangzhou chyrsanthemum tea
汤面	soup noodles	茉莉花茶	jasmine tea
炒青菜	fried vegetables	酒	wine
白米饭	white rice	啤酒(冰的)	beer (chilled)
牛肉	beef	红葡萄酒	red wine
鸡肉	chicken	白葡萄酒	white wine
猪肉	pork	绍兴酒	Shaohsing rice wine
鱼	fish	茅台酒	mao tai
虾	shrimp	橘子水	orangeade
豆腐	beancurd	矿泉水	mineral water
茶	tea	冰开水	cold water
绿茶	green tea	开水	hot water
红茶	black tea		

SHOPPING

Canton's main shopping areas are Beijing Lu, Zhongshan Lu, the downtown section of Jiefang Lu, and Xiuli 1-Lu and Xiuli 2-Lu. Beijing Lu is a most prestigious thoroughfare by Chinese standards. Although prices are fixed in the government stores, always bargain in the privately owned shops! Check prices in the department stores as a guide to what you should pay.

Department Stores

If you need something, the big department stores are the places to go. With the rebirth of consumerism these stores are stocked with all types of goods – daily needs and sometimes luxuries. Before you buy something in the Friendship Store, it's worth checking to see if it's available in the local department store, as it may be cheaper there.

On the north-west corner of the Zhongshan/Beijing Lu intersection is the large, general-purpose *Zhongshan Department Store*. Canton's main department store is the *Nan Fang*, which is opposite the Cultural Park on Liuersan Lu. The store is popular with Hong Kong people and there's a currency exchange counter at the rear of the ground floor.

Friendship Stores

These stock goods which are either imported from the west and/or are in short supply in the ordinary stores. You usually have to pay for goods in these stores with Foreign Exchange Certificates – which have become the subject of a black market since possession of them enables ordinary Chinese to buy goods which are otherwise unobtainable or may require a long wait – like televisions or bicycles.

The Canton Friendship Store is next to the Bai Yun Hotel and has two or three levels selling everything from Moskovskaya Osobaya Vodka to life-size replicas of the terracotta soldiers at Xian. They'll take a number of credit cards, including American Express, Federal, Visa and Diners Club. Their packaging and shipping service will send stuff home for you, but they only handle goods bought from that particular store. You should be able to find a few good bargains in the Friendship Store. There's another in the China Hotel but it's generally more expensive, and there's an arts and crafts store in the New Garden Hotel.

Antiques

The Friendship Stores have antique sections, but prices are high so don't expect to find a bargain. Only antiques which have been cleared for sale to foreigners may be taken out of the country. When you buy an item over 100 years old it will come with an official red wax seal attached – this seal does *not* necessarily indicate that the item is an antique! You'll also get a receipt of sale and you must show this to Customs when you leave the country; otherwise the antique will be confiscated. Imitation antiques are sold everywhere. Some museum shops sell replicas of pieces on exhibit.

For antiques try the Friendship Stores and that other major tourist trap, the *Guangdong Antique Store* at 575 Hongshu Bei Lu, in front of the Guangxiao Temple.

From Zhongshan Lu turn into Wande Lu. Not far down on the left side of the road at No 146 is the *Canton Antique Store* – not as large as the Guangdong Antique Store, but worth a look in.

Arts & Crafts

Brushes, paints and other art materials may be worth checking out – a lot of this stuff is being imported by western countries and you should be able to pick it up cheaper at the source. Scroll paintings are sold everywhere and are invariably very expensive, partly because the material on which the painting is done is expensive. There are many street artists in China, who often sit out on the sidewalk making on-the-spot drawings and paintings and selling them to passersby. Beautiful kites are sold in China and are worth getting, just to hang on your wall. Paper rubbings of stone inscriptions are cheap and make nice wall hangings when framed. Papercuts are sold everywhere and some of them are exquisite. Jade and ivory jewellery is commonly sold in China – but remember that some countries like Australia and the USA prohibit the import of ivory.

Along Zhongshan Lu, across Beijing Lu and opposite the entrance to the Children's Park, is the *South China Specialities Store* which specialises in regional handicrafts. Look for the sign in English saying 'native products.' It sells a few interesting, inexpensive items.

The *Jiangnan Native Product Store* at 399 Zhongshan Lu has a good selection of bamboo and baskets.

On Beijing Lu, next door to the Foreign Languages Bookstore at No 326, is Canton's main art supply shop, the *Sanduoxuan*. Apart from art materials it sells original paintings.

Books, Posters & Magazines

Try the *Foreign Language Bookstore* at 326 Beijing Lu – almost directly opposite the Sieko Store. As well as translations of Chinese books and magazines, foreign magazines like *Time, Newsweek, Far Eastern Economic Review* and even the *Reader's Digest* are sold here.

The *Classical Bookstore* at 338 Beijing Lu specialises in pre-1949 Chinese string-bound editions.

The *Xinhua Bookstore* is at 336 Beijing Lu, and is the main Chinese bookstore in the city. If you want to investigate the state of the pictorial arts in the country today, this is a good place to come; there are lots of wall posters as well as reproductions of Chinese paintings. They also sell comic books, voraciously read by young and old alike.

All over China you'll see sidewalk vendors presiding over shelves full of little books. These are the Chinese equivalent of comic books and are about the size of

your hand. People rent them from the stall-keeper and sit down on benches to read them. The stories range from fantasies about animals to tales from classical China and episodes from the Communist revolution. They're all in Chinese but they make nice little souvenirs – you can buy them in the shops for around 20 fen each.

The fashion magazines printed in Beijing and Shanghai are interesting mementoes, with their pictures of western and Chinese beauties whose looks, hair-styles and dress are eons away from the blue-garbed socialist women of the Maoist era. Like the posters, the magazines make good souvenirs.

Theatre & Music

For theatre costumes, drop into the *Theatre Shop* almost next door to the Zhongshan Department Store. Here you can pick up Chinese opera costumes, masks and swords. Part of the shop specialises in Chinese musical instruments. Instruments are also sold in the depart-ment stores, and quite a few private shops manufacture and sell them. If you have a liking for Chinese music, you can buy records and cassettes in music stores.

Other

Good souvenirs are the discarded PLA caps (or imitations) which can be bought from the street markets, along with the blue so-called 'Mao caps.'

China issues quite an array of beautiful stamps – generally sold at post offices in the hotels. Outside many of the post offices you'll find amateur philatelists with books full of stamps for sale. These are worth checking out.

If you want tacky statues, there are opportunities to stock up in China! Fat Buddhas are everywhere, and 60 cm-high Venus de Milos and multi-armed gods are not uncommon. They're all incredibly crass, but the Chinese haven't had these things for 30 years so the market for them is booming.

Around Canton

A couple of places around Canton make good day or half-day trips. Buses to some of these places depart either from the long-distance bus station on Huanshi Xilu – a 10-minute walk west of the main railway station – or from the provincial bus station across the road from the long-distance bus station. For some destinations you have to get buses from smaller bus stations around the city.

BAIYUN SHAN (WHITE CLOUD HILLS)

The White Cloud Hills are in the north-eastern suburbs of Canton. They are an offshoot of Dayu Ling, the chief mountain range of Guangdong Province. They were once dotted with temples and monasteries, though no buildings of any historical significance remain today. The hills are popular with the local people who come here to admire the views and slurp cups of tea – the Cloudy Rock Teahouse on the hillside by a small waterfall has been recommended if you want to do the same. At the southern foot of the hills is Luhu Lake – also called Golden Liquid Lake – which was built for water storage in 1958 and is now used as a park.

The highest peak in the White Cloud Hills is Moxing Ling (Star Touching Peak – which only rises 382 metres, but anything higher than a kiddie's sandcastle is a mountain in eastern China). From it you can see a panorama of the city – the Xiqiao Hills to one side, the North River and the Fayuan Hills on the other side, and the sweep of the Pearl River.

The Chinese rate the evening view from Cheng Precipice as one of the eight sights of Canton. The precipice takes its name from a story from the Qin Dynasty. It is said that the first Qin Emperor, Qin Shi Huang, heard of a herb which would confer immortality on whoever ate it. Cheng On Kee, a minister of the emperor, was dispatched to find it. Five years of wandering brought Cheng to the White Cloud Hills where the herb grew in profusion. On eating the herb, he found that the rest of it disappeared. In dismay and fearful of returning empty-handed, Cheng threw himself off the precipice, but having been assured immortality from eating the herb, he was caught by a stork and taken to heaven. The precipice, named in his memory, was formerly the site of the oldest monastery in the area.

North of the Cheng Precipice, on the way up to Moxing Ling, you'll pass the Nine Dragons Well – the origins of which are also legendary. One story goes that Canton officials came to worship twice yearly, and also in times of drought, at the Dragon Emperor Temple that used to exist on the spot. During the 18th century, the governor of Canton visited the temple during a drought. As he prayed he saw nine small boys dancing in front of the temple, who vanished when he rose from his knees. A spring bubbled forth from where he had been. A monk at the temple informed the amazed governor that these boys were in fact nine dragons sent to advise the governor that his prayers had been heard in heaven and the spring became known as the 'Nine Dragons Well.'

Getting There

Baiyun Shan is about 15 km from Guangzhou and is a good half-day excursion. Express buses leave from Guangwei Lu – a little street running off Zhongshan 5-Lu just to the west of the Children's Park – every 15 minutes or so. The trip takes about 30 minutes.

XIQIAO HILLS

Another scenic spot, these hills are 68 km south-west of Canton. Seventy-two peaks make up the area, the highest rising 400 metres, keeping company with 36 caves, 32 springs, 28 waterfalls and 21 crags.

At the foot of the hills is the small market town of Guanshan, and around the upper levels of the hills are scattered several centuries-old villages. Most of the

NUMBER 12 STYLE TRACTOR

area is made accessible by stone paths. It's popular with Chinese tourists, but Europeans are rare.

Getting There

Buses to the hills depart from the Foshan Bus Station on Daxin Lu, which runs west off Jiefang Nanlu.

CONGHUA HOT SPRINGS

The springs are about 80 km north-east of Canton. Up to now, 12 springs have been found with temperatures varying from 30 to 40°C – the highest being over 70°C. The water is supposed to have a curative effect on neuralgia (severe spasmodic pain along the course of one or more nerves), arthritis, dermatitis and hypertension, and one tourist leaflet even claims relief for 'fatigue of the cerebral cortex' (headache?) and gynecological disease.

Getting There

Buses to Conghua depart all day from the long-distance bus station on Hongyun Lu near Canton East Railway Station. There are also buses all day from the provincial bus station on Huanshi Xilu. The first bus is around 7 am, the last about 5.30 pm. The fare is about Y2. As soon as you get to the springs, buy a ticket for the return journey to Canton, as buses are often full.

The place is thick with bodies at the weekend, so try to avoid going then.

FOSHAN

Just 28 km south-west of Canton is the town of Foshan. The name means 'Buddha Hill.' The story goes that a monk travelling through the area enshrined three statues of Buddha on a hilltop. After the monk left, the shrine collapsed and the statues disappeared. Hundreds of years later, during the Tang Dynasty (618-907 AD), the Buddha figurines were suddenly rediscovered, a new temple was built on the hill and the town was renamed.

Whether the story is true or not, from about the 10th century onwards the town became a well-known religious centre and because of its location in the north of the Pearl River Delta with the Fen River flowing through it, and its proximity to Canton, Foshan was ideally placed to take off as a market town and a trade centre as well.

Since the 10th or 11th centuries Foshan has been notable as one of the four main handicraft centres of old China. The other three were Zhuxian in Henan Province, Jingdezhen in Jiangxi and Hankou in Hebei. The nearby town of Shiwan (which is now virtually an extension of Foshan) became famous for its pottery, and the

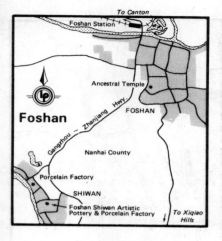

to Qingping Market in Canton, but it's worth wandering through if you're in Foshan. Here you can stock up on fish that have been sliced in half with the heart left intact and pumping, or on turtles, crabs or skinned and roasted dogs. A few shops up from the Lianhua/Kuaizi Lu intersection is one selling snakes, and across the road from it is a building housing the main meat, fish and poultry market. At the far end of the street are a few miscellaneous stalls selling clothes, oddments, furniture, flowers, birds and goldfish. (Pets are back in favour in the People's Republic; during the Cultural Revolution the keeping of goldfish and birds was regarded as a bourgeois pursuit and activists tried to wipe out the hobby. Come the end of the Cultural Revolution even the animals had to be rehabilitated.)

Ancestors Temple

Located at the southern end of Zumiao Lu, the original temple was built during the Song Dynasty in the later part of the 11th century, and was used by workers in the metal-smelting trade for worshipping their ancestors. It was destroyed by fire at the end of the Yuan Dynasty in the mid-1300s and was rebuilt at the beginning of the Ming Dynasty during the reign of the first Ming emperor Hong Wu. The Ancestors Temple was converted into a Taoist temple since the emperor himself worshipped a Taoist god.

The temple has been developed through renovations and additions in the Ming and Qing dynasties. The structure is built entirely of interlocking wooden beams, with no nails or other metal used at all. It is roofed with coloured tiles made in Shiwan.

The main hall contains a 2500-kg bronze statue of a god known as the Northern Emperor (Beidi). He's also known as the Black Emperor (Heidi) and rules over water and all its inhabitants, especially fish, turtles and snakes. Since South China was prone to floods, people often tried to appease Beidi by honouring him with temples and carvings of turtles

village of Nanpu (which is now a suburb of Foshan) developed the art of metal casting. Silk weaving and paper-cutting also became important industries, and today Foshan papercuts are one of the commonly sold tourist souvenirs in China.

The bus from Canton heads into Foshan from the north. First stop is Foshan Railway Station (the railway line starts in Canton, passes through Foshan and heads west about 60 km to the town of Hekou. The bus then passes over the narrow Fen River, where a few decaying barges huddle, and a few minutes down the road pulls into the long-distance bus station.

Walk out of the station and turn left; you're on the Canton-Zhanjiang Highway and that's no respite from the bustle of Canton! Turn left again down any one of the side streets. Walk for about 10 minutes and you'll come to one of Foshan's main streets, Song Feng Lu. A right turn into Song Feng Lu will point you in the direction of the town centre and Lianhua Lu.

Lianhua Market

This market on Lianhua Lu can't compare

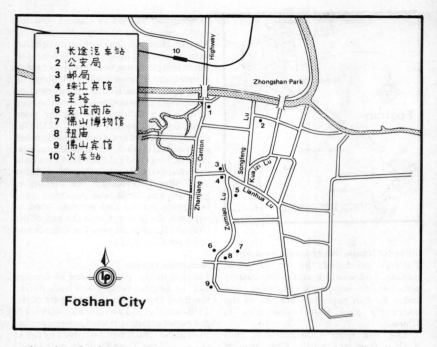

1 长途汽车站
2 公安局
3 邮局
4 珠江宾馆
5 宝塔
6 友谊商店
7 佛山博物馆
8 祖庙
9 佛山宾馆
10 火车站

Foshan City

and snakes. In the courtyard is a pool containing a large statue of a turtle with a serpent crawling over it, onto which the Chinese throw one, two and five fen notes – plus the odd soft-drink can.

The temple also has an interesting collection of ornate weapons used on ceremonial occasions during the imperial days. The Foshan Museum is in the temple grounds, as is the Foshan Antique Store and an arts and crafts store. The temple is open daily from 8.30 am to 4.30 pm.

Intriguing enterprise

Places to Stay

Centrally located is the big and fairly inexpensive *Pearl River Hotel* (tel 86481 or 87512) in the centre of town. The *Overseas Chinese Mansion (Huaqiao Daxia)* is at 14 Zumiao Lu, also a good central spot. The town's tourist joint is the *Foshan Hotel*, rather inconveniently situated at the far end of Zumiao Lu.

Places to Eat

Cheap food stalls in front of the bus station serve rice noodles with meat and

Vibrator Factory, Foshan
Dunhou, Shijiao 86-765
0617 FOSHAN
佛山振动器厂
市郊敦厚

soup for about 50 fen a plate. There's a cheap canteen on the road when you turn left out of the bus station, and a number of similar places on Lianhua Lu down from the market. You might give the *Qunyingge (Hero's Pavilion) Restaurant* in Zhongshan Park or the *Meiyuan (Plum Garden) Restaurant* near the Temple of the Ancestors a go. In Shiwan you could try the *Taodu* across the road from the bus station.

Getting There

Buses from Canton leave from the Foshan Bus Terminal at the corner of Daxin Lu and Jiefang Nanlu. The ticket office is on Daxin Lu just a few minutes walk down from Jiefang Nanlu. The fare to Foshan is Y0.55 and the trip takes 50 to 60 minutes. It's an interesting ride, and if you're up from Hong Kong only for a few days you'll at least get a glimpse of the countryside.

GONGBEI

Gongbei is the Chinese border town with Macau, and like its big brother Shenzhen, it's been built from the soles up in the past few years, with numerous office blocks and apartment buildings sprouting a km or so back from the border. Yet for all this, a bus ride from Gongbei to Canton brings back the fact that China is very much a rural society, where peasants water their fields with cans slung on poles over their shoulders, boatmen make their way up rivers standing on their boats and

Watering the fields

pushing their way along with two oars, motorcyclists transport basketloads of geese in panniers, and slaughtered pigs are carried slung over the pack-racks of bicycles. There's also a surprising number of beggars in Gongbei, scraping a bit of their own off the Four Modernisations.

Places to Stay

There are a couple of hotels near the border. As you come out of the Customs Building from Macau, turn to the right and then make a left.

First up is the *Jiu Zhou Hotel* on the right; singles and doubles run from Y50.

Next door, the *Gongbei Palace Hotel* (tel 23831) has a disco, billiards room, swimming pool, sauna and video games. Funny, three years ago I was standing on Rua dos Pescadores across the bay in Macau wondering what was on this side of the border. No singles, but doubles start from Y190, plus 10% service and 5% tax.

Across the road is the *CTS (China Travel Service) Hotel*; no singles but doubles are Y36.

Getting There

There are direct buses between Canton and Gongbei – see the 'Getting There' section at the start of this chapter for details.

SHENZHEN SPECIAL ECONOMIC ZONE

The Shenzhen municipality stretches right across the northern border of Hong Kong from Daya Bay in the east to the mouth of the Pearl River in the west. Though hardly a place to linger, Shenzhen town is worth stopping off in for a few hours to look around, since this is the centre of one of China's major Special Economic Zones.

The Special Economic Zones have been set up to promote foreign and overseas Chinese investment in China using reduced taxation, low wages, abundant labour supply and low operating costs as encouragement – the theory being that China can be modernised quicker and more easily if it imports foreign technology and expertise. The SEZs are a sort of geographical laboratory where western capitalist economic principles can be tested using cheap socialist labour. These zones are not a new idea; they bear some resemblance to the Export Processing Zones to be found in almost 30 countries around the world.

The SEZ was set up in a small part of the Shenzhen municipality in 1979. The area was chosen for several reasons: it is adjacent to Hong Kong, thus allowing easier access to the world market; most Hong Kong businesspeople speak the same dialects and maintain kinship relations with Shenzhen and other parts of southern China; there is easy access to the port facilities of Hong Kong; and the area itself has level land suitable for settlement and the construction of industrial plants plus a ready supply of raw materials suitable for use in the construction industry.

In the SEZs foreigners can invest in anything which the state deems useful for the country, be it production of goods for export or construction of private-housing estates. These can be joint ventures, cooperative enterprises or wholly foreign-owned operations. A uniform income tax rate of 15% is applied. Whether the SEZs actually benefit China is debatable. The zones were conceived as a means of obtaining foreign technology and capital, and producing exports with a minimum of disruption to the rest of the country's economy. The problem has been that these zones are importing equipment and raw materials but most of their output is ultimately sold in China, not exported. The amount of money they produce for China may be far less than the money that the government puts into them to keep them running. What's more, most of the foreign industries set up in Shenzhen in the five years after it opened in 1979 have been relatively simple ones – like electronics assembly – which falls well short of the

Happiness Soft Drink Factory, Shenzhen
Tianbeicun 23-223
Tx:44223 SZHSD CN   23-418
Lee, Kuo-Kin Suarez, JG   23-379

Happy drinking!

capital– and technology-intensive investment China has been seeking.

Other problems have been produced by
unleashing this laissez-faire capitalism on
a pocket of Chinese territory, not least of
which is the booming black market in just
about everything. One of the main problems
in Shenzhen has been that the Chinese
Hong Kong 'compatriots' as well as PRC
Chinese sell Hong Kong currency at a
higher black market rate than the official
rate, then go to buy Chinese produce at
the free markets, thus undercutting the
official export prices, and ship the produce
off to their markets in Hong Kong and
Macau. It's also said that one of the things
that has upset many big-wigs in the
Chinese government and administration
is that black market dealing has been
putting their own business enterprises in
Shenzhen at a disadvantage.

Various plans have been conjured up to
solve these problems. One is to introduce
a whole new currency for use solely in
Shenzhen and thus halt the black market
dealing in foreign currency there; once the
new currency was in place all other
currencies in the SEZ – renminbi, Foreign
Exchange Certificates and Hong Kong
dollars – would be withdrawn. Whether
this plan will go ahead is not known at this
time. However, one thing the Chinese
have already done in anticipation of it is to
literally fence off the whole Special
Economic Zone from China and Hong
Kong!

The showpiece of the SEZ is Shenzhen
town, once a fishing village but transformed
in just a few years into a small town of
high-rise blocks spreading north of the
border with Hong Kong, among them the
600-bed, 33-storey Asia Hotel Complex
topped by – you guessed it – a revolving
restaurant. There are Friendship Stores
and air-conditioned restaurants (the locals
pause in the doorways for a breath of cool
air), and at nearby Xili Reservoir there are
holiday resorts and golf courses for Hong
Kong people searching for more breathing
space.

Places to Stay
The *Overseas Chinese Hotel* is immediately
across the tracks from the railway station,
and you'll be looking at around Y45 for a
single or a double room.

Getting There
Shenzhen is the border town with Hong
Kong. There are trains from Canton to
Shenzhen, and you can then pass through
Customs and catch the electric train from
Lo Wu (the Hong Kong border station) to
Kowloon. There are bus services from
Hong Kong to Shenzhen. By the time this
book is out it may even be possible to drive
across the border and all the way to
Canton on the highway which is being
built. For details of transport see the
'Getting There' section at the start of this
chapter.

Index

Maps references are in **bold** type.

Lonely Planet travel guides
Africa on a Shoestring
Alaska – a travel survival kit
Australia – a travel survival kit
Bali & Lombok – a travel survival kit
Bangladesh – a travel survival kit
Burma – a travel survival kit
Bushwalking in Papua New Guinea
Canada – a travel survival kit
China – a travel survival kit
Ecuador & the Galapagos Islands
Fiji – a travel survival kit
Hong Kong, Macau & Canton – a travel survival kit
India – a travel survival kit
Indonesia – a travel survival kit
Japan – a travel survival kit
Kashmir, Ladakh & Zanskar – a travel survival kit
Kathmandu & the Kingdom of Nepal
Korea & Taiwan – a travel survival kit
Malaysia, Singapore & Brunei – a travel survival kit
Mexico – a travel survival kit
New Zealand – a travel survival kit
North-East Asia on a Shoestring
Pakistan – a travel survival kit
Papua New Guinea – a travel survival kit
South America on a Shoestring
South-East Asia on a Shoestring
Sri Lanka – a travel survival kit
Tahiti – a travel survival kit
Thailand – a travel survival kit
The Philippines – a travel survival kit
Tibet – a travel survival kit
Tramping in New Zealand
Travel with Children
Travellers Tales
Trekking in the Indian Himalaya
Trekking in the Nepal Himalaya
Turkey – a travel survival kit
USA West
West Asia on a Shoestring

Lonely Planet phrasebooks
Indonesia Phrasebook
China Phrasebook
Nepal Phrasebook
Thailand Phrasebook

Lonely Planet travel guides are available around the world. If you can't find them, ask your bookshop to order them from one of the distributors listed below. For countries not listed or if you would like a free copy of our latest booklist write to Lonely Planet in Australia.

Australia
Lonely Planet Publications, PO Box 88, South Yarra, Victoria 3141.
Canada
Milestone Publications, PO Box 2248, Sidney, BC V8L 3S8, Canada.
Denmark
Scanvik Books aps, Store Kongensgade 59 A, DK-1264 Copenhagen K.
Hong Kong
The Book Society, GPO Box 7804.
India & Nepal
UBS Distributors, 5 Ansari Rd, New Delhi.
Israel
Geographical Tours Ltd, 8 Tverya St, Tel Aviv 63144.
Japan
Intercontinental Marketing Corp, IPO Box 5056, Tokyo 100-31.
Malaysia
MPH Distributors, 13 Jalan 13/6, Petaling Jaya, Selangor.
Netherlands
Nilsson & Lamm bv, Postbus 195, Pampuslaan 212, 1380 AD Weesp.
New Zealand
Roulston Greene Publishing Associates Ltd, Box 33850, Takapuna, Auckland 9.
Pakistan
London Book House, 281/C Tariq Rd, PECHS Karachi 29, Pakistan
Papua New Guinea see Australia
Singapore
MPH Distributors, 3rd Storey, 601 Sims Drive #03-21, Singapore 1438
Spain
Altair, Riera Alta 8, Barcelona, 08001.
Sweden
Esselte Kartcentrum AB, Vasagatan 16, S-111 20 Stockholm.
Thailand
Chalermnit, 108 Sukhumvit 53, Bangkok, 10110.
UK
Roger Lascelles, 47 York Rd, Brentford, Middlesex, TW8 0QP.
USA
Lonely Planet Publications, PO Box 2001A, Berkeley, CA 94702.
West Germany
Buchvertrieb Gerda Schettler, Postfach 64, D3415 Hattorf a H.